GERMANS FOR A FREE MISSOURI

Naked Truth, memorial to Carl Schurz and Emil Preetorius, editors of the *Westliche Post*, and Carl Dänzer, founding editor of the *Westliche Post* and editor of the *Anzeiger des Westens* from 1863 to 1898. Compton Hill Reservoir, St. Louis.

GERMANS
FOR A FREE MISSOURI

TRANSLATIONS FROM THE
ST. LOUIS RADICAL PRESS, 1857–1862

Selected and Translated
by Steven Rowan

With an Introduction and Commentary
by James Neal Primm

University of Missouri Press
Columbia, 1983

Library of Congress Cataloging in Publication Data

Main entry under title:

Germans for a free Missouri.

    Bibliography: p.
    Includes index.
    1. German Americans—Missouri—History—19th
century—Sources. 2. Slavery—Missouri—Anti-
slavery movements—History—Sources. 3. Missouri
—History—Civil War, 1861–1865—Sources.
4. Radicalism—Missouri—History—19th century.
I. Rowan, Steven W. II. Primm, James
Neal, 1918–
F475.G3G47 1983   977.8′00431   83–6627
ISBN 0–8262–0410–4

Meinem Schwiegervater
Herrn Aloysius James Schuster,
einem Amerikaner deutscher Herkunft,
gewidmet.
SR.

Preface

The revolutionary generation that fought on the barricades and battlefields of central Europe in 1848 and 1849 passed through its last uprising in Missouri in 1861. Nowhere else in American history has a single group of foreigners or a single cohort of leaders made such a difference in the course of a region as in St. Louis between April and June 1861, when the government of Missouri was defied and then overthrown by an uprising licensed by the United States government. The organizers of this legal rebellion were officers of the United States Army and leaders of the Republican party, but the armed force was made up largely of Germans, with revolutionaries as officers and staff.

The purpose of this book is to recover the peculiar mental processes of the German radicals during the secession crisis in St. Louis. The goal is to show how it came to make sense for a German to place his life in peril to defend the American republic in Missouri. A radical cohort, the true Forty-eighters, managed to convince thousands of others, ordinary German workers, shopkeepers, and farmers, to participate in an armed rebellion against the legally constituted government of a state on behalf of a distant federal government. The chief means of this persuasion was the German-language political newspaper.

The Forty-eighters constituted a community of exiles whose positive political ideas ranged from liberal reformism to communistic socialism, but they shared a symbolic language, an experience, and a separation from their homeland. This makes them both attractive and maddening to study: they were often brave and gallant in their services to their new country, but at the same time they were pompous and bitterly critical of much they found in America. This is precisely because few men have ever loved America so deeply. They had sacrificed everything for revolution, and America was—at least in symbol—the last refuge of that revolutionary ideal for which they had fled their first homeland. So the chief theme of this book is a love story, and as with all love stories it will also prove to be a tale of foolishness, suffering, disappointment, and death.

The articles which have been translated here were selected in order to give the reader a reasonable sampling of the range of news and editorial opinion in the two major radical St. Louis German newspapers, the *Anzeiger des Westens* and the *Westliche Post* (with its Sunday supplement *Mississippi Blätter*). Comments on the articles have been kept to a minimum, and no effort has been made to cover all happenings in the eventful times between the founding of the *Westliche Post* in 1857 and the battle of Pea Ridge in March 1862. All articles were translated in their entirety, and the only principle of order has been chronological. It appeared to me from the outset that the internal logic of the material itself provided five major divisions:

1. *St. Louis Germans, 1857–1860.* During the relatively placid and uneventful period between the end of nativist agitation and the start of the presidential campaign of 1860, the Germans were given a chance to explain themselves.

2. *The Republican Crusade, 1860.* In the eyes of politically active Germans, the Republican National Convention of 1860 decided that the Germans would have a lasting place within that party. The campaign for Abraham Lincoln was doubly significant for Missouri Republicans because it marked the first time they dared to campaign outside St. Louis. Victory appeared to promise the eventual end of the control by slaveholders of national and state policies.

3. *Secession Winter, 1860–1861.* From the election of Lincoln until the arrest of units of the Missouri State Guard at Camp Jackson on 10 May 1861, there appeared to be little to stop the secession of the state. Germans looked at the prospects for a Confederate Missouri and found them utterly unappealing. In April they were being armed by federal authorities to secure St. Louis against the hostile state government.

4. *The Missouri Putsch, 1861.* During May and June 1861, a largely German force participated in the Camp Jackson raid, securing St. Louis for the Union, and then the same force executed a coup d'etat expelling the administration of Governor Claiborne Fox Jackson from the seat of government at Jefferson City.

5. *Beyond Heroism, 1861–1862.* In the nine months after the capture of Jefferson City, the United States government pulled back from any suggestion that it follow in the war the revolutionary principles demanded by the radical Germans. This policy decision was expressed in Missouri by the removal of General John C. Frémont as commander of the Western District. By the spring of 1862, the war had become an industrialized undertaking, and the St. Louis Germans had been reduced once more to spectators. Ger-

mans would continue to fight and die, but they would no longer play a central role.

This book began in a conversation I had some years ago in the apartment of my friends Rainer and Renate Liessem on Jacobistrasse in Freiburg im Breisgau, West Germany. On the wall hung a florid proclamation calling upon all friends of the German Republic to rise up and strike down tyranny. The broadside was dated in 1849 and bore the name of one General Franz Sigel. The odd spelling of the name at once called to mind the equestrian statue in Forest Park in St. Louis. Could they possibly be the same person? This elementary question started me off, and when my friend Kathy Corbett of the Missouri Historical Society asked me to look at some German materials from the St. Louis area and give a talk, I started to look at microfilms of the *Westliche Post*. My first plan was to edit a collection of articles from the St. Louis German press to be published in Germany, since citizens of the Federal Republic today are deeply interested in recovering the story of their liberal exiles. I was convinced to undertake a translation project by my colleague Dr. Howard S. Miller. Mr. Anthony Crawford of the Missouri Historical Society graciously allowed me to buy splendid microfilms of the *Westliche Post*, and the State Historical Society of Missouri allowed me to keep films of the *Anzeiger des Westens* for a period beyond all reason. The illustrations have come from various sources, as noted in the captions.

It was a great honor to be able to obtain the help and cooperation of my colleague Dr. James Neal Primm, certainly the greatest living authority on the history of St. Louis. If others have half as much pleasure reading this collection as I have had making it, all the effort will have been well spent.

An honest question that should be asked is what should be done next. Some readers might find this collection so tantalizing that they will want more. There is certainly a great range of materials from the Missouri Germans that merits translation, including novels, memoirs, and newspaper columns. Friedrich Münch's political comments from the 1840s to the 1880s, Heinrich Börnstein's picaresque memoirs, Gert Göbel's chatty reminiscences, immigrants' guides, the muscular frontier novels of Otto Ruppius or Adolph Douai, all merit translating or editing. There is also room for selected translation from each of the major German-American journalistic traditions of the nineteenth century. But in the last analysis what is most pressingly needed is not a bookshelf of translations but an increasing number of bilingual historians of America. The concentration by American historians on English to the exclusion of all the other languages historically spoken and written in North America both destroys our usable past and impoverishes our present.

S. R.
St. Louis
March 1983

Contents

Abbreviations

A Note on the Spelling and Americanization of German Names

The Germans who lived in St. Louis in the nineteenth century participated in two distinct linguistic cultures at the same time, and they routinely used names that were given in their American or German forms depending on convenience, so that Karl Ludwig Bernays was also Charles Louis Bernays, Franz Sigel Francis Sigel, and so on. The umlaut forms *ä*, *ö*, and *ü* were normally rendered *ae*, *oe*, and *ue* in English texts as well, so that Heinrich Börnstein was also Henry Boernstein. German orthography was also looser then than it is today, so that *Karl* could also be spelled *Carl*. In the texts that follow, the form of the name used in the original text has been preserved.

Part I

Introduction

Missouri, St. Louis, and the Secession Crisis

James Neal Primm

A few Germans were scattered among the six thousand border Southerners, Creoles, Pennsylvanians, Irish, and Yankees who lived in St. Louis in 1833. Of the fifteen or so German families, most were second-generation Americans, primarily from Pennsylvania, who were substantial propertied citizens, comfortably at home with the local leadership. Henry Von Phul, a leading merchant, moved among the economic and social elite; Charles Wahrendorff, a commission merchant, was a major figure in the Western trade; and the talented Henry S. Geyer was a rising legal and political star. Like the pioneering Musicks of the Spanish period, these Germans were assimilated, hardly more concerned with the affairs of central Europe than other St. Louisans.

Within a few years, a dramatic change was under way. Rapid settlement of the Illinois and Missouri River valleys enhanced St. Louis's position as an agricultural entrepôt and wholesaling center, and more Germans began to come, first by the hundreds and then by the thousands. Economic change and dislocation in the post-Napoleonic era had created a large class of impoverished or dissatisfied people in the German states, which had impelled a young lawyer-official, Gottfried Duden, to seek in America a haven for his restless compatriots.[1] Duden came in 1824 to Warren County, Missouri, some fifty miles west of St. Louis, and hired labor to clear and work a farm. After three years, Duden wrote his *Report of a Journey to the Western States of North America*, portraying the lower Missouri valley as a Western Eden, a better Rhineland especially suited to Germans. He recommended that immigrants should come in groups, with sufficient funds for a good start, but thousands of German readers did not always notice his reservations.[2]

Responding eagerly to Duden's enthusiasm, Germans swarmed to Missouri in the 1830s, with most intent on farming. At first, only a few artisans and professionals stopped in St. Louis, with most of

1. George H. Kellner, "The German Element on the Urban Frontier: St. Louis, 1830–1860" (Ph.D. diss., University of Missouri, 1973), 9–10, 47–50.
2. Ibid., 25–33; James W. Goodrich, "Gottfried Duden: A Nineteenth Century Missouri Promoter," *MHR* 75 (1980/1981): 142–43. A translation of Duden's work was published in 1980 by the State Historical Society of Missouri and the University of Missouri Press.

the immigrants heading upriver to St. Charles, Warren, Franklin, and Gasconade counties. Individuals with capital and mutually supportive groups succeeded in farming.[3] Those with slender resources, faced with failure or at best unremitting toil for a bare subsistence, returned to Germany if they could, or more often to St. Louis or other Western towns, where demand for labor was strong. By 1837, according to the *Missouri Republican*, there were thirty thousand Germans in Missouri, six thousand of them in the city.[4] This figure was probably exaggerated, but by conservative estimates, a third of St. Louis's fifteen thousand residents in 1840 were Germans.

St. Louis more than doubled in population between 1840 and 1845, with the Germans maintaining their share. By 1850, with an industrial base forming and with undisputed mastery of the river and Western trade, the valley metropolis had doubled in population again, to 77,860. St Louis was twice as large as Pittsburgh, slightly smaller than Cincinnati and New Orleans, and still three times the size of upstart Chicago.

During the 1840s another immigrant group arrived in strength. Spurred by repeated potato famines and another failed rebellion against the British, the Irish fled to America by the hundreds of thousands, some eleven thousand of them to St. Louis.[5] Affluent Irish families had been in St. Louis since territorial days; many of them—Mullanphys, Walshes, Connors, Bradys, Christys, Charlesses, and others—had intermarried with the Creole elite. The new Irish, most of whom were destitute, were a different lot.

Germans and Irish together in 1850 comprised more than 40 percent of St. Louis's population. During the next decade, both groups doubled in numbers again, more than keeping pace with St. Louis's overall growth. By 1860, if their American-born children are included, these ethnic groups comprised three-fifths of the city's 161,000 population.[6]

This influx of immigrants provided a substantial labor force that virtually destroyed the economic utility of slave labor. Slaves were 10 percent of St. Louis's population in 1840, but less than one percent in 1860. In absolute terms, the dramatic decline came during the 1850s, from 2,636 to 1,542. Free blacks, a part of St. Louis

3. Goodrich, "Gottfried Duden," 144; Kellner, "The German Element," 27.
4. *Daily Missouri Republican*, 30 August 1837.
5. In 1850, German-born persons numbered 23,774 and Irish-born 11,256 in St. Louis. See William Hyde and Howard L. Conrad, eds., *The Encyclopedia of the History of St. Louis* (St. Louis, 1899), 3:1782–83.
6. St. Louis's population in 1860 was 160,733, with German immigrants numbering 50,510, Irish 29,926; United States Bureau of the Census, *Census of Population, 1860* (Washington, D.C., 1864), 29, 32, 299–300.

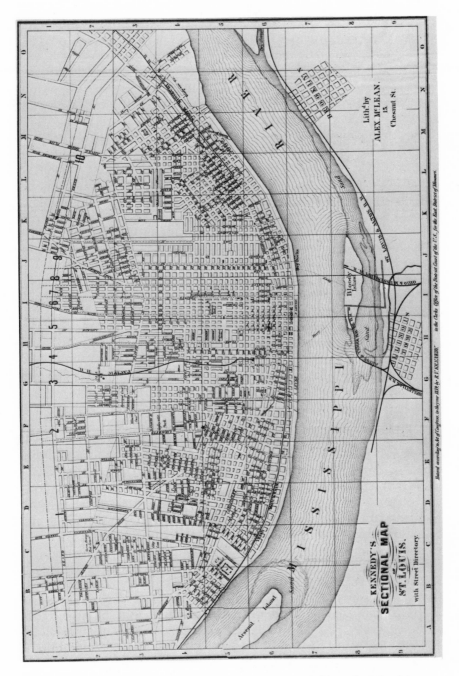

Map of St. Louis in 1859. Courtesy of the Missouri Historical Society.

since the Spanish period, were slightly more numerous than slaves in 1860. The vast majority of St. Louisans had never owned slaves, but antislavery rhetoric was unpopular, and the decline of slavery reflected economic realities rather than humanitarian sentiment. With Irish and German labor available at $200 a year, only those with a sentimental attachment to the institution or to individual servants could resist the temptation to sell their slaves at high prices to Southern planters.

During the 1850s, with their ethnic consciousness raised by an assertive German-language press, Germans became a potent political force in St. Louis. Veterans of the failed political revolution of 1848 in the German states, determined to achieve their liberal agenda in America, flocked to St. Louis and other American cities, many of them as founders or editors of newspapers. Slavery, as the most visible contradiction in a nation of free institutions, came under their editorial fire frequently.

From the time of their initial surge into Missouri in the 1830s, the mass of German voters identified with Sen. Thomas Hart Benton and the Democratic party. The Jackson-Benton Democrats' equalitarian rhetoric and consistent opposition to nativism commanded the Germans' loyalty.[7] In the late 1840s, Benton split with his powerful allies, the central Missouri planters' clique led by Claiborne Fox Jackson, chiefly over the slavery question. The Central Clique, taking its cue from John C. Calhoun of South Carolina, held that slavery had a right to exist in all American territories before they became states. Since this position contravened the Missouri Compromise, which Benton argued had held the Union together for thirty years, he refused to obey instructions from the clique-dominated Missouri legislature to oppose all restrictions on slavery in the territories.[8]

In 1850, anti-Benton Democrats, by combining with the Whig minority in the legislature, replaced Benton in the United States Senate with the pro-Southern Whig Henry S. Geyer. During the next few years, Missouri politics revolved around the struggle between Benton and anti-Benton forces. Benton returned to Washington in 1853 for one term as congressman from St. Louis, leaving Missouri in the charge of his "Lesser Ajax," Frank P. Blair, Jr. Blair, an attorney, was a native Kentuckian and the scion of one of the most powerful political families in the nation. His father, the leading member of President Andrew Jackson's "Kitchen Cabinet,"

7. William N. Chambers, *Old Bullion Benton: Senator from the New West* (Boston: Little, Brown, 1956), 369; Kellner, "The German Element," 210–12.
8. Chambers, *Old Bullion Benton*, 341, 344–46.

was soon to be one of the founders of the Republican party, and his brother Montgomery was an influential Washington lawyer.

With his cousin and fellow-Kentuckian B. Gratz Brown, Frank Blair helped to found the *Missouri Democrat*, a "Benton" newspaper which soon became strong competition for the long-dominant *Missouri Republican*.[9] The *Republican*, founded in 1808 as the *Louisiana Gazette*, was a Whig paper that had been fighting Benton since 1817. Its coeditor, Nathaniel Paschall, who had started with the *Gazette* in 1814 as a twelve-year-old apprentice, was an expert on Benton's shortcomings. Since the 1830s the *Republican*'s columns had reflected the crosscurrents and ambiguities of St. Louis's political and economic environment. On the one hand, the paper was pro-development, boosterish, and thoroughly Whiggish in its commercial-industrial nationalism. On the other, it was sentimentally and somewhat snobbishly attached to Southern institutions, including slavery.

The *Republican* welcomed the immigrants as additions to the labor force, necessary to the city's future as the great city of the West.[10] Yet it could not resist sneering at the Germans' outlandish ways, especially their clinging to their native customs and language, their churches and schools, and their lager beer.[11] The brawling Irish and their vile "doggeries" (saloons) were deplorable, too. But the immigrants' greatest sin was their affinity for Benton's agrarian democracy, with its antibusiness, antibanking overtones. After the German press began to harass the Missouri political and economic establishment, the *Republican* professed to be worried that Missouri might become a new Germany.[12]

In the 1840s when the immigrants seemed to be relatively docile additions to the labor supply, the *Republican* had resisted the Whig tendency toward nativism; that is, the denial of full civil and political rights to the immigrants, including the condoning of violence to that end. But in the mid-1850s, having endured several seasons of the *Anzeiger des Westens*'s onslaughts against the local power structure, the principal organ of the economic elite flirted briefly with nativism.[13]

Know-nothingism, the final version of antebellum nativism, was the Whig party's death song. Unable to hold both its Southern and

9. Ibid, 387; Norma L. Peterson, *Freedom and Franchise: The Political Career of B. Gratz Brown* (Columbia: University of Missouri Press, 1965), 17; Jim A. Hart, "The Missouri Democrat, 1852–1860," *MHR* 55 (1960/1961): 127–41.

10. *Daily Missouri Republican*, 28 March 1840.

11. Ibid., 20 September 1854.

12. Ibid., 9 August 1851.

13. Ibid., 30 July, 1, 3, 5 August 1854.

Northern constituencies by taking sides on the slavery-extension question, the party temporized, an infallible formula for losing everything. The Republican party, formed in 1854 after the Kansas-Nebraska bill had destroyed the Missouri Compromise, captured the Northern antislavery Whigs. The Southern Whigs went to the Democrats, and border-state Whigs, still unwilling to commit themselves, flocked to the Know-nothings, who refused to discuss slavery as a political issue.

Missouri Whig leaders, such as James S. Rollins of Columbia and Edward Bates of St. Louis, flirted briefly with Know-nothingism, and in the city the Know-nothing Washington King was elected mayor in 1855. King quickly installed as much of his party's agenda as possible. He expanded the police force, primarily as a weapon against Irish and German "mobs," and installed and enforced Sunday closing laws (against Irish pubs and German beer gardens, but not against "respectable" hotel bars).[14] But in 1856, the *Republican* disavowed nativism, knowing it could not prevail for long against half the community, and King's bid for reelection was defeated by the Bentonite John How.[15]

Slavery also created havoc in Democratic ranks, but the Democracy survived by adjusting. Its troubles had started with the Benton–anti-Benton split in 1849, after which the state party was dominated by the pro-Southern ultras of the Central Clique and its border-county allies David Rice Atchison and Benjamin F. Stringfellow. Bentonites, who were increasingly identified as free-soilers and were supported by the *Democrat* and usually by the German press as well, mostly prevailed in St. Louis. With the presidential administrations of Democrats Franklin Pierce (1853–1857) and James Buchanan (1857–1861) tilting southward, Missouri's anti-Bentons dubbed themselves "National" Democrats.

By 1856, Benton's lieutenants in St. Louis faced a dilemma. "Old Bullion" himself, already in the grip of the cancer that was to kill him but still determined to regain control of the state, failed in 1856 and 1857 to capture the governorship and then a United States Senate seat. Clinging to his vision of a tranquil Union achieved by restoring the principles of the Missouri Compromise, Benton would not face current realities. Elsewhere, men of Benton's views had helped to found the Republican party, but the old lion, for thirty years the West's Democratic leader, hoped to return his party to its Jacksonian origins. Thus he refused to endorse the Republican

14. John C. Schneider, "Riot and Reaction in St. Louis, 1854–1856," *MHR* 68 (1973/1974): 183–84.
15. Ibid., 182.

ticket in 1856, despite the presence of his son-in-law, John C. Frémont, at the head of that ticket. He campaigned throughout Missouri for Buchanan, a weak man as Benton acknowledged, but an old Jacksonian who would try to save the Union.[16]

Frank Blair and Gratz Brown, regarding Buchanan as a tool of Southern slave interests, saw that the logic of their free-soil views demanded that they endorse Frémont for president. But there were good reasons for not doing so. They did not want to risk Benton's wrath, and in Missouri, now tightly held by the National Democrats, a Republican ticket would have been merely a quixotic gesture. With Benton's support, a modest base for Republicanism might have been established, but without it, there was not a chance. So Blair and Brown did not endorse Frémont, but they would not campaign for Buchanan.[17]

In 1857, Gratz Brown, still a nominal Democrat, shocked his fellow legislators and the nation by proposing in the General Assembly that slavery be abolished in Missouri. It was not that slavery was immoral as the Massachusetts abolitionists claimed, said Brown, but that the economic health of Missouri was at stake. Emancipation would attract capital, stimulate business, raise land prices, and increase the population. Slavery's only contribution to Missouri, he argued, was to identify it with the backward South. The state's principal trading partner was the Northeast, and that relationship should be enhanced. As the leading Western state, Missouri should pass laws favoring immigration, manufacturing, commerce, railroads, and free land. This was the whole Republican platform, with emancipation thrown in for good measure. The legislature rejected Brown's resolution, but the speech rang true with the Germans and with some elements of St. Louis business.[18]

The young lawyers and merchants who had coalesced around Benton in the early 1850s—Blair; Brown; John How; Barton Able; Giles, Oliver D., and Chauncey Filley—were fully, if not quite openly, committed to Republican principles by 1857. Blair, whose father chaired the Republican National Convention in 1856, won a congressional seat that year as a Free-Soil Democrat, and How was elected mayor. In 1857, How was succeeded by John Wimer, a German blacksmith who headed the Emancipation ticket. The *Missouri Republican* mourned that St. Louis's new mayor was committed to agitating the slavery question until Missouri became a free state. Once in office, Wimer tried to placate the *Republican*, which

16. Chambers, *Old Bullion Benton*, 420–26.
17. Peterson, *Freedom and Franchise*, 65–66.
18. Ibid., 72–75.

irritated his friends, who replaced him in 1858 with O. D. Filley. Thomas Hart Benton died in 1858, removing a major deterrent to the Republican label.[19]

With the Whig party virtually a nullity after 1856, the *Republican* went over to the National Democrats, promptly qualifying it as the major press spokesman for the Southern interest in the upper Mississippi Valley and the West. It did not identify with the Southern "fire-eaters" who would destroy the Union, but editor Paschall and the paper's principal owners, the brothers George and John Knapp, were well satisfied with Southern ascendancy in the national and state governments. In the *Republican*'s columns, the enemy were "black Republicans" who would abolish slavery and promote racial amalgamation. This emphasis, standard in the state's Democratic press, made it virtually impossible even in St. Louis to win an election, practice a profession, or do business as an avowed Republican.[20]

As they eased toward Republicanism, the Bentonite cadre had the warm support of the German press and the mass of German voters. But as the antislavery trend emerged, the Irish refused to follow. Catholic leaders in St. Louis were often pro-Southern, and the Irish did not welcome the prospect of competing with free black labor. But this defection was more than counterbalanced by other developments in St. Louis. Chief among these was the influx to the city beginning in the late 1830s of young and enterprising Yankee businessmen. There had been a New England and middle-states element in St. Louis since territorial days, but these earlier families, through long association and intermarriage, could hardly be distinguished politically from their Creole and Southern friends. William Carr Lane, for example, a Pennsylvanian who became the city's first mayor in 1823, was a thoroughgoing Southerner in outlook, fiercely proslavery and finally pro-Confederate.

The mid-century Northerners were different. They had come to St. Louis after exposure at home to antislavery views, and they established businesses that relied on access to Eastern capital. They had an East-West rather than a North-South orientation, believing that the city's and their own futures depended on strong transportation and financial links to the East. They supported railroad construction with their influence and with their own money. Many businessmen of Southern origin agreed with them on

19. Ibid., 80–81; William E. Smith, *The Francis Preston Blair Family in Politics* (New York: Macmillan, 1933), 1:404–6.
20. See B. B. Lightfoot, "Nobody's Nominee, Sample Orr and the Election of 1860," *MHR* 55 (1960/1961): 145.

economic matters, but the Yankee merchants carried no sentimental Southern baggage with them as the political crisis deepened.

The Filleys, of the Excelsior Stove Company, natives of Connecticut and active in St. Louis politics from the early 1850s, were exceptions to the general run of Yankee merchants who stuck to business. Thomas Allen of Massachusetts, who shared with native St. Louisan James H. Lucas preeminence among local businessmen, served briefly in the Missouri Senate in the late 1840s, but only for the purpose of establishing the state's railroad network. Hudson E. Bridge, a Vermonter, who founded the Bridge-Beach Stove Company, was twice president of the Pacific Railroad and served on the boards of several banks and horsecar lines. He had powerful financial and business connections in New York City and investments in a half-dozen Iowa, Illinois, and western Missouri towns. Bridge was a parishioner and friend of William Greenleaf Eliot of Massachusetts, pastor of the Unitarian Church of the Messiah, who was one of the few open abolitionists in St. Louis before the mid-1850s. With the help of Bridge, John How, and others, Eliot founded Washington University in 1857. From the beginning, the university had a strong Yankee flavor. Carlos Greeley (New Hampshire), George Partridge (Massachusetts), Henry Ames (New York), and a dozen more New Englanders and New Yorkers were also in the front ranks of St. Louis and Western business in the 1850s. Less active personally in politics than the Filleys and John How, these men shared free-soil views and sensitivity to any threat to the Eastern economic connection.

Far less numerous than the Germans in the city, and less ideologically driven than the German editors, these Yankee merchants, with their ranks strengthened by a few powerful Southerners such as the Virginian Henry Taylor Blow, president of the Collier White Lead Company, put their economic muscle behind the political leadership of Frank Blair. As large employers of labor, buyers of raw and semifinished products, major customers of the banks, investors in railroad and other public enterprises, and creditors of hundreds of individuals and businesses, this coalition could claim at least equal influence with Democratic businessmen in the local economy's structure.[21]

21. For a fuller discussion of the origins and attitudes of the St. Louis business elite, see James Neal Primm, *Lion of the Valley: St. Louis, 1764–1980* (Boulder: Pruett, 1981), 233–38. The Hudson E. Bridge Papers at the Missouri Historical Society, St. Louis, illustrate in striking detail the amazing range of economic activities and political interests of a leading Yankee merchant.

As the national and state elections of 1860 approached, Frank Blair and his allies struggled to create a Republican party in Missouri. With little initial support outstate, a conservative image was required. Despite a personal preference for Abraham Lincoln, Blair joined his father and Horace Greeley of the *New York Tribune* in backing the presidential candidacy of Edward Bates, a St. Louis lawyer who had been prominent in the national Whig party for two decades. Blair knew that the Germans did not like Bates, whose short affair with Know-nothingism had offended them, but he believed they would not stray far. Bates, an ex-slaveowner whose long career as a political conservative was known to every Missourian, could hardly be portrayed by the Democrats as a flaming radical.[22]

Missourians in 1860 were moderates usually, loving neither abolitionists nor fire-eaters. John Brown and William Lloyd Garrison, and even William H. Seward, the preconvention Republican favorite for the presidency, were anathema to many Missourians, who resented attacks on the immorality of slavery as destructive of good order and the sectional balance. But even outstate, slavery was not the norm. Most Missouri counties had few slaves; only 5 percent of the state's white families owned even one. Slaves, which comprised 10 percent of the state's population, were concentrated in the river counties along the Mississippi north of St. Louis and along the Missouri from Callaway County to the northwest border.[23]

Missouri politics reflected national divisions in 1860. Sen. Stephen A. Douglas of Illinois, the nation's most powerful Democrat, had lost his Southern following by repeatedly rejecting federal protection of slavery in the territories. Southerners bolted the Democratic National Convention in 1860 and nominated their own presidential candidate, John C. Breckinridge of Kentucky. When the regular (Northern) Democrats nominated Douglas, Claiborne F. Jackson, the leading gubernatorial candidate in Missouri, found himself in a box. If he endorsed Douglas, his most dedicated supporters, Missouri's proslavery "Ultras," would desert him. If he did not, moderates would be offended. Jackson stalled until Nathaniel Paschall of the *Missouri Republican* threatened to enter his own Douglas candidate if Jackson did not come to the mark. Jackson

22. Marvin E. Cain, *Lincoln's Attorney General: Edward Bates of Missouri* (Columbia: University of Missouri Press, 1965), 98–115.

23. Of 24,320 slaveholding families in 1860, 17,349 held fewer than 6 slaves, 540 held 20 or more, and only 191 families held more than 30. U.S. Bureau of the Census, *Agriculture in the United States in 1860* (Washington, D.C., 1864), 220–21.

disliked Douglas's politics and hated Paschall, but he acquiesced.[24]
The Ultras promptly nominated a Breckinridge ticket, with Hancock Jackson at its head. Many conservative Democrats and ex-
Whigs, doubting the sincerity of Claiborne Jackson's conversion,
supported a political unknown, Sample Orr of Springfield, on the
Constitutional Union ticket. Orr stressed preservation of the Union
and compromise on slavery extension in his campaign. The Republicans, with little credibility outside St. Louis, chose James Gardenhire as their candidate.

In the gubernatorial race, Claiborne Jackson barely defeated
Orr, with Hancock Jackson and Gardenhire a distant third and
fourth. For president, Douglas won in Missouri (his only complete
state victory). Constitutional Unionist John Bell was a close
second, with Breckinridge and Lincoln trailing. The Republicans
carried St. Louis for Lincoln and reelected Frank Blair to Congress
and O. D. Filley for mayor.

Missourians had chosen the middle ground. The Constitutional
Unionists' strong showing reflected the voters' longing for an un-
attainable past. Only because he has suppressed his real views had
Claiborne Jackson barely won the governorship. The Southern
Democrats and the Republicans, who shared a clear perception of
the direction of events—toward a climactic clash of the sections
over slavery—had captured between them less than one-fifth of the
electorate. In the months after the election the futility of the neu-
tralist view was repeatedly demonstrated.

During the campaign Frank Blair, whose life had been
threatened many times, went nowhere without his "Wide-awakes,"
several hundred glazed-hatted, caped, singing and shouting young
Germans—a combination bodyguard and cheering section.[25] After
South Carolina seceded in December 1860, the omnipresence of this
group, which looked suspiciously like a small army, aroused un-
favorable comment in the Democratic press and open hostility
from a secessionist paramilitary unit called the "Minute Men."
Taunts and threats, rather than violence, were the chief manifesta-
tions of this rivalry. On New Year's Day 1861, the Wide-awakes
broke up the last attempt to sell slaves at public auction in St.
Louis. For their part, the Minute Men harassed the "black Dutch"
and flew the Confederate flag from their downtown headquarters.

After the deep South states organized the Confederate govern-

24. Walter B. Stevens, *St. Louis, The Fourth City* (St. Louis: Clarks, 1909), 1:220–
21.
   25. Peterson, *Freedom and Franchise*, 98.

ment in February 1861, Missourians divided generally into secessionists, conditional unionists, and unconditional unionists. Relatively small in number, the secessionists included a majority of
the legislature, a congressman, and a United States senator. In St.
Louis, Lt. Gov. Thomas C. Reynolds, John A. Brownlee, president of
the Merchant's Bank, and Basil Duke, a Reynolds political lieutenant who headed the Minute Men, were the leading secessionists.

Conditional unionists, initially the largest of the three groupings,
opposed secession for Missouri but also rejected coercion of the
seceded states. The *Missouri Republican*, for example, opposed
secession for economic and military reasons. Notwithstanding the
ties of blood that Missourians had with the South, the state was
bound to the North and East by the more powerful ties of railroads,
markets, and capital. If war came, Missouri as a Confederate state
would be a peninsula bounded on three sides by Union territory,
likely to be engulfed by Illinoisans, Iowans, and Kansans. If the
Confederacy survived, with or without war, the Republicans would
be in full control of the Union, free to erect trade barriers that
would ruin Missouri.[26] But these economic realists would not
countenance interference with slavery nor the shedding of blood in
the name of union.

Businessmen of Southern origins—such as Virginian George R.
Taylor, president of the Pacific Railroad, Kentuckian Derrick R.
January, wholesale grocer and land speculator, and native St.
Louisan James H. Lucas, banker and transportation magnate and
reputedly the richest man west of the Appalachians—and Missourians James Harrison and Charles P. Chouteau, proprietors of the
Chouteau, Harrison, and Vallé Rolling Mills, were all of this persuasion. Hamilton R. Gamble, a leader of the St. Louis bar, and Sterling
Price of central Missouri, governor from 1853–1857, both professed
conditional unionism. For their pains, such men were taunted in
the Republican press as "dishrag unionists." Secessionists called
them turncoats or "yellowbellies."

Frank Blair, leader of the unconditional unionists, rejected the
constitutionality of secession. Since states *could not* secede, they
had not seceded; their lands were simply held temporarily by insur-
rectionists. The authority of the United States must be reestablished in all of its territories, by force if necessary. Hudson Bridge,
the Filleys, and most of the Yankee merchants generally held this
view, as did William Greenleaf Eliot; Isidor Bush, the city's leading
Jewish politician; William McKee, principal owner of the *Missouri
Democrat*; B. Gratz Brown, second only to Blair in influence with

26. *Daily Missouri Republican*, 22 March 1861.

the Germans; and of course Henry Boernstein of the *Anzeiger des Westens* and the Germans generally.[27] Even Robert M. Stewart, a long-time anti-Benton Democrat, bowed out as governor in January with the following: "Missouri to surrender her prosperity for the mad chimera of secession, to be followed by revolution, battle, and blood? Never!"[28]

Although he had not yet taken a public stand for secession, Governor Jackson, following the lead of the deep South, called upon Missourians to elect delegates to a convention "to consider Missouri's relations with the Union." Now certain of the governor's intentions, Frank Blair reorganized his Wide-awakes and members of the German *Turnverein* into an armed and drilling Home Guard. To maintain federal authority in Missouri, Congressman Blair set up a Committee of Safety, which included Giles Filley, O. D. Filley, Hudson Bridge, Samuel Glover, Barton Able, James O. Broadhead, John How, and the German Julius Witzig. Abraham Lincoln was kept informed of the Missouri situation by Blair's brother Montgomery and Edward Bates, both members of Lincoln's cabinet.[29]

On 18 February, Missouri's voters elected the entire slate of unionist delegates to the state convention. Secessionists had been rejected, 110,000 to 30,000. Eighty percent of the ninety-nine delegates were slaveholders, some were shaky unionists such as the convention's chairman Sterling Price, and a few were disguised secessionists such as attorney Uriel Wright of St. Louis, but the outcome was a shocking blow to the governor. Breckinridge Democrats had won a plurality in the legislature only a few months before, supported by many of the voters who had given the governor his victory. Jackson had not perceived the chilling effect on the electorate of the actuality of secession.

After a day in hot, crowded quarters in Jefferson City, the convention moved on 4 March to the Mercantile Library in St. Louis. Wavering unionists now heard, instead of the seductive Southern intonations of the legislature, unionism preached at dinner or at the bar of the Planter's House or Barnum's Hotel. Merchants, railroad men, and shippers, with their talk of Eastern markets and capital, were all around. This move, a masterstroke, had been arranged by Edward Bates's brother-in-law, Hamilton R. Gamble, and other St. Louis delegates. As chairman of the Committee on Federal Relations, Gamble wrote a report finding no present

27. Primm, *Lion of the Valley*, 244–47.

28. Quoted in Duane Meyer, *The Heritage of Missouri* (St. Louis: State, 1963), 344–45.

29. Cain, *Edward Bates*, 138–39; James O. Broadhead, "St. Louis During the War," unpublished manuscript, Broadhead Papers, Missouri Historical Society.

grounds for secession, which the convention adopted with only one dissenting vote.[30]

Having lost the battle of ballots, Governor Jackson was forced to develop a new approach. Confederate President Jefferson Davis at Montgomery and the governor kept in touch by courier, and they agreed that St. Louis was the key to the control of the state and the West. Assuming that outstate Missouri would go with the winners, Jackson thought that seizure of the federal arsenal in St. Louis and neutralization of Frank Blair and his followers would guarantee a Confederate future for Missouri. To achieve the latter, Jackson requested and the legislature passed a police bill transferring from the mayor to the governor the power to appoint members of the police board. Jackson promptly chose John A. Brownlee, a secessionist banker, to head the board.

After the Confederate attack on Fort Sumter on 15 April 1861, President Lincoln called upon the states for seventy-five thousand volunteers to suppress the insurrection. Governor Jackson indignantly (and predictably) refused to meet Missouri's quota of four thousand, stigmatizing the request as "illegal, unconstitutional, and revolutionary." Frank Blair promply offered to honor Lincoln's call from the ranks of the Home Guards. Shortly thereafter, Blair's German legions were sworn into the federal service as "Missouri Volunteers."[31]

His earlier efforts to take over the arsenal by various ruses having failed, Governor Jackson, following the Confederate president's advice, decided to seize it by surprise assault. He would call the eastern Missouri State Guard to its annual encampment, this time to be conveniently located on the hills overlooking the St. Louis arsenal. Once there, siege guns (to be furnished by President Davis) could break down the walls surrounding the arsenal and drive out the garrison. Unfortunately for this plan, when the militia general Daniel Frost arrived to reconnoiter the site, he found federal troops occupying the hills. Police Commissioner Brownlee then ordered the troops removed as trespassers, but Capt. Nathaniel Lyon, their commander, brushed him off.[32]

Lyon, a New Englander of abolitionist leanings, had been trans-

30. William Roed, "Secessionist Strength in Missouri," *MHR* 72 (1977): 421; Primm, *Lion of the Valley*, 247.

31. U.S. War Department, *The War of the Rebellion: A Compilation of the Official Records of the Union and Confederate Armies* (Washington, D.C., 1881–1901), vol. 3, part 1, 82–83, cited in Arthur Roy Kirkpatrick, "Missouri in the Early Months of the Civil War," *MHR* 55 (1960/1961): 235, 238.

32. Thomas L. Snead, *The Fight for Missouri from the Election of Lincoln to the Death of Lyon* (New York: C. Scribner's Sons, 1888), 148–49.

ferred from Kansas to the arsenal on 6 February at Frank Blair's request. His experience with Missouri "border ruffians" in Kansas had confirmed his political views. Blair and his associates had smelled out Jackson's intentions, and Lyon's disposition of his troops had prevented a state seizure of the arsenal. As a further precaution, Lyon had quietly transferred most of the military stores not required by his troops and Blair's Missouri Volunteers to Illinois.[33] Frustrated but determined to play out his hand, Frost set up his state militia camp at Lindell Grove, near the western edge of the city.

Some nine hundred militiamen gathered at Camp Jackson early in May, set up their tents, and began their military routines. About three hundred of these troops, called the "Southern Guard," were Basil Duke's Minute Men, augmented by several dozen unemployed stevedores and roustabouts from the levee. A few unionist guardsmen attended the encampment, but more of them shunned it or melted away after a day or two. The remainder of the militia were a mixed lot, many of them as yet uncommitted. A majority eventually served the Confederacy, in part because of their experiences at Camp Jackson.

Although they knew that the encampment posed no real threat to the security of the arsenal, Blair and Lyon were determined to assert federal authority as forcefully as possible in order to instruct the community and the governor. A few days after Camp Jackson was established, the steamer *J. C. Swon* arrived with Jefferson Davis's siege guns, seized from the federal arsenal at Baton Rouge. The guns were crated with misleading labels and unloaded at night, but Lyon was expecting them. His agents observed their unloading and transfer to Camp Jackson, but the captain made no attempt to interfere, since the guns represented opportunity. Dressed in clothing borrowed from Blair's mother-in-law and riding in her carriage, Lyon toured the camp on 9 May, noting the unmistakable crates and crude street signs lettered Jeff Davis and (Confederate General) Beauregard Avenues. With this evidence, he met with Frank Blair and the Committee of Safety, which had written authorization from Washington to act for the United States. Although Samuel Glover pointed out that the guns could be seized on a judicial writ by federal marshals, this would not have served Lyon's purpose, and a committee majority approved a military confrontation.[34]

33. William E. Parrish, "General Nathaniel Lyon, A Portrait," *MHR* 49 (1955/1956): 7.
34. Ibid., 10–11.

On 10 May, several hundred regulars from the arsenal and four regiments of Missouri Volunteers, some seven to eight thousand in all and under Lyon's overall command, converged upon Camp Jackson from several directions. The regiments were commanded by Frank Blair, Nicholas Schuettner, Henry Boernstein of the *Anzeiger*, and Franz Sigel, another Forty-eighter. Ignoring Frost's plea by messenger that the encampment was legal and his intentions were peaceful, Lyon continued the march and surrounded the camp. Frost promptly surrendered, and his men were marched out of the installation to Olive Street, flanked on both sides by Lyon's troops. There they stood for several hours, while Lyon and his regimental commanders conferred about their disposition.

News of the marching men and their objective had spread rapidly through the city, and a substantial share of the mobile population was at the site before Lyon arrived, having come by carriage, horsecar, or on foot, many of them bringing their lunch and their beverages and others their pistols, apparently intending to participate if there was to be action. Accounts of the denouement vary widely, but according to William Tecumseh Sherman, who looked on with his young son, a drunk with a pistol tried to break through the line of soldiers. A scuffle ensued, then a shot from the crowd struck Volunteer Capt. Constantine Blandowski (an expert instructor in the Prussian military drill). Having endured ethnic slurs and flying missiles from trouble-seekers for hours, some of the nervous and angry Volunteers fired low into the crowd, killing fifteen persons immediately and seriously wounding another dozen or so, several of whom eventually died, as did Blandowski. The troops then marched away with their prisoners, but there was hell to pay. Lyon had made his point, but at great cost. Stories that the "black Dutch" would murder citizens in their beds circulated, and many families fled to Illinois. For the next few days, Germans in uniform were targets for snipers.[35]

Camp Jackson polarized opinion in the state. At first it seemed that Lyon had converted the whole population to secession, and there were several well-publicized converts, such as Sterling Price, who accepted the command of the State Guard from Governor Jackson. But that angry reaction was soon calmed by the sober realization that Lyon and Blair had the upper hand. Neutrality was still the favorite theme of conditional unionists such as Paschall of the *Missouri Republican*, but neutrality for Missouri had never been a realistic option, and after Camp Jackson, it was even

35. James Peckham, *General Nathaniel Lyon and Missouri in 1861* (New York: American News, 1866), 136–51.

less so. Lyon's show of force, despite the tragedy and the angry reaction, had put into bold perspective Blair's (and Lincoln's) position that the nation could not relinquish ultimate authority over part of its territory and remain a nation. If secessionists did not care whether the United States survived, a large majority of Missourians did.

After Camp Jackson, Gen. William S. Harney, commanding the Department of the West, whose judgment (but not his loyalty) had been questioned by Blair, returned from Washington and publicly endorsed Lyon's conduct at Camp Jackson. Yet Harney continued to talk with Jackson and Price as though peace could be maintained in Missouri. Blair believed that these negotiations were a sham as far as the governor was concerned. After Harney agreed not to move federal troops outside St. Louis County in return for Jackson's guarantee to protect unionist persons and property, President Lincoln gave Blair Harney's dismissal papers, to be dated and presented to the general if and when Blair thought it necessary. On 30 May, Blair handed Harney his notice, and Nathaniel Lyon, just promoted to brigadier general, assumed command of the Western Department.[36]

Governor Jackson, still playing for time and Confederate assistance, sought a conference with Lyon, hoping to confirm his arrangements with Harney. Lyon agreed to meet only as a concession to conditional unionists such as Hamilton Gamble and James Yeatman, who had tried to prevent Harney's dismissal. Blair and Lyon, Jackson and Price, and their respective staffs exchanged views at the Planter's House in St. Louis on 11 June. After several hours, Lyon angrily announced that he would accept no restrictions on federal authority or movement.[37] Having no doubts about Lyon's next move, the governor and general returned to Jefferson City as fast as the Pacific Railroad could travel, burning the Gasconade and Osage bridges behind them. The governor grabbed the state seal and key records and decamped for Boonville, believing it easier to defend than the capital. In less than forty-eight hours Lyon, Blair, Henry Boernstein, and two thousand troops disembarked from steamboats at Jefferson City. Pausing only to install Boernstein as commandant at the capital, Lyon proceeded to Boonville, where his troops routed Jackson's State Guard after a brief skirmish.[38]

The governor and his retinue then retreated to southwest Mis-

36. Parrish, "General Nathaniel Lyon," 14.
37. Ibid., 15–16.
38. Snead, *The Fight for Missouri*, 206–11.

"Volunteers attacked in St. Louis," riots at Fifth and Walnut on 11 May 1861. *Harper's Weekly*.

souri, where he established a temporary capital at Neosho. Jackson still claimed to be merely defending the state from invaders (in December, the rump legislature passed a secession ordinance). In late July, declaring the elected state officials in rebellion, unionists recalled the state convention, which established a provisional government and elected Hamilton Gamble as governor. President Lincoln immediately recognized the legitimacy of this procedure and its results.[39]

Governor Gamble, James Yeatman, and other conservatives (former conditionalists), reconciled to war but fearing Lyon's boldness and his abolitionism, persuaded Lincoln to remove Lyon as commander of the Western Department, but the bulldog general continued as field commander. With the Blairs' advice, the president selected John C. Frémont to replace Lyon at St. Louis.[40] On 10

39. Kirkpatrick, "Missouri in the Early Months of the Civil War," 247.
40. Peterson, *Freedom and Franchise*, 104.

August, General Price's State Guard and Confederate troops from Arkansas defeated a smaller Union force at Wilson's Creek south of Springfield, killing General Lyon in the battle.

During his one hundred days in command of the Western Department, Frémont failed both politically and militarily. The Union defeat at Wilson's Creek and another at Lexington might have been averted by prompt movement of reinforcements on his part, and in St. Louis he alienated Blair and the merchants by awarding desirable military contracts to Californians. Already a favorite with the Germans, Frémont cemented their allegiance in late August by emancipating all slaves owned by rebel sympathizers in Missouri. Though he was an emancipationist himself, Blair (and Lincoln) thought this abrupt action would endanger the Union cause in Missouri and other border states. After Frémont refused to withdraw his proclamation, Lincoln rescinded it. Blaming Blair's reports for his troubles with Washington, Frémont jailed him twice for insubordination, but each time the War Department ordered his release. The *Missouri Republican*, despite its distaste for radicalism (emancipation), applauded the jailings of its old enemy.[41]

By November, Frémont was gone, having repeatedly demonstrated his incompetence, but the breach between Blair and most of the Germans was permanent. Only Henry Boernstein among the German leaders stayed with him. Blair never wavered in his commitment to total victory, but he found new allies on his right, emerging eventually as the leading conservative unionist in Missouri, stressing gradual emancipation and national reconciliation.[42] As a major general commanding an army corps under General Sherman, Blair performed with distinction, a rarity among civilian volunteer generals.

B. Gratz Brown succeeded to the radical leadership after Frémont's departure, and most of the Germans followed him, but the majority of the Yankee merchants and lawyers preferred Lincoln's and Blair's moderate course. James Yeatman, a Tennessean and former slaveholder, and the New Hampshire–born merchant and railroad promoter Carlos Greeley, for example, demonstrated the unity of purpose among the business elite as they worked indefatigably with William G. Eliot in managing the massive relief, supply, and medical adjunct to the Union army, the Western Sanitary Commission.

With the enthusiastic support of the German volunteers, Frank Blair and his Yankee businessmen and Nathaniel Lyon frustrated

41. Ibid., 105–8.
42. Ibid., 109.

the secessionist plans of Claiborne Jackson in 1861. In the long run, the residual unionism of a majority of Missourians was equally or more important, but in the crucial weeks after Fort Sumter, clear vision and decisive action tipped the balance. Blair had to have the Germans, but without his leadership and his connections in business and in Washington, the dedicated German minority would have floundered. That he became estranged from his mass support was a personal tragedy for Blair. His anger and grief when the Germans marched off behind their bogus hero was monumental, but for the Germans, Frémont epitomized an uncompromising commitment to human freedom, a commitment eventually required of Abraham Lincoln and the entire nation.

The Continuation of the German Revolutionary Tradition on American Soil

Steven Rowan

What happened in St. Louis in 1861 can be explained from the German side in terms of the experience of a generation that was aware it was reaching the limits of its active life. From this point of view, the German rising of 1861 was an episode of a European revolutionary tradition that drew on shared language and symbols going back at least to the era of the French Revolution and the wars of liberation against Napoleon I of 1812–1814. It was a tradition with both social-revolutionary and nationalist elements. The defeat of the German states by Napoleon I had led to the suppression of the ramshackle Holy Roman Empire of the German Nation and the reduction of sovereign German states from hundreds to dozens. This rapid transformation made drastic social and political change the order of the day and increased the level of political awareness. The shock of defeat by the French generated intense German nationalistic feeling, which emerged in such odd forms as the combination of gymnastics and nationalism promoted by Friedrich Ludwig Jahn and his Turners. Some governments briefly exploited these nationalistic feelings, but after the final defeat of Napoleon, the princes sought to retreat to authoritarian normalcy. The result was the development of a true culture of opposition in universities and towns all over the territories of the reactionary German Confederation. In 1819 the murder of the reactionary poet Kotzebue led to the promulgation of the Carlsbad Decrees, which placed all newspapers and universities in German central Europe under uniform blacklisting and censorship. Repression sent the culture of opposition underground, to surface occasionally in mass demonstrations such as the Hambach Festival in 1832 or the Frankfurt putsch in 1833. The revolutionary movement of the 1830s promoted a romantic nationalism with few concrete social or political goals beyond justice and brotherhood in a united German nation. In the 1840s, however, a few intellectuals who cultivated variations on the philosophy of Hegel began to move beyond liberalism to more radical ideologies, including forms of communism. By the middle years of the 1840s the full range of opposition opinion had already developed.

23

The common heritage that linked the journalists who propelled the normally inert German community of St. Louis into action was the great European revolution of 1848, or rather what they eventually came to believe about that revolution. This series of revolts began with the fall of Louis-Philippe in Paris, and a concatenation of mishaps led to the momentary retreat of the authoritarian regimes in central Europe and the apparent triumph of the Liberal opposition, which was then the only viable alternative to princely rule. The most radical social-revolutionary and republican groups, centered in southwest Germany, staged two fitful risings about a year apart, in 1848 and 1849, before final collapse. The revolutionaries who participated in these risings in the southwest achieved almost legendary fame in the opposition press, so that Friedrich Hecker, Franz Sigel, and August Willich—all future Union officers in America—became universally known. The Liberals who dominated the German uprising outside the southwest were soon shown to lack a strong hold on popular loyalties and were swept away by the revived princely governments.[1] As a result, a sizable group of rebels of differing political beliefs joined the flood of economic refugees emigrating overseas.[2]

These political refugees, the Forty-eighters, had as little unity in emigration as they had had in Germany, but they shared a common past and a common political culture. The choice open to them at the outset was whether to cluster near their country in hopes of an early return—an alternative soon narrowed by expulsions from Switzerland and France—or to set out to make a new life in distant America. Those who preferred to keep a watch on the Fatherland tended to gather in the expatriate community in London, where Karl Marx and the socialists honed their doctrines in acrimonious purity. Others went to America but hedged their bets by settling in the cosmopolitan European bridgeheads of New York, Boston, or New Orleans. Passing into the interior of the United States, to the Middle West of farmers and traders Gottfried Duden had extolled in the 1820s, was a decision that implied the desire to leave Europe forever and start over.[3]

1. The best general outline of the risings of 1848–1849 is still Veit Valentin, *1848: Chapters of German History*, trans. Ethel T. Schaffauer (Hamden, Conn.: Archon, 1965).

2. Mack Walker, *Germany and the Emigration* (Cambridge: Harvard University Press, 1964); Carl Wittke, *Refugees of Revolution: The German Forty-Eighters in America* (Westport, Conn.: Greenwood, 1952); Stephan Thernstrom, *The Harvard Encyclopedia of American Ethnic Groups* (Cambridge: Harvard University Press, 1980), articles "Germans," "Germans from Russia."

3. Gottfried Duden, *Report on a Journey to the Western States of North America and a Stay of Several Years Along the Missouri (During the years 1824, '25, '26, and*

In the chief city of Duden's promised land, St. Louis, they found a German community well on its way to absorption into American life. Germanic purity of a sort was represented in the region by encapsulated Hermann on the Missouri and by Latin-Farmer settlements such as Augusta or Marthasville in Missouri or Belleville in Illinois.[4] German emigration to Missouri in the 1830s and 1840s had achieved momentum through the settlement of homogeneous groups with goals ranging from social reform (the Giessen settlement society under Paul Follenius and Friedrich Münch) through a search for cultural survival for German-Americans (the Hermann settlement from Philadelphia) to the maintenance of sectarian orthodoxy (the Old Lutherans from Saxony under Martin Stephan). Even in the 1850s, some educated Germans would follow the example of Friedrich Hecker and turn to the soil in the New World. Rural Germans in Missouri had a self-conscious and vigorous culture all their own. St. Louis Germans, on the other hand, were haphazardly collected and on their way to piecemeal Americanization. The leaders of the German community were largely self-selected businessmen, with a scattering of lawyers and other professionals.

Some of those who arrived with ready-made reputations as popular leaders intended to make their stay brief, since they were certain that the final collapse of old Europe would come any day. The mass rallies that greeted the heroes of 1848 gave some illusions of power out of all proportion with reality. Gottfried Kinkel, who had been rescued from Spandau by Carl Schurz, sought to promote bonds payable on the faith and credit of the German Republic, and the former Hungarian dictator Louis Kossuth tried to raise American and ethnic support for a general European rising. The era up to 1855 was replete with spasms of what has been called "German Fenianism," but the failure of these pretentious efforts soon discredited quick American solutions to European problems. Efforts to enlist the United States directly as an agent of world revolution or as the center of a world republic also failed.[5]

What was left in the 1850s once these possibilities had been disproved was the hard business of setting priorities for a large and fluid German-speaking population in English-speaking North America. Each year delivered a new mass of German immigrants,

---

1827), trans. James W. Goodrich et al. (Columbia: State Historical Society of Missouri and University of Missouri Press, 1980).

4. For a preliminary survey of types, see Charles van Ravenswaay, *The Arts and Architecture of German Settlements in Missouri* (Columbia: University of Missouri Press, 1977).

5. Wittke, *Refugees of Revolution*, 92–108.

but the often-brutal economic and cultural environment also did rapid work. Once the enthusiasms of the great revolt had passed, Germans went back to their normal pattern of being almost impossible to unite on anything, since they were profoundly riven by social class, religion, political persuasion, and past experience. Unlike the Irish, they shared neither a common faith nor a common social deprivation. The Forty-eighters provided an impetus for social and political organization, but many Germans long in the United States agreed with some recent arrivals that the Forty-eighters were bearded wild men prone to impractical schemes. The Forty-eighters were largely religious skeptics or freethinkers at a time when many Germans still took their confessions quite seriously. They were intensely involved in political questions in a German population chiefly interested in making a decent living. Their chief strength with their fellow Germans was their talent for writing and speaking, their eagerness for organizing and leading at a time when group action appeared pressingly necessary even in individualistic America. The ethos of the Forty-eighters was strong enough to draw to them many educated Germans who had crossed the ocean before 1848, and the glamor of these gallant fighters for a lost cause made others long for their own great adventure.

Some of the radical leftists promoted profoundly dark visions of America, but they saw possibilities in its Hobbesian chaos. The communist novelist Adolph Douai declared in 1858:

> Democracy in this Union has only *this much* importance, namely, that everyone who happens to win the power to keep himself alive in the perpetual struggle of each against all earns the right to stomp on the heads of those who happen to be weaker, and they in turn can defend themselves as best they can. In the Old World they are not allowed to do that: they have to allow themselves to be trodden down; they can bite the chains which bind them, but they are not allowed to try to break them. In the Union they *are* allowed to break them if they can, that is, if they have the natural strength to do it. They also have come far enough for a general feeling of equality to reign, and for a relatively large number of people to be able to rise above the average, so that *actual* equality is expanded, not just equality in the abstract, and *progress is possible.*[6]

In the mid-1850s the concern of Germans was concentrated on defending themselves from nativist assaults on their enjoyment of ordinary citizens' rights. Most Germans probably felt more concern about pressure against their German life-style than about political restrictions, and it was always easy to get a crowd together to protest temperance laws or restrictions on Sunday entertainment.

6. Adolph Douai, *Fata Morgana. Deutsch-Amerikanische Preis-Novelle* (St. Louis: *Anzeiger des Westens*, 1858), 127.

The demonstrations and riots of the mid-decade made manifest a need for a common defense. The German-language press focused the opinion of the German reading public on the measures needed to defend the German ethnic community in the midst of an often-hostile American community. The American penchant for violence provided its own cure through counterviolence: the revolutionary general Franz Sigel wrote extensively on small-unit tactics for German-American militia units, and the Turner Societies were only one variety among many of self-defense organizations.[7]

One of the major results of the capture of ethnic leadership by the Forty-eighters in the course of the 1850s was the solidification of a German presence in the Republican party. Several factors impelled Germans to bolt the Democratic party in the middle of the decade, including disgust at the presence of the slaveholding aristocracy of the South, fear of Irish competition, discomfort over the importance of Catholics in the party, and distress at the readiness of the Democrats to tolerate a soft currency. The Republican party had its own negative elements as far as the Forty-eighters were concerned, particularly nativists and New England prohibitionists. The party the Forty-eighters wanted to build resembled nothing so much as that which Eric Foner has described under the rubric of *Free Soil, Free Labor, Free Men.*[8] The Republican party was not nearly so simple even in 1856 and 1860, but a coalition of Germans at the national convention in Chicago in 1860 did their best to act as if it were and to ignore whatever did not fit. For better or worse, the Republican party would be the chief channel by which the Forty-eighters entered the mainstream of American politics. Their contribution to the formation of the radical wing of that party is a story that has not yet found its historian.

The chief symbol of Republican principles for many Germans was John C. Frémont, a man who seems to have excited love and enthusiasm out of all proportion with his abilities. This enthusiasm can be explained at least in part by the fact that the presidential campaign of 1856 was the first in which the German Forty-eighters found their voice at the head of an increasingly powerful German voting bloc. Missouri Germans, particularly those in St. Louis, had been serving their own apprenticeship in the arts of opposition under Thomas Hart Benton, B. Gratz Brown, and Francis P. Blair,

7. Franz Sigel edited a journal in New York on militia companies (Carl Wittke, *The German-Language Press in America* [Lexington, Ky.: University of Kentucky Press, 1957], 190–91); a pamphlet by Sigel was published in 1859 entitled *Kavellerie-Reglement für deutsch-amerikanische Miliz-Compagnien.*

8. Eric Foner, *Free Soil, Free Labor, Free Man: The Ideology of the Republican Party before the Civil War* (Oxford: Oxford University Press, 1970).

General Franz Sigel. Courtesy of the State Historical Society of Missouri.

Jr., since 1851. The nativist Know-nothing movement had peaked in 1855, but its memory continued to spur immigrants to rally to defend their civil rights. Col. John C. Frémont, soldier, explorer, and former United States senator from California, was an ideal candidate to catch the enthusiasms of Germans. Unlike most American politicians, he seemed a dashing man of action, an apostle of principle. No stump orator or slick lawyer, Frémont appeared to represent a fresh start in American political life even while serving as a link to the traditions of Jacksonian democracy. His opposition to the expansion of slavery in the territories combined well with his support for a homesteading policy favoring smallholders and his advocacy of a Pacific railroad. Since the presidential candidate was required by custom to maintain a dignified silence through the entire campaign, Frémont was allowed to do what he did best—stand as a symbol for ideals imposed on him by others. By 1856 enough German political leaders had earned citizenship rights to be an effective force, and by then the "German Fenian" vogue had receded. Few Germans were as yet sure enough of their position to stand as candidates in their own right—that time would come only after 1861—so they supported sympathetic American political figures. John Frémont was their first love, and he drew broad German support in 1860 and 1864.[9] In 1856 the voters of Missouri were unable to vote the Republican ticket because it was not made available in the state, so they were encouraged by the *Anzeiger des Westens* to vote for the Know-nothing candidate Millard Fillmore using tickets marked "Under Protest." In 1860 many Germans supported Edward Bates and similar favorite-son candidates at the Republican National Convention in Chicago, but they harbored the hope that a deadlocked convention would turn to Frémont. The Blairs engineered the assignment of a western military command for Frémont in order to bolster their own influence in Missouri, but the explosive combination of a political Messiah with a revolutionary upheaval led to catastrophe. The removal of Frémont from his command after three months in power destroyed the political front the Forty-eighters had patched together. From that time, Frank Blair's party and the Frémont radicals were distinct, warring groups. The result was that Blair was forced out of the Republican party into a revived Democratic party. The ultimate doom of the radical movement that would come to power in Missouri at the end of the Civil War was probably already sealed by the split between Frémont and Blair in the summer and fall of 1861.

Abraham Lincoln, too obviously an old Whig, never excited more than lukewarm enthusiasm as a candidate among the Germans. They doubted until his death his commitment to the abolition of slavery and to the destruction of the retrograde society of the old South.

The crucial juncture between the ideology of the German Left and the ideals of the Republican radicals always lay in a similar perception of the parallels between social and political power. The German leftists believed the concentration of privileges and property in the hands of a ruling caste robbed the economy of its vitality and brought political despotism in its wake. The historians of the period often sang the praises of smallholder democracy and lambasted those who undermined the position of yeoman citizens through monopolizing markets and through controlling labor. To cite only one example, Theodor Mommsen underscored the disastrous effects of the defeat of the populist Gracchi by the senatorial aristocracy of ancient Rome. These historians were preaching

9. Ruhl J. Bartlett, *John C. Frémont and the Republican Party* (Columbus: Ohio State University Press, 1930).

a text set for them by the classic economists of England and Scotland. Gottfried Duden, who had lived in Missouri in the 1820s, had thought of slavery as a mildly distasteful necessity in a land where hired hands were hard to come by. In the 1830s and 1840s, on the other hand, slavery was seen by Germans as the instrument for massive concentration of economic and political power. Much of the vocabulary that would be applied to the capitalist order in the second half of the century was used first on the agrarian capitalists of plantation states in the United States.

When transferred to an American setting, the German leftist vision required only a few analogues with European institutions to mobilize German-Americans. First, the old European landed aristocracy was to be equated with the plantation-masters of the South. The mechanization of cotton spinning and weaving in the first half of the nineteenth century had made the South a world economic power, an agrarian outlier of Lowell, Massachusetts, and Manchester, England. The plantation-owning class regarded itself—and was regarded by others—as a preeminently political group, dominating much of the nation through its control of the Democratic party. To German leftists, the spread of slavery would doom the realization of the promise of the American Revolution, and with it the best remaining hope for a redemption of mankind. The America they saw themselves saving was a mythic democratic republic perceived through the writings of Jefferson, Franklin, and Paine. Slavery threatened both the livelihood of the immigrant farmer and the hope for the ultimate liberation of Europe.

The early 1860s was the last period in which the politics of the Forty-eighters were still generally expressed in terms of mass rather than class, in which the ultimate object of desire was a union of the whole populace against an external despotism. There was a problem of how the myth of popular revolution could be applied to the harsh realities of America, particularly with a powerbase linked to a single ethnic group. Workers' movements were still relatively rudimentary, and it was common for socialists to work with Liberals for common ends. The whole revolutionary spectrum still shared both outlook and language, if not specific remedies: Marx and Engels are the only part of that tradition normally read today, but many of their supposedly trenchant views were no more than commonplaces—even banalities—of German radical journalism in the mid-nineteenth century.[10] Friedrich Engels would

10. Most of the opinions on American matters registered in the collection of Karl Marx and Friedrich Engels, *Der Bürgerkrieg in den Vereinigten Staaten* (Berlin/

tremble with quiet jealousy over communist friends and Liberal enemies who had won colonels' eagles and generals' stars in the United States Army during the Civil War.[11] By the 1870s this sort of common purpose among revolutionaries would be a thing of the past, with St. Louis being the only place where the myth of the popular uprising was put into practice in an American setting. Soon the central revolutionary myth held by the Left would be the general strike, the ultimate confrontation between labor and capital; St. Louis would have its turn for that in 1877.

Another contributing factor to the events of 1861 was the simple passage of years. By 1861 the ranks of the true Forty-eighters had begun to thin, since many had died or lost the faith. Amnesty in Germany had enticed many to return to take up their disrupted lives in Europe. Involvement in American life had caused some to go completely native and give themselves over wholly to the pursuit of private fortunes. The great war that began with such lightheartedness would be the last putsch of the revolutionary generation: the industrialized hell of the long Civil War Americanized the German intellectuals in a way peacetime would never have done, so that they came out as American as the G.A.R. By 1865 the days of *Freikorps* and of street barricades were gone forever, and the men of 1848 were dead, maimed, or irredeemably middle-aged. The Forty-eighters had always lived on myth and bluff, and the growing religious and social fragmentation of the German population left the freethinkers and radicals increasingly isolated from any power base. Even the most successfully Americanized Forty-eighter of them all, Carl Schurz, would find St. Louis an inhospitable place after the mid-1870s. Some reform-minded German-speaking writers, like Joseph Pulitzer, would go over completely to the dominant English-speaking culture, while others, such as Emil Preetorius and Carl Dänzer, became mere critics of a state that was becoming increasingly backward. Börnstein commented at the end of his life that Missouri would never live up to its promise until it returned to the ideals of Thomas Hart Benton and the young Frank Blair. In much the same way the abandonment of Börnstein, disreputable as he was, made the St. Louis Germans all

---

East: Dietz, 1976), are found in abundance in both the *Anzeiger* and the *Westliche Post.*

11. Ibid., 214–15, letter of Engels to Joseph Weydemeyer in St. Louis, 24 November 1864: "[August] Willich seems to me to have done the best of the Germans who have gotten into the war, [Franz] Sigel, on the other hand, has unmistakably documented his mediocrity. And [Carl] Schurz, bold Schurz, that dumb fart *(Furz)* who leaps into the hail of bullets, how many foes has he destroyed so far?"

that much poorer. They continued to fragment and Americanize until those who remained were a quaint precipitate of something once great. The events of 1861 have marked Missouri ever since, but the ultimate irony is that the true winners in Missouri would prove to be the followers of Claiborne Fox Jackson and Sterling Price.

In retrospect, the spring of 1861, the "honeymoon of the war," would be the last time the men of the German March Revolution could strut with feathers in their hats and feel once more like boys storming the heavens. The long adventure that had begun in the streets of Berlin, Dresden, or Freiburg would end on the slopes of Bloody Hill by Wilson's Creek or at some other shambles, where romantic revolution met bullets and cannonballs for one last time.

St. Louis German radical newspapers in the early 1860s were a mature hybrid of German and American journalistic styles, for they shared characteristics of both along with a flavor all their own. The German periodical press had existed in St. Louis for a quarter of a century, despite the fact that the fund of common experience drawn upon by the writers and readers in the New World rarely went before 1848. Prior to 1848, German newspapers in St. Louis were often short-lived and highly personal organs of particular editors, or they might be financed by a political party for the duration of a campaign before being dropped. The lonely radical Heinrich Koch, for example, was associated with no fewer than three newspapers of a revolutionary bent between 1843 and 1848, with some time off to fight in the Mexican War: *Der Antipfaff (The Priest-Hater), Der Communist,* and *Vorwärts (Charge!).* Strictly religious weeklies flourished, but they had little to say on matters concerning the community at large. The Old Lutheran periodicals *Lehre und Wehre* and *Der Lutheraner* would join the Catholic *Der Herold des Glaubens (Herald of the Faith)* in surviving into the twentieth century, but they would only persuade those who were already converted to a particular sect.[12] The beginnings had been made of a political journalism of more general significance, but the direction it would take was still unclear as late as 1850.

In 1859 the Nestor of the Missouri Germans, Friedrich Münch, tried to explain the state that St. Louis journalism had attained:

12. Karl J. R. Arndt and May E. Olson, *German-American Newspapers and Periodicals, 1732–1955: History and Bibliography,* vol. 1 (Heidelberg: Quelle & Meyer, 1961), 247–77; see generally Wittke, *German-Language Press,* and *Refugees of Revolution,* 262–79; on St. Louis, George Hellmuth Kellner, *The German Element on the Urban Frontier: St. Louis, 1830–1860,* Univ. of Missouri–Columbia Ph.D. Diss., 1973, esp. pp. 175 ff. Less helpful is Audrey J. Olson, CSJ, *St. Louis Germans, 1850–1920: The Nature of an Immigrant Community and Its Relation to the Assimilation Process,* Univ. of Kansas Ph.D. Diss., 1970.

Friedrich Münch of Marthasville, Missouri: farmer, politician, publicist. Photograph taken in 1856. Courtesy of the Missouri Historical Society.

Missouri shows some attempts at authorship already, both in English and German—but the main reading material is supplied by public newspapers, which concern themselves with many more matters alongside politics (such as science, economics and personal concerns) than is normally the case in Germany; they also have a periodical literature for poetry and short stories on a scale which one has to get used to reading and seeing. —Since newspapers are deeply involved in political affairs, and since considerable capital is invested in them, only the most capable men are chosen as editors. The main newspapers have excellent high-speed presses.

I could hardly describe the number and names of the English papers. At the head of those which represent the free-state movement is the splendidly edited "St. Louis Democrat." The chief partisan of the conservative direction is the "St. Louis Republican." The nativist persuasion is also represented.

But the reader will want to know more about the German newspapers in order to be able to form an opinion about the intellectual efforts of his countrymen in Missouri. —The "Anzeiger des Westens," which appears in St. Louis, was the first German newspaper west of the Mississippi, and from that day to this it has been in capable hands. A bit more than a year ago the "Westliche Post" was founded in the place of other newspapers not worth remembering; both newspapers, though different in tone and attitude, support the cause of progress, of making Missouri a free state, of the rights and interests of the Germans here, and of the reorganization of federal politics, all with equal warmth, and they are not only the most influential German organs in the entire West, but they can be compared directly with the very best of the Eastern newspapers. —The "St. Louis Chronik" is conservative and opposes any alteration of the current system of slavery—it is read mostly by Catholics. —The "Herold des Glaubens" is an utterly Catholic newspaper. The "Mississippi-Handelszeitung" is trying to fulfill its mission with laudable zeal. —The German newspapers in the countryside—the "St. Charles Demokrat," the "Hermanner Volksblatt" and the "St. Joseph-Zeitung" are all on the liberal side.

The newspapers here cannot be expected to preserve the restrained tone of European journals. Not only do they subject the conditions and events of the Old World, of which they are kept well informed through numerous correspondents, to a scathing critique, but the parties hew at one another with a two-edged sword—the President himself is spared no more than the least citizen, and deeds and personalities are discussed which seldom come to be spoken of in public in Germany. Anyone who stands out for any reason must expect to be subjected to public criticism, and few are able to win friends without also gaining open rebuke as well. The searching investigations miss nothing, and a so-called public man had better cover himself well lest he show his weak spots. It is worst of all for a candidate—the opposing party will leave no artery unslashed. —I would not be so bold as to assert that decency is observed in every case, or that the limits of good taste are not frequently overstepped in the course of this mud-slinging, but until people learn to master their passions, republicans cannot allow themselves to be too touchy. Here people prefer to put up with the abuse of the press rather than give up their unrestricted right to do what they want; people think the evils committed by the press can also be corrected by the press, and only the continuous vigilance of all can preserve freedom and secure progress.

Newspapers here are very cheap; the "St. Louis Democrat" already mentioned can be had in a mammoth format printed in very fine type for a dollar a year (with thirteen cents postage within the state); the best German papers (with a smaller circulation, to be sure) cost two dollars. There are few American families where a newspaper is not read; Germans in the countryside read too little—unfortunately the so-called farmer is satisfied with a church bulletin. —There is also a French newspaper in St. Louis.[13]

Münch gives a reasonably accurate account of the form German journalism had achieved by the end of the 1850s, though the rates he quotes are for weekly rather than daily editions. A daily subscription to the *Anzeiger* in 1860 cost eight dollars a year, a rate which included two additional weeklies, the Sunday tabloid *Westliche Blätter* and the literary newspaper *Der Salon*, edited by the novelist Otto Ruppius. The rates for the *Westliche Post* were the same, though this only included a single Sunday tabloid, *Mississippi Blätter*. *Kennedy's St. Louis Directory* lists nine German newspapers by counting the supplements as separate periodicals, out of a total of twenty-eight newspapers in all languages. The cheapest subscription listed in 1860 was for the freethinker monthly *Gottes Freund, der Pfaffen Feind (God's Friend, the Priests' Enemy)*, which went for only fifty cents a year.[14]

The St. Louis journalistic tradition that would achieve virtual establishment status in the latter half of the nineteenth century with Emil Preetorius, Joseph Pulitzer, and Carl Dänzer began with the *Anzeiger des Westens*, founded in 1835. The *Anzeiger* set the caustic, progressive style that would always mark the St. Louis German press, including such English-language spin-offs as the *St. Louis Post-Dispatch*. The true founder of the *Anzeiger*, which was launched in October 1835, was Wilhelm Weber, who was the first journalist in St. Louis to speak out against the lynching of blacks and the evils of slavery.[15] Weber would edit the *Anzeiger* from March 1836 until March 1850, during a period when its main German competition was the Whiggish *Deutsche Tribüne* and the Catholic *Tages-Chronik*.

The figure who came to dominate German journalism throughout the 1850s, as either hero or horrible example, was Heinrich

13. Friedrich Münch, *Der Staat Missouri geschildert mit besonderer Berücksichtigung auf teutsche Einwanderung* (New York, St. Louis: Farmers' and Vine-Growers' Society, 1859), 166–68.

14. Richard Edwards, ed., *St. Louis Directory, 1860* (St. Louis: R. V. Kennedy, 1860), "Newspapers."

15. A. A. Dunson, "Notes on the Missouri Germans on Slavery," *MHR* 59 (1964/1965): 355–66.

Heinrich Börnstein, publisher of the *Anzeiger des Westens*. From a *carte de visite* of 1873, Vienna. Courtesy of the Missouri Historical Society.

Börnstein (1805–1892).[16] It was Börnstein, part revolutionary, part bigot, part culture vulture and wholly sensationalist, who provided the radical press with both a model and a whipping boy. His energy and entrepreneurial drive left a profound and ambiguous legacy, yet he is the key to the convolutions of the German element in St. Louis down to 1861. Those who came after him tried their best to live him down, but this rather disreputable figure is at the bottom of almost every story worth telling about St. Louis Germans from the day of his arrival in 1850 until his final departure in 1862. Why should this be so?

Heinrich Börnstein was born in Hamburg in 1805 as the son of a mixed marriage, his father a Catholic actor from Austrian Galizia and his mother a Protestant. When his father took the family home to Galizia to escape the tumult of the last phase of the Napoleonic wars, young Heinrich was forced to submit to a Catholic education in Lemberg against his will, due to the operation of the Austrian law on mixed marriages. This helped to instill in him a hatred of Catholicism in general and the Jesuit order in particular that was to be one of the connecting strands of a complex public life. Börnstein served a long stint in the Austrian army before devoting himself to the stage, and he lived in Paris in the 1840s as a cultural rather than a political expatriate. There he set up a "translation factory" to work French plays into a form suited for the German stage, and in 1844 he launched the weekly *Vorwärts!* as a liberal reformist review of culture and politics. Börnstein edited the small paper along with his lifelong friend Karl Ludwig Bernays (1815–1879), who would also be his colleague in St. Louis. After a few months of publication, the journal took a sudden lurch leftward when Börnstein took in the famed exile poet Heinrich Heine and a group of socialists including Arnold Ruge, Karl Marx, and Friedrich Engels. This metamorphosis of Börnstein into a red menace is understandable only when one considers both his pique over the continued banning of his innocuous cultural review by German authorities and the personal magnetism of the young Marx. The Paris *Vorwärts!* published Heine's most radical poetic attacks on the German social order, along with Karl Marx's first "scientific socialist" writings. Despite the growing influence of communists in the newspaper, it was Bernays—a future secretary of the Missouri Republican party!—who seems to have precipitated the closure of the newspaper by praising an assassination attempt on the Prussian King Friedrich Wilhelm IV. Since the French King Louis-

16. Alfred Vagts, "Heinrich Börnstein, Ex- and Repatriate," *BMHS* 12 (1955/1956): 105–27.

Philippe had suffered assassination attempts on a roughly annual basis, the Paris government listened to the demands of the Prussians and shut *Vorwärts!* down. In the end only Marx had to go into exile, in Brussels; Börnstein stayed in Paris until the February revolution in 1848 seemed to promise the dawn of a new order.[17] He avidly collected the newspapers of that revolt day by day (the collection is still in the St. Louis Mercantile Library), and he played a role in organizing a German Legion to aid the revolution in Germany. When all turned sour at the end of 1848 with the election of Louis Napoleon as president of France, Börnstein decided to join his friend Bernays in America.

In early 1849 Heinrich Börnstein arrived in New Orleans, from whence he traveled via St. Louis to the Swiss settlement of Highland, Illinois. Ever a man of many talents, Börnstein subsisted by working as a pharmacist and physician. In March 1850, he was asked to cross the Mississippi to St. Louis to edit the *Anzeiger des Westens*. He at once set about researching and writing a scandalous anti-Jesuit novel in the style of his French old friend Eugène Sue: *Die Geheimnisse von St. Louis*, translated in 1852 by Dr. H. W. Gempp as *The Mysteries of St. Louis, or, The Jesuits on the Prairie de Noyers*, dedicated to no less a personage than former United States Senator Thomas Hart Benton.[18] This would be the first of a series of popular political novels published on Börnstein's initiative, notably Adolph Douai's *Fata Morgana* and Otto Ruppius's *Der Prairie-Teufel*, a sequel to *The Mysteries*.[19] Besides serializing popular German or translated novels in his daily and weekly editions, Börnstein made an intense effort to fill gaps in the literary culture of the German reading public in the Midwest. His semiannual *Haus-Bibliothek des Anzeigers des Westens (Home Library of the "Anzeiger...")* ran from 1855 to 1857 before being replaced by the weekly *Der Salon*.[20] He always had a strong predilection for plays translated from French, and the *Haus-Bibliothek*, which presented material Börnstein apparently brought from France, had

17. See Heinrich Börnstein, ed., *Vorwärts!*, reprint with an introduction by Walter Schmidt (Leipzig: Zentralantiquariat der DDR, 1975).

18. Heinrich Börnstein, *Fünfundsiebzig Jahre in der Alten und Neuen Welt: Memoiren eines Unbedeutenden* (Leipzig, 1884), 2:99; the English edition is preserved in several places, including the Mercantile Library and the Missouri Historical Society in St. Louis.

19. Adolph Douai's *Fata Morgana* won a competition given by a committee consisting of Berta Behrens of St. Charles, Missouri, Friedrich Münch of Marthasville, and Karl Ludwig Bernays of St. Louis. Otto Ruppius, *Der Prairie-Teufel: Roman aus dem amerikanischen Leben* (St. Louis: Meylert, 1861), was published earlier in serial form and by the *Anzeiger* press.

20. Heinrich Börnstein, ed., *Haus-Bibliothek des Anzeigers des Westens*, vol. 6 (St. Louis: *Anzeiger des Westens*, 1857), last page, announced the demise of the series.

Karl Ludwig Bernays, editor of the *Anzeiger des Westens*.
Courtesy of the Missouri Historical Society.

those as well as curiosities, poems, and sensationalist accounts of murders. The most jarring note to modern eyes is the inclusion of anti-Catholic as well as anti-Semitic tales. The Jewish ghetto culture he encountered in Galizia offended Börnstein as profoundly as did the convent culture of Catholicism.[21] The *Haus-Bibliothek* makes the scabrous side of freethinker journalism palpable.

Börnstein prided himself in his memoirs for having raised the level of German journalism in St. Louis, but his main accomplishment in politics was to act as the local agent of parallel changes taking place all over German America. German journalists everywhere in the 1850s were calling their wayward countrymen back to the purity of their language, and the influx of educated refugees determined to avoid manual labor at all costs added a certain urgency to this appeal. In most communities, some Germans had already begun to find fault with the traditional party of the immigrants, the Democrats, but in Missouri this transition was particularly sharp; it is a tribute to Börnstein's agility that he saw the change and rode the new political movement to prominence.[22] In 1850 the Missouri Legislature refused to elect the veteran Senator Benton to a new term, and in 1852 Börnstein threw his full support behind Benton in his run for a St. Louis seat in the United States House of Representatives. While most of the older immigrants opposed Benton, the younger immigrants apparently were attracted to the chance to join a mass opposition to the slaveowners who dominated Missouri. Benton Democracy would provide a stepping stone to the Missouri Free Soil movement, which would eventually form the kernel of the Republican party in Missouri. In the early and middle 1850s the *Anzeiger* managed to use this cause to overwhelm its competition, and the *Deutsche Tribüne* and its successors finally died. In the Know-nothing era of the middle 1850s Börnstein made himself a name as a leader among the St. Louis Germans, refusing to support efforts to fund dubious revolutionary schemes aimed at Europe, but keeping up an assault on organized religion and establishment politics at home. He alienated almost as many as he attracted, since he threw money at speculative invest-

21. Ibid., vol. 3 (1856), 33 ff. for *Schief Levinche und seine Kalle oder Judenthum und Katholizismus* by a Dr. Schiff, which was defended on the grounds that it had been recommended to Börnstein by Heinrich Heine in Paris; vol. 4 (1856) for *Die Ermordung des Pater Thomas in Damascus*, a blood-accusation tale also presented with a certain amount of special pleading.

22. Vagts, "Heinrich Börnstein," is surprisingly weak on Börnstein's politics, which are reviewed in his memoirs with large gaps. Every memoirist and publicist of the region made some sort of comment on Börnstein, usually negative. See, for example, Daniel Hertle, *Die Deutschen in Nordamerika und der Freiheitskampf in Missouri* (Chicago: *Illinois-Staatszeitung*, 1865), 52 ff.

ments in hotels, saloons, and breweries while earning a reputation as a cheapskate with his own employees.[23] In the late 1850s he was back with his first love, the theater, by organizing a full-scale legitimate repertory theater company, the St. Louis Opern-Haus on Market Street. He confidently launched an annual for the Opera House in 1861, fronted by a lithograph portrait of his wife Marie.[24]

In the later 1850s the *Anzeiger* was near the height of its influence, though it seems to have grown more cautious with age. Börnstein boosted circulation by offering cheap run-of-press novels he had sponsored as well as complete sets of the *Haus-Bibliothek*. In 1857 the list of agents authorized to accept subscriptions for the *Anzeiger* gives an idea of the newspaper's reach: the greatest number of agents (forty-six) were in southern and western Illinois, from Springfield and Urbana to Cairo. There were agents scattered all over Missouri, with concentrations on the banks of the two great rivers, but the total number (thirty-seven) was still lower than that in Illinois. Seventeen agents resided in Iowa, even in communities as diminutive as Sigourney. Six agents were found in Indiana, four each in Minnesota Territory, Wisconsin, and Ohio, two each in Kentucky, Kansas, and California, while one agent each sufficed for Michigan, Tennessee, and Nebraska Territory.[25] Börnstein boasted that he was offered sixty thousand dollars cash for his newspaper in 1860, and he regarded that as less than the undertaking was worth.[26] It seemed to be an invincible concentration of journalistic power.

In 1857 Börnstein's former editor-in-chief, Carl Dänzer, organized the *Westliche Post*, which would soon be the premier newspaper of the German midwest and would survive until 1939. Although the *Post* was modeled on the *Anzeiger* and both were radical Republican papers, there were also strong differences. The *Post* never had Börnstein's pretense of being a medium of culture for the masses, and its anticlericalism was muted. The *Post* under Dänzer, a former member of the Frankfurt National Assembly of 1848–1849, and his 1860 successor Theodor Olshausen, a leader in

23. William Hyde and Howard L. Conard, eds., *Encyclopedia of the History of St. Louis* (New York, Louisville, St. Louis: Southern History Co., 1899), 4:1636.
24. F. Kreuter and C. Börnstein, eds., *Bühnen-Almanach des St. Louis Opern Hauses*, vol. 1 (St. Louis, 1 January 1861), no subsequent issues. Besides theatrical pieces Börnstein published in the *Haus-Bibliothek*, he authored a one-act farce entitled *Deutsche Einwanderer und Deutsche Gesellschaft! Lebensbild in 1 Aufzuge—Aufgeführt von der deutschen philodramatischen Gesellschaft im Varieties-Theater zu St. Louis* . . . (St. Louis: *Anzeiger des Westens*, 1853).
25. *Anzeiger des Westens*, Wochenausgabe, Sunday, 1 November 1857 and following, in the first column, first page of each issue.
26. Börnstein, *Fünfundsiebzig Jahre*, 2:383.

Carl Dänzer, editor of the *Westliche Post* from 1857 to 1860.
Courtesy of the Missouri Historical Society.

the Schleswig-Holstein revolt against Denmark, was more narrowly political and ideological than the flamboyant *Anzeiger*, with its editors who prided themselves more on their literary than on their political pretensions.

With the onset of the war, Heinrich Börnstein was off on a new adventure as a colonel of volunteers, then as United States consul in Bremen. The newspaper he left behind tended to drift, and his brief return in 1862 to promote the fading political fortunes of Francis P. Blair, Jr., who was suffering the political consequences of his destruction of John C. Frémont's radical military administration, precipitated the *Anzeiger* into closure in early 1863. Börnstein, whose business interests in St. Louis collapsed due to neglect and mismanagement in his absence, remained in Europe to pursue yet new careers as a photographer and as a theatrical manager in Vienna. He would return to America in spirit only by means of his sprightly and often misleading memoirs of 1881. The name of the *Anzeiger* was soon revived under its old editor Carl Dänzer, who would lead the newspaper as a Democratic daily until it was absorbed into the *Westliche Post* in 1898. The *Anzeiger* would survive as the evening variant of the *Post* until 1912.

The only foil for the radical Republican press of St. Louis was provided by self-consciously Christian newspapers, both Catholic and Protestant. The *St. Louis Tages-Chronik* represented the conservative Catholic position from 1849 to 1861, but its role would not be filled again until the Catholic daily *Amerika* appeared in 1872. Lutherans were warned by Pastor C. F. W. Walther against the "Satans-Presse" of St. Louis, and a stock company was set up to float the *St. Louis Volksblatt* in 1855 in order to provide a Protestant daily newspaper. To Walther's great chagrin, Börnstein managed to buy the *Volksblatt* in 1857 and use its pages to deride religion. Walther had to advise his flock that there was now no daily newspaper in St. Louis he could recommend.[27]

The *Anzeiger* and the *Post* were equal participants in the German radical journalistic culture. They presented editorials and news items composed with an acerbic pen, and the domestic and European correspondents they published were profoundly critical of the established governments of virtually the entire globe. Beyond such original material, the editors provided articles taken from other German-American newspapers or translated from the English-language press. Laws and decrees were translated on a daily basis, and close attention was paid to economic and financial news. The

---

27. Arndt and Olson, *German-American Newspapers*, 1:272. Walther scathingly denounces the change in *Der Lutheraner* in 1857.

Theodor Olshausen, editor of the *Westliche Post* after 1860.
Courtesy of the Missouri Historical Society.

advertisements included official notices, real-estate schemes, notices of theaters and restaurants, and announcements for fraternal organizations.

It is important to realize that these newspapers were not ethnic papers in the modern sense: their first task was not to describe the comings and goings of a particular community but rather to cover all of the news for their readers. They shared many of the faults of the hyper-politicized press of the United States in the 1850s, and these faults were even exaggerated through their freedom from official censorship. Writers relied heavily on a body of experience shared with their readers, and intense feeling animated every line. From 1857 to 1862 the great adventure of a generation would reach a crescendo in their pages.

The German radical press as it developed in the United States in the 1850s produced some of the best journalistic writing in either the German or American traditions of that time, and that press provides us with a rare opportunity to view from within a world usually seen only from outside. Even the sensitive Francis Grierson saw the Germans as enigmatic automata when they shuffled down the streets of St. Louis toward Camp Jackson.[28] These newspapers help us to put a little color into the gray mass American historians call "the Germans," and the result is that they can be seen as much less orthodox Unionists than is usually thought. As the secession crisis developed, the Union was at first less important to German writers than was the survival of a free economic and political system. Several times the concept of a "Central States Union" focused on St. Louis beguiled these men. Their interests were concentrated on the middling whites, and blacks were seen more as walking problems than as people. Their plans for dealing with freed blacks ran the gamut from colonization abroad to training as yeoman farmers and soldiers in a new South. The binding thread was the great dream of 1848, now translated into an American idiom, even if still written *auf Deutsch*. The Union was worth dying for precisely because the American republic was bound up with the survival of republican liberty itself.

28. Francis Grierson, *The Valley of Shadows*, ed. Harold P. Simonson (New Haven, Conn.: College & University Press, 1970), 187–92; the original edition was published in 1909.

Mississippi Blätter

Sonntags-Blatt der „Westlichen Post."

4. Jahrgang.	St. Louis, Mo., Sonntag, den 19. Mai 1861.	No. 34.

Feuilleton.

Friedemann Bach.

Von J. C. Puchvogel.

Dritter Theil.

(Fortsetzung.)

A typical front page of the *Mississippi Blätter*, the weekend supplement of the *Westliche Post*. The date is 19 May 1861.

Part II

Translations

I.

St. Louis Germans

1857–1860

"... What Germany has given America up until now is like a down payment which would be lost if subsequent payments were not kept up."

Friedrich Münch, *Mississippi Blätter*, 27 March 1859

Westliche Post, Daily Edition, 27 September 1857

To Our Readers*

Despite the fact that the undersigned editors of the *Westliche Post* are well known to the reading public through their participation in the German-American press for many years, so that the direction of this new publication could hardly be in doubt, yet even in this case it seems advisable to uphold the old custom and tell the readers in a few words what they should and should not expect from this undertaking.

The *Westliche Post* has the liberal support of a few *personal* friends to thank for its appearance, friends who happen to belong to various political persuasions and thus could not hope to commit us once and for all to any particular political party. The *Westliche Post* is *independent* of all current political parties or cliques and owes support to *no one* who could turn it away from its mission to serve the truth and *only* the truth; it is solely the "organ" of its publishers and producers.

From this independent position the *Westliche Post* will openly and autonomously review the positions of all parties, recognizing the good wherever it is to be found, but also opposing lying, humbug, and corruption everywhere; but this will most sharply and radically be so when self-seeking, office-jobbing, and bribery hide behind the shingle of a popular cause or pursue their self-obsessed plans under the sign of progress and freedom. No country has greater need for an unsparing critique of all public measures and

*This is the editorial statement of the *Westliche Post* in its premiere edition. SR.

all public men from a *truly* independent press than does this Union, where party discipline is the worst enemy of *truth* and the interests of the people.

Of the two great questions that have concerned the Union most in the last few years, at least one can be considered settled, and settled to the benefit of freedom. *Know-nothingism* as an organized party is dead. The attempt to depress the immigrant population to the status of a pariah has quickly and completely failed. Some isolated outbursts of nativist spirit that still show themselves here and there, particularly in the New England states, hardly deserve serious attention. As far as we can see, equal rights for the adoptive population, as well as the current legislation on behalf of immigration, are secured for years to come. The political and social influence of the German element is on the rise, and nowhere more so than in the western states. The more lively the participation of German citizens in public life and the more energetic their efforts at founding educational institutions, the more lasting will be this newly won victory over Know-nothingism. Especially in the northern states, it depends wholly on the Germans themselves how much or how little of the achievement of German life and spirit will be preserved and domesticated. The German press cannot stress often enough that *education is power* and that the foundation of a single educational institution is worth more for the German element than a dozen "democratic" victories. In this sense the *Westliche Post* will still continue to oppose the "dead" Know-nothings.

The *Slavery Question* will certainly prove to be the theme of party struggles here for a series of years, and it will only end with the definitive victory of the system of free labor. For the time being, the ruling party has proclaimed it to be Democratic doctrine—in the Cincinnati Platform, in the Dred Scott decision, and in the latest letters of Buchanan—that Negro slavery is a *federal institution,* and as such it rightly stands under the protection of the Constitution of the United States in all of its territories. The Southern wing of the party has not hesitated to use any means to translate this theory into practice in Kansas. It is, however, a long way from the Cincinnati Platform and the election of Buchanan to the organization of Kansas as a slave state. Despite cowardly acts of violence and the maneuvers of Governor Walker, we do not believe that they shall succeed in overcoming the resistance of the free-state population of Kansas, even if the entire Democratic party lends a hand. It is the "manifest destiny" of slavery to be pressed *southward*—and the German immigration to the northernmost slave states and the new territories is one of the surest ways of accelerating this trend.

We believe that Kansas must be a free state, and we hold it to be the duty of the current generation to free Missouri from slavery as well. We are convinced that if slavery is not the greatest crime, then it is certainly the greatest misfortune the Union has inherited from the "Fathers." The abolition of this evil in the northern slave states is not only possible but, when we consider the beneficial results of such a measure, which are tied with no more than minor sacrifices, the time for making practical proposals for the elimination of Negro slavery in Missouri has come. We consider it to be one of our main duties to consider all measures that seem suitable for bringing us closer to the goal of transforming Missouri into a flourishing *free state*.

To represent the principles of freedom and the well-being of the people against every form of injustice, oppression, monopoly, and aristocracy is the task which the editors of the *Westliche Post* have taken on themselves as the political responsibility of the newspaper.

The demands that the German public places on its press have grown so in recent times that the editors of a newspaper have no easy task before them if they are to follow their readers' desires. It will be our goal to publish the *Westliche Post* in such a way as to meet all reasonable expectations, though we are entirely aware how difficult this is.

A precise and complete review of the latest news of the day, as well as telegraphic dispatches, will keep our readers continually aware of current events. Several respectable literary talents from various parts of the Union have assured us of their collaboration, and in order to keep our readers up to date with conditions in Europe, we have won for our undertaking European correspondents whose messages will be seen every day.

We shall give special attention to local events as well as to the commercial and financial conditions in our city, and we shall spare no effort to win the interest of the public in our newspaper.

We do not know whether the establishment of a new German newspaper is a deeply felt need here, but we have been encouraged by the enthusiastic support that the business world has already shown us at the outset, so we will get down to work without further ado.

C. Dänzer and F. Wenzel*

*Carl Dänzer was born in Odenheim, Baden, in 1820, studied law at Heidelberg, and served as a delegate to the National Assembly in Frankfurt am Main, 1848–1849. He

Westliche Post, 27 September 1857

(ADVERTISEMENT)

E. C. Angelrodt*
Consul General
for the
Kingdom of Saxony and the Grand Duchy
of Hesse,
Vice-Consul
for the
Empire of Austria
and Consul for the Kingdoms
of Prussia, Bavaria, and Württemberg,
the Grand Duchies of
Baden, Oldenburg, and Mecklenburg,
the
Electorate of Hesse
and finally the
Duchies of Nassau and Brunswick.
Consulate Bureau:
Main Street, between Market and Walnut Streets,
south of the new Exchange Building.

---

was associate editor of the *Anzeiger des Westens* in the mid-1850s, resigning after disagreements with the proprietor, Heinrich Börnstein, in 1857. In October 1857, he launched the *Westliche Post* in partnership with Friedrich Wenzel, but after a year Wenzel was replaced by Daniel Hertle. Dänzer sold the newspaper to Theodor Olshausen in 1860, when he returned to Germany. He took over the *Anzeiger des Westens* after it had been closed due to mismanagement by Börnstein's representatives in 1863, and he edited it as a Democratic newspaper until it was merged with the *Westliche Post* in 1898. Dänzer then retired in Germany. See William Hyde and Howard L. Conard, eds., *Encyclopedia of the History of St. Louis* (New York, Louisville, St. Louis, 1899), 1:540. SR.

*E. C. Angelrodt was an immigrant of the 1830s who struck it rich as a wholesaler. He was a partner with Emil Mallinckrodt in the development of New Baden, a community on the northern border of St. Louis established in 1844 and incorporated into the city of St. Louis before the Civil War. SR.

Anzeiger des Westens, 22 October 1857

What Should Be Done with Unemployed Workers?*

A large number of factories have already ceased operations and laid off their workers, and many more will soon follow. At the present time, for example, only *three* mills are running in the entire great city of St. Louis. Thousands of workers are looking ahead to the arrival of winter without work, hence without income, without the means for making a living. There is no other work for them, and the usual counsel that they leave the city and seek work on the farms, where there is a chronic shortage of hands, is a bitter mockery in the present circumstances, since winter is coming and the time for farm work is past.

Yet something has to be done for these thousands who will otherwise starve, sicken, and freeze, or even die. The mayor has mentioned it in an address; he says that the public officials and wealthier citizens should help by providing charity.

We can expect nothing from the charity of individuals—each would prefer to help himself and his own—and how much does the municipal budget have to deal with such a problem? Perhaps $10,000. What good will this do when there are ten thousand unemployed workers to be kept through the winter—one dollar per man for the whole winter!

What turns us even more decisively against this charity is the fact that it degrades a worker into a beggar.

This would amount to a public distribution of alms at the expense of the municipality and private donors, and what honorable upstanding worker is going to accept *alms*? A worker wants to *earn* his bread, through the labor of his hands and the sweat of his brow, but he certainly does not want alms.

True workers will reject alms out of hand, but the news that support is available for the unemployed in St. Louis will draw in hordes of those shiftless, lounging good-for-nothings who wander routinely from place to place. They would settle here as unemployed and soak up the greater part of the alms available.

Who is to prevent this? Who is to differentiate the suffering true workers from these shiftless, lazy troublemakers when *thousands* are applying for support?

*The brief, sharp financial panic that began in fall 1857 gave the German press a chance to subject American banking and trade institutions to a scathing critique. Despite the severity of the bank crash and the business slump that followed, recovery would be surprisingly swift in the Midwest. SR.

It would be necessary to have special officials for this purpose, and along with this would come fat paychecks, nepotism, and patronage—and then, as always in this country, embezzlement, party favoritism, and waste.

Away with such alms! They serve no purpose. They do not help, and they would demoralize the people.

Give the worker work. That is all that he wants and all that he needs. Admittedly the factories cannot be started up again, since even if the engines could be stoked with coal and the raw materials found, there would be no buyers for the finished goods, so the artificially activated factory would soon have to close down again.

But you could still provide the worker with work, and it is the duty of the city government to *see to it*; this is much better and more profitable than simply passing out alms.

Let the city undertake some large, useful project to benefit the *city*—something that can be done in wintertime—so that every worker, whatever sort of factory business he worked in before, can have work and a wage to get through the winter.

We turn to the two boards of the city council and discover that they have done little or nothing in the first six months in office. Three-quarters of the sessions have been given over to *buncombe speeches* or sniping disputes between north and south St. Louis. Every useful proposal has been tabled. Mayor Wimer, an energetic and active man who seriously desires reform in the municipal administration and whose efforts cannot be praised enough, has seen all of his undertakings from the nomination of officials to the construction of City Hall harassed and lamed. Was this done by his political enemies? No! They were men who ran with him on the same ticket and were elected with him. Considerations of clique, calculation, and private benefit all seem more important now than the welfare of the city and its citizens.

We have observed the activity of the present council through its entire tenure, but until now we have been silent, since we hoped for a turn for the better. But now that six months have passed fruitlessly—even while we have been attacked by the most fearful conditions this country has ever experienced—now silence would be a crime, and as the organ of a large portion of our population, all citizens of this city, we lift our voices and beseech the boards of the current city council to drop their wrangling and petty dispute and apply themselves to our present pressing needs and to the critical situation in which our city now finds itself.

Consider, gentlemen, as you lounge in your curule chairs, that the people will be electing new representatives again in April—and believe us, we have a good memory and will help the people remember who their friends and foes might be. We beseech our German countrymen on both boards to work with their American colleagues with this end in mind and to seize the initiative if necessary. If the others refuse your recommendations, then they will earn unpopularity.

But what should we do, you ask? —*Give the worker work*! we answer. We even demand it; undertake a useful project that will employ thousands. What could it be? There are many possibilities. We will even suggest one, *just as an example.*

Every year many steamboats winter along our levee, and almost every year the ice floe sweeps away dozens of these vessels, smashing them to pieces and causing damage in the millions. *A safe harbor* for the winter is a necessity for any trading city such as St. Louis—behind the old Duncan's Island to the south is a shore that serves as a small wharf for St. Louis; this is where a safe harbor could be built that could be protected by using the surviving point of Duncan's Island as a breakwater.

We are no engineers to demonstrate this matter to you mathematically, but go to the city engineer and have him draw up a plan; he will understand what we are saying and carry it out. Put thousands of unemployed to work digging a harbor-basin for fifty or sixty, even a hundred steamboats in this flat, sandy, and moist ground, and surround the whole with a wall of stone.

This harbor-basin would have to have a stone bulwark higher than the Mississippi high-water mark to guard against flooding and silting. Two canals with locks would lead from the river to the basin, which would be dried out and cleaned in summer, or a *swimming school* could operate there, which could also function as a *bathing establishment.*

All steamboats could pass the winter there without having to risk ice, and the owners of the boats would gladly pay fourfold fees for wharfing there. Insurance companies, which would have lost thousands through ice damage, would surely contribute, and within three or four years the wharfage fees, insurance contributions, and bathing fees would have paid off all original investments.

But the means? Where would we get the money to pay off the workers? Think of the excavation for the Southern Hotel on Fourth Street, only wider and deeper, and you have an idea of the safe harbor.

Now a *private* firm could undertake this work and raise the money—why does the wealthy city of St. Louis not do this? It is true that the city cannot float any new municipal bonds, since they cannot be sold now, but they could issue city scrip under the condition that the scrip would be accepted by the city treasurer in payment for municipal taxes in 1858 and 1859. If you restrict other expenditures, apply all possible resources, and administer the city with strict economy, you would not only have enough to get thousands of workers through a hard winter, but you would enrich the city with a great and important project.

Members of the city council! The time for jesting and discussing is now past! Now is the time to act! If you *want*, get *going*. Thousands of unemployed workers look to you and expect an answer at your next session to their *demand* for *work!*

Anzeiger des Westens, 22 October 1857

Germans and the Crisis

When we look around the city and the countryside and ask after the affairs of our German friends during the current business difficulties, we have to confess that we find only a very few who have serious concerns about survival. Those few who are in peril of being drawn down into the pit of bankruptcy are precisely those who have flown too close to the blazing sun of credit and have singed their wings—or they are those who have surrendered themselves to the American "show" of luxury and overconsumption and have paid out more than they could bring in.

There is a special technique to becoming American. It seems to us that the right way to become American is to evaluate the relationships here correctly, to learn from their errors and derive benefit from them, to avoid their excesses, and to desist from applying one's own narrowly European concepts of order to this young, untrammeled land, but also not to take as granted the injustices and humbug found here just because they have been accepted by earlier settlers and their descendants. The alternative to this is not Americanization; it is ruin and decadence: to give oneself up to the American style of loafing; to wander the streets spangled with gold but with empty heads, hearts, and pockets; to participate in swindles of all descriptions; to waste one's talents and energies on the false values of lotteries; to be obsessed by humbug; and to lose one's own mother tongue and pass the day mangling English instead.

After all, America belongs to *us* just as much as it does to them, and *our* spirit, *our* way of getting something out of life, and *our* concepts of economy can find a place in this country, its resources, and its development just as well as what the natives seem to think is predestined.

Germans are more careful in business and less excessive in their enjoyment than Americans. When immigration was less intense and Germans lived here as isolated individuals rather than as organized groups, the Americans called them "small souls." The American tolerates a peculiar individual only with misgivings, but as soon as such persons reach a certain mass and are present in large numbers, then he does not withhold recognition. For instance, if the majority of the population here were indifferent to religion and there were only a Methodist dolt or some other sectarian here or there, there is no doubt that the population would laugh these fools to scorn. But since this foolishness is held by many and has become a social necessity, they are spared. How much more must German thriftiness and honesty in business compel recognition when not just a few isolated persons but an entire division of the population sails secure and undamaged through a crisis that arises from the reverse of these virtues, from the excessive luxury, euphoria, and irresponsible self-aggrandizement of the natives.

Becoming American means becoming self-supporting and proving our principles in these circumstances. What we have already done politically should be an encouragement and a model for what we could achieve in the economy. Our independent and unshaken survival through the crises created by the failings of others will provide us with a valuable tool. Just as no shift of parties and no political changes can shake us from our principles and their exercise at the ballot box, and just as we have always sworn allegiance to principles rather than to parties, so also we should allow ourselves to be moved by the ebb and flow of commerce and industry only when we are sure that the vehicle we have chosen is inevitably going straight ahead against all the currents.

So our struggle against the currency is a German-American struggle; so our attacks on the anarchic banking system* are German-American attacks; so our demand for security and control is a German-American demand.

*At this time, most of the city's unregulated note brokerages (called banks), which performed most banking functions except that of note issue, had closed because they were overextended. They could not be rescued by New York banks, which were similarly embarrassed (Panic of 1857). When the largest local bank, James H. Lucas and Company, closed in October, credit virtually dried up in St. Louis. Large firms such as the Chouteau, Harrison and Vallé Rolling Mills, which employed eight hundred men, could not operate without short-term credit. By late fall, some ten thousand workers (one-fourth of the labor force) were unemployed. Since the Bank of the State of Missouri, the only firm which could issue bank notes in the state, was

We have made people listen to German-American convictions in political matters, and we will not rest until our economic demands are equally respected.

Anzeiger des Westens, 29 October 1857

Fear of the Slaveholders for German Settlers

We have often printed expressions of concern about Germans from the papers of the slaveholders. None has ever been as candid or as naive as what we find in the *New Orleans Crescent.* It concerns the Germans in western Texas, who appear to us to be not particularly dangerous, if the *Neu-Braunfels Zeitung* is any indication. The newspaper says:

> These alien votes are already powerful enough to dominate elections in Texas, since alongside the Europeans settled in the western part of the state there is a large Mexican population. The fact that the enormous German population of western Texas is radically opposed to the institution of slavery, and the fact that the Democratic party owes its success to these votes is clear to every intelligent resident of this state ... The leaders of the Democratic party in Texas not only know that there is a large antislavery mentality in the western part of this state, but also that it is increasing so rapidly that if it is not stopped it could have such a decisive influence on this state within five years that it could bring about the partition of the state by declaring the western portion independent. And the same leaders know that the last legislature created a new county where most of the land belongs to a few Germans who plan to bring over a colony of four thousand of their countrymen and settle it there.

It is remarkable that these slaveowners look upon the possibility of a free state in Texas as something almost impermissible, as if there were no provision for the people of a state declaring themselves "totally free" ever since the suspension of the Missouri Compromise and the "grand principle" of the Nebraska Bill.

---

very conservative, it was not much of a factor in the St. Louis economy. Thus the private banks, such as James H. Lucas's, dealt in the often speculative notes of Illinois and Kentucky, which were heavily discounted or worthless during economic crises. Early in 1857, the Missouri legislature had passed a limited "free-banking" law, which authorized ten regulated banks of issue but was too late to be useful in the 1857 crisis. Eventually, the new banks eased the credit squeeze somewhat, but they did not eliminate the problem. When the New York banks restricted credit, St. Louis shuddered. JNP.

Anzeiger des Westens, 15 November 1857

Jefferson City Correspondence of the *Anzeiger des Westens*

(Delayed because of our splendid postal service)

Jefferson, 5 November 1857

The National Democrats gave yet more evidence of their famous tolerance and love for their German adoptive citizens in the session on the fourth of this month.

Mr. Burke called his bill for the incorporation of the Missouri-Ansiedlungs-Verein to the floor of the House out of the custody of an *ad hoc* committee, and it excited a long and animated debate. By means of this bill, several Germans were seeking to incorporate themselves in order to buy a piece of land in Missouri and establish a town on it. Each shareholder was supposed to receive at least two town lots. The main goal of the corporation was to provide a large number of their countrymen a home in a healthful location at a cheap price and thereby increase the number of prosperous towns in the state. The advantages of such an undertaking were so obvious that only the National Democrats in the House could have overlooked them. The people who asked for incorporation were, of course, Germans, and they might be Free-soilers or emancipationists; they might belong to that group of electoral officers who believe in free labor and free speech; such people should not be allowed to found towns or increase the wealth of the state or even promote immigration. Then the difference between free and slave labor might become too obvious; the advantages might all fall on the side of free labor, and that would be too dangerous!

Oh, the National Democrats are not intolerant—they are the friends of the Germans—the Know-nothings are the professional bigots, after all; vote for us, Germans, help us win office and rank, Germans, but when you want anything at all, such as the foundation of a colony, of which there are so many in the United States, then rest assured—we will reject it out of hand!

And the National Democrats buried the bill. The vote was:

Yeas		Nays	
Benton	25	Benton	1
Americans	7	Americans	8
Old Whigs	4	National Democrats	39
National Democrats	7		
	43		48

Thirty-nine National Democrats voted against an innocent bill because it asked for a charter for some Germans who wanted to better and enrich this state, although the Germans are known as the best colonists in the countryside. Why? Because these Germans are not entirely satisfactory concerning that peculiar institution that provides such blessings for our state and whose representatives are the most hypocritical, most intolerant race that ever disgraced a legislative organization.

Anzeiger des Westens, 15 November 1857

The Annexation of Cuba

We have no idea of the source used by our colleagues at the *Democrat* when they said that President Buchanan was once more thinking about annexing Cuba. If this is indeed the case, then our president can prepare himself for a great political defeat.

We have always opposed this annexation; the advantages that they say would come from it are out of all proportion with the innumerable difficulties it presents for us. The necessary creation of a new slave state, the alteration and expansion of our army, the addition of a sizable Catholic population, whose pretentions would be concentrated in a very small space and could not be ignored, these have been the themes of our polemic up to now. But now these have been strengthened by new conditions arising from the current situation of our country.

It has been demonstrated beyond a shadow of a doubt that the growth of our territory has exceeded our disposable strength; the maintenance of authority by force in the manner of that island would bring us military and financial problems alongside of which the Utah expedition would be a bagatelle, and the demand for forces would be almost impossible to put off in view of the current situation of that country.

Our trade and industry do not need this expansion; on the contrary, large amounts of capital would be drawn there that would be more useful and more secure if they remained here.

So we should hope that England's problems shall not tempt our own central government to sacrifice the good of the country for one of the president's pet ideas; it is certainly a better idea for the government to set a good example of moderation for the country than for it to get big ideas about Cuba.

Anzeiger des Westens, 29 November 1857

(ADVERTISEMENT)

A German Hotel

On the first of June we will open our newly furnished German hotel under the name:

*Germania Hotel**
Corner of Market and Third Street,
St. Louis, Mo.

Sixty elegantly furnished rooms, a good, healthful German buffet, cleanliness and comfort, friendly and pleasing service, and a convenient location in the center of the city's business district will certainly make this German hotel a gathering place for all German travelers from Missouri, Illinois, and the entire Mississippi valley.

Soliciting your friendly inquiries,

S. Jacobi and Co.
Owners of the Germania Hotel

Westliche Post, 30 December 1857

The Administration and the Filibusters

The partisan efforts of the cabinet in Washington on behalf of the Filibuster-general Walker,* as well as the measures against Com-

---

*S. Jacoby joined with his friend Heinrich Börnstein to establish this hotel, which failed to prosper because German travelers were not interested in paying premium prices to stay in a first-class German hotel. See Heinrich Börnstein, *Fünfundsiebzig Jahre in der Alten und Neuen Welt: Memoiren eines Unbedeutenden* (Leipzig, 1884), 2:236. SR.

*William Walker, a Tennesseean, in the name of America's manifest destiny led a band of American adventurers to Nicaragua in 1855 and maneuvered himself into the presidency. The Pierce administration considered recognizing his government, and there was discussion of admitting Nicaragua to the United States as a slave state. Fear of a negative British reaction apparently dissuaded Pierce. Encouraged by Cornelius Vanderbilt, whose transportation interests in Central America were threatened by the filibusterers, Nicaragua's neighbors invaded and ousted Walker. Walker was acclaimed by Southerners as a hero, and in November 1857 he led another invading party to Nicaragua. Shortly after landing, his forces were broken up by an American naval detachment and Walker was arrested by its commander, Commodore Hiram Paulding. Incredibly, Paulding was reprimanded and relieved of his command by President Buchanan. In August 1860, Walker tried again, this time in Honduras, where he was captured and executed. JNP.

modore Paulding, who has a different concept of international law than that held by his masters who sent him ambiguous instructions, will have to disillusion all of those who expected that Buchanan would alter the pitiful policies of General Pierce. Self-abasement toward the South and its policy of expansion was the chief reason Pierce—whom the people raised to the presidential chair by an almost unexampled majority—quickly squandered his great reputation, even the respect of his country, without achieving his goal of reelection.

The example of his predecessor seems to have made no impression on Buchanan, for he is just as much a self-abasing servant of the South, and just as the formidable Jefferson Davis really pulled the strings of the administration under Pierce, so now Howell Cobb, the most capable member of the cabinet, is the one who sets the tone in Washington. Perhaps the South is playing again the old comedy with Buchanan and is trying to make him pliable with hopes for another nomination. The usually well-informed *New York Evening Post* says that even Buchanan is figuring on his reelection. So Buchanan is nothing more than a continuation of Pierce, both domestically and externally.

Domestically the Kansas swindle, which the administration has ended up favoring, is even more offensive than the indifference with which Pierce allowed the Missourians to fool around in Kansas.* There is not a trace of an autonomous, manly action in either case.

Externally Pierce inaugurated the policy of Filibusterdom *en gros*, admittedly on the direct urging of Buchanan, through approving the Ostend Manifesto,* and only the general disapproval that broke out on all sides forced Pierce to play a gentler tune. Throughout the world there reigns only one voice of astonishment over the

---

*Proslavery men from western Missouri, headed by Senator David Rice Atchison and Benjamin Stringfellow and urged on by Claiborne F. Jackson, organized secret, oath-bound societies known as Blue Lodges, Social Bands, or Sons of the South for the purpose of making Kansas a slave state. They specialized in burning, looting, occasionally murdering, and voting in Kansas elections. Antislavery men called them "border ruffians." On 30 March 1855 hundreds of armed Missourians marched into Kansas and elected a proslavery legislature, and on 21 May 1856 Missourians sacked the antislavery town of Lawrence, Kansas, killed several persons, and destroyed two free-state newspapers. JNP.

*On 9 October 1854, Pierre Soulé, John Y. Mason, and James Buchanan, United States ministers to Spain, France, and Great Britain, with the approval of President Franklin Pierce, sent a dispatch from Belgium to the state department that was later called the Ostend Manifesto. Declaring Cuba essential for the security of American slavery, the ministers recommended that the United States should buy it from Spain. If Spain refused, the United States should take Cuba by force. When the dispatch became public knowledge in March 1855, Republicans seized upon it as evidence that the administration was dominated by slavery extremists. JNP.

open proclamation of a theory that offends every concept of law. Pierce was overcome by the storm, but Buchanan, who won points with the South with the Ostend Manifesto, kept quiet until the storm had passed. During the election Buchanan's Northern friends swore by all that was holy that the old man was too smart and too experienced to bring the country into any dangers to which the execution in practice of the Ostend Manifesto might lead. Many an honorable Democrat who would normally have been driven into the camp of the opposition by Pierce's stewardship let themselves be fooled by these assurances and voted for Buchanan.

Not even a year has passed since the formal installation of Buchanan, and yet he has achieved almost as complete a bankruptcy in popular opinion as his predecessor, whom he has sought to copy.

Right on the heels of the contemptible actions in Kansas follows open partisanship for the Filibusters, for lawless bands who overrun peaceful countries with robbery, murder, and plunder in contempt of all international law, despite the fact that they write such hypocritical slogans as *Manifest Destiny* or "Civilization" on their banners. The action against Commodore Paulding, who has done nothing but his duty, is the first official confirmation that Buchanan has not been separated from the principles of the Ostend Manifesto. As a true body-servant of the South, he must do something for the darling of the Southern Cavaliers. In the end Walker is certainly nothing but an arm that carries out independently the ideas that Buchanan has already proclaimed to the world in a document that has become famous and notorious.

Anzeiger des Westens, 3 January 1858

The Next Municipal Elections

Our readers may have noticed that the *Republican* has been suffering from a recurring disease ever since the demise of the Whig party. This illness consists of the fixed idea that the city of St. Louis will go to its ruin if the *Republican* does not hold its blessing hand over the community and grace it with an "independent ticket." The first symptoms of this illness are already starting to make their appearance, and in yesterday's issue of the *Republican* there was already an article calling on the citizens to cast aside all party organizations and nominations and support "a good independent ticket" (concocted out of pure National Democrats and slavelords). —Through a peculiar coincidence, the central committee, together with a dozen or so National Democrats from St. Louis under the leadership of Dougherty and Penn, held a conference on the next municipal election only the day before yesterday, and lo, the very next day the *Republican* comes out and presents its inevitable "independent ticket." —How far both are symptoms of the same disease, we have no idea; but we do believe that the Nationals and the *Leader* will be in the same woe over the next municipal elections as the *Republican* and its clique.

A victory for the administration must be won at any cost, particularly here in a slave state and in the most important city of the West; the ruin of the party of emancipation in Missouri and the triumph of the proslavery party of the Union is desired also at any price, and yet these gentlemen know full well that this has not the slightest chance of realization. The "American Party"* will *no longer* present a ticket—and since there will only be two tickets in the running, it is clear that the ticket of the National Democrats will lose by a majority of three to four thousand votes.

Under the pressure of this disturbing perception, they are trying out the old trick of an "independent ticket" just as it has been tried and found wanting before so many times, and by this means they hope that at least a third ticket will serve to split the votes of the freethinker majority.*

Pointless effort! The freethinker population of St. Louis knows full well that the imposing position won so far in Missouri for the emancipation party is the result of hard struggle and is not to be frivolously played away—the freethinkers know *that the future belongs to us*, and that we need to do nothing except to be *unified*, to keep our organization intact, and to benefit from the errors, weaknesses, and divisions of our enemies.

And since our freethinker majority knows this, it will not allow itself to be misled by anyone, whoever he might be, or allow its strength to be scattered, but most of all it will not consider accept-

*The American Party was the "Know-nothings." JNP.
*Freethinker was the general designation for a person who was rationalist in religion, and it seems to have embraced positions reaching from something akin to Unitarianism or ethical humanism all the way to atheism. Heinrich Börnstein established a "Bund freier Männer" on his arrival in St. Louis that sponsored a school, but the membership of this group seems to have merged with the "Freie Gemeinde von Nord-St. Louis" by 1859, when his name appears on the rolls. See the papers of the Freie deutsche Gemeinde, Western Historical Manuscripts, University of Missouri-St. Louis; also Carl Wittke, *Refugees of Revolution: The German Forty-Eighters in America* (Westport, Conn.: Greenwood Press, 1952), 122–46. SR.

ing a so-called "independent ticket" from the hands of its mortal enemy, the *Missouri Republican*.

Mississippi Blätter, 8 March 1858

Reintroduction of the Trade in Negroes

The *Cincinnati Republikaner* has presented the following musing, half in earnest and half in jest, about this very serious current question:

In Louisiana it has been decided to reintroduce the trade in Negroes legally and in the best possible form. Negroes are to be *bought* in Africa and *sold* in America. But the purchasers are supposed to grant their charges their freedom after a service of fifteen years; until that time the Negroes have to work for their lords free of charge but afterward they can figure out how to survive on their own.

A black war-captive costs about $90 on the African coast; the cost of transporting such a person across the ocean could be figured to be $25. The Negro would thus have to work for fifteen years to pay off the $115 invested in him—not too much, indeed, for the splendid freedom that awaits him when his term expires.

Many believe that this last condition was inserted in the Negro trading treaty just to get around the law. It certainly would be easy enough to get around this condition. Since the Dred Scott decision, a Negro is a head of cattle like any other, and cattle have no standing in court.*

Still, we fully believe that the Louisianans are dead serious about this clause. It is even to their advantage.

In fifteen years a person can exploit the labor of a Negro to such a degree, can so expend him and squeeze him, that afterwards he is good for nothing—except freedom. After fifteen years, the fellow gets his freedom, whether he wants it or not, and precisely there is the profit. You buy a grown rascal of thirty years of age and throw him to the devil when he is forty-five and getting stiff—what could be more advantageous?

Now the question is whether this well calculated business can actually be carried out?

*In 1857 the United States Supreme Court ruled in the Dred Scott Case that Negroes, free or slave, were not U.S. citizens. JNP.

The law of 1808 forbids the African slave trade, and treaties concluded with the seagoing powers condemn it and punish it as a crime—but the attorney general will issue an opinion showing that the law and the treaties do not apply in this case, and Buchanan will declare his hearty agreement; then the august Supreme Court will sweep away all scruples.

Much more sensitive to any suspension of the protective measures against the importation of humans would be the *nigger-breeders* of Virginia, Maryland, and North Carolina.* These nigger-manufacturers, like all manufacturers, are decided enemies of free trade insofar as it applies to the articles they themselves produce. They would all go bankrupt if the importation of the black and yellow articles in whose production they have been protected up until now should be opened up, since their wares would immediately drop by about 50 percent in value, and they would fall to a price at which they could not be produced in America. These gentlemen are looking upon the new trade undertakings of the Louisianans with concern—and there will be a high time when the producers and importers of black flesh start to fight it out with one another.

Mississippi Blätter, 17 May 1858*

SPRING FESTIVAL
for the
German Institute
in
Concordia Park

———

On
Pentecost Sunday
and
Monday
the 23rd and 24th of May, 1858,

*These states, and Missouri too, exported slaves to the lower South. Renewal of the African slave trade, which had been legally suspended since 1808, would ruin the interstate slave trade by lowering prices. JNP.
*This is an advertisement for a popular festival to raise money for the Deutsches Institut, the most ambitious educational program for Germans in St. Louis. Note the importance of building lots as prizes. SR.

the great German popular festival will be held to benefit the German Institute in Concordia (formerly Scholten's) Park.*

The arrangements committee, encouraged by the enthusiastic support that has blessed the German Institute in the past and in view of the great success of last year's festival, has not spared the greatest expense to make this year's festival even better than ever before.

The festival opens on
Sunday at 2 P.M.
At 4 P.M. an
Oration
will be held.
A large *Band*
has been engaged under the baton of
Director Vogel.
A special committee has arranged for
favorite Popular Shows
to entertain the public during the afternoon.
Target Shooting for Ladies,
with lovely prizes,
Climbing Contests,
Sack Races,
Marionettes,
such as will allow no boredom to appear.

———

☞ *The Dancing Area is very large,*
and the ball committee will make every effort to assure
that the Ball shall not be disturbed.

———

In the Evening
The Festival area will be totally illuminated and
Brilliant Fireworks
shall be set off.

———

For the Second Festival Day
the theatrical section of the St. Louis Turnverein
has prepared
a theatrical presentation

*Concordia Park was a popular German private park located at Wall Street and Carondelet Avenue (now Broadway). See Richard J. Compton and Camille N. Dry, *Pictorial St. Louis* (St. Louis, 1876; reprint St. Louis: Knight, 1979), plate 30. SR.

on the festival grounds
to be announced.

———

Combined with the festival there is
A Great Lottery
in which a hundred prizes to the value of $800 will be offered,
including the following
Big Items:
1) A lovely house lot in the City of St. Louis
2) ⎤ 3 lots in Blairsville
3) ⎬ on the
4) ⎦ Iron Mountain Railway
5) A lady's brooch watch
6) A handbag with brooch and earrings
7) A golden watch-chain
Other prizes, up to a total of a hundred,
Consist mostly of
valuable items in Gold,
ladies' handwork
made especially as gifts for this festival
and
worthwhile books.
Each ticket to the festival is a lottery ticket which entitles one to
play this lottery, but only those present at the drawing may claim
prizes.
The complete lottery scheme will be published a few days before
the festival.

———

Tickets to the Festival
50 Cents Each
Can be purchased from members of the
Arrangements Committee
Or the office of the
German Institute
Or in the Office of the
Westliche Post.

———

Each ticket is good only for
One Day
and
no return tickets
shall be sold.

Mississippi Blätter, 2 August 1858

125,000 Tickets, but No Votes!

We hear that no fewer than 125,000 tickets lie in the office of a German newspaper here with the name of one Louis Kessler as jailer on them. We will not envy that newspaper the honor of supporting a *German slaveowner* and *slave breeder* as an emancipation candidate. But we are really curious about how many Germans will vote for such a man.

German voters, read the following documents:

    *   *   *

Louis Kessler, the sole German candidate

A Voice from Warren County on the St. Louis Elections

Germans make up a large proportion of the Free State party in Missouri, so it would be only fair if they asserted their right to hold a corresponding portion of the public offices. Yet they are told to abstain from running on their own lest the virginal banner of the new party be soiled and the nativists be given grounds for complaint. —Mr. *Louis Kessler* is the candidate for county jailer in St. Louis. The contributor of this letter cannot think it proper that the delegates of a party that writes "Emancipation from Slavery" on its banner should present a candidate who is a notorious friend of that institution. K. is a slaveowner, a slave trader, and a slave breeder, not due to education or inheritance but because the business is profitable, comfortable, and pleasing for him.

And yet this is not the chief argument against his candidacy. K. lived about fifteen years in Warren County and is known by all the inhabitants there, but of all of them you could hardly find five who would witness to K. being an honest man; everywhere one hears that he belongs in a jail, but behind the bars rather than in front of them. I am no lover of scandal, so to avoid the accusation of libel I am compelled to state some facts. K. is a gambler in the worst sense of the word and has been severely chastised for that many times.

He was *dishonorably* discharged from the volunteer company formed in Warren County during the Mexican War. His own uncle litigated against him for years for issuing *false notes* and for busi-

---

*This is an example of a personal attack carried out in the context of the rivalry between the *Anzeiger des Westens* and the *Westliche Post* (of which *Mississippi Blätter* was the Sunday issue) over the candidacy of a German for jailer on the Free State party ticket. The *Anzeiger* had supported a slaveowning German but had to withdraw the endorsement when the man's past caught up with him. SR.

ness fraud; K. finally terminated the litigation and paid seven hundred dollars in costs. One could best inform himself there about a long and dirty litigation with a Mr. Ellis of St. Louis concerning the taking of wagons and horses.

I think what has been said should suffice to show that Mr. Kessler is unworthy of the support of the Free State party and should be dropped from the ticket. If not, we are ready to accompany this and all further contributions with signatures of respected residents of several counties. —We are upset enough already about the shameless corruption of the Democratic party in distributing public offices; let us avoid letting the same shame fall on us.

Let the *Anzeiger des Westens* copy this, in the interests of the party in general and of Germans in particular.

*   *   *

Warren County, Missouri, 22 July 1858

To the editors of the *Westliche Post*

Dear sirs:

I send you the above as an expression of the voice of the people, to be printed in your newspaper. I have been most restrained in my treatment of Mr. K., and it would be wise not to ask me to send any more fodder. I stand behind what is said, and I will reveal my name to the public *as soon as this is necessary or useful.*

With respectful regards, yours,
*Georg Münch**

*   *   *

Warren County, Missouri, 27 July

My Dear Friend Dänzer,

I have only a few moments free, so I can only tell you the following on the matter in question in response to your letter.

The first contribution was made with my full knowledge, but I prefer not to have *my* hands in too *many* things, and so I left the matter to Mr. G. Münch alone. I confirm every word he has written—everything in it can be confirmed by witnesses, though Kessler will never let it go so far. To gather affidavits would be too difficult because time is short, and because the most important witnesses no longer live in the neighborhood. I would like to make a

*Georg Münch was born in Hesse-Darmstadt, settled in Warren County, Missouri, in 1833 with his older brother Friedrich, owned a winery in Augusta, St. Charles County, and died in 1879. SR.

few additional comments on the accusations, which have been made *for your information*:

1. It is no crime to be a gambler, but it can be shown that Kessler has worked professionally at *cheating at cards* for several years, and he has suffered for it occasionally, though not as much as he has deserved.

2. Kessler wrote out a false ballot for his own uncle, who couldn't read English (I was present at the election), and he would have been ripped limb from limb by the Americans if he had not fled away. The case was brought before the circuit court by the grand jury and shown by a slick lawyer to have been in error on a technicality. Kessler thus escaped unscathed, but it is certain that fraud was actually committed, and the uncle is ready to testify to that effect.

3. The dishonorable discharge from the volunteers actually took place, and there are dozens of witnesses to it.

4. The litigation on the fabrication of notes initiated by his uncle came before a court in St. Louis, though I don't know which one. The most shameful things were brought to light, and in the end Kessler thought it best to satisfy his uncle and pay the heavy court costs.

5. The matter with Ellis played itself out in St. Louis as well as here, and it was such a complex and extensive piece of tomfoolery that a quire of paper would be needed to portray it. The basic facts can be proved, partly here, partly in St. Louis.

The best approach would be to accuse Mr. Kessler privately and tell him this will be printed if he does not withdraw, and he will probably do so. He will suspect that the contribution came *from me*, since I often write for your newspaper, and you know what to say about that. The actual contributor isn't afraid of any suit for libel Kessler might bring, but he insists on publication if Kessler doesn't withdraw. Perhaps Kessler will lay aside any future plans about running for office.

Fr. Münch*

*Friedrich Münch, 1799–1881, makes a rather unfortunate debut here, but he was one of the leading figures of the older generation of Missouri Germans. He emigrated to Missouri with Paul Follenius as a member of the Giessen Settlement Society, settled in Warren County, and prospered as a viticulturist. He was well known as a philosophically inclined columnist and political commentator under the pen name *Far West*. His *Gesammelte Schriften* (St. Louis, 1902) contains some of his least interesting writing. See the filiopietistic account of Julius Thamer Muench, "A Sketch of the Life and Work of Friedrich Muench," *Missouri Historical Society Collections*, vol. 3, no. 2 (April 1908), 132–44. SR.

Mississippi Blätter, 2 August 1858

A Contribution to the Natural History of the Alderman.

The Alderman is a warm-blooded biped and, since he sucks the public teat, he belongs to the family of mammals. He bears his offspring alive, and he has incisors all the way back to his wisdom teeth (which are blunt). As soon as he is in office he broadens his belly, just as he does many of the streets of the city, at public expense.

Mississippi Blätter, 28 November 1858

Back from Europe. Mr. N. Schäffer,* partner of the noted firm of Schäffer, Anhäuser and Co., returned here after six months in Europe and was greeted with two serenades, one performed by Frank Böhm's Band.

More immigrants. Yesterday evening 350 German immigrants arrived on the steamboat *Morrison* from New Orleans. They are almost all from the region of Osnabrück and Prussian Westphalia. They crossed the ocean in two Bremen ships, the *Ernestine* and the *New Orleans*, and they had a rather long and stormy passage. Despite this there were no deaths on board, and the new arrivals are all healthy and cheerful. Most of them expect to make their homes in Missouri, so far as we could discover.

Mississippi Blätter, 13 February 1859

Negotiations in the Missouri Legislature. Among the bills that passed the house without debate we note a "Bill for Removing Free Negroes from Missouri." Is this the Boulware Bill, which intends to force all free Negroes from the state by 1860?* Where are they to go?

---

*Nicholas Schäffer of Schäffer, Anhäuser and Co. had his residence in 1860 on the south side of Christy between Twentieth and Twenty-First. See Richard Edwards, ed., *St. Louis Directory, 1860* (St. Louis: R. V. Kennedy, 1860). SR.

*The bill passed both houses, but it was vetoed by Governor Robert M. Stewart. The governor was politically in transition at this time. Elected in 1857 as a proslavery "Ultra," he opposed secession in 1861 and was a staunch Unionist during the war. His railroad interests and secession were not compatible. JNP.

The session of the senate that took place on the ninth saw bitter debàte over a special message of the governor concerning the Hannibal and St. Joseph Railway.* It is well known that the governor used to be president of the railway and still has a strong interest in it. But now the senate passes a bill that withholds from that company the right to dispose of lands given to it until certain improvements in the rail line are made. This condition is redundant, since the original grant to the company stipulated that the rail line had to be constructed and operating as a *first-class* railway before the rights of property would be transferred to the company. The reason the Senate bothered to pass such a special law on keeping this condition is because the company is widely known to be in difficulties. It appears that the governor was upset by this action and sent a message to the legislature that effectively threatened that the bill would be vetoed if it passed the house.

This attempt to exercise direct influence over the debate of a legislative body, as well as the effort to influence its proceedings by threatening a veto, raised a veritable storm and ended with yet another defeat for the governor. His friends barely managed to have the governor allowed to withdraw his message. Most wanted to leave it on the table. The governor later sent the same message to the house, where it will doubtless receive a similar, but not quite so hostile, reception.

We see it as an example of unwise thrift when an increase in the salary of judges on the Missouri Supreme Court is rejected. The salary is now $2,500, which is certainly an inadequate salary for members of the state's highest court, which is more overloaded with business than any other court in the state.

Mississippi Blätter, 27 February 1859

The Prosperity of Carondelet. There are few if any of the small towns along the river whose rapid rise can match that of Caron-

---

*The Hannibal and St. Joseph Railroad, a key line in the Missouri system planned by Thomas Allen of St. Louis in 1849 and promoted by R. M. Stewart and others from St. Joseph, had received $3 million in Missouri railroad bonds to aid construction, in addition to a substantial federal land grant. Construction began in 1853 and was completed in 1859. John Murray Forbes of Boston and his associates, who had gained control of the road in 1855, made it a part of their Burlington system, serving Chicago rather than St. Louis. Not only had the road helped attract thousands of free-state settlers to north Missouri, but also Forbes was an abolitionist. The *Blätter* should have been friendlier. JNP.

delet. There is an imposing number of new buildings, and just during this year a new city in miniature has been built. The recent discovery that Illinois coal can smelt the iron ore of Iron Mountain and Pilot Knob as well as charcoal—which is getting expensive due to the clearing of the forests—is of great importance for Carondelet. The ease with which iron ore can be brought to Carondelet, where the best Illinois coal can be had for a cheap price, has to make Carondelet one of the centers of the iron industry in Missouri.* The favorable situation on the river that it enjoys, the ease of shipping, all go to assure a great future for our little neighboring town.

Mississippi Blätter, 27 March 1859

Emigration from Germany to America

Missouri, 16 March 1859

The German nationality has already planted itself so deeply in the western states of the Union that the traces of German blood, German industry, and German spirit can never be obliterated; and yet what we regard here as our mission will be imperfectly fulfilled if we keep to ourselves and survive without further additions from our old homeland. Our descendants would be *happy* enough in this country even if they were to be thoroughly Americanized in custom and language, and mixed with the rest of the population in the course of fifty or a hundred years; but, in terms of the whole, the only benefit then would go to the people here, and the old Fatherland would have nothing to show but a loss of lifeblood. In such a context it would be proper for the Fatherland to oppose sending anyone except those who are a burden to others.

In keeping with this, anyone who wishes to bring the currently stagnant German emigration to America into motion again will have to convince the German people that those who leave would improve their economic situation; that an important human need could be fulfilled *here* that would be worth the sacrifice; and that some sort of compensation would be offered to the German people in exchange for strength lost through emigration.

As far as the first point is concerned, we must concede that there are those who are inclined not to emigrate, particularly members of

*It was easy to bring iron ore to Carondelet because the Iron Mountain Railroad had been completed from St. Louis to Pilot Knob in 1858, financed by $3.5 million in state bonds, $1.5 million in stock subscriptions by St. Louis City and County, and $.5 million in subscriptions by St. Louis and Madison County businessmen. JNP.

the better classes enjoying privileges of birth over those in the masses, and yet even they feel better here than they did in the old country once they have adjusted to local conditions. In exchange for the struggle with the yet raw and unconquered forces of nature, one is compensated by the greater bounty of natural resources; the lacks in society—the continual swindling, moral decadence, and prejudice—do not overcome the fact that the individual can live here in greater independence and security, untroubled by the care and need that is the lot of half the inhabitants of the Old World. The fact that our compatriots who came here with nothing quickly rose to prosperity can be held up as an encouraging example for the rest. Compared with what is squandered in Europe on princely courts, state servants, soldiers, and so on, what is lost here through the poor administration is hardly worth considering, and the shocking rawness here is a small fault compared to the torment experienced over there because of perpetual wardship, military service, the ruination of war, compulsion of every sort. In short, Germany can let a portion of its population go off to America every year without great concern for their future well-being; they will take care of themselves perfectly well without the Federal Council or the princes doing a precious thing for their survival or shadowing them with a protective wing.

If the Germans here are to accomplish anything at all beyond improving agriculture, horticulture, and viticulture, or lifting the level of several crafts, then they will have to preserve their language and education against the onslaught of English speech and the American style of education. They must be ready to apply themselves so as not simply to give a special tone to the life here, but to put the best of German style, German thought, and German feeling into practice. In this case the mission the Germans face here is harder than that which they would face in their homeland—they must master two complete educations. —Experience teaches us that the preservation of German ways (language and education) is harder for the second generation to accomplish than the adoption of American ways, and it is to be expected that the latter—which is easier and more comfortable in practical terms—will push the former out more and more, especially if there is no continuing pressure of immigration to maintain an inner spiritual link with the Mother Country that refreshes our Germanity. Accordingly, what Germany has given America up until now is like a down payment that would be lost if subsequent payments were not kept up. In the same way we would disappear if left to ourselves. —Further, we are still too weak to have an important effect here and need to be reinforced considerably, and this could be done without causing the old Fatherland any harm. If we were strengthened as we should be, we would have an easier time maintaining our ethnic identity, since we are no more than a sixth of the population here and now. —Anyone can see that it would be better to intensify the German element in order to make it viable and influential here than to scatter it to all corners of the world so that it is overcome by aliens and wastes away.

As far as Germany is concerned, a reduction of the total population would be a good deed for those who remained, even if those who left were swallowed by the sea; feeding, clothing, and warming forty million people within such narrow borders is a task that demands so much exertion, such anxious saving, and such intensified exploitation of too little land that the higher level of prosperity demanded for a civilized and civil society is hardly possible. But I do not want to go on with ideas that have already been explored frequently enough.

Germany does not control an inch of land outside its own borders. What is to prevent those who emigrate from joining other nationalities? Which is the most suitable? Which is most like our own? Which is in the course of mastering a country that is most suited to our German ways? —Everything points to the United States. Here we neither can nor will found any colonies that could pay taxes to the Mother Country, but the relations of sentiment and trade that arise between our new and old homelands, that are already there and promise to grow in the future, are a gain for both sides of the exchange. A new German life of a special sort can and shall unfold in the New World and work its effect on the old Fatherland, so that we shall freshen and strengthen it from here. It is inevitable under the present circumstances that we should combine with the Yankees, but just as it is in the interests of those in the old homeland that we do not disappear in the process, so it is in Germany's interest that its excess population come here rather than to Brazil, Australia, the Black Sea, or anywhere else.

The future development of humanity will have the effect of melting the vast number of present nationalities down to a small number. In the future theater of world history, the chief roles will go to the Romance, Germanic, and Slavic nationalities. If the Germanic nationality can hold its various branches together, it will hold a commanding position in Europe, and together with the British it will have a similar position in all other parts of the world. The younger branch of the British, the North American, is on its way to overtaking the older in height, and it is a matter of world-historical importance that the long-separated Anglo-Saxon and old Germanic peoples reunite. A resurrected, truly free Germany, England, and North America united in close association could force the rest of the world to strive for humane institutions and clear away the last vestiges of barbarism. The more the German element in British life and, most of all, in North American life asserts itself, the more it assumes decisive influence over the future course of human history.

It is not an accident but rather a property of the folk character of the Germanic nationality (which includes the British, Netherlandish, and Scandinavians) that it asserts Protestant principles, while the Romance nationalities stand for stationary Catholicism and the Slavs are dominated by a Christianity of mere outward forms that has a more oriental character. So a common lineage, spiritual direction, and mission bring together the Germans, Americans, and British more than any other peoples.

Another point has yet to be raised. The current Union will probably no longer exist by the time the population has risen to hundreds of millions. The plantation states are currently the ripest for separation; then the states along the Pacific will certainly form a league of their own; the states along the Atlantic as far as the Alleghenies would be suitable for another grouping of states together with Canada, etc., and the states along the Mississippi valley for yet another. This last association would fall heir to a large region of good soil and natural resources that could be compared with no other region of its size in the entire world. St. Louis will some day be the capital of an empire of fifty million free people, an empire that could match strength with any other in the world.* It lies in the Germans' power to make this coming Mississippi Union essentially German, so that it could reach a helping hand across the ocean to a coming German Republic. —Whereas the German element has usually been sacrificed when merged with the Romance nationality (as is the case in all the countries of South America), and when it encounters the Slavs it achieves importance only when it overwhelms them, it can combine with the British stock in the western states of the Union so as to win an equal right to exist. Thus these states are now and shall always be the most suitable homeland for those Germans who are inclined to emigrate for whatever reason.

Far West [Friedrich Münch]*

*St. Louis as the capital of an enormous economic empire stretching to the Pacific and even to China was a common booster theme, but Far West's suggestion of political separation was unusual if not unique. JNP.

*Friedrich Münch promoted emigration with great zeal in the late 1850s, particular-

Mississippi Blätter, 3 April 1859

The Week in Review

The life and activity of the city of St. Louis presented a particularly lively scene during the week just past. There are several factors that contributed to this.

The *election campaign* gained intensity toward the end of the week. There was furious activity on all sides, but particularly among the National Democrats and the Know-nothings. Some of the demonstrations drew large crowds, and party wire-pullers were actually able to raise some enthusiasm. The National Democrats have been much in evidence with their raucous parades, including the famous bear band, Chinese lanterns, and signs—mostly with stale slogans—carried about by half-grown boys. Colonel Bogy is doing his best to provide the usual "fun" for his Irish teenager Young American Supporters.* These efforts are of little avail, and we would lose our faith in the good sense of the citizens of St. Louis if they should fail to elect Oliver D. Filley,* candidate of the solid, honest people, as Mayor. The business world is almost unanimous in supporting him.

In order to prevent disturbances during the election tomorrow, all bars in the city have been closed for the day by the mayor's proclamation. We do not believe that serious disturbances of the peace will take place, but there are fears that there will be a battle over the ballot boxes for the Ninth Ward. In general this election campaign has proceeded rather quietly, since the people of St. Louis are growing tired of party humbug, and some day we hope to see an election when this sort of nonsense with pompous parades, Chinese lanterns, and pitch torches will fail to draw crowds and be dropped. They are not an encouraging gauge of the people's political maturity. The *business world* of St. Louis was as active as or even more active than the politicians in the week just past. Business is

---

ly by a tour through Germany in summer 1859, reported in columns published in *Mississippi Blätter*. For the occasion he published an immigrants' guide, *Der Staat Missouri geschildert mit besonderer Berücksichtigung auf teutsche Einwanderung* (New York, St. Louis: Farmers' and Vine-Growers' Society, 1859), which was issued in new editions in 1866 and 1872. SR.

*Louis V. Bogy, a prominent businessman of Creole descent, was an anti-Bentonite. Senator Stephen A. Douglas of Illinois was the most noted advocate of Young America, which stressed aggressive expansion, especially into Latin America, and free trade. Membership did not require approval of William Walker's tactics, nor of slavery extension, but Douglas used the movement to gain Southern support. JNP.

*Oliver D. Filley, a wealthy stove manufacturer with New England origins and an active Free-Soiler since 1848, was a close political associate of Frank Blair and B. Gratz Brown. JNP.

excellent; our wholesale houses on Main Street can hardly keep up with the orders, and towers of chests and boxes loom in front of every store like wooden walls. German wholesalers have done business during the last week in the hundreds of thousands of dollars. The harbor is full of boats; the levee crammed with products; in short, everything reflects a boom that enlivens all of St. Louis.

A third peculiar element that has given a lift to the life of our city is the *Pike's Peak emigration*, which was particularly numerous last week. Each boat going up the Missouri carries a number of adventurous golddiggers who hope to apply their labor more profitably on distant Cherry Creek or Pike's Peak, and who already dream of being as rich as Croesus. Many are already acting out their romantic fantasies of the Plains and the Rocky Mountains in their present attire, and one tall Teuton was held in awe for his grizzly-bear cloak and elegant moccasins. A great swarm of swindlers, tricksters, and counterfeiters has come along with the emigrants, as the crime statistics abundantly show. —Emigrants allow themselves to be swindled and robbed particularly often by mock lotteries and sideshows on the levee, and every day brings new examples as well as new victims. A single policeman has the duty to oversee all the shows at once, but the police here seem to be unable to do anything even about fraud committed right under their own eyes.

Important changes have taken place in the last week on the *stage*. The Varieties-Theater, which has recently been satisfying all friends of the theater with its really excellent productions, closed with last Sunday's performance.* Mrs. Dremmel and Mrs. Petosi, who were especially loved by the public for their performances, left in the middle of last week for Milwaukee, where they will be performing. Part of the personnel of the former company at the varieties has gone over to Mr. Fischer's Flora-Theater, and part has been engaged by Mr. Bechtner's Stadttheater. The theater in the Floragarten has drawn a particularly good crowd recently. The repertory company there has some excellent members; Madame Otto has long earned considerable recognition; and Mr. Höchster shows himself capable of playing many different roles. The distinguished director of the Varieties, Mr. Schwan, has had a guest engagement there since last week. Next Tuesday, as a tribute to Mr. Schwan, "Catherine Howard, or the Royal Crown and the Scaffold"

*The closing of the Varieties-Theater was soon followed by the establishment of the St. Louis Opern Haus in the same building, under the management of Heinrich Börnstein. Börnstein had long been associated with the Varieties-Theater, since that is where his farce *Deutsche Einwanderer und Deutsche Gesellschaft!* was first performed by the "Deutsche philodramatische Gesellschaft" in 1853. SR.

will be presented, with Schwan as King Henry VIII and Mr. Höchster as Ethelwood. We cannot neglect to inform friends of the theater about this.

Bechtner's Stadttheater has also gained several very useful members from the old Varieties company, including Mr. Wetzlau and Mrs. Rudolph. —The artist Steffen, who has made such memorable portrayals of the Grand Inquisitor and other villains, now performs in Ruedi's Garden. Almost all the smaller theaters will benefit from the Varieties' collapse. A reopening of the Varieties-Theater before next fall is out of the question.

We have to report a few events in *social* life that cast a rather darker hue on social conditions.

The shocking infanticide that a Swiss girl of seventeen committed, in which she disposed of a newborn child in a privy after slitting its throat, betrays a coarsening of the spirit that one would have thought impossible. The degradation of a German girl of fifteen and the suicide of the German Sachs, combined with the memory of Downie's murder, which is called to mind by the sentencing of the young murderers Nick Trautwein, Anton Leise, and Theodor Deobold, should cause Germans to be deeply concerned. Germans appear all too often in the crime reports.*

The *health conditions* in the city were worse than in the previous week. The number of deaths rose significantly, from 52 to 78. Of those who died, 45 were white males, 29 white females, 2 free colored, and 2 slaves. The number of children dying under the age of five was 35, which was good in view of the fact that this number usually accounts for 50 percent of the total. The arrival of the milder season and the end of bad weather will soon improve health conditions, although St. Louis already has considerably better conditions than other large American cities, including Cincinnati and Chicago.

Mississippi Blätter, 3 April 1859

Pictures of St. Louis

Lunch and Lunchers in St. Louis

The lunch is an American invention, at least in the breadth and importance it has achieved in the United States, since it supports a

---

*German crimes were only rarely and reluctantly admitted in the German press, which took great glee in reporting deeds of the Irish, particularly drunken Irish.

large number of people. It is an achievement for humanity and socialism of which America can be justly proud. European efforts to organize lunch by state initiative, such as the Rumford soup kitchens in Munich, are worlds apart from the lunch American style. Rumford soup kitchens only serve starving proletarians, but in America lunch has the twofold mission of providing at a single setting breakfast and dinner for true proletarians, while providing an opportunity for the wealthier luncher to escape the store or office for a few moments to take a bite to balance off his beer or wine. At lunch all differences of rank are abolished and socialistic equality reigns supreme; the fancy luncher, who sees the lunch as a luxury or as an occasion for entertainment, stands shoulder to shoulder with the poor devil who fate has treated unkindly and whose rumbling tummy would soon sing elegies or even dirges if lunch did not still that longing which has no name. The difference between a Rumford soup kitchen and a free lunch is identical to that between a monarchy and a republic. The poor man who slurps the soup in a Rumford kitchen has to see this philanthropy as an act of grace, but the luncher is a free man who demands his rights, which in this case consist of soup, sausages, meatloaf, liver dumplings, and on and on.

The American lunch might also be compared with the romantic French public pots, where one buys for a pittance the right to dip a large fork into a vast stewpot that is filled like a witch's cauldron with food remnants of every sort, some weighing whole pounds a piece, such as half ducks and leftovers from hotels and restaurants, all in a wild, disordered stew. If one is lucky, he will land a big catch (half a duck), or if not, then, a booby prize (a bare bone). The lunch is an American invention, and by no means the least, since many thousands are preserved from hunger by it, particularly in the larger towns.

The greatest elaboration of the lunch system is found in harbor cities, and the true El Dorado of the luncher is New Orleans, a fact that was established after our long wrangle with German newspapers in New Orleans some years ago. Since those days the lunch has borne its victorious banner northward and westward, and soon it shall be unfurled on the furthest limits of civilization, though everywhere modified by local conditions.

Suicides by immigrants appear to have been extremely common, and the strict sexual morality expected by the German community of its own female members (there were virtually no prostitutes of German extraction) placed a heavy burden on German women to avoid being sexually compromised. See Audrey J. Olson CSJ, "St. Louis Germans, 1850–1920: The Nature of an Immigrant Community and Its Relation to the Assimilation Process" (Ph.D. diss., Univ. of Kansas, 1970), 54. SR.

St. Louis, for example, has rather few true professional lunchers. Here there are no establishments so liberal as the City Hotel in New Orleans, where one can have salad and three courses, but St. Louis specializes in the "extra lunch" and the "free lunch." Those few professional lunchers that we do have are physicians with big tummies, hungry clerks, poorly paid actors, and other artists short on bread. For such lunchers we can recommend the establishments of Mr. Schreiner and Gustav Wolf. A higher-class lunch, such as is eaten by the political and commercial bigwigs, is served around the corner of Market and Second Street. The patrons of these lunches do not eat out of necessity but to pass the time. Lunch is served in beer halls in form only, since it serves as an accompaniment to the sale of beer. In this context lunch in St. Louis could never be compared with lunch in New Orleans, but it was the Germans in St. Louis who gave lunch a role to play in family life. As readers of our advertisements well know, a baptism or a wedding is often the occasion for a special lunch, which anyone can join on the payment of ten cents. The literature of the lunch in St. Louis has made significant progress, as can be seen from a glance at the newspapers. A special species of lunch is the "election lunch," which is given before the election so that the patriots can go off to their ballot boxes in a suitable frame of mind. The election lunch is one of the exceptions to the rule. The categories of lunch in St. Louis are not as strictly ranked as they are in the port towns, and here lunch is more a pleasantry than a necessity.

Mississippi Blätter, 1 May 1859

Monthly Crime Report. In the course of the month of April just past, St. Louis police made 605 arrests, 285 by the day watch and 320 by the night watch. The grounds for arrest were as follows:

Crimes or Misdemeanors against state laws: murder, 1; assault with intent to kill, 3; passing counterfeit currency, 7; street robbery, 3; theft, 46; shoplifting, 2; obtaining money under false pretenses, 4; receiving stolen goods, 1; illegal exercise of the right to vote, 3; Negroes in the state without permission, 18; riot, 5; altogether, 98.

Misdemeanors against city ordinances: reckless driving, 4; carrying concealed weapons, 13; mistreatment of animals, 1; disturbing the peace, 136; drunkenness on a public street, 187; indecent exposure, 7; brawling and fighting, 31; Negroes out at night without a pass, 6; unlicensed pets, 2; resisting arrest, 15; vagrancy, 64; other misdemeanors, 42.

Mississippi Blätter, 10 July 1859

Our Levee. Strangers and even those who live here will be somewhat surprised when they see the condition of our levee, where the retreating river has left behind a deposit of mud mixed with potatoes, onions, corn, and grass seed, which sprouts and grows vigorously and is then ripened by the fiery rays of the sun. It appears that our city fathers are perfectly happy to let the levee become a farm and are little concerned that the muck raises a pestilential odor.

Mississippi Blätter, 18 September 1859

The Sale of Slaves from Missouri into the South continues without letup. Ever since the last coup of the slaveowners failed in Kansas, the owners of black human property have become convinced that the "peculiar institution" has become more and more untenable in Missouri, especially along the borders. Material interests are taking the upper hand, and the slaveowner prefers to send his property to the sunny Southland rather than face increased competition with free labor, which has grown increasingly powerful with the establishment of Kansas as a free state. There has been a particularly large movement of slaves through Missouri to the South in most recent times. The *Lexington Express* says there is not a single county in the state where slaves have not been sold South. One slaveowner named White shipped forty at one time down the river. In the week before last, the *General Davis* arrived at Lexington with a hundred slaves, all being taken to the South. The demand for slave labor created by the high cotton price has had a great influence on the purchase of slaves for the Southern market. As long as the price for a pound of cotton stands at twelve cents, labor will simply be worth more in Louisiana, Mississippi, and Alabama than in Missouri, and this is the principal explanation for the forced migration of blacks into the South.

Mississippi Blätter, 18 September 1859

*Horace Greeley** was expected to arrive in St. Louis yesterday on his return journey from California. Since he left San Francisco with the Overland Mail on 26 August, he should have been able to reach here yesterday evening.

Greeley must certainly be satisfied with his visit to California, since the entire state received him enthusiastically and all the newspapers are filled with his accomplishments.

Despite jokes that cling to him, Horace Greeley is one of the few leading American political figures who has maintained a reputation for integrity, and that is saying a great deal in the land of corruption *par excellence*. Greeley sometimes makes a fool of himself, but his American nature impels him to get excited about things that lead him astray even with the best of intentions.

Greeley, with his white coat, is one of the most important phenomena of the contemporary American world. —Although merely a newspaper editor, he exercises a powerful influence over the country's public opinion, and the jubilation with which he has been greeted everywhere on his cross-country tour, not to mention his reception in the mines at Denver City and in California, or in Salt Lake City, where he tried to come to terms with Mormonism, is enough to show that Greeley's name is equally respected throughout this vast Union.

In California, the way he spoke out for the completion of the Pacific Railway assured him a role in the undertaking.

With his white coat, Greeley is a sort of modern Diogenes, though he does not lounge in a tub as the Greek philosopher did, and he is much more presentable despite the fact that he only drinks water. With his traveling bag to hold some extra linen, he goes off on journeys lasting months, talks with miners at Cherry Creek, with Brigham Young in Utah, in every place in California. He has already visited Europe with the same carpet bag and the same white coat.

With all his eccentricities, Horace Greeley is a character who lives out his convictions, a man of broad knowledge, a paragon of American journalism. When he comes to St. Louis, he will not want for a warm reception.

P.S. The Overland Post did not arrive yesterday. The Mail is expected tonight, and Horace Greeley along with it.

*The German press in America used and respected no English-language newspaper so much as the *New York Tribune*, edited by the eccentric Horace Greeley. SR.

Mississippi Blätter, 9 October 1859

The Ultimate Destiny of the White and Black Races in America

It is a question of basic importance for the white race what will become of the black race in the United States, since the white race regards itself as a more noble, intellectually superior, and ruling race, as has been the case *de facto* and *de iure* until now. If the two races coexist primarily in the South as at present, they will continue to mix, and eventually a homogenous people will emerge. The proof of this assertion can be seen by anyone who has traveled in America and has eyes to see. In 1850 the ratio of blacks to whites was about one to six in the entire Union. The census of 1850 simply gave the number of whites and blacks without making any distinction of degree among colored people, with few exceptions. One can assume, however, that at least a third of the four million colored people were mixed: mulattoes, quadroons, and the other differentiations up and down the scale between the two races.

If we accept it to be a fact that the African race has lived in America for two hundred years and that during this time has become increasingly mixed, then it follows that the remaining two-thirds will be absorbed or born mixed during the next four hundred years. Further, we can assume that during this long period those already mixed will continue to be absorbed into the more numerous white race, so that six hundred years from now both races will have utterly vanished into one another and a uniform people of one color will be formed. We expect that the census of 1860 will not neglect to make a distinction between blacks and mixed persons in order to establish when they shall all be mixed. Only once we have the census of 1870 and know the rate of mixture in the intervening ten years will we be able to predict with any precision the time when the entire race will be absorbed when the white and colored races will become a single people.

This evaluation takes on a completely different form when we apply it to the slave states alone rather than to the entire Union. In the slave states the ratio of blacks to whites is about one to two, and there race mixture is the order of the day, especially in the towns and villages, where at least half of those of African race are mongrels. Since there are about two whites for every black in the South, it follows that the complete mixture of both races would produce a race the color of a dark quadroon. This assumes that neither race is increased by immigration. If the South reintroduces the slave trade, the result would favor the dark color even more than otherwise. Using the enormous resources of modern commerce, anywhere between a quarter-million and half-a-million slaves could be imported annually. In twenty years this would make the numerical relationship between the races almost equal, and by the end of the century the colored would constitute about three-quarters of the population of the South. The utterly mad agitation of the fire-eaters for the reintroduction of the slave trade would lead to this result, hardly to be desired, and the South struggles against its own interests and for its own ruin when it seeks to reactivate the import of slaves.

The sole means against this unwished-for result would be the restriction of slavery, since proposals for exportation have all proved impractical. If the black race could be concentrated in a few states, the sexual mixing would soon cease. But if the system of slavery and the black race with it spread even wider across the continent, then racial mixture would accelerate along with it, and the blacks would be absorbed into the white race in a few centuries. The white residents of the slave states are trying with all their might to remedy a too-great increase of blacks in the old slave states by expanding the region of slavery, and this only works to speed up amalgamation and the demonstrated result of a mongrel race. The North is not willing to promote this goal through appeasement, and it has the right of self-defense to ward off such an undesirable eventuality by all available means. What has been said shows that it is the Democratic party that promotes racial amalgamation, while the Republican party's principles work to restrict slavery and with it racial amalgamation.

Mississippi Blätter, 23 October 1859

An African "Dutchman." Under this title the local reporter of the *Republican* announced it as something especially "amusing" that among a group of white German immigrants arriving from the old Fatherland on the evening of the day before yesterday there was a colored man who had the same clothing as the others, spoke German, and smoked a German pipe. —We have no idea what could be *amusing* about this "occasion."

We never saw our supposed black compatriot, so we cannot say what accident brought him to Germany in his youth. We can only hope he brought good papers with him so some trader in human beings does not seize him as "fleeing goods" and sell him South. We also hope he subscribes right away to the *Westliche Post*.

Mississippi Blätter, 6 November 1859

The City of St. Louis

No one could ever accuse St. Louis of having been built according to a standard pattern and having no character of its own, a jibe which would fit most other American cities. The city presents an imposing image when viewed from the opposite bank of the Mississippi, and its further limits are lost in the mists. It rises in terraces from the brim of the Father of Waters, and its domes and church towers rival the tall chimneys of factories and shops, whose black coal smoke threatens to besmudge the heavens.

When we step onto the levee, we are at once in the midst of a whirl and activity that appears to be chaotic confusion but that indeed has system and reason. The rumbling of the great haulage wagons, the truly terrifying shrieks of the teamsters, who seem engaged in a perpetual battle of wills with their mules, the demonic puffing of steam boilers, the thick enveloping dust—all of these contribute to a picture that is interesting but hardly pretty. The levee is a great peaceful battlefield during working hours; the colossal steamers that dump and take on wares are the heavy artillery, the teamsters and loaders the cavalry and infantry that throw themselves into the fray in a great colorful confusion.

But on a Sunday morning we can see the banks of the Mississippi in their true festive dress. When the morning sun has risen victorious over the swamps of Illinois and reflects its rays on the swell of the majestic river, we can breathe in the mild autumnal air on the same spot where dust and hubbub was the order of the day through the week. Now at last we come to feel the inner well-being that only repose and the harmony of nature, not the striving of men, can bring. On Sunday the full splendor of the Mississippi emerges from the shroud of coal smoke and dust that covers it during the week. The steamers have ceased to spit out their thick pall, teamsters and their titanic wagons have stayed at home, and loaders are resting from the exertions of the week in the murky den of some boarding house. The solid walls of warehouses glare down darkly on the empty place, only a few pedestrians are scattered across the broad expanse, and even the cyclopean rings that held boats during the week lie useless, testifying only to their strength and inertia. We are seized by the same feelings that strike one who wanders over a battlefield after the deed has been done. Over there are a few chests belonging to poor, helpless immigrants; here is a twitching drunk who shows how far the divine human species can sink as he sprawls in the misty glow of the morning sun. We know that thousands have worked and struggled here through the entire week to earn their bread by the sweat of their brow; we know that products of the whole world are shipped in and out of here; we know the battle will soon be taken up again with renewed verve, and that every day will lay a new burden on the flywheel of this vast machine. All the more we feel ourselves graced to sense the peace of this Sunday—a picture of a humane nature well formed—which sweeps away all obstacles in its path.

The majestic forest on the far shore, with its idyllic cabins, could hardly indicate to the stranger that two of the great arteries of traffic spread their arms northward and eastward in its shadow, making a frame for the picture our weak pen is trying to trace.

We go on. If the levee is to be compared with the heathen under-world, with Dante's inferno, during the week, and the Mississippi with the River Styx, and the sole difference is that those who cross it pass not to the realm of the dead but to that of the free, then soon we reach the higher regions and the Elysian fields of trade, Main Street. Here the canny merchant receives his goods out of the chaos of the levee; here we begin to see that all of this seemingly crazed effort has a certain sensible end. Here the wholesaler stacks with care the goods of the East, the fruits of the South, and the grains of the North to ship them out to the whole world. Great blank chests and boxes hem in our path here, and among them move the generals and the corporals of trade, as if on the eve of a battle, cold-bloodedly figuring their value, aware of themselves as functioning parts of society. But away from here, away from this all-too-earnest if honorable class.

Now we pass to the next street, Second, or rather to the lower part of it, since the upper part belongs as much to the wholesalers as does Main.

Here we hear the German tongue, or rather the German *dialect*, everywhere. Here resides happy mediocrity, a self-assured prosperity that worries little about the blows of fate; here the German barman serves beer and wine; here the honest German craftsman does his best for a customer; here the earnest seamstress leans over her work, and the apprentice works his way up to prosperity. Here we are pleased to see this or that man who could tell us he had to work on the railroad or on the roads for a while, but that he now no longer has to worry about where his next meal is coming from. Here we find the older settler of the thirties in high style alongside the refugee of '48 and '49, who has already worked his way out of the depression of exile, of *Elend* as the Germans call it. It is true that many fell by the wayside in the hard struggle for survival, through death or moral collapse; that makes these survivors all the prouder for having made it through and reached their goal.

When we go down a bit along Second and Main streets, the stranger will be surprised at the peculiar form and grouping of houses, many of a quite archaic form. Here we see a modern brick house, and next to it is a one-story hut about twelve feet tall with rotting shingles on the roof and signs of decay abounding. The door is usually open, and in the interior we can spy a seamstress or worse. Next door is an old French house, one story high and surrounded by a covered porch, and it usually still shelters a descendant of the people of Saint Louis. The whole bonhomie of French character and its penchant for tradition that often decays into dirtiness jumps out at us; there we see a shingle, "Pension française" of "La Tante Marie." What patriarchal charm is contained in this yellowed sign! One seems to be set back a good hundred years when he sees these houses of an earlier generation, which owe their survival to the fact that the business world has moved its activities elsewhere.

Now we climb up to Fourth Street; here the air is clearer, the street wider, and the broader space permits greater cleanliness. Now we are on the boulevards of St. Louis. Glittering shop windows invite us to look and to buy; broad sidewalks give us the chance to stroll, and pleasant restaurants offer the finest culinary enjoyments. Yet such things are found in every town. Let us go a bit higher and turn into Broadway, which extends itself without end toward the north.

We have never seen anything like it in any city in America. A broad street, covered on both sides, with broad sidewalks giving the pedestrian a place to walk and the sellers a place to display their wares. But what wares! On a walk of four or five blocks on either side you will indeed find in a colorful mixture everything for sale that human imagination or mood is capable of conceiving. We would need someone like old Homer to describe the splendor of the world offered here to any man who loves modest prices. Wholesale, retail, clothing shops and notions, shoemakers and tailors—everything is represented here. Next to a cart full of dried deerskins we see

shining apples and pears; next to shoes and socks there are cran-
berries and tomatoes; fresh meat of all sorts, rabbits and squirrels;
onions and lemons, oranges and garlic; hats of the latest style and
Swiss cheese; readymade dresses and silverware; live bunnies and
salted butter; crowing roosters and salt pork; a sodawater stand
sells stockings, a clothing shop sells fresh potatoes; there are shops
that sell anything that has ever been sold or ever shall be sold—in
short, a true microcosm of all human wants. One Saturday afternoon reminded us of the lively comings and goings of a German
annual fair. "People live to shove and get shoved." The careful
German housewife with a chicken for a Sunday soup jostles an
American gourmet seeking a prairie hen or a quail. An Irish work-
man hauls roast beef for half a week, while a descendant of the
French carries home the best varieties of fish. Yet all are seized
with a special sort of good cheer that announces the coming of the
peace and joy of Sunday. Each must admit that he is part of a happy
people.

A step further and we are closed for the day. Down to the river in
the upper part of the city is to be found no retailing, no friendly
faces, but only blackened, vulcanic, grotesque forms. Nothing but
factories, foundries; nothing small, everything huge; smoky buildings with smudged windows from which machines whir or steam
governors shriek; in front of the doors lie anchors, pieces of
machine iron and such, fallen to the earth by their own weight. A
workshop for Vulcan, a black, smoky underworld that thumps and
clangs and nourishes thousands, makes thousands of the tools of
comfort and travel, and even provides the missing link in the chain
of factors that holds our world together.*

We can see that St. Louis is a great center of industry, and it will
be even greater some day; here are the proofs of wealth and human
industry; here is the great nerve of the social body of our city.

On the whole, the exterior of the city has preserved a strongly
French appearance in the older quarters. The narrow, irregular
streets of the business district speak of this; the upper portion
bears a clear, American character that gives the eye no place to
rest.

St. Louis is rich in peculiarities that are barely indicated by what
we have said, and for that very reason it is the most interesting city
there is for one who is wont to watch people living and striving.

*Before the completion of the Iron Mountain Railroad, St. Louis's main source of
iron blooms and pigs was the Maramec Ironworks, seventy miles to the southwest.
Maramec iron reached St. Louis via the Missouri River, to the upper city where
Chouteau, Harrison and Vallé, and the steamboat and railroad engine manufacturers were located. After 1858 heavy industry gravitated to the Carondelet area. JNP.

Mississippi Blätter, 24 December 1859

A Calculated Assault on the Freedom of the Press

What follows is the text of the bill which Mr. Thompson of Clay has filed in the senate of the Missouri legislature:

> Section 1: Any person who writes or prints a book or any other writing, or has it written or printed, which incites Negroes in this state to rebellion, revolt, or resistance against the property rights of their masters, and any person who intends to distribute such a book knowingly, is guilty of a felony and after conviction is to be punished by imprisonment in the penitentiary for no less than two and no more than five years.
>
> Section 2: If a postmaster or his deputy becomes aware that such a book or writing is in the mails, he is to inform a justice of the peace of that fact, *and the justice of the peace is to investigate the matter and have such books or writings burned in his presence.* If it appears to the justice of the peace that the person to whom this book was being sent subscribed to the book knowing its character or had promised to receive it in order to further the goals of abolitionism, he should arrest such a person and have that person brought before him, and if the guilt of the person appears probable, he should have that person imprisoned to be tried by law. Any person who commits such an act is guilty of a misdemeanor and if convicted by a jury is to pay a monetary fine of no more than $500 or to serve a prison sentence of no more than three months, or both. The postmaster or his deputy who do not enforce this law will be compelled to pay a fine of no more than $200.

We should not linger over the provisions of Section 1 of this bill, since this is something to be expected in a slave state. But what of Section 2? This is a direct, brutal assault on freedom of the press. Anyone can see at first glance that Section 2 of this law would require the destruction of all books and newspapers directed against slavery, and any which are not written in favor of the proslavery party are delivered up to the arbitrary decision of a postmaster and a justice of the peace. Any justice of the peace could make a summary decision of life and death over any books or newspapers that show up in this or that post office.

Accepting and carrying out this act would put an end to freedom of the press in Missouri, and in its place there would rule censorship and inquisition by postmasters and justices of the peace.

We fully believe that even this act could be passed by our current legislature. Since the *Negro Bill* was passed by the Senate we hold anything to be possible.

The Negro bill stomped on all human rights, the Sunday bill destroys the freedom of religion, the police bill obliterates the right of communal self-government, so why should the despotism that calls itself the National Democratic party not try to set an ax to the strongest support of freedom, a free press?

Since one member of Buchanan's cabinet finds a similar law in Virginia to be entirely in order, why should National Democracy shrink from such an act when it also is willing to sell native-born citizens of Missouri back into slavery?

Go ahead, gentlemen, the crazier the better; then your despotic rule will end all that much sooner.

Mississippi Blätter, 1 January 1860

From Jefferson City. Our regular correspondent in Jefferson City sent nothing yesterday. We interpret that to mean that nothing happened, which is always the *best* news that can come from Jefferson City. Citizens who arrived yesterday evening from the "capital" told us that Drake made a second attempt to bring up his metropolitan police bill, but it did not succeed.* The man is killing himself.

The house discussed the railroad question,* and the debate will demand several more days. The result is totally uncertain, since opinion in the legislature is evenly divided.

Mississippi Blätter, 15 January 1860

Colonization of Free Negroes in Central and South America

Where are the unfortunate free Negroes to go? They have been driven out of the Southern states, they have not been accepted by the North, or, if they are tolerated, they are still dealt with politically and socially in such a way that their progress among white people is encumbered and their elevation to a higher cultural level

---

*Charles Daniel Drake, a Democrat from St. Louis, sought to transfer control of the St. Louis police board from Republican Mayor O. D. Filley to Democratic Governor Stewart. By 1865 the political chameleon Drake was the acknowledged leader of Missouri's Radical Republicans, with a strong German following. JNP.

*Claiborne F. Jackson and other central Missouri agrarians wanted the state to exercise its lien on the state-aid railroads, all of which, except the Hannibal and St. Joseph, were in default on their interest payments. St. Louisans, led by Nathaniel Paschall of the *Republican*, opposed the bill, which was defeated. As the next governor, Jackson would have been in a position to close down the roads and sell off their assets. JNP.

is made almost impossible.* This question has been forced to our attention again by the latest measures of the Southern states, and in fact it is one of the most pressing questions of humanity in our times. It is well known that several Southern states have barred most if not all free Negroes from their territory and that similar measures are pending in several other states. Negroes from Arkansas, for example, are wandering about the West and North without a home. Many states are now closed to them by law, while in others the population is decisively hostile to their settlement. Every new exile of Negroes increases the difficulty and resistance to their reception on the part of the population of the North. One might complain bitterly about this fact on philanthropic grounds alone, but one also has to admit it to be a fact that will not go away. The Anglo-Saxon race simply *has* this hostility to the black race, and the laws in the South and the social treatment of free colored people in the anti-slavery North demonstrate the immutability of this racial hostility. The same phenomenon is even beginning to emerge in Canada, which had been the last refuge of the blacks. One could go further and say that the Anglo-Saxon race has in essence less potential for solving the race question than any other, and that there is simply no future for the subordinated black race in the midst of primarily Anglo-Saxon and Celtic Americans but slavery in the South and belittlement, persecution, and decline in the North.

It is not necessary to go any further, or to accept the notion that the coexistence of both races would have a corrupting influence, to see the need for solving this question. The fact is that the free Negro population in the United States is damned to the position of a pariah by measures of both North and South, that they are hunted and driven through the land, and that the inevitable result for blacks is nameless misery, let alone political and social disadvantage for the whites. Some sort of solution is necessary, and soon, for the sake of humanity. From the point of view of the Republican party, which is trying to limit the territory of slavery and which expects slavery to be ended in the Northern slave states in the near future, the solution of the racial question is completely unavoidable insofar as it concerns free Negroes.

*"Black laws" in Illinois, Indiana, and Ohio required blacks to post bond before taking up residence. By the late 1850s Oregon, Illinois, and Indiana excluded black newcomers altogether. Abraham Lincoln in 1858 declined to sign a petition permitting blacks to testify against whites in Illinois courts. In only a few free states could blacks vote or serve on juries, and even in Massachusetts in 1860, they were excluded from all but the most menial occupations. Everywhere in the North, the race was segregated, caricatured, and ridiculed. JNP.

People are also starting to come seriously to grips with this problem, so it seems. The old proposal to establish Negro colonies on this continent in Central or South America rather than in distant Africa, whither a mass migration is impossible, is ever more actively discussed. This was the subject of a speech in the latest session of Congress by Francis P. Blair.* In the last few days the governors of Ohio, Indiana, and Wisconsin expressed themselves in a similar way in favor of Negro colonies. These three governors are all Republicans. But the arguments that are raised in support of the proposal are also presently directed at the interests and prejudices of the South. Free Negroes in the free states are a peril for the South, as Southern newspapers repeat often enough. The Southern states cannot demand that the North accept as an act of charity a population they have expelled. If we want to ban free Negroes as well, then it is our duty to find a new homeland for these unfortunates.

So the creation of colonies for free Negroes makes sense, and from the point of view of humanity it is a necessity that cannot be avoided, even by the Democratic party if it is capable of gazing into the future at all.

The colonization of free Negroes is the sole means conceivable for a peaceful solution of the slavery question. This question will soon become the main concern of politics here.

Mississippi Blätter, 12 February 1860

A Conservative Voice

Today we are publishing Far West's defense against attacks aimed at his last article on the position of the parties in the Union. One will find a great deal here that is original. If Far West is opposed, as he says, to every harshness and excess due to his long experience, we have nothing against that; but the same experience must have told him that a partisan struggle cannot be handled with kid gloves if it intends to overthrow that which is old.

*In 1858 Blair unveiled an elaborate plan in Congress for gradual emancipation and colonization. He reasoned that fear of and dislike for blacks were so strong in America that no plan of emancipation could succeed without their simultaneous removal. In the warmth of the Caribbean area, they would thrive in freedom, and in their absence, white labor and business would thrive in the United States. Most slaveowners were no more enchanted by Blair's scheme than by William Lloyd Garrison's abolitionism. JNP.

We cannot agree with him when he speaks of the division of the Union; his vision of a Negro state in fifty years is extraordinarily novel, but we are not currently in the position to work out the principles of a vision of the future that would be different. Fifty years is too long a time for our talents of prognostication, so we leave the fate of these states in those days to the next generation.

Further we assume that, when all is said and done, the South will submit, since experience up until now confirms this assumption. Most recently, the election of a Republican Speaker shows this. We do agree with our esteemed correspondent that the conflict is beyond reconciliation, and that it cannot be ended by political speeches alone.

*   *   *

South and North

Missouri, 1 February 1860

The essay that I published under this title in the *Cincinnati Volksblatt* (whose editors announced themselves to have been enthusiastically in support) was republished in the *Westliche Post* together with comments that can be found in the daily editions. The *Anzeiger des Westens* took the opportunity of these "marginalia" to make an attack on this newspaper, with which I had nothing to do, and it went on to describe my own essay as extremely *mal à propos* (perhaps it has never published anything *mal à propos?*). I shall not dispute the right of anyone to have an opinion of his own in such matters, but it is usually better to support a harsh public evaluation by giving *grounds*—they do not even burn a heretic before asking him *why*. As matters stand right now, a reader of the *Anzeiger* would know only that I wrote an article that journal thought *mal à propos*, and they would have to believe it for good or ill, since they did not get to read it for themselves and they had no idea what was being condemned. —And yet the quintessence of the article was the notion that one should evaluate the actual situation in the South coolly in order to deal with the South firmly and without passion—and this is substantially what the *Anzeiger* said already on 25 January: "It is only necessary to make the proper (hence passionless) description of Republican principles to bring the Southern people to reason."

Reason is what we need, now more than ever, and if one who is attacked is supposed to be brought to see it, then one who attacks should have it totally in his own grasp. In the current struggle the attacker is the Republican party. Whoever wishes to deny this should consider the following:

After the North tolerated the importation of slaves until 1808 and held it to be legal, after it permitted new slave states into the Union almost without protest or allowed them to be carved out of federal territory,* and after it approved a second round of fugitive slave laws much harsher than the first, now suddenly there stands a unified, powerful party competing for supreme power in the Union whose platform proclaims slavery to be an evil no longer to be tolerated, an insult to the entire republic, and which declares it to be its principle that not one foot more shall be conceded to slave-owners.* At the same time the requirements of the Fugitive Slave Law passed by Congress have been made incapable of being carried out in eight states; along with that, as none denies, there is a plan to suspend slavery in the District of Columbia, to forbid slave trade between individual states, even to free individual Southern states of the evil of slavery.

Is that not aggressive politics? —I know it all must come to that eventually, and one can hardly criticize the North for the fact that it has at last perceived the true situation and decided to act accordingly, but at the same time I believe that it would have been better if the North had acted from the outset—even at the peril of dividing the Union—according to the principles of the Northwest Ordinance of 1787 and had made no concessions that contradicted the demands of humanity, had not conditioned the South to expect appeasement, had not helped the South along its way or funded its mammoth expansion. Now all of these errors are supposed to be made good at one time—and high time, too—and what was given away freely long ago is now to be taken back by fiat, without compromise, even, we might say, without pity or grace.

Nothing is to be done about it, but the source of the present state of affairs—to be precise—is the long-term cowardly self-serving of the North, which has always had the superiority in votes and power, and it is almost more to blame than the South, which has always

---

*There was a serious protest by the North only once, in the case of the reception of Missouri. Sad to say, the North eventually gave in. [Münch's note.]

*The writer overstates the Republican position. Neither the 1856 nor 1860 platform attacked slavery where it already existed, although most Southerners regarded restrictions on the spread of slavery as tantamount to abolition. "Personal liberty" laws in Ohio, Vermont, and other Northern states, in defiance of the federal Fugitive Slave Law, forbade state and local officers to assist in capturing runaways. In some states Southern slave-catchers could be arrested for kidnapping—if they were not mobbed first. Despite the furor about fugitives, they were only a small fraction of the slave population. JNP.

done no more than what was to its immediate advantage, as all men do too often.*

Southerners can tell the party of the North with full conviction from their own point of view: we have an institution that was in part imposed on us by the North, on which our continued existence depends as a result of long accommodation, of which there is as yet no adequate means of freeing ourselves. This institution we are now supposed to regard with shame, and every day the power grows of a party that desires to make us impotent for ever; that is more than we can bear. The North says, You *must* bear it, and we can do nothing but punish you, the present generation, for the sins of earlier generations both North and South; before we were blinded and weak, but now we comprehend that only our Northern institutions are correct, and in the future you will have to respect them.

Here it is, one point of view against another. There is no chance for reconciliation, and the very party that is the most prudent (free from passion and exaggeration), persistent, and courageous will win the victory; but no one should multiply the evils of this irrepressible conflict beyond necessity, or ignore the terrible position of the defeated party with proud arrogance. "We will subdue you," Douglas said not long ago; it was a needless threat, and in the meantime he has fallen to the ground; no one can tolerate being subjected to the will of another.

If one simply recalls the horrors that go along with the damned institution, it takes no great rhetorical gift to paint it as black as one pleases; but even more infamous than the treatment of a recalcitrant slave is the fact that Northerners outfit God knows how many slave ships every year; by no means are all the moral offenses suffered by the Union committed by the South.

Since I favor a just and humane perception of things, I freely admit that those who count the most in your party are those who flail pitilessly away with the greatest true or simulated passion. For that very reason this has been the most irreconcilable dispute

*All of Helper's books in the world will not convince the South that slavery is not profitable so long as new territories are being created for it to order. I know that someone leased a Negro last year in Texas for $300, paid the Negro $100 for overtime work, and still made $300 on the deal. Let the American slaveowner conquer southeast Mexico, Central America, and Cuba and you will soon see the trade of the whole world dependent on him. —The North believes that *free* labor suffers accordingly when slave labor prospers, but the South does not accept that as truth. [Münch's note. Hinton Rowan Helper was a Southerner noted for his severe critique of the effects of slavery on free labor. He was a severe Negrophobe as well. His book *The Impending Crisis* raised a violent public debate in the late 1850s. See *Dictionary of American Biography*, 8:517–18. SR.]

in the world, and in the end raw force will decide because neither party will listen to reason. The harshness of our condemnation is least toward those who assign the thought, the will, and the deeds of men to their economic organization (for which individuals cannot be made to account), and it is no grounds for marveling when we find that people organize themselves differently in Georgia than in Massachusetts. Who has any idea what effect this has within the brains of our four hundred thousand slaveowners?

I am personally opposed to harshness and exaggeration on principle, from long experience, and from observation of human beings, I never approve of harshness and exaggeration (I always hold them to be *mal à propos*). Since I do not wish to be a party leader, and since I am not striving for public office, I have no need to struggle against competitors or to cut opponents down to size, nor do I have to sound alarms, so what in the world would have to happen before I would give up my habit of evaluating things quietly and cause me to shoot off in a so-called extreme direction? —I hope I can convert all of my compatriots both in and out of St. Louis to a somewhat cooler appreciation of things; we have already had enough fireworks.

I want to add this to what I have already said: the census of 1860 will probably show that we have six million Africans in the Union.* The whole people, North and South, is opposed to their *intermingling*, with few exceptions; *colonizing them externally* appears to me to be totally impractical. If the North is determined—as it should be—to wash the shame of slavery away from the Union, what will be the definitive solution for the slave question? I think it is this, and the next fifty years will prove it one way or the other: the South will separate itself; some of the agrarian slave states will stay with the North at the start, and others will return and transfer their black population southward. Then the plantation states will fall into the hands of the Africans, since whites will withdraw more and more from the South, and people will leave them to their fate, perhaps by raising a barrier against them.

One must not mistake the true spirit of the South—it will not submit! The sole really conservative party faction in the South that will hold to the Union is the little remnant of the former Whigs (now so-called Americans). The nonslaveholding whites in the South almost all belong to the Democratic party and blindly follow their fire-eating leaders. One must remember that it was precisely this class that voted down Henry Clay's emancipation plan in Kentucky years ago, while the majority of the slaveowners supported it.

*The census of 1860 showed just over four million persons of African descent in the United States. JNP.

These people keep themselves going with the hope that they shall someday be slaveowners, and the more ignorant and uneducated they are the more they value the fact that there is a class below them into which they cannot sink. Education makes people humane, but coarseness is always inclined to repression. Most of the recent Missouri border raiders were as a rule nonslaveowners.

The current game in the House of Representatives is a prologue to the dissolution of the Union. An irreconcilable conflict has commenced between the North and the South, not just in interests but also in emotions, sensibilities, and ways of life, and in this conflict the South has by far the poorer position. For the South the alternatives are division or submission. The former has great perils, but it is more in tune with the sense of the South than the latter; there are a few conservative voices in Kentucky and Tennessee who will counsel submission. Even Missouri seems to be represented at this moment only by men of the most extreme tendency; they would love to lead our state into the Southern league of states if they could possibly do it. —No person foresaw more clearly than Calhoun that all of this had to come to pass; now the whole South seems to see him as its Messiah.

Far West [Friedrich Münch]

II.

Republican Crusade

March–November 1860

> "What good fortune it was that no Americans were there
> to watch this scandal—I would have died of shame."
>
> Karl Ludwig Bernays, *Anzeiger des Westens*, 17 May 1860

Anzeiger des Westens, 22 March 1860

Our First Choice!
As Presidential Candidate of the
Republican Party
J. C. Frémont
Subject to the decision of the
Republican
National Convention

*   *   *

On the Presidency

The Democrats can go right ahead and nominate Douglas or Breckinridge or Alexander H. Stephens of Georgia—it is certain that the debate in the Republican convention will rotate around three names, and these are Seward, Frémont, and Bates. If Seward is out, which would seem to be the case due to his latest speech, then only Frémont and Bates remain on the list, and it would take a miracle for *Frémont* not to be the man on whom the hearts of the delegates can unite. There are no questions about whether *Frémont* is a good Republican, whether he wants a homestead bill, whether he wants complete equality of rights for all citizens without reference to nationality or belief, or whether he is for a central railway to the Pacific. We *know* everything about Frémont, and there is no doubt about either his past or his future, and the only thing that can be said against him is that he ran honorably for president once, and there are men who are stupid enough not to vote for him *now* because they voted *against* him then.

It is an entirely different matter with Mr. Bates, and even if there are well-intentioned men who believe that Mr. Bates believes in all the Republican articles of faith, there are still enough well-founded doubts about him, and until he settles these he will have to rely on the support of *personal friends* and *politicians* who are concerned about the outcome of the election, not about the voice of the people.

So we expect answers to the questions we have posed to Mr. Bates within the next week. These answers will deal with the questions so often asked, namely whether the nomination of Bates by the Republican convention would be an abandonment of principles, or whether the whole debate is a matter of personalities to be settled by personal preferences or hositilities.

For us it is all the more clear that nothing, including declarations by Mr. Bates, can drive the name of John C. Frémont from the hearts of the German population. But we also know that if these declarations are satisfactory, then the Germans will not stand in the way of the victory of the Republican party, even if the Chicago convention chooses a Republican of *today* rather than a Republican of *yesterday* on the grounds that he can be elected.

Mississippi Blätter, 29 April 1860

☞ Mr. Theodor Olshausen of the *Davenport Demokrat*, whose recent presence in our city was briefly reported, has recorded his impressions in the following article.* It is certainly not without interest to learn the views of such an experienced and penetrating observer.

*   *   *

St. Louis

Anyone who visits St. Louis again after an absence of as little as two years is astounded at the expansion, beautification, and improvement that has continued to take place here. For years people have been saying that St. Louis had hit its peak, and that if it did not actually decline it would at least stand still. Here in the Northwest the view is often expressed that the turning point has already

---

*Theodor Olshausen, a leading participant in the 1848 revolution in Schleswig-Holstein, had been editor of the *Davenport Demokrat* but would soon purchase the *Westliche Post*, which he would edit until 1864. SR.

come, reflected in a decline in business. I was unable to detect any evidence of this during my recent visit. Certainly some merchants were heard to complain about a lack of business and the low payment of debts, but the precise opposite is also often heard, and I would like to believe that things here are as they are everywhere, with some branches of trade and traffic suffering while others boom.

If one looks at the many new buildings, including some truly splendid ones of the first rank, he will be reinforced in the opinion that St. Louis is growing rapidly, that it is in truth the capital of the West, that it has surpassed New Orleans, and that Chicago will have a hard time catching it. This is the result of the vast capital centered only in St. Louis due to its propitious central location for trade and industry. St. Louis dominates the river trade of the Missouri, which promises an as yet unlimited expansion and increase; gradually its trade southward grows, and it is the linch-pin of the vast traffic between the Ohio, Missouri, and the upper and lower Mississippi systems. To be sure St. Louis has lost some of its trade on the upper Mississippi, but this is but a small part of its total trade and has been more than compensated by new acquisitions elsewhere. In the case of trade with Iowa in particular, people often hear merchants saying they would be glad not to have anything to do with this state in the future, since it is in such financial straits; but at the same time there are other highly influential businessmen who think otherwise. They argue and trade in these terms: Iowa has survived its toughest times, and soon the wealth of its resources will make it well again. Insolvent businesses have gone under in the last few years; those which survive are more dependable and creditworthy than was the case before the crisis. Since many wholesalers still withhold their business from Iowa as a result of erroneous prudence, now is the perfect time to invest on very advantageous terms that have prospects of great profits in good time if not right away. If we do nothing in St. Louis now to keep Iowa with us, we will probably be conceding the region utterly and forever to Chicago as far as commerce goes. —It seems to me that this reasoning is well founded and deserves to be heeded by several St. Louis houses.

The population of St. Louis is estimated at a minimum of 180,000; if the immediate vicinity is counted in this, including the city of Carondelet on the southern border and the factory settlement of Lowell on the north, then the number of people living there mounts to 200,000. The city of Carondelet has doubled in the last two years, enlivened by several industrial undertakings.

St. Louis has the character of a city of a free state, a virtual enclave in this region of slavery. This circumstance places it in political isolation, at least for the moment, and cripples its influence. If St. Louis were the capital city of a free state, there is no doubt that the intelligence, wealth, prosperity, and composition of the population, which is half German, would not only exercise dominant political influence in the state but set the course of public life for the whole West. But in the slave state of Missouri, St. Louis is in a decided minority and will be so for the foreseeable future. Outside its immediate vicinity the free-spirited population of St. Louis runs up against elements too heterogeneous to be absorbed quickly. This explains the difficulty of its position, but also the great service the Free-Soil party is performing in making a reasonable compromise between opposing principles of free labor and slavery in one of the largest states of the Union. As dim as hopes for a peaceful solution appear to be in the Union as a whole, it is more likely in Missouri than in any other border slave state. The number of slaves is relatively small,* and the existence of free states on three sides makes it more difficult every single day to protect slave property and hold it in awe. It is not out of the question that there could be an inner reform that could abolish the Southern institution here, an emancipation based on general support, however wildly the Missouri slaveowner aristocracy has raged in recent times.

I would have laid my worries about the candidacy of Bates to rest after coming to St. Louis if I had not already done so before. No man who has so little support in his own state could hope to be nominated in Chicago. The German population is particularly concerned because it knows nothing about him. Even though the *Anzeiger des Westens* babbles on about the love and respect the Germans of Missouri have for Bates, this is just a silly self-deception under the best of circumstances. The truth is that there are not a dozen Germans in St. Louis who know Mr. Bates personally, and what they have heard about him is calculated to turn them away from him. His earlier nativist statements and deeds are generally known, and there is no proof that he has ever changed his mind— not even a sign. The weak position he has taken on slavery disgusts committed Republicans. To nominate such a man for the presidency, one who has stood outside of any party until now, despite the fact he is nearing his seventies, is certainly the oddest thing any party leader could dare to offer his party.

*Though Missouri had the largest free population of any of the fifteen slave states in 1860, it had only 115,000 slaves, compared to Kentucky's 225,000, Louisiana's 332,000, and Virginia, Georgia, and Mississippi's 400,000 plus. JNP.

Anzeiger des Westens, 10 May 1860 (for 9 May 1860)

The Blairs

Since we had the occasion recently to speak of the two "grand and glorious houses" of the Washburnes and the Lovejoys, it did not appear to be out of order to discuss a family of half-Southerners that has done no small service for freedom in an even less favorable setting.

The whole world knows who Frank P. Blair, Sr., is, and since we are not writing for children, we will avoid touching on his life history beyond its largest contours. He was known during Jackson's administration in his role as editor of the *Globe* as the third power in the government behind the president and the two houses of Congress—a third power which, like a third estate, gained the hearing of those in power because it virtually made public opinion. Beyond that he was the trusted adviser and virtual oracle to "Old Hickory," as Alexander Hamilton was to Washington, so that once the victor of New Orleans said that all the justices of the Supreme Court did not have as much authority with him as Frank P. Blair alone. He was also the first Republican from a slave state, and he was the first, most enthusiastic, and most influential friend and supporter of John C. Frémont, both before and during the electoral campaign of 1856. In those days the whole Republican world—even the German Radicals—sang his praises. But now—still, the man also has two sons.

Montgomery Blair and Frank P. Blair, Jr., are two apples that have not fallen very far from the tree. Both are virtually Republicans born and bred, and both have dedicated themselves to this calling with a love and a self-sacrifice as have few others. We shall not speak of brother Montgomery Blair, who has spent less time on the stage of national politics than in his professional career and is further away from us—but who does not know the accomplishments of our own St. Louis Blair? Who does not know that he rose from being the friend and successor of the "Great Missourian" Thomas Hart Benton to a position far above that of the grand old man by leading the first open Free-Soil party in a slave state (the small if high-principled beginnings under Cassius M. Clay hardly deserve to be called a party), and he has led the party to victory several times in this district. Who does not recall how his imagination and his maiden speech in Congress led at once to his being mentioned as a vice-president of the United States? Then there was only jubilation—but now——

Now all three distinguished Blairs have declared for the candidacy of Edward Bates for president, and that is enough for all of the German *Criminal [Zeitung]* Radicals to shout "Stone them!" in unison. Blair Sr., who stood closer to the latter-day Jackson, Frémont, than anyone else and who would have been his leading adviser had he won in 1856—and Frank P. Blair, Jr., who would have the first option on the vice-presidency if Bates were out of the way—both have been proclaimed traitors simply because they have declared for Bates.

Anzeiger des Westens, 17 May 1860 (for Wednesday, 16 May)

The Republican National Convention

(Editorial Correspondence of the *Anzeiger des Westens*)*

Chicago, 15 May

Mr. Carl Schurz* has given a formal promise to the St. Louisans to visit St. Louis and speak there in the course of the coming campaign. He is one of the most important figures here, along with the elder Blair, Tom Corwin, and Horace Greeley. The respect he excites among the Americans even exceeds the love and honor he receives from his own countrymen. No wonder! Americans are only Know-nothings about strangers, people who keep to themselves; Germans act the same way toward their own countrymen when they dare to appear to be an inch above mediocrity. And Carl

*The passage of a bill restricting the right of newly naturalized citizens to hold office in Massachusetts had profoundly disturbed those Germans considering making their political home in the Republican party. Some former revolutionaries, such as Adolph Douai, promoted the idea of a separate German political party, but such leading immigrant political figures as Carl Schurz and Gustav Körner preferred to try to have the Republican National Convention formally renounce nativism in its platform. The result was a caucus of German political representatives held at the German House in Chicago immediately before the Republican Convention. The following accounts, written largely by Heinrich Börnstein's editor Karl Ludwig Bernays, illustrate the tensions between the Germans from the Northeast, where the Republican party had a strongly nativist component, and those from the Midwest. SR.

*Carl Schurz, 1829–1906, a media hero during and after the 1848 revolutions, settled in Watertown, Wisconsin, and set about becoming the Americans' favorite German. He would come to St. Louis as editor of the *Westliche Post* after the Civil War and serve as United States senator from Missouri before becoming Interior secretary under Rutherford B. Hayes. He worked very hard at being the conscience of the Republican party in the later years of the century. See *Dictionary of American Biography*, 16:466–70. SR.

Schurz stands feet above the best. Even if Schurz has been unable to save Seward,* he has still completely destroyed the other side, and there is no more talk of Bates, Banks, McLean, or Cameron. Still, he is not a Seward man to the last gasp; he knows the man's weaknesses thoroughly, and he is inclined to seek a compromise candidate *between* the two extremes, so that he is ready to settle on Lincoln, Frémont, Wade, or even Read of Pennsylvania. That is how it will turn out.

Later: Mr. M. Pinner was moved to tender his resignation after a stormy meeting of delegates from Missouri. It was, of course, accepted, and Dr. Bruns,* our brave compatriot, was elected in his place. Mr. Barton Able* was also elected to fill another vacancy. He resigned as well, and his place was taken by Dr. A. Hammer.*

I shall restrain myself from describing Pinner's conduct at this meeting, or the accusations made against him. It is better to be silent where speaking would compel one to say distasteful things.

F. P. Blair assembled a large rally for Bates in the courthouse this morning. After Mr. Krekel* expressed himself for Bates in the

*William H. Seward of New York had endeared himself to radicals and alarmed moderate Republicans by his "irrepressible conflict" speech in 1858, predicting that the nation would emerge from the sectional struggle wholly free or wholly slave. Ex-Democrats in the party, however, disliked him for his past assaults on Jacksonian economic policy. As the Republicans sought to broaden the Western political base, they shunned extremes, both in their platform and in their nominee. Edward Bates of Missouri, Nathaniel Banks (Speaker of the House) from Massachusetts, Supreme Court Justice John McLean of Ohio, and Simon Cameron of Pennsylvania were much less aggressive about slavery than Seward. Frémont and Benjamin Wade of Ohio, presented by the writer as moderates, proved to be far more radical than Seward during the Civil War. JNP.

*Dr. Johann Bernard Bruns was the founder of the community of Westphalia, Missouri, before moving to Jefferson City. During the Civil War he served in the Medical Corps, and he died while serving both as a major in service in a hospital in Jefferson City and as mayor. See State Historical Society of Missouri, Vertical File for Westphalia. SR.

*A native of Illinois, Able was an active Free-Soiler and a close associate of Frank Blair, with mercantile and steamboat interests. JNP.

*Dr. Adam Hammer, who died in 1878, had fought in the Swiss Sonderbund wars, then in the Baden revolution as a follower of Friedrich Hecker, where he won respect as a military surgeon. In St. Louis, he established the Humboldt Institut, a German medical college, and organized his faculty and students to fight in 1861. He was lieutenant colonel of the Fourth Missouri Volunteers in April 1861, and he headed military hospitals during the war. After the war he was a professor at the Missouri Medical College in St. Louis. See Wilhelm Kaufmann, *Die Deutschen im amerikanischen Bürgerkrieg (Sezessionskrieg 1861–1865)* (Munich, Berlin: Oldenbourg, 1911), 506–7. SR.

*Arnold Krekel, an 1830s immigrant who published the *St. Charles Demokrat* from 1852 to 1855, was a slaveowner and leading Republican in St. Charles and led a much-feared Home Guard regiment called "Krekel's Dutch." He was president of the 1864 state convention, and he was finally appointed as United States circuit judge of western Missouri. SR.

warmest terms, Mr. G. Körner* took the floor and expressed the
highest regards for the character and principles of Mr. Bates but
said he doubted Bates could be elected because of the prejudices the
Germans held against him, which could not be cleared away in time.
On the other hand, when he mentioned the name of *Lincoln,* loud
applause broke from the crowd.

Chicago, 15 May, 6 p.m.

Latest News: This evening the German convention broke into
complete uproar. I have never even been to a peasant fair where
such things went on as among these troublemakers in the German
caucus. All hell broke loose when the eight from the East demanded
that voting be by states rather than by delegates. When this did not
pass, they tried to have everyone voting identify himself by name
and state—obviously so the *New York Demokrat,** which stands
behind these fellows, can attack the voters at W. Kopp's good pleasure. When the discussion moved on to the instructions for the
delegates, the delegates fell into a fight *over the very first line,*
where it says that it had been decided by an assembly of *delegates*
and citizens of various states. They fought over these lines for two
hours, and everything else stopped. President Kopp, on whose
shoulders the Lord God put a bushel of stupidity for a head, declared that the defeat of the word *delegates* was an insult to the
Eastern Germans and threatened to resign his presidency. The
confusion that reigned was beyond description—the sixty-two persons assembled were transformed into a single raging mob, and I
am sure it was on its way to clawing itself to death when I managed
to escape the hall with a few friends. What good fortune it was that
no Americans were there to watch this scandal—I would have died
of shame. Douai* alone remained in the battle—he got into a spat

*Gustav Körner (1809–1896), a lawyer by training, fled Germany after participating
in the Frankfurt putsch of 1833, settled in Belleville, Illinois, and was briefly an
associate justice of the state supreme court. Körner was lieutenant governor, 1852–
1856, and he served as an aide to Governor Yates and General Frémont in the early
part of the war. He was minister to Spain, 1862–1864, and wrote an important
account of the early phase of German immigration to America. His memoirs are a
major source of the history of Midwest Germans in the secession crisis. See *Dictionary of American Biography,* 5:496–97. SR.

*The *New York Demokrat,* also known as the *New Yorker Zeitung,* was published
from 1845 to 1876. Its editor at this time was Wilhelm Kopp. See Karl J. R. Arndt and
May E. Olson, *German-American Newspapers and Periodicals, 1732–1955, History
and Bibliography,* vol. 1 (Heidelberg: Quelle & Meyer, 1961), 345, 410. SR.

*Adolph Douai, radical communist agitator, publisher, and pedagogue, is notable as
one of the few German radicals to take the question of black rights seriously. In
1859–1860 he advocated the formation of a separate German party. His proletarian
novel *Fata Morgana* won a prize as the best German-American novel presented in a

which was less his concern than mine. Pinner, who had been driven out of the Missouri delegation that morning, was the worst trouble-maker of the afternoon.

I never spoke in the bedlam—Schurz and Körner did not even attend. They were justifiably afraid for their reputations for *common sense*.

Special Dispatch to the Anzeiger

Chicago, 15 May, Evening

Carl Schurz, C. L. Bernays,* Judge Körner, and Mr. Hatter-scheidt of Kansas have been named to the platform committee.

Indiana is for Lincoln. The highest possible vote for Seward is ninety-five. The resolution concerning naturalization in the draft of the platform was moved by Carl Schurz, and as powerfully and decisively as anyone could wish! The German ratpack-caucus has become a thorough nuisance.

*   *   *

From the Theater of War

the dispatches are already streaming and pounding like hail, like schools of fish, like flocks of pigeons.

One proof that it is war being waged in Chicago is the following list of dead and wounded.

The first death, or collapse, was that of the lamented "German Preconvention." The death was brief but painful, poor beast! After it had raised its great heathen shout in splendid, truly radical style, the only sound that echoed from the mass of Germans in reply was a laugh of disdain. It still tried to turn its words into deeds against all expectations of more rational men, even against the chance to make a little "show." Eight persons bearing the sacred character of delegates from associations, five from the distant East and three from Louisville, Kentucky, appeared at the site of the Republican Convention to challenge the rights of many times their number in regularly elected German delegates to speak for the Germans. On

---

competition sponsored by the *Anzeiger des Westens* (see Introduction, part 2 above). See also Wittke, *Refugees of Revolution*, 306–8. SR.

*Karl Ludwig Bernays, Heinrich Börnstein's colleague on the *Vorwärts* in Paris, came to the United States in 1848. He returned to Germany for health reasons in 1861 but returned in 1862 with Börnstein to try to save the congressional seat of Francis P. Blair, Jr. He received the rank of colonel during the war, and he served as United States consul in Zürich. See Kaufmann, *Deutschen im Bürgerkrieg*, 483, Wittke, *Refugees of Revolution*, 272. SR.

one side were Messrs. Douai, Kopp, and Stengel,* the *Pionier** and *Demokrat* clique, on the other Messrs. Körner, Schurz, Hassaurek,* Münch, Schneider,* Bernays, Kreismann, Dr. Hammer, Vogel—it was really hard to choose! And they intended to sit in judgment over these men? They wanted to dictate terms to the great convention about what it was to do with the Massachusetts delegation, whose leader they refused to recognize even if it meant breaking up the party! —But the attempt to operate as an "isolated cell" was a stillborn child, and the effort to operate as a special convention was the end of the song. They could not even get organized. Despite the fact that it is often the case in clubs in Germany and German America that there are more officers than ordinary members, they could not even elect a chairman. They marched up the hill only to march down the other side with equal pomp. It was to be expected, and it was predicted by everyone. But instead of proceeding quietly and carefully so that Germans as a whole would not be held up to ridicule, they ran off to the English press and declared that every state would send a delegation to this German convention, and then they stormed the Chicago convention, where they were sent home with catcalls. *May the earth rest lightly on it.*

The second death we have to report is much more troubling and important. This is the declaration that the California delegation is supposed to have in its pocket according to which *Frémont* has ceased once and for all to be a candidate at this convention, which he never really was. We hope that he shall surrender to the call of his country. And we are still convinced he would do this if he did not think his place could be adequately filled. So there is hardly a hope left, though we will continue to hold his name up at the head of our ranks as the first and only chosen one until a final and irreversible decision, and we shall parade until then for Frémont alone.

*Wilhelm Stengel was a Forty-eighter and a journalist in Cincinnati before serving as a freethinker chaplain and as an officer with an Ohio Volunteer regiment. After the war he worked with Emil Preetorius on the *Westliche Post*. See Wittke, *Refugees of Revolution*, 230, and *The German-Language Press in America* (Lexington, Ky.: University of Kentucky Press, 1957), 96. SR.

*Pionier was a radical journal edited in Boston by Karl Heinzen, an independent communist publicist. See Wittke, *Against the Current: The Life of Karl Heinzen (1809–1880)* (Chicago: University of Chicago Press, 1945). SR.

*Friedrich Hassaurek, a participant in the Vienna revolution in 1848, was a virulently anti-Catholic editor in Cincinnati in the 1850s but turned to the law after 1857 and reemerged as a conservative Republican at the end of the war. See Wittke, *German-Language Press*, 109. SR.

*Georg Schneider edited the *Illinois Staatszeitung* of Chicago. See Wittke, *German-Language Press*, 91–93. SR.

There have also been many wounded. The most seriously hit seems to be William H. Seward of New York, although he is still called the frontrunner. Wade is already mentioned as his substitute, and we have less against him than against anyone else who was not our first choice.

But let us not linger over such subtleties, since our correspondents on the scene will do that better.

Anzeiger des Westens, 24 May 1860
(for Thursday, 17 May 1860)

Special Dispatches to the Anzeiger

Chicago, 17 May 1860
12 Noon

The German members of the platform committee celebrated a proud triumph today. The committee accepted the following resolution by a majority of all against one.

Resolved, that the national Republican party is opposed to any alteration of the existing naturalization laws as well as any act of state legislation that would alter or limit the civil rights of immigrants from foreign lands, insofar as it supports a full and effective protection of the rights of citizens of all classes, whether native-born or naturalized, both here and abroad.

With this act, the Republican party has thoroughly purged itself of all accusations of nativism.

C. L. B. [Karl Ludwig Bernays]

(Second Special Dispatch)

Chicago, 17 May 1860, Evening.

An amendment against the draft of the paragraph in favor of maintaining the present naturalization law was withdrawn after two speeches by Schurz and Hassaurek. Each speaker was met with warm applause. The stocks of Seward and Lincoln are high.

C. L. B. [Karl Ludwig Bernays]

Anzeiger des Westens, 24 May 1860
(for Wednesday, 23 May 1860)

The Nominations in Chicago

Chicago, 19 May 1860

I still have enough time before my departure to say something about the most recent events here. The disappointment of Seward's friends was very great. Never did anyone come to the place of decision so certain of victory as they did, and this contributed to their defeat, since it hindered them from seeing what was taking place right before their eyes. The great majority of the Republican party decided to set aside the *claims* of a single man in view of the consideration that the party was not interested in another great demonstration (as in 1856), but in victory. There shall be other occasions to discuss what stood in the way of Seward's nomination, but it can only be explained by the accidental course of events. One has to confess that Seward was defeated by a combination of elements formed into a movement that was in itself absurd. One of these elements was the Bates movement in Missouri—an important part of the opposition, though, taken on its own terms—it never had a real chance. I myself had to concede its importance for the state of Missouri as well as its importance as a means of counterpressure, and I supported it all the more intensely because the respectable old man had nothing against the use of his name. Fine, then: the more *earnestly* and honestly we worked to bring about the victory of the good cause, the more satisfied the German delegates of Missouri have returned from the convention, since we have accomplished *everything we* wanted. I saw hundreds of long faces— but on our faces, young and old, there was only satisfaction, hope, even certainty of victory, and, though our position in our own state is always difficult, we go to the hard labor before us with elevated and freshened courage.

It must be said that the Eastern politicians, after their hopes were so intensely disappointed, went on to promise cooperation, and they outbid everyone else in their enthusiasm. I hope that our German compatriots in the East will be no less patriotic and tactful. In this convention the Germans have won a position, have achieved a weight, have attracted attention to their views, which no foreign element has ever won in any country in the world. A single step further (which has to be understood by everyone, since the Westerners have long since learned it) could have ruined *everything*, and whoever demands more under the present circumstances belongs to those who achieve *nothing* because they do not recognize the limit beyond which excess begins.

Through the energetic and measured activity of the Germans at the convention (despite the fact that the East was not represented at all, which was wrong), the German element was recognized for all time as a vital part of the party of freedom and progress here. Who can deny that the West has finally had its claims recognized by the nomination of Lincoln? Except for the administration of Polk and the few months when Harrison and Taylor sat in the presidential chair, this republic has been ruled since Jackson's time by men who had their residence east of the Alleghenies. And yet the center of gravity of the Union has already moved to the Mississippi valley, and steadily the further West has begun to assert its power. It is beyond a doubt that the sympathy of the masses (which alone decides elections here) is with the man who once "walked barefoot driving his ox across the prairies of the West," who then raised himself to the same level as the greatest in his country through the power of his talents and a rare level of intellectual exertion—with this man on whom no corrupt clients depend, who is as honorable as he is simple, as open as he is unshakably solid, who stands before the people impervious to intrigue, who may not *bring along* the most elevated statesmanlike capacities one usually obtains in aristocratic circles (which derive from a long and thorough education, hence depending on riches and social position) rather than in the Western primeval forests. Yet I believe more and more in the continued good health and freshness of our life as a republic when the people do not hesitate to raise the best from its own midst, precisely when the needs of the hour demand it rather than letting politicians decree a leader for them—no matter how good he may be. I have said too much about him already, since he has already been described in such promising terms that his nomination now seems to the whole world to be self-explanatory. Lincoln is truly a man of the people, just as Jackson was for his supporters, though Jackson's last great service in the eyes of the people had been the victory at New Orleans. Lincoln is seen by the people as the man who will see his way through a great struggle yet to come, the struggle with the most dangerous and ruthless enemy of freedom, with those self-seeking tricksters, those high and mighty sneerers at all the truth and justice that ever appeared in this land.

I want to add to this that the German delegates from Missouri demanded that the votes of Missouri be given to Lincoln on the third ballot, but they were unable to prevail before another state corrected its votes; also, in the second ballot for vice-president we gave our votes to Cassius Clay; finally, the committee on resolutions issued a statement in which a clause on the rights of immigrant citizens and the naturalization laws was literally demanded, which now is in fact found in the platform.

I return to my homeland not to rest but to go into battle with an earnestness that has more to do with deeds than with words.

Far West [Friedrich Münch]

Anzeiger des Westens, 24 May 1860

Disappointed

Our readers already know the impression that the nomination of Abraham Lincoln as candidate of the Republican party has made on the editors of the *Anzeiger des Westens*. We have greeted this naming in the most enthusiastic terms, and we have been just as completely pleased with the platform as with the candidate.

Our two German colleagues in this city, on the other hand, have declared themselves bitterly disappointed, and this is no surprise, since both of them worked so anxiously for Seward's nomination. It is astounding, though, that on this great occasion they were more interested in the *Anzeiger des Westens* than in the *candidate for the presidency*. The *Chronik** says the following:

The Chicago Convention
We were deceived. We actually believed that the Republican party had enough character to name a candidate who represented principles.

We were deceived. We honestly believed that Frank P. Blair was a smart fellow and that the *Anzeiger des Westens* was cunning.

We were deceived. The Republican party *has no* principles; Blair is not a smart fellow, and the *Anzeiger des Westens* is anything but cunning. We will take this occasion to express an opinion, out of courtesy to our colleagues.

Abraham Lincoln
Hannibal Hamlin
This is the name of the two candidates! God protect us from such names! Abraham and Hannibal! What would you put past such names?

But the nomination is worthy of the party. Abe Lincoln, as he is called, or *honest old Abe* (as a joke) is an honorable fellow, as they say; he was once a member of the Illinois legislature, and as chairman of the finance committee he made a little arrangement for $100,000, so that the credit

*The *St. Louis Tages-Chronik* was a Roman Catholic newspaper published from 1849 to 1861, as a daily during 1860–1861. Its publisher was Franz Saler, and the editor was Adalbert Löhr. See Arndt and Olson, *German-American Newspapers*, 271. SR.

of the Missouri Bank rose, to be sure, but Illinois lost something more than $100,000. But as Mark Antony said in his own day:

We are all honorable men. (Shakespeare)

Lincoln is a splendid candidate, and we could hardly portray our amazement when we saw that after the news of his nomination arrived, the *Westliche Post* (generally said to be a Lincoln organ) let fly with only two rockets and dime firecrackers. We thought they would spend at least a dollar *anyhow*.

The *Westliche Post* spoke in this manner out of the midst of its affliction:

The Impression of the Nomination

of Mr. Lincoln was, as far as we could tell, received by the German Republicans more with surprise than joy. Everywhere they say, "Seward would have been better." Except for a few rockets fired off in front of our offices, there were no particular demonstrations. The *Anzeiger* required an entire day to recover from its astonishment and remove the double constellation of Frémont and Bates from its flagstaffs,

Etc., etc., in anti-*Anzeiger* ravings.

At another point in the same issue, in the editorial letter from Chicago:

Well, now we have as the standard-bearer of the Republican party old, honest, straightforward Abraham Lincoln, the same Lincoln against whom the "Missouri Democrat" clique conspired in 1858, and against whom the *Anzeiger* openly fought, using even forged letters, etc.

I hope and desire that Lincoln gets elected. *But the impression of visitors here—except for those from Illinois and Indiana—is not favorable.* People cannot forget that the most important man in the party, the most talented and loyal representative of Republican principles, the warm lasting friend of immigration, has been sacrificed for the sake of expediency.

Note: Even in Chicago Mr. Dänzer did nothing but drag St. Louis *Anzeiger* and anti-*Anzeiger* linen through the muck. One would have to be a Hogarth or a Lichtenberg to draw a true picture of the shameful goings-on in the dispute between the Teutonic East and West in Chicago—but enough of this; the Germans earned no honor from it.

Anzeiger des Westens, 28 June 1860 (for 22 June 1860)

The "Criminalzeitung" and the Chicago Convention

Missouri, 14 June 1860

As long as the Union lasts, there will be no occasion when the German element will have had more impact here than it had at the convention in Chicago. No one can doubt that we have used the *right method* for exercising as much political influence as we could when our number and power are taken into account. This convention taught us an important lesson, so it is all the more important not to put what happened in a false light or to interpret it confusedly. Instead it is important for an historically correct picture to be multiplied and preserved for all time. I take it to be my duty as an eyewitness and participant to help in the process of telling the truth.

The *Criminalzeitung** says that the Republican party in Chicago "accepted all the proper demands of the German citizens," and I agree wholeheartedly with this. This paper disputes the silly assertion of the *Tägliche Beobachter* of Albany that nothing for the protection of immigrants would have been done without the Eastern delegates, and that it was these delegates who forced Mr. Schurz to take such surprisingly energetic action. They say further that the Germans showed "more good luck than understanding" in this affair, and that they finally attribute the fortunate success to the "glorious inconsistency" of Mr. Schurz.

What is an educated German either here or abroad to make of the course of events when this is the most substantial information he can get? What follow are the simple facts.

During the first days of the convention week there was a great deal of talk among the Americans about the German caucus, and the idea that a German rump was trying to control the whole Republican convention and dictate terms excited the highest degree of hostility. If this feeling had persisted it would have been impossible for the German delegate to have any influence at all. When I came to Tremont House many Americans asked me about this. I told them that we Germans have no special political interests, and I didn't know anything about a *German party*, since the Germans who had gathered here came as *Republicans;* our ethnic group was not strongly represented in the convention, and it was only proper for Germans to gather here, especially from the East, where they were not represented, to speak with one another and with the German delegates who were here. There was one question that concerned us as *naturalized* citizens more than you, and you must concede that it is natural for us to be concerned about it and

*The *New Yorker Criminal-Zeitung und Bellettristisches Journal* was a cultural weekly that began as a German version of the *Police Gazette* but soon became a leading literary and political journal, published 1852–1911. See Arndt and Olson, *German-American Newspapers*, 345–46. SR.

discuss what would happen in regard to that question, etc. —Other German delegates spoke in the same manner, and it dispelled the hostile attitude toward us, and in fact we were treated very well on every occasion. It then behooved us to make the German caucus precisely what we promised the Americans it would be, a friendly discussion among Germans from various parts of the Union. Even if this discussion was not always friendly, nor always even civil, then at least no one will ever hear me condemn it. My own great goal was to make it *harmless*—either to the great cause or the German name—since I never expected anything effective to come of it, and I think this was accomplished, even though we should have done without many of the expressions of hostility.

The most important thing that took place for Germans in Chicago and the source of all the successes was *the assembly of all German delegates* in the May Hotel on the morning of the first day of the convention. A more unanimous gathering of Germans never has taken place before and probably never shall again. It was everyone's opinion that we should apply all of our influence to achieve as liberal a statement on immigrants in the platform as possible. A proposal was drafted, discussed and adopted; it had—in a few more words—everything that is now found in the platform on immigrants. Then the question was *how* it could be accomplished. If possible our demand must be gotten through the resolutions committee first, and to accomplish this as many Germans as possible had to be elected to that committee. In response to the question how to get people on that committee, Messrs. Bernays, Körner, Schurz, and Hatterscheidt (of Kansas) answered that they believed they could get on, and they all managed to do so. At the same time the question was raised about what to make of the German caucus, and the opinion was expressed and defended that it should be left to itself. I proposed (and it was adopted) that those chosen for the committee should not attend the caucus, and that the others might do so in the sense already determined. At this point I want to remark incidentally that I attribute the fact that the whole thing went its way tolerably and did not degenerate into a riot to Mr. Butz of Chicago,* who made an agreement with Mr. Douai. It is inconceivable that there has ever been anything more pointless than what took place there.

---

*Caspar Butz, 1825–1885, was a Forty-eighter and a poet who wrote elegies for John Brown and Abraham Lincoln. His *Deutsch-Amerikanische Monatshefte für Politik, Wissenschaft und Literatur*, published in Chicago, was a leading opinion maker during the war years. See Wittke, *German-Language Press*, 189. SR.

If it had been necessary to treat the matter of the rights of immigrants *in the convention*, it would have been left to those who had the greatest ability of arguing in English: Schurz, Körner, and Hassaurek said they would do it. —It was asked how many votes the German Republicans would have if the Americans asked. We did our best to gather the numbers from all the states, and it was about three hundred thousand. When Mr. Schurz speaks of a possibility of three hundred thousand more votes, then this is certainly no exaggeration with six million Germans in this country, and his figures make sense.

As readers can plainly see, everything that took place had to be discussed and considered, means weighed, duties distributed, and for this the committee of four men worked together with united energy and drive for a common goal (Mr. Greeley offered his assistance), and since the proper effort was made in accordance with a solid plan, it was crowned with success. It is thus clearly at variance both with truth and with justice to say that success was a result of "more luck than understanding," and to ascribe it all to the "glorious inconsistency" of one man is wrong. The success was more a result of *consistency*, and even if there was nothing particularly *glorious* when all arises from the nature of the situation, still it is proper to say that everyone who had a part in it was to be commended.

The Germans were the only immigrant group represented at the Chicago convention, and German participation in the party of progress is assured for all time to come if we determine to proceed with tact and moderation. If we had gone a hair's breadth further we would have lost everything; one inch back and the bowline would have snapped. It has been demonstrated beyond a doubt that faithful collaboration with Americans can be successful, but that ethnic separatist organizations will not work. They will not deny us access if we act as American citizens, but they will oppose us if we try to act as if we were something alien. It is more necessary with the passage of time for more of us to participate routinely in English debate, since they will not care what we argue among ourselves in German. It is not necessary for us to lose our German character, but it is extremely important that we keep it pure without making ourselves continuously obvious in an improper manner. Our mission is difficult, but the goal that stands before us is doubly worth the effort.

Far West [Friedrich Münch]

Anzeiger des Westens, 12 July 1860 (for Monday, 9 July 1860)

The First Republican State Ticket in Missouri

Republican voters of Missouri can still recall the joy with which we presented you the ticket of Lincoln and Hamlin. Today we have a much more important event in the political history of this state to announce to you, and this is the first Republican state ticket in Missouri.* In keeping with the most pressing wishes of the German Republicans of this city as well as energetic demands of Republicans from the interior of this state for the unfurling of the party banner over all the counties, the Central Committee has decided to take up the powers delegated to it by the last convention and yesterday proclaimed a *purely Republican state ticket*, which is found at the top of the page today.

It is obvious that there has never been a more propitious occasion for our party to organize across the entire state than right now. Everywhere the fragments of the old parties are feuding, secure in the notion that the votes which go to the Republican ticket will weaken their opponents, so that all the personal danger for Republicans when voting has disappeared. The first step has already been taken, and it is inevitable that the Republican party, strengthened by the defeated Douglasites who have been excommunicated from the Democratic church, will spread across the land like an avalanche.

We wish to encourage our German party members in St. Louis County to stay the course in this struggle, now that the Republican party has made such progress. You are primarily responsible for the introduction of liberal principles into the politics of this state, and you must not abandon the banner of your party until these principles triumph. To the Germans in the interior of the state, we urge you to rally again around the flag for whose unfurling you have so much longed. The time of compromise is past; we no longer ask to be supported by a third party; whoever wishes to be *with* us can fight under our banner; whoever wishes to fight us knows where we stand. Courage and persistence is all we ask of the Ger-

---

*The first Republican state ticket in Missouri was headed by James B. Gardenhire for governor and James Lindsay for lieutenant governor. The Germans on the ticket included Arnold Krekel for attorney general, Dr. [sic] Henry Boernstein for superintendent of public schools, and Frederick Munch [sic] for the board of public works. See a ticket in the membership books of the Freie deutsche Gemeinde, Western Historical Manuscripts, University of Missouri–St. Louis. SR.

mans in the interior of the state, and even though thrice beaten, we will win the fourth time.

The slightest suspicion of inclination to Know-nothingism has been cleared away from the Republican party; all accusations made against those who proposed the presidential candidacy of Edward Bates have been stifled by bold political action—for the same men were guilty of the same act. Today nothing divides the men of the party of the future, and it needs nothing for its final victory beyond valiant persistence along the path already traced.

Look into the future—and if you see Missouri as a free state at the end of all our efforts, a free and happy homeland for *your* countrymen whom the next bloody decade shall expel hither—then, steadfast and loyal Republicans of St. Louis, strike your chests and say, "*We* have done our best to achieve this!" And no one will dispute you this honor.

Anzeiger des Westens, 26 July 1860

People's Justice, or St. Louis by Night!

Clearing of the whole Bordello Quarter!

The long-term nuisance of houses of ill repute on Almond Street from Main to Fifth has had an almost instantaneous end.* Yesterday evening the people of the neighborhood, assisted by many other fed-up and shocked men, took the law into their own hands and wrecked house after house with pitiless energy. There was a roar as if the last judgment were underway, and the novelty and liveliness made an astonishing scene. The people themselves finally did what Police Chief Rawlings has long wanted to do.

A column of more than a thousand men gathered on Main Street and proceeded up to Second toward Almond Street, and they cleared all of the bordellos without mercy. Furniture, beds, sofas, and chairs were all piled into the middle of the street and set afire. When we departed the scene of this people's tribunal due to the lateness of the hour, *six* houses had already been pulled completely down; large numbers of firemen were gathered in front of the demolished houses, under the captaincy of Mr. Sexton, to prevent the flames from spreading to neighboring houses. The mob then

*Almond Street was located between Spruce and Poplar streets running between the levee and Fifth. The bordellos there were frequently the object of popular riots in the 1850s. SR.

moved to Convent Street to minister a dose of fire and water to purge the shame that had run out of control there as well. Good luck to them, since nothing else seems to work!

An especially dramatic and picturesque scene was staged over the destruction of the little tobacco shop on Fourth Street near Almond. The birds had just flown and the nest was still warm when the grim hand of these moral judges descended on this establishment and tore everything to shreds. The head policeman sat by on horseback listening to the cheers of the embittered crowds, the crash of falling walls, the tinkling of shattered windows, and the snapping of flames as if all was as it should be. —At this point the mob held a council of war: "What next?" —At that moment there was only one house left. Those who knew said that *one* house had been spared in Almond Street on purpose. The opinion was that this one house would be spared so long as there was no bloodshed. There was great tension in the air, since no one knew where the mob would turn next. Suddenly there was a smashing of windowpanes, twice, three times, followed by a report! —a shot! a shot! they cried—but the sound was more like the slamming of a door. A few more blows and Judge Lynch had taken control of another house. Thus was Almond Street cleared out. We cannot yet say whether the people's justice will go further, say into Myrtle Street.

*   *   *

Skirmish at Barnum's Hotel. About eleven o'clock the police arrested and led away fifteen fellows who had participated in the demolition of the bordellos. When the column passed Barnum's Hotel a policeman had been struck on the chest by a heavy stone, and they doubt he will recover. His name is Joseph Fries. Those who had been arrested got away in the excitement, so a genuine pistol battle broke out between them and the police; many shots were fired, there were several wounded on both sides, and one was even killed. More tomorrow.

Anzeiger des Westens, 2 August 1860
(for Thursday, 26 July 1860)

Prostitution and Mob

Prostitution and mob have long been correlative concepts, not only for St. Louis but also for the entire world. But the rule is usually that the mob arises from the dens of prostitution themselves, since alongside the female nymphs these dens always harbor a corresponding number of male fellow-travelers as pimps and all-purpose bullies supporting themselves with robbery and murder, and they perform real work only under duress. Is it any wonder! In contrast to the women, who are either innocent and lucklessly seduced or brought to their ruin by force, these fellows are simply the excretion of human society, collecting in the enclosed and hidden chambers of this most depraved of occupations. This is a scum that does not live off of prostitution for want of something better to do but that speculates and intends to get rich on it. —A scum that exists for the purpose of sundering families, seducing innocence, smearing good names, ruining patrons, and worse is certainly capable of anything and everything. These dens thus are wellsprings of crime, starting-points for all sorts of assaults. This brood has raised its hand against everyone else, so it is no marvel that the hand of everyone is also raised against it.

Such a permanent state of war exists between these dens of vice and society at large that the only thing that prevents the outbreak of true hostilities is an effective police, such as is found in European cities. There these "houses of joy and lust" (a pretty name indeed!) are so strictly controlled that very little can take place other than joy and lust, and one can taste of this cup without risking further harm. This is how institutions of that sort arise and are tolerated in Europe even in small towns. But here there is hardly a police force at all to undertake such continuous supervision. The houses of prostitution in America are everywhere injurious to society, and unless the energetic fist of government presses and restrains them, as under Mayor Wood or Mayor Wentworth,* there is nothing left but for the people to rise up and strike with the mob as its two-edged sword. "Who sows the wind reaps the whirlwind."

For this reason we saw St. Louis in the hands of the mob for three hours last night. There was no more authority. The reign of the *populace* over this great city was absolute.

However lamentable and depressing all of this is, or perhaps because of it, we still have to say that after intensive investigation of the facts we have found that, despite appearances to the contrary, this action did not follow any preconceived plan. The outbreak yesterday did not have even the slightest resemblance to the Regulator movement, which spread from county to county in Iowa a few years ago.

*Fernando Wood, mayor of New York City, and "Long John" Wentworth, mayor of Chicago. JNP.

The origin was as follows: A respected citizen of this city discovered his two minor sons on several occasions in a disreputable dancè hall in the company of girls with painted cheeks and beflowered hair. When this happened yet again the day before yesterday, he fell into an argument with the proprietor of the bar, who had him thrown out the door. Once he had been so dispatched, the man rushed home, gathered his neighbors, and they began an attack on the dance hall, which was the first establishment to be torn down. Since dissatisfaction and bitterness over these bars due to offense against public morals had grown and spread so much over time, and since complaints about these establishments had been ignored by the authorities, a great mass of people soon gathered. People are like lions: the taste of blood drives them wild. And once people overcome the limits of the law and perform an act of violence, then everyone knows that more will follow. It might be hard to get such a movement underway, but once begun it is much harder to end it. What is one man's justice is another man's fun— then they think, "Strike while the iron is hot," if anyone actually bothers to think at all. And so destruction followed destruction until it was horrible to look on.

No good citizen can enjoy such a scene. Any reasonable man must condemn it unequivocally, no matter how inevitable or provoked it might have been. It was no surprise that many innocent people suffered in the wholesale destruction of property, even if we do not consider that the city has to be held responsible for damages caused by a riot the police did not suppress. The city might have to pay compensation of some fifty thousand dollars, which the taxpayers will have to finance—a burden that is greatest on the poorest. Such an example also has all sorts of evil results, since it encourages the satisfaction of many types of suppressed passions.

So we earnestly warn against any repetition of these scenes, and we entreat people not to participate in them. A cry of astonishment, injury, and offense will pass through the entire Union over what happened the day before yesterday, and the police will be compelled to try to prevent the recurrence of similar incidents at any price.

It would be better if the police applied its attention to these and similar nuisances of public life here and reconciled itself with public opinion by enforcing the letter of the law to the last jot and tittle against such social abuses.

But if this does not happen, then the people can have its revenge at the ballot box. It would do well to vote for no one who has not pledged himself in advance in the most detailed terms not to tolerate these dens in the city.

Even if all this is done, we are still not finished with what happened the day before yesterday. This could already be seen yesterday morning. As the ruins of the destruction still lay about, as the trashheaps of burned furniture still smoked and the people stood about in clusters, the birds were already back in their filthy nests, displaying themselves half-naked in the windows, seemingly enjoying their notoriety. When a group of housewives returning home from market stopped to show their disapproval by shaking their heads or saying a few words, each of the women protesting knew in their hearts and souls that the people were experiencing a sort of hangover that would make it hard to do similar things in the near future. So the prostitutes are sinning even more boldly, as if they had received absolution in advance.

Will the police—will the officials—continue to slumber until the scorn of the people is awakened again? Now they should know the peril that is even greater than these dens of vice. Think about it yourself for a while, even if the people as a whole will not.

Anzeiger des Westens, 16 August 1860
(for Tuesday, 14 August 1860)

Slaveowners and Proslavery People

The tendency to doubt the motives of any slaveowner who is trying to achieve importance in the Republican party has always seemed to us to be an irresponsible error. If we had not personally experienced the fact that it is often precisely the slaveowners who belong to our party who are the most deeply principled Republicans, we ourselves would never have realized it to be possible.

Who do the Republicans fight in the *free* states? Are there slaveowners there? Certainly there are none there at all. The people they fight are *proslavery people,* and *what* they fight are the politics of proslavery.

It is the system of free labor that is fighting with the system of slave labor; it is true democracy that opposes the oligarchy of the South and the rule of a destructive system; humanity is battling barbarism; small property in land and rational agriculture is in conflict with aristocratic exploitation, and those who want the territories given to the free white man and not to the slaveowning baron of the South; but it is not the nonslaveowners who are struggling with the slaveowners for the freeing of slaves.

This struggle will not be settled by the political doctrines of the South and North, but rather it will be resolved within the states themselves as a result of economic studies, perceived interests, increased education, and enlightenment. It will be fought in the hearts of men, just as the Jew Jesus Christ fought and reformed Judaism, or as the Franciscan [*sic*] monk Martin Luther reformed Catholicism.

The free states do not want to be dominated by the slave states; they do not want to give proslavery principles any more terrain than they already have by strict interpretation of the law. By doing this they are declaring war on political and social systems, but not against their reputed property, their duly obtained rights. It is in the nature of things, but not in the nature of the political struggle, that their property will become worthless with time and that their rights will turn into a burden too heavy to carry.

Conditions will be ripe for a definitive decision within each of the slave states when a majority of the slaveowners stand on the Republican side. In Missouri right now there are more than five hundred slaveowners who are antislavery people at the same time. These are persons who do not hold slaves out of haughtiness, as so many others do, but in order to get their fields worked. In part they have inherited slaves, and they have been trying to make use of their inheritance. We receive more and more of these people in our movement every day, for experience has taught them that slave labor is not as productive in Missouri as free labor, and all that keeps them from emancipating their slaves is a fear of further losses, the impossibility of finding enough free white workers, and often a certain piety that hesitates at placing inherited slaves in strange hands or seeing them go to ruin in freedom. They are all antislavery people—and probably no Republican from a free state knows as well the curse of slavery or discusses it more openly or more thoroughly than this type of slaveowner. Until recently Mr. Francis P. Blair was one of their number, since he only freed his slaves about a year ago; among them now is our mayor, Mr. O. D. Filley, our compatriot Arnold Krekel of St. Charles, and hundreds of other Americans and Germans we know, who are as good (and some better) Republicans than those who have never owned a slave. The solution to the slavery problem would not be a bit closer, the future of the Negro not one fraction brighter, the effort for emancipation in this step not a single step further if every single enlightened slaveowner in this state freed his slaves. On the contrary, the proslavery slaveowners would only hang onto their peculiar institution even more vehemently, would pass even more infamous laws against free Negroes, and the whole movement, which has begun so well and is obviously destined to win, would be set back decades, as is the case in Kentucky and Virginia.

But we are not interested here in a recapitulation of party positions or efforts for emancipation in Missouri, but rather in distinguishing between the slaveowner and the proslavery man. The great majority of slaveowners are proslavery people—but that is no reason why a slaveowner cannot be the best possible Republican!

Anzeiger des Westens, 3 September 1860

The Bissell Case

The long-term rivalry between Chicago and St. Louis is currently being expressed in the bitter struggle over the Rock Island Bridge, in which Chicago represents its interests in railroads and St. Louis its interests in rivers in the crudest and most unremitting manner. It seemed to us for a time that it was St. Louis that was going too far when it demanded that the bridge be removed at all costs. Since then, the argument that the bridge hinders navigation has begun to make more sense, and since Chicago arrested Mr. J. W. Bissell, the agent for the chamber of commerce here who was collecting data about the bridge, on charges of arson and of plotting the bridge's destruction, and since the court has denied bail on all sorts of pretenses, it has become a matter of honor for St. Louis to bring his cause to public attention with all of its power.* We will restrict ourselves to the incontrovertible fact that the man has been systematically denied his freedom despite the fact that the whole chamber of commerce here has offered to go surety for him, and despite the fact that some Chicago capitalist with business dealings here could easily have bailed him out. We have no idea how high the bail is, but we do know that any amount could be raised. We do not blame the court, which follows prescribed procedure no matter how

*The *Anzeiger* account is misleading here. The Rock Island Bridge episode reflected the St. Louis–Chicago commercial rivalry, rather than river against railroad. Bissell was a railroad bridge promoter himself. His proposed bridge at St. Louis in 1855 did not materialize because the Ohio and Mississippi Railroad, which terminated at East St. Louis, was heavily in debt and could not afford the $1.5 million estimated cost. Local investors had tied up their funds in railroads, mining projects, and land, and Eastern capitalists favored northern routes through Chicago. The trumped-up arson charge was based on the burning of the first wooden drawbridge at Rock Island when the St. Louis steamboat *Effie Alton* crashed into it. JNP.

reprehensible, so much as we blame the public spirit of Chicago expressed by it, since all considerations of friendship have been overridden to satisfy a petty grudge. This is doubly unworthy of Chicago, since its spirit of enterprise has already won it enough advantages over St. Louis that are worthy of recognition. Yesterday evening there was another meeting of the chamber of commerce, where $8,000 in cash was raised to give Mr. Charles D. Drake to take to Chicago to obtain J. W. Bissell's release. Should not the Chicago correspondents of St. Louis businesses be ashamed of themselves for this $8,000 cash?

P.S.: The best possible proof that there is a conspiracy against a citizen's freedom is the open statement that they will prevent Mr. Bissell's release through bail by immediately arresting him again on another charge. This is not administration of justice but revenge.

Anzeiger des Westens, 10 September 1860

Highly Interesting Statistics from Warren County, Missouri

The following comparison of the census of 1860 with that of 1850 is not without interest. Warren is one of the smaller counties (342 square miles) with not a square foot of homestead land left; since the land is already rather expensive, few have come into the county from outside in recent years, and part of its population has begun to move further west despite the fact that there is a great deal of uncultivated land left. In twenty years the population here has risen from 5,860 to 8,760, a growth of 50 percent. The black population has only grown by 87, from 939 to 1,026; in 1850 they were 16 percent, and now they are 12 percent of the total population. It is obvious that many blacks have been exported, since their natural increase would have been much greater than that, and none have been brought in. Only about 200 of the 1375 families in the county own slaves, and yet the slave interest rules everything up to the present day. One can see how hard it is to overcome an evil that has deep roots, and also how little the majority understands its advantages once prejudice enters the picture. The great majority puts up with the continuance of slavery simply because slaveowners tell them, "Would you rather have the blacks who are among you set free?" The number of poor supported at public cost (*paupers*) is only three, that is, one in three thousand residents—a remarkable situation! The value of property is given as about $3,250,000, that is, $500 per capita. The death rate in the last year was 128, that is, one in 67, which indicates such a poor health situation that one is inclined to suspect an error in the figures. The number of dwellings is the same as the number of families; churches, 21 (one for every 417 persons).

Far West [Friedrich Münch]

Anzeiger des Westens, 17 September 1860

*The Introduction of the German Language
into the Public Schools*

In another part of this newspaper is given the account and minority opinion of Dr. Pope, as reported by the *Evening News*. This is only one side of the matter—one-sided opinion telling us that the "true Americans" are very aroused, and that neither they nor we are very sure about the new organization of "our" public schools. It is to the credit of the board, by the way, that personal friends of Messrs. Pope and Robbins have not allowed themselves to be misled by the anxiety and excessive concern of these gentlemen, and they have set aside the one-sided arguments of a party politician and a nativist to do some justice for just demands. In order to be complete, we give the names of those voting:

For: Barlow, Fichtenkamp, D'Oench, Levy, Sigel, Wyman, Green,
    Corbitt, Pasquier, Ravold, Jennings, and Carr.
Against: Robbins, Robison, Patrick, and Pope.

Washington King registered in favor in the course of the debate, in the French manner. Dr. Hammer was sick of a fever but had himself recorded in favor of the Levy motion. Holmes and Sickles, of whom nothing good could have been expected, were absent.

As can be seen from the majority opinion printed here, the original motion was limited to introducing the German language to *four* schools; the way the classes were to be organized is also not entirely in keeping with the spirit of the members who were most deeply involved with the question, but more was accomplished than one could have expected. During the committee session that preceded the plenary session of the board, opinions were still so divided that it hardly seemed possible to achieve any results at all. Mr. Pope was *"against the whole thing."* —Mr. Jennings only wanted to experiment in *one* school, while Barlow and Sigel insisted on their four schools and Mr. Corbitt wavered from one side to the other under the pressure of the urgent importance of the question. To free himself from this predicament, he got up his courage and set the proposal at *two* schools, which was adopted by four votes (Barlow, Jennings, Sigel, and Corbitt) to *one* (Pope).

It is interesting how Mr. Pope entered the lists even at the last moment in the plenary session of the school board to say he was *"against the whole thing."* Mr. Pope is without a doubt what he said of himself in so many words, *"one of the best French scholars"* in the city of St. Louis, but he seems to respond to the Germans the same way Emperor Charles V did at the mention of the "hellish" Luther. We had never believed that such a fat, bearded man could be so weak-nerved that the mere thought of Teutonic pronunciation could send him into convulsions. Perhaps he fears that the German spirit will escape from the primary schools into the medical colleges and grab him there? Has old Humboldt visited him in a dream to examine "one of the best French scholars" on scientific subjects, or to ask him to translate a German medical article? Even if the French language did stand "high above German" as the good doctor believes, and even if he understands French thoroughly, still we believe that German has some things to say that Mr. Pope would not know how to answer in French. Incidentally, Mr. Pope apologized to the one German who voted *against* the introduction of German on the board several years ago. Small comfort! There are even a few Hindoos among the Germans who allow themselves to be used as the tool of those more clever than they are.

Anzeiger des Westens, 15 October 1860

St. Louis Republicans Pay a Visit to Abraham Lincoln

(Editorial Correspondence of the *Anzeiger des Westens*)

Springfield, Illinois, 10 October

We could not have chosen a better day than yesterday to make our long-delayed visit with our presidential candidate. (The party consisted of Messrs. Henry T. Blow, Barton Able, Peter L. Foy,* Ch. L.

---

*Henry Taylor Blow, a native Virginian and president of the giant Collier White Lead Company, was a staunch Republican and antislavery man. Peter L. Foy, a loyal follower of Frank Blair, was editor of the *Missouri Democrat* in 1860. JNP.

Bernays, along with a Captain Lee of the United States Navy, a brother-in-law of Frank P. Blair.) We first met Mr. Lincoln late in the evening at 11 p.m. in the state house, surrounded by friends from all parts of the country awaiting news of the elections in Pennsylvania, Indiana, and Ohio. As we entered, Mr. Lincoln was soothing the timid by saying that he was not only morally convinced that the people of the North, East, and Northwest would teach the Fusionists a hard lesson,* but that he had precise forecasts and reports from the best-informed men in Pennsylvania, New York, and Indiana showing that his election was beyond a doubt in those states.

As soon as we were introduced to Mr. Lincoln, he greeted us in the warmest manner and said, "You are my most welcomed and esteemed guests on this, the day of the first round of elections. But I must confess to you that since Frank's election* I had a great longing to see my friends in St. Louis again. I count that day as one of the happiest in my life, and I would have liked to have shared my joy with you *then*. Why didn't you come then?"

We excused ourselves by saying that we had been exhausted by the August elections, and this splendid man accepted our excuses— which were justified in *every* way.

And then the messages of victory began tumbling in one after another. Dispatches arrived from every part of the country where anyone could have expected good news; from St. Louis, from Cleveland and Columbus in Ohio, from Louisville in Kentucky, from Cincinnati, from New York, from Harrisburg, from Pittsburgh, from Indianapolis—in short, from all nooks and corners friends of Lincoln vied to be the first to bring him messages of victory. All doubts lifted between midnight and 1 a.m. when the decisive announcements arrived from the presidents of the state central committees of Ohio, Indiana, and Pennsylvania.

Joy was now as lively as worry had been before—only Lincoln remained the same. His face was no more flushed than it had been before; his movements were just as calm, his language as cheerful and prudent. He only allowed himself a moment of triumph when he read out the dispatch (published yesterday—eds.) of General

---

*Fusion was a last-ditch scheme concocted in September 1860 by Breckinridge Democrats and Constitutional Unionists, chiefly in New York and Pennsylvania, to deny Lincoln victory in the electoral college by combining to support a joint slate. Douglas supporters did not cooperate, and even if they had, the plan would have failed. Only Oregon, California, and New Jersey among the free states failed to give Lincoln an absolute majority. JNP.
*Frank Blair was elected to Congress in August 1860. JNP.

Cameron, saying: "Now Douglas might learn a lesson about what happens when one tries to get people opposed to slavery to *vote* for slavery. It is not my name, it is not my personality which has driven Douglas out of Indiana and Pennsylvania, it is the irresistible power of public opinion, which has broken with slavery."

We only departed at 3 a.m., satisfied with our day's work. —Let the South talk about *secession* until the sixth of November—then we will see that *submission* will be closer to the truth.

And now a word about the impression which *Abraham Lincoln* made on us and about his external appearance.

If the painters and lithographers have succeeded in portraying Abraham Lincoln as one of the ugliest men imaginable in their caricatures, then that is the fault of their lack of talent, not that of Mr. Lincoln's head. Not a single portrait has given more than the rawest contours, the most general lines of Lincoln. Lincoln's profile is not at all handsome, due to the lack of flesh on his chin and the unfortunately long neck—only when he is facing one directly does his face give its extremely pleasing impression. Mildness, friendliness, and modesty have been poured into that face; his smile is especially benevolent, and everyone wants to believe him when he assures us that he harbors not a grain of bitterness in his character, but that he is deeply hurt by the doings of Crittenden and the Old Whigs in Kentucky, who have tried to separate him from his former fellow party members and to get them to vote for Douglas.

It would be hard to find a more open, more intelligent brow or a more intelligent mouth than his. Even if he juts out his lower lip when he has finished an argument, still his movements bespeak an utter conviction that expresses something irreversible, a decision to stick to his convictions without altering them. Certainly, despite the fact that the portraits of Lincoln that are circulating lead one to expect him to be extraordinarily ugly, personal contact with him fills one with a feeling of trust and good will, with security, and with the comfortable feeling one invariably gets from strength and decisiveness paired with good cheer and mildness.

*   *   *

The next morning we passed a few hours—among the most pleasant in our life—with Mr. Lincoln; we then visited his lady in that small, three-story frame house that is Lincoln's only property, and we also paid our respects to Governor Bissell's widow.

Another powerful impression was not withheld from us! We were seized with the irresistible desire to see the interior of the palace of that man who so shamelessly abused his trust at the head of the government of Illinois that he burdened his state with six hundred thousand dollars in debts to his own benefit. So we betook ourselves to Governor Matteson's residence and had ourselves shown the interior of this fabulously rich palace. From the cellar to the last step of the tower, every corner is filled with rich sculpture and painting, with the most splendid rugs and gilded work, the finest of French mirrors and furniture—in this palace lives a Matteson, alone, abandoned and abhorred—and that little frame house that is furnished not poorly but with the great simplicity of an Illinois farmer holds old honest Abe and his modest, well-respected wife.

Anzeiger des Westens, 22 October 1860*

A German Proslavery Democrat

Since this species is rapidly dying out, we hold it to be our duty to exhibit the following self-portrait of such a person in our newspaper for the edification of the living and for posterity. We hope all Germans of *this* sort belong to the National Democratic party, both now and forever! The portrait our countryman has drawn of himself as a slavery man can be observed stroke by stroke:

Independence, 11 October 1860

I have been awaiting the date of the expiration of my subscription to this infamous lying Black Republican newspaper with increasing impatience and abhorrence. Since the time seems as if it shall never come, I am compelled as a white man to demand of Schwarz, Lincoln, and that Negro-thief Seward never to send your rag to a white man again, for Germans are all white except for those who pull a black pelt over their lying faces.

W. C. Rodewald

*This letter is marred by errors of grammar and spelling that cannot be rendered in translation. Mr. Rodewald transformed Schurz into Schwarz (black), obviously on purpose. SR.

Anzeiger des Westens, 22 October 1860*
(for Friday, 19 October 1860)

The First Quarter Century of the *Anzeiger des Westens*

has been completed *today*. On 20 October 1835, the prospectus for a little German weekly newspaper appeared, and on 31 October following that there appeared the first number of the *Anzeiger des Westens*.

Our readers already know the biography of this newspaper, and many Germans still are living in this city who have held with it from its first day to this very hour. Its history is virtually identical with that of the German element in the West. Starting small and short of money but rich in good intentions, persistence, and energy, as did the German immigrants themselves, it struggled with all the difficulties that can be placed in the path of a foreigner with alien ways and an alien language. The *Anzeiger* had to struggle through many years of apprenticeship before it achieved a position just as secure and independent as the best English newspapers, in the same way as the expanded German population has assured the survival of the German element.

One of the most important duties of the *Anzeiger des Westens* since its creation has been to fight the laming and corruption of the German language, which was the inevitable result of a less well-educated immigration to the older states. The corruption of language had a tendency to spread to the inland areas, placing a destructive barrier in the way of basic knowledge and the acquisition of philosophy, diplomacy, and literature.

In other states Germanity withdrew in shame before the spread of Anglo-Saxon culture, its language rendered disgraceful and decadent by the adoption of English words and the English use of German words. The *Anzeiger des Westens* has always striven to place the German language *here* on a level with the modern literature of the Fatherland, and this was successfully accomplished by an unbroken succession of capable and literate editors, aided by the two gifted immigrations of 1830 and 1848. Excellent German primary schools, first-rate German political orators, reproductions of German classics and the best works of our modern authors, finally in our own days a German legitimate theater, all have tended in the

*This article is the closest approach to a general statement of editorial policy by the *Anzeiger des Westens*, and it can be compared with the inaugural statement of Carl Dänzer's *Westliche Post* on 27 September 1857. SR.

same direction, so that we need only to continue along this path for Germanity in the West to reap the fruits that only an advanced culture and the most fruitful cultivation of our mother tongue and customs can produce.

The culmination of the first quarter-century of this newspaper coincides with the election of the first Republican president, with the victory of the party to which all enlightened Germans belong and whose principles and interests have always been promoted by the *Anzeiger des Westens.*

The *Anzeiger* is so well situated that it has never needed the favor of any party, but through the years up to this hour it has always supported the antislavery party, since this party had principles and perceptions that coincided with those for which the two great German emigrations strove and fought in their homeland. Association with that party as then constituted was often trying and uncomfortable—very often it took sidesteps or tangents against the wishes of the editors—but just as no one should try to achieve utterly abstract goals in such a realistic country, this is doubly the case with a *German* newspaper, lest it wallow in its theoretical pride with neither effect nor respect. It must also try to ward off the old characterization of the Germans as impractical dreamers, an accusation that is not always unjustified.

The work completed is a praise to its maker, and a German newspaper has no reason to apologize for belonging to the Republican party as it has developed, and we do not have to repent a single step we have made *in* or *with* this party.

We hope it will remain forever what it is now—tolerant, humane, and unprejudiced against immigration; truly democratic and republican in its political undertakings; a defender of the many against the few; a bulwark against the expansion of human slavery—then it can count on our continued support. But when the times are ripe for the internal liberation of the American spirit, or if a new party arises to redeem the *white* race of the shroud of prejudices, superstitions, and abuses imported from old Europe to the land of the free, then men will certainly be found in this newspaper to support it, carrying forward the successes of a whole series of editors up to the present day.

No special mention need be made of the financial situation of this newspaper as it enters its second quarter-century. Everyone knows what it was twenty-five years ago, and what it is now. Due to the special nature of the journalistic business, it has often prospered on the bad fortune of others, and in the bad times of 1857 it suffered less than most other businesses, though it did not escape unmarked. This was a reason for the temporary suspension of the monthly edition. It will appear as soon as trade and mercantile prosperity make the monthly possible and useful once again.

A newspaper that has been so widely sold and that has operated as long as the *Anzeiger des Westens* is an infallible barometer of the intelligence and political importance, but also of the material rise, stagnation, or fall, of a whole circle of readers. It is only right that we should participate in the joys and sorrows, the achievements and the losses of the German population. Without doubt our hardest days lie behind us now, and we step forward into our second quarter-century with the greatest certainty and confidence that the good old days will return.

May this newspaper always be entrusted to hands as faithful as those it has had until now; may it always *earn* the support of the German populace as it has until now, and may *the man* who has guided it so well across the rocks during the last decade be able to dedicate at least a portion of his powers to it. He was, if not its actual founder, then at least the creator of its importance for German life in this state and the whole West.

We remember with fondness on this day all those who have dedicated their strength to the *Anzeiger* for twenty-five years; but we must not abstain from recognizing the man who has sinned so much against himself through his attacks on us since his withdrawal [Carl Dänzer]. But we only pay the truth its due when we grant the whole sum of our respect to *Heinrich Börnstein*, the soul and driving force behind this newspaper. May he be able to celebrate with many of our German fellow citizens our first *half*-century with the same good health and force of spirit he enjoys on this splendid day.

St. Louis, 20 October 1860

Karl L. Bernays

Georg Hillgärtner*

Anzeiger des Westens, 22 October 1860

Republican Rallies in the Interior of Missouri

The sixth of October was an important day for the beautifully situated, wholly German town of Augusta in St. Charles County. It

*Georg Hillgärtner, a Forty-eighter and lawyer who came to America as secretary to Gottfried Kinkel on a tour to raise money for German revolution, became an

had been announced that Mr. A. Krekel and the undersigned would speak there in the afternoon, and for that purpose the inhabitants made the most splendid preparations. The roomy hall could not hold everyone, so the open doors and windows were filled with listeners. The understanding as well as the emotions of those present were addressed, so that everyone broke into a seemingly unending jubilation at the conclusion. Night had come upon us in the meantime, and now the German band (which has reached a perfection rare in such a small town under the leadership of Mr. Fuhr), the speakers, the committee, and the listeners were fêted; the Turners bore flags, lights, and lanterns, and the procession of enthusiastic people wound through all the streets of the town while eight bonfires lit the sky. Whoever heard the cheering and saw the fires from afar would better have understood Seward's words, "Missouri is Germanizing itself to make itself free."*

The guests were treated to a brilliant supper, in which Augusta's Catawba played a prominent role. Among the toasts, that for Garibaldi excited the greatest enthusiasm. The great crowd dispersed only after midnight, and everyone certainly said to himself: we must not give up our *German* way of life here, for only Germans can enjoy themselves in such a way by putting thought, heart, and hand to any cause they support.

The same orators spoke on the eighth of October at *New Melle*, a German village in the same county. We spoke to a totally agrarian population there; many traveled miles to come, and everyone listened with rapt attention. I believe we succeeded in answering all the questions those present had to ask and that they will all go to the election as Lincoln men.

Since the Hurrah-for-Douglas boys had no opportunity to disrupt festivities, both of these rallies went on without the slightest disturbance.

On the thirteenth the same orators will speak in Dutzow—currently the residence of the undersigned—and then in other parts of Warren County.

Friedrich Münch

---

important editor, serving at times with the *Anzeiger des Westens*, the *Illinois Staatszeitung* of Chicago, and the *Westliche Post*. See Wittke, *Refugees of Revolution*, 273. SR.

*William Henry Seward, 1801–1872, leading Republican figure before the war, in making this statement raised the hackles of the English-language press in Missouri and made himself a hero to many Germans. SR.

Anzeiger des Westens, 22 October 1860

To Republican Voters of Missouri

Since the post offices of Missouri are all in the hands of Democrats who will doubtless seize all Lincoln tickets, the undersigned
requests that all those who wish to vote the Republican ticket next
6 November should inform him how to send them the tickets with
security.

St. Louis, 20 October 1860

K. L. Bernays

Secretary, Republican State Central Committee

Anzeiger des Westens, 29 October 1860

St. Louis, 25 October

Every day we hear what the South will do or have done if we elect
Lincoln as president. They are trying to frighten us with fears
about a civil war; they want to make us believe that South Carolina,
Mississippi, and Alabama are only waiting for the news that a
Republican president has been elected in order to depart from the
Union. Very well, then, we will do what we think is right and let
happen what may. We ourselves believe that they will never take
their fists out of their pockets down there; we are convinced that
the interests of the majority of the white population go hand in
hand with our interests and that the burned-out and demoralized
mongers of human flesh will quickly be brought to reason—but we
are much more interested in what shall become of the North and
the West, especially what becomes of our own state, than what will
become of the South.

The shirt is closer to us than the coat, and if Lincoln's election
supports the interests of the North and the West, then we are only
sad at second hand that the South might suffer for it.

First of all, Lincoln's presidency will at last get a *homestead bill*
through.* It will reduce excessive, unproductive urban population
and drive it into the countryside. It will make virtuous farmers out

*Cheap or free land for (white) farmers, long a Benton Democratic theme, was a
basic tenet of Republicanism. JNP.

of thousands of those who have fallen almost to the level of petty thieves. It will fill the West with immigrants from the older states and from the old continent, and it will bring us people who produce raw materials and consume our manufactures, the best, most desirable market for our large inland cities.

Slavery will lose its offensive nature under Lincoln's presidency, since all prejudices and concerns will fall from the one side, and all of the expectations of the other side will be fulfilled. The country will be able to turn its attentions to the improvement of its interior facilities without being bothered any further by the specter of civil war that has haunted it for so many years.

Freedom will once again be the rule, repression the rare exception.

Cheating and bribery will cease to be the sole rudder of the machinery of government, and talent, patriotism, and true service shall again be prime requirements for those seeking office; the interests and the needs of the country will become necessary conditions for those contracts that are granted.

This country will no longer have to be ashamed of its own administration, and the contempt foreigners have heaped on us during the last two administrations will go to those who really deserve it.

But Missouri in particular will be moved a half-century forward in its effort to emancipate. Once brutality has to submit itself to authority, it loses half its power. Instead of shouting us down or threatening us with death, soon they shall be begging us and offering us money. Soon people will be able to speak and write freely whatever they wish in the interior of the state without fear of being lynched; Democratic postmasters will no longer seize and burn our newspapers as revolutionary documents; free immigration will no longer be hindered by impediments of any kind, and the struggle will proceed peacefully and quietly until at the end we shall see Missouri a free state, homeland of many millions of happy citizens.

What do such hopes matter in the face of the rage of a handful of slaveowners, what matter their injured pride, their shaking and quaking at the thought of losing their human cattle? Their putative loss is compensated more than a hundredfold by the happiness of millions!

Anzeiger des Westens, 5 November 1860

The Future Position of the Parties in This Country

Missouri, 27 October 1860

No thinking person depends only on what is available at a particular moment; our attention moves back to the past, both to compare the past to the present and to investigate how the present emerged. Human cleverness also likes to exercise itself in forecasting the future from what exists today by playing the engrossing game of making pictures of the future. Precisely this is one of the peculiarities of the intellectual nature of man: great energy is continuously being expended in rescuing the past from oblivion—and hardly a fact emerges from the most recent times but that all thinkers are hard at work determining what results will follow.

Today we see the victory of the Republican party as certain; what comes next? This is too broad a subject for such a limited space, so I shall consider a more restricted question: what system of parties shall prevail in this country in the near future?

Before the most recent splintering of the Democratic party there were *four* parties, and this is the natural situation found everywhere in every human community with an active political life; a fifth party is one too many and will not survive. —In accordance with the model of the French chamber of deputies, one distinguishes the various parties as (1) extreme left, (2) center left, (3) center right, and (4) extreme right. Parties are distinguished in a similar fashion in German parliaments, and here as well the same phenomenon can be observed wherever the interests of the masses are involved in a public question. The source of this distribution is found in irrevocable psychological laws.

(1) *The Extreme Left:* A young person, whose fire has not yet been dampened by cool experience, raves for his ideals, believes they can be fully realized, and is ready to challenge the whole world on their behalf. But there are also older people who remain youthful throughout their lives on such matters (we usually call them abstractionists here); often what drives them forward are religious ideals. Their strong will often excites admiration, but they lack practical talent insofar as they are unable to judge particular circumstances adequately. Often there are desperate types or true swindlers in their midsts. The further Left, made up of persons of the sort described, demands rapid progress and reckless upheaval of such conditions and institutions as do not function or which are

not as good as they could be, and here they are represented by the *abolitionists* of the North. People will have to pay more attention to this party than they have up until now, despite its small size, for the parties shift steadily in the course of time: party number 1 goes to position 2, party number 2 to position 3, party number 3 to position 4, and party number 4 is passed out of the system entirely, so that an entirely new party of the future appears in position number 1.

(2) *The Center Left* generally approves the ideas of the previous party but undertakes to turn them into reality only insofar as appears possible under the existing circumstances. It is happy with the *better* if it cannot have the best of all, and it does not choose to risk the better to get the best. It follows the path of *reform* and rejects revolution except for situations where no progress whatsoever is possible (in this case it temporarily allies with number 1). It makes specific, moderate demands in keeping with the occasion after careful investigation, and it never loses its footing while taking the next step. In the natural course of things it loses some of its supporters to number 3 and gains new ones from number 1. Here and now it exists as the *Republican party*, and it is stronger now than the other three together because moderate progress has now become a pressing necessity in this republic due to its history over the last several years. It will lead the Union for a number of years as the Democratic party has in the past; may it not reach a similarly pitiful end!

(3) *The Center Right* is always the party of men of caution and care, the keepers of what is there, the *conservatives*. Their electoral slogan is *Blessed be the possessors*, that is, whatever one has must be kept and not waged to win something better for oneself or others. This party of restrictions has won great strength in most countries through something in human nature similar to inertia in physics. Although the level of thought is lower in this party, its power lies in its aristocracy, which sees its interest to be a lack of change and which has the means to make its influence felt on the masses. —Here the center Right has no true support or unity at the moment since the Whig and Know-nothing parties have dissolved, but it will certainly recover after the elections. The Douglas party is something unnatural and abnormal, a true fifth wheel on our political wagon that is there simply because of the ambition of one man with whose political *death* it will necessarily cease to exist. The *doctrine* of squatter sovereignty,* as unclear as it is and as impractical as it

*Douglas's popular (squatter) sovereignty left the status of slavery to the voters of a territory at the time it was organized. This doctrine had struck down the Missouri Compromise in 1854, and it was in turn made obsolete by the Dred Scott decision in 1857, which opened all of the territories to slavery. JNP.

is now even with the intervention of the Supreme Court, serves neither progress nor conservatism and remains a stillborn child. By far the majority of the Douglasites in the free states are Free-soilers who approve squatter sovereignty out of blind respect for democratic principles, but only with the understanding that Northern voters will always be strong enough to keep the evils of the slave economy from their own borders. After the election most of them will find their home in the Republican party while the remnant will go over to the so-called *Union-party*, which will henceforth represent the center Right between the progressive parties and the Southern Ultras. In order to justify itself, it will keep the Republican party under close watch, placing as many difficulties in its way as possible, but it will also seek to repress Southern hankerings for division, approve nativism after a fashion, and represent the principle concerning slavery that the residents of a territory can decide whether the institution will exist there at the time it becomes a state.

(4) *The Extreme Right* consists of people who are not satisfied to have the wheel of time stand still (which never works in reality), but who wish it to turn backwards. The party of reaction is formed by despots and obscurantists; but it is in keeping with human nature that there are always such, so the powers of society are always kept fresh and strong through struggle. Breckinridge is only a tool of the Southern Ultras, not their head, and their standard bearer is said to be Yancey or somebody much like him.* These people cast their eyes back to the time *before* the Revolution, when the expansion of slavery and the trade in slaves went on as they wished. Nothing is more hateful to them than the principles of the Declaration of Independence. The slavery interest wants to be lord in the state as well as in the federal government or it will dissolve the Union; for them there is only *one* honorable position in the world, to be owner and lord of hundreds of people in servitude.

The extreme Right triumphed in Germany in the reaction of 1849. In free political societies it is only dangerous when temporarily allied with the center Right (which will probably be tried in 1864). In some circumstances both *centers* join against one or another extreme party that has become overly mighty, or the extreme Left and center Left join to push through a particular measure. There can even be a temporary alliance of both extremes to realize some temporary goal. In our republic the center Left usually has the political power, interrupted by brief triumphs of the true center

---

*William L. Yancey of Alabama, a proslavery "fire-eater" and early secession advocate. His political power was usually exaggerated by Northerners. JNP.

when the center Left has misused its power (as when the Whig party won briefly here in 1840 and 1848), or when the people want a temporary respite from progress.

Gradually it has become clearer that the two old chief parties had elements in their makeup that no longer could operate together. The Whig party broke apart first, and the Democratic party was able to win two more times before a new progressive party could mature. The Know-nothing party had to step in in order not to be utterly without strength, and now it stands at center Right as the Conservative Union party. The Democracy had earlier been the center Left, and under Douglas it tried in vain to move to the center Right, but now its name has passed to the Southern Ultra party.* Republicans, who grew out of the Free Democrats who held their convention at Buffalo in 1848 and issued a splendid platform there, reappeared greatly improved as Free-soil men at a convention in Pittsburgh in 1852. In 1854 it finally took on its present name as a party seriously contending for victory, which promise has been fulfilled in 1860 to a degree exceeding all expectations. As the party of prudent progress it now occupies the center Left and will resolve at last the questions that are now at issue, despite all opposition. What comes beyond that can be left unconsidered today.

Far West [Friedrich Münch]

---

*The platforms of the Democrats and Whigs in 1852 agree completely on the matter of slavery insofar as they forbid all further agitation. In this way the victory of Pierce was a great *conservative* victory. His administration and that of Buchanan led the Democracy over to the most extreme Right as the center Left developed itself anew. [Münch's note.]

III.

Secession Winter

1860–1861

"Have you honestly asked yourself—and honestly answered—how
much St. Louis, Missouri, and its German adoptive citizens
have to lose by leaving the Union?"

Anzeiger des Westens, 4 February 1861

Anzeiger des Westens, 3 December 1860*

Minutemen in St. Louis

Not all the fools are dead, not even the dangerous ones, and not
all of them are off getting involved in the border war.

We discover this from the resolution of the "Ninth Ward Washington Minute Men" printed yesterday in the *Bulletin.* We give only
two of the resolutions here:

> *Resolved,* that we are Southern men and that we wish to uphold and
> defend our interests and institutions with our lives, to the exclusion of all others.
> *Resolved,* that we regard the election of Abraham Lincoln to the presidency as a sufficiently "open act" to move the South to take
> action, and that the positions taken by South Carolina, Georgia,
> and other Southern states are in complete agreement with our
> own views and that we place ourselves in readiness to march to
> their aid as soon as they need it.

And these people have christened themselves with the name of
Washington and assert that they are friends of the Union and of the
Constitution! It would not be easy to be any bolder or any crazier.

*In the presidential election of November 1860, Missouri cast its electoral votes for
Stephen Douglas, who had won a narrow victory over Bell, with the open secessionist Breckinridge and Lincoln trailing far behind. Claiborne F. Jackson, a reluctant
Douglas man whose heart was with the South, was elected governor, with Thomas C.
Reynolds as lieutenant governor. Lincoln had carried St. Louis, with Douglas a close
second. Unionist and secessionist quasi-military clubs, formed during the campaign,
drilled and paraded after the campaign as tensions rose with the open withdrawal of
slave states, led by South Carolina. SR.

So it is good that the Wide Awakes have kept their organization in being to keep an eye on each step of these fanatics for secession and civil war.

Anzeiger des Westens, 3 December 1860
(for Thursday, 30 November 1860)*

Yesterday morning we received the following lines from Major Fr. Schäfer:*

Camp Gentry, 27 November

Dear Mr. Bernays,

Since yesterday we have been camping here in the most extreme misery. We are not to stay here long, since we just received orders to decamp at four a.m. tomorrow. Where we are going and how long we shall march nobody knows. The governor says only that we should leave any extra baggage here in order not to overload the wagons. The condition of the men's health is better than one could have expected in this wet, stormy weather. We have less news about the border troubles than you do, and we only learn about them through St. Louis newspapers forwarded to us.

Your Friend,

Fr. Schäfer, Major

*   *   *

The Levy of Our Militia

has shown itself already, on the third day of the expedition, to be precisely what we called it publicly at the first moment: the irresponsibly childish prank of our drunkard governor. Our St. Louis friends languish about fifteen miles west of Jefferson City wallowing in the muck, longing for warm stoves and their families, con-

*The Southwest Expedition, a militia force sent by Gov. Robert M. Stewart to close the Kansas border to raiders from both states, went with weapons loaned from the United States Arsenal in St. Louis. The demand that these arms be returned would be a minor pretext for the seizure of Camp Jackson, 10 May 1861. SR.

*Friedrich Schäfer, a police officer in Germany, was street inspector for the heavily German First Ward in St. Louis and a major in the Missouri State Guard before resigning due to the secession sympathies of the state government in April 1861. He was lieutenant colonel under Heinrich Börnstein in the Second Regiment, Missouri Volunteers. He became colonel of the regiment when it was reorganized for three years' service, and he died at the battle of Murfreesboro, Tennessee, in 1862. See Kaufmann, *Deutschen im Bürgerkrieg*, 548. SR.

cerned about their businesses, and universally convinced that they have been driven into this winter campaign for no reason at all. The dispatches say nothing about any officials being driven out; the court there has not been interrupted for a single minute, and Judge Williams's flight is seen by everyone as an overreaction justified by no factual cause. Governor Stewart knows that just as well as we do, and it is only shame that keeps him from sending the poor benighted fellows home after three days under arms and putting a quick end to this foolishness.

This is precisely how our state has earned general derision, and no wonder if some of the contempt directed at Governor Stewart lands on the citizens who have been so ready to be taken in by his silliness.

The slaveowners and Union destroyers needed their own *John Brown* for once to prove that the victory of the Republicans would lead to raids on a daily basis into slave states to free Negroes. But there was no John Brown to be found. So they decided to choose one brave man in Kansas for ridicule and rebuke, until in the end they were convinced he was a villain or a madman—that had to draw Montgomery in.* The telegraph collected lies upon lies saying that Montgomery's "raid" was about to happen—at last a companion to John Brown's "raid" had been discovered.

But to the despair of Buchanan and his fire-spitting friends, Missouri is not a secessionist state where every spark of truth has been extinguished. All that was needed was *to present the facts*, and the more light shed the more clearly the assertions were shown to be lies and sheer fabrications.

But these lies have cost Missouri fifty thousand dollars and a good piece of its reputation. Responsibility lies with those who approved and carried out this maneuver. *We* wash our hands of it.

Anzeiger des Westens, 10 December 1860
(for Thursday, 6 December 1860)

Missouri Against Secession

Obviously the fire-eaters of the cotton states have nothing to expect from Missouri. A state that gives 17,000 votes to Lincoln and

---

*James Montgomery of Fort Scott, Kansas. Not only Governor Stewart but also Governor Denver of Kansas and the army at Fort Leavenworth patrolled the border to prevent raids from both directions. JNP.

only 31,317 votes out of 165,518 cast to Breckinridge, but which gives Bell and Douglas almost 120,000 has already declared itself unshakably for the Union. And when one considers that the sole large city in the entire state, St. Louis, gave only 610 votes to Breckinridge out of 24,755 cast, while giving more than 24,000 votes to Union candidates, then there is no basis for the fear that a temporary government might be imposed, or a reign of terror such as now rules in New Orleans, where the secessionists were just as much in the minority as here. Breckinridge's party in this town is not even a party; it is too poor, too weak, and too lacking in respect to form the basis of real trouble. There are certainly some secessionist newspapers in the interior of the state—the *Boonville Patriot*, the *Lexington Expositor*, the *Washington County Mirror*—but the greatest number declare themselves for the Union. We do not pay much attention to one or the other of these newspapers, for they are not in a position to see the situation as a whole.

Missouri is currently in the midst of a struggle for the revision of its constitution as a slave state. It is obvious that the latest turns in this struggle have not been favorable—but they will not alter the course of public opinion, let alone turn it in the exactly opposite direction.

The question of where Missouri should turn *if* the other slave states form a special confederation seems premature and difficult to answer. It is premature because there is as yet no effort to separate the so-called border states from the Union; it is difficult to answer because one would have to know the international relations of a Southern and Northern Union to one another and to foreign countries. If it were the case that the Southern Union would set the same tariff against all foreign countries, including the Northern Union, as was the case with the whole Union before, then St. Louis would be ruined, or it would have to establish a smuggling industry that would transform our current border running into pure piracy. What role Missouri and St. Louis would play in a Southern Union in this case is unpredictable. But if the South only levied tariffs against the Northern Union and none against other foreigners, then our city would bloom and have a great commercial future under the Southern banner! But at what price? At the cost of all education and civilization, at the cost of all pressure for progress of an intellectual sort, at the cost of freedom of speech and of the press, and certainly at the cost of equality for all ethnic groups!

It is certain that every advantage lies with keeping the Union as it is now—and the great majority of our fellow citizens think this as well.

Anzeiger des Westens, 17 December 1860
(for Wednesday, 12 December 1860)

What Is the Mission of the German Element in the Present Crisis?

Whoever understands the effort that has been expended over the last six years to get the German element where it is today in the United States, whoever knows the interests that drew the German nationality here and that bind it to this country, whoever understands the German character for its humaneness, tolerance, and prudence, and lastly whoever knows the depth of the German love of freedom will know what the mission of Germans in this crisis must be.

It can be condensed into very few words: steadfastness in our principles and in the Union!

The German character is not aggressive, but it is tenacious and steadfast about its rights. The role of the German element since the moment the situation of our country became clear has been that of a defender. In keeping with this character, the Germans are protecting the principles of freedom upon which they believe this league of states was founded, and they are defending their own position as guaranteed by the Constitution. Germans found themselves surrounded by a land in continual conflict, and only their strict insistence on the principles of law and Constitution has brought them through without injury.

Germans never were aggressive. Filled with more intensive concepts of freedom, with more expansive notions of humanity than most peoples of the earth, Germans are more likely to promote their principles through an intense insistence and defense of their rights than through hostile attacks.

The German is no border raider and no thief of Negroes; no German had anything to do with the Harper's Ferry raid, nor has he ever disturbed the borders of a slave state in the guise of an abolitionist leader. Yet the German is an opponent of slavery, and the German is always unfailingly there when free labor is being defended through law and Constitution against the pressure and dominance of slavery and the despotic principles of government it brings with it.

At this moment the defense of these principles coincides with the defense of the Union against those states that desire to smash it because their own principles can no longer rule, and because the people have spoken out in favor of the spread of freedom and against the expansion of slavery.

Defending freedom and defending the Union are one and the same thing. It is still *possible* for the Union to be preserved. It is still *possible* that the South will see how poorly it is prepared to guarantee its own security and how little it can depend on foreign protection if it separates from this Union. It is still possible that the division is a trial the schismatics will give up after three months.

But if this is not the case, then the Germans in the Western states—to which Missouri belongs—must take their stand on freedom and right and oppose this state entering the *Southern* confederation, so far as their strength reaches. Germans must support Missouri joining with those states where Germans form a sizable bloc and in which they have won considerable influence *through* the defense of their own principles. If the Union falls to pieces and Missouri cannot stay with the North, then a *Central States League* to which Germans and border slave states would gravitate would not be impractical or unrealistic.

It has always been the case in revolutionary times that extraordinary measures become necessary, so we have considered the possibility of separating this city and its immediately surrounding area from our state. But we still hope that the Union will be able to come through this crisis undamaged, so we only touch on such eventualities in vague, general terms, and we stress the great fact of the pressing danger that now threatens this country. The first matter of importance is to preserve what now exists, and we call on the Germans to do just that. If our effort to accomplish this fails, then the second act of the great drama will begin—the reconstruction of a new state system, and the Germans will make their presence known so that they are not cheated of their due when the prizes are handed out.

Westliche Post, 9 January 1861

Jefferson City and the Legislature

The journey from St. Louis to the capital city of our state, where the concentrated wisdom of the people is currently gathered, is very engrossing. The extraordinary difficulty of the terrain with which the civil engineers had to struggle while the railways were being built is more than compensated by the picturesque beauty of nature, whose contemplation shortened the hours of this traveler's trip. A few miles after leaving the city, the railway touches the banks of the Meramec River and snakes its way along its left bank, following the winding course of the river, with the steep bluffs on one side and the river on the other. At the village of Glencoe, where the river takes a great bend, the area resembles the Saxon Switzerland or the banks of the Elbe in Bohemia. The railway hangs directly from a steep cliff of considerable height, and the turn of the river permits the passenger to see both banks of the Meramec. The right-of-way then cuts through the heights between the Meramec and the Missouri, as the train moves to the northwest, until it comes out on the right bank of the Missouri shortly before Washington. The high bluffs accompany us from there on our left all the way to Jefferson City, while the river remains in view most of the way on our right. The usually wild and uncontrollable Missouri presented an impressive picture of pleasing grandeur, which was made even more dramatic by its coat of ice. We saw more banks than water in its vast, wide riverbed, and only a few arms of water snaked slowly along.

Soon our iron horse brought us to the goal of our journey, and we saw Jefferson City—a great exception for America—built on the top of an impressively high hill. As soon as we climbed the hill, we saw on our right the Capitol, rising impressively high above the waters of the Missouri, and on the left we saw the dark walls of the state's penitentiary. The Capitol, with its colonnade and dome, though battered and by no means a masterpiece of esthetic architecture, still rises proudly above the little town and makes a grand impression. This is because it stands alone on a high mound, similar to an earthwork, so that it has a place of prominence on the hill in front of the rest of the town. From the great open staircase of the Capitol there is a splendid view of the banks of the Missouri, and here as nowhere else one can see high bluffs crowned with forest on the left bank as well. The town itself has a quaint character, though it clearly puts on its Sunday best during the time when the legislature is in session. A stranger is surprised to find the streets and houses of the little town so peaceful; there are no gangs of loafers, no demonstrations here. Only here and there are utterly harmless gatherings of saviors of the Fatherland having a drink and enjoying life quietly. If one gazes at these peaceful faces, which even greet a stranger on the street, thinking you are a colleague, it seems impossible that these people could be pulling the state of

Missouri into the disaster that awaits the fire-eaters. Most of them, the vast majority, are more like fat, cheery old Crassus than the thin Cassius whom Caesar feared, or the Catiline whom Cicero detested. These good fellows seem to have written on their foreheads the motto of those who do not know what they want, "Something must be done," which is in fact inscribed on the portals of every hall of legislation from Washington down to Tallahassee and on west to Jefferson City. The delegation from St. Louis County has decided to take a passive position, justifiably, as long as the secession fever lasts. This movement is like all fevers—it must be waited out, just as with the Know-Nothing fever, the Kossuth fever,* or the revival fever. During the crisis there is no point in trying to restrain the sick man, any more than a madman can be convinced by sensible arguments. Secession is the fashion now, just as the crinoline is with the fair sex; even the ladies have changed their colors, it is an offense against fashion in stylish circles to be against secession. All snobs and loafers, all politicians and office seekers are for it, and who can stand against it? Enough of this Capitol of secession, so it is suitable for us to cross over to the penitentiary. It consists of several large buildings surrounded by a high, encircling wall of a rectangular shape. There are 511 convicts of all sorts working in various halls; we saw cooperage, wagon repair, carpentry, cobbler, and saddlery shops, all filled with workers. The great majority of the prisoners are young. Each works without manacles, and there are only a few guards in the halls. Cells for the prisoners rise up in the American fashion six or seven stories high, and their great number shows that the size of this class is expected to grow. The finest parts of the building were constructed as recently as 1859 and 1860. Prisoners are used outside the prison as well, under the control of armed guards. Some of them were cutting stone at the Capitol, and others cut ice at the river's edge.

On the whole the picturesque location of this little town and the friendliness of the residents, two-thirds of which are Germans, make the greatest impression on a stranger.

---

*Louis Kossuth, the deposed revolutionary dictator of Hungary, made a triumphal tour of the United States in 1851–1852, which raised great enthusiasm among ethnics and native-born Americans for the liberation of Europe. SR.

Anzeiger des Westens, 14 January 1861
(for Tuesday, 8 January 1861)*

The Facts Speak! The Position of St. Louis, Especially of Its German Adoptive Citizens, with the Legislature

First Fact

In the session that took place last Saturday, the question was debated whether the farewell address of the departing governor and the inaugural address of the new governor were to be printed in German.

This motion was *defeated*. The senators hostile to the Germans declared:

(Translated literally from the *Missouri Republican:*)
Germans should learn English as soon as they come to this country; *they have most recently shown such a hostility to the institutions of this country that they do not deserve any special favors from the state;* they have no greater claims to translation into their own language than any other ethnic group, and the legislature is thus not justified in supporting, even indirectly, *the plan of some Germans to Germanize Missouri.*

(Translated literally from the *Missouri Democrat:*)
Some ultra-Democrats denounced the Germans in the most bitter terms because they had voted in massive numbers for the Republican ticket, and for the time being the terms Black and Red Republicans were the order of the day. The wholesale attacks on the Germans that had become epidemic in both houses should open the eyes of the world to how narrow-minded and proscriptive the ruling party in the legislature is.

The great majority of the members of the Senate share this hatred of the Germans, and to punish them for being unfriendly to the institution of slavery, it has been decided not to do them any favors, so the addresses were not printed in German.

But let us see what happened in the house. There the motion was *passed*, but only after the Germans were denounced and rebuked in the most infamous way by a large portion of the Democratic members. Let us listen to a literal translation of part of the report in the *Missouri Republican:*

Mr. Moore of Laclede says that he opposes printing the addresses in German. Should people who neglect to learn the American language be

---

*Upon his inauguration as governor in January 1861, Claiborne F. Jackson declared that Missouri would stand with the South. It was an established practice to print the governor's proclamations and addresses in German as well as English, in a ratio of one to two. SR.

kept informed by this means despite their error? We are supposed to put *our* literature into their hands? To what end? *So they might rip it up and light their Meerschaum pipes with it. My Bible tells me not to cast pearls before swine.*

Messrs. Moore and Partridge of St. Louis, Lawson of Platte, and Thomas L. Price all flailed away at the Germans.*

This is how two hundred thousand Germans in Missouri are treated by the senate and the legislature of this state. They were not criticized for some injustice committed but rather for the free exercise of their rights as American citizens by expressing their convictions and consciences through their votes. For this reason they have been deprived of a "grace," as they call it, extended to them for years. They are even called "swine" for whom the address of the governor is too fine.

But these Germans are not too fine to put thousands upon thousands of acres of swamp and hillside under the plow; to introduce viticulture to Missouri; to pay their taxes conscientiously; to have built a good third of this city of St. Louis. They are good enough to be *white Negroes*, but they are too bad to be free voters.

Fine, then, one will not go without the other. As fine as the Germans are as industrious and law-abiding citizens, then they must also be held to be politically equal citizens. If you do not want this, then have the courage to pass a law to expel them, seize their property, and close the borders of the Missouri Republic to them forever. No German in Missouri has ever led a Negro astray; no German has ever come into the state in order to free slaves; there is no state law the Germans have ever violated in a treasonous manner. What is it, then, that they want to punish? Our sentiments? Our convictions? Our legally exercised expression at the ballot box? Is that what they mean? Good—say it, then; frame laws in this direction; drive us out and ruin us, then, since you can no more rob us of our sensibilities and convictions than you can take away our right to vote, our freedom of expression, and our free press. Stop being an American and become an Austrian or a Neapolitan—then we could understand that sort of legislation and could either yield to superior force or go to our ruin with honor.

Second Fact

Mr. Churchill of St. Louis filed a resolution in which the Committee for Federal Relations was ordered to draw up a bill calling for a state convention.

*George Partridge, a member of the St. Louis business elite, and Thomas L. Price were former Benton Democrats who disliked Blair's and the Germans' emphasis on emancipation. They were both strong unionists, however. JNP.

At this moment the calling of a state convention can mean nothing other than a proclamation of the separation of this state from the Union. Whoever is for the Union has no need for a convention.

The next news item leaves no room for doubt:

Messrs. Churchill and Johnson,* senators from St. Louis, have spoken out in favor of the immediate withdrawal of the state of Missouri from the Union.

Who authorized these gentlemen to take this step in this Union-loving city? Has there ever been the slightest demonstration here in St. Louis that might lead one to believe that St. Louis is inclined to withdraw from the Union? What do we call it when two men decide the precise opposite of what their constituents wish? When they decide to take the state in precisely the opposite direction from that in which the overwhelming majority of residents in their districts wish to go?

It means nothing less than that St. Louis is being *forced* in a direction in which it does not wish to go, and that this is well known in Jefferson City. Hence we have

The Third Fact

(Literally translated from the *Missouri Republican:*)
Mr. Johnson (senator from St. Louis) has filed an act that alters an act of March 1855 concerning the suppression of riots. This act *withdraws from the mayor or other officials of a town all power and authority in a community in which a riot is taking place and bestows it on the governor,* with the exceptions of sections 17 and 18 (which allow the mayor to close saloons on election days and to keep children off the street). It also extends the effect of the act to the entire state. The ordinary rules were suspended, the bill was given three readings, and it passed by a great majority.

(Literally translated from the *Missouri Democrat:*)
This bill takes all disposable power to suppress mobs out of the hands of municipal and county officials and delivers the people of the city and the county of St. Louis to the tender mercies of rioters and a governor rabidly in favor of separation.

Let us hear what the *Missouri Democrat* has to say about this law:

The Disunion Conspiracy in Missouri
The drama being played out in Jefferson City opened after the prologue of Governor Jackson's traitorous and incendiary address, and it has unfolded itself with surprising speed. The General Assembly has

---

*Samuel B. Churchill and Waldo P. Johnson. Within a few days, the legislature elected Johnson to the United States Senate; after his expulsion from the Senate in 1862 for secessionist activities, he accepted a commission in the Confederate army. JNP.

barely been organized before it has been called upon to approve revolutionary measures. War projects are already on the calendar. Bills to transform the governor into a military dictator, to arm the state, to call a convention to separate the state from the Union, all have already been thrown onto the senate's table. The disunionists seem to have adopted Danton's motto, "Boldness, boldness, boldness!" The first step was obviously to rob local officials of all the power they have exercised until now and to centralize it in the hands of the governor. Mayors, sheriffs, judges, etc., are supposed to be stripped of all their power. An autocrat who resides, as it happens, in Jefferson City and lives among the classic Scots of Saline County is supposed to replace the various municipal authorities as keeper of the peace. The throne of the despot is to be raised up in the ruins of citizen self-government. Henceforth the citizens of St. Louis are to be subject to the will of a dictator who openly confesses his design to plunge the people who elected him as governor into a civil war. The bill that makes all these recommendations for the erection of a military dictatorship into law is also a bill to authorize riot and disorder. It is a law that grants to people with a blue cockade an unlimited license to commit violent crimes of every sort without punishment. It is a bill for the suppression of every legal demonstration and every Unionist rally.

And this dreadful and tyrannical bill was introduced by one of the bogus senators from our county, Johnson by name. The other bill that called for the convocation of a secession convention was introduced by Churchill, that other pillar of the state from St. Louis. The new army law, whose originator, Monroe Parsons,* is infamous for his plan to finance the education of the youth of Missouri on the profits of exploitation, is what the General Assembly has spawned in its first weeks, and it is mild to say that it is the most wicked and senseless thing ever to be presented for consideration by the people of Missouri and its representatives.

We endorse every word of this article. This is the program that is being forced on this state and particularly on this city. Consider for a moment the fact that for weeks it has been the general practice to see the Unionists in this city as primarily, if not exclusively, Germans, and to describe the Germans as a group as enemies of the state; consider that it must be the obvious plan of the senate to raise up mobs against the Germans and to strip authorities of the city and county of the power to suppress these mobs, and then we can see precisely the situation of the German population of St. Louis. Yet we are not even allowed to express disappointment over the situation.

On the other side stands the fact that our *native-born* fellow citizens here know the Germans better than do the gentlemen in Jefferson City, and we have nothing to fear from these plans being

---

*Monroe M. Parsons of Jefferson City, a rabid secessionist, had run for lieutenant governor of Missouri in 1860 on the Breckinridge ticket. He became a brigadier general in the Confederate army. JNP.

hatched outside the city as long as the native-born citizens of St. Louis are not made into slaves by being stripped of their constitutional rights through terrorism from outside. Then at least the Germans will share the fate of their native fellow citizens.

*   *   *

We wrote this article with serenity and cold blood because we hold it to be our holiest duty always to inform the German population of this city and state of *the true state of affairs*. Far be it from us to upset people, but it is our duty not to mislead our fellow citizens about imminent peril. Only an ostrich is so dumb as to think that he can avoid danger from hunters by burying his head in the sand. A serene, determined man looks danger straight in the eye and diminishes it by so doing. Indifference and coolness are the greatest possible misfortunes, and only a person who lets himself be cowed into silence can be terrorized. The only way we adoptive citizens can get through this political crisis and be happy and secure is to fulfill all legal duties faithfully, to hold with the Union and the Constitution, and to work together with our American fellow citizens to preserve peace, order, and law. The gaze of the entire Union is directed at the German citizens of Missouri, so let us show ourselves worthy of the expectations that rest on us.

Anzeiger des Westens, 14 January 1861
(for Saturday, 12 January 1861)

United States Troops Arrive in St. Louis to Protect the Sub-Treasury

The arrival of a unit of United States troops under the command of W. J. Robinson excited no small amount of concern in our city yesterday. The troops entered the new Customs House or Post Office, where the Sub-Treasury is located, at 8:30 A.M. The Sub-Treasury usually stores a large amount of silver and gold.

Large groups gathered around the Customs House, drawn more by curiosity than anything else, but as soon as the crowd had gathered, a few secessionist leaders appeared and denounced the arrival of the United States military as an attempt to place the city under a military despotism, and they distributed an extra of the secessionist *Bulletin* that sought to raise the level of agitation by casting doubt on the plans of General Scott.*

Naturally all this failed due to the native good sense of the people. Everyone felt that the central government was compelled by the developments in this state and city to show determination to protect United States property.

Since the governor of Missouri has openly declared himself for secession;* since the legislature of this state has passed laws depriving the mayor of St. Louis of all power to suppress mobs, thus enticing all robbers and murderers to form mobs; since there is no doubt whatsoever that terrorists have plans to seize all United States property; since armed companies of Minute Men are forming, which all believe would cooperate with any such mob; since such an influential newspaper as the *Missouri Republican* still spreads the crazy idea that the Germans want to take over the Arsenal; since the telegraph has magnified all of these stories even more, is it any marvel that General Scott is concerned to protect the property of the United States?

Certainly if General Scott knew the local population well enough he would not have bothered to place a single man here. But since he gets so much of his information through lying and deceptive officials, since exaggerated newspaper accounts work their effects on him just as they do on other men, and since he is doubtless preoccupied with complex plans for defending Washington, he should not be criticized for extending his caution as far as here.

Those who keep their hands off the Arsenal and the Sub-Treasury are in no danger of being bothered by the troops stationed there; —those who shout their complaints about them appear to be disappointed—and the protection against them is more than justified.

Anzeiger des Westens, 19 January 1861
(for Thursday, 14 January 1861)

The Birthdays of Thomas Paine and Benjamin Franklin

will be celebrated in the hall of the St. Louis Turners on the twenty-ninth of this month.

Two names whose sound filled the world almost a hundred years

---

*Lt. Gen. Winfield Scott, general-in-chief in Washington, had been the Whig nominee for president in 1852. JNP.

*In his inaugural address, Gov. Claiborne F. Jackson had declared the destiny of all the slaveholding states to be one and the same. JNP.

ago and which are among the noblest man ever carried—and yet they are today almost forgotten by the very people to which they dedicated all their thought and feeling. Now and then printers still celebrate the birth of Franklin with a mindless dance party, now and then the old guard, the enlightened of an earlier generation, quietly celebrates the clear, brilliant, and liberating writings of Thomas Paine in lonely privacy—but on the whole it cannot be denied that the present generation of indifferentists or religious headhangers is not one that can recall these two great Americans with a joyous heart!

It is all the more welcome to learn, then, that *German youth* in the United States, in this age of acquisitiveness and self-indulgence, have committed themselves to venerating these two names that had almost been banished from the hearts of the people. One of them represents all the civic virtues of the American republic, together with all its wisdom and knowledge of everyday life; the other represents free pursuit of knowledge against the claims of blind faith; and each has earned the eternal thanks of the citizens of this country!

The people of the United States have abandoned the path set for it by the great men of the Revolutionary period; and as much as we commend the Turners for honoring these two names of republican simplicity, courage, and righteousness as is proper for young, enthusiastic, and virtuous German youths, we still cannot abstain from making the troubling confession that they are celebrating *past* virtues that are now seen as almost *ludicrous* in this country.

Friends, do not make any mistake about the value of your festival! You are trying to keep a tiny spark of republican virtue alive, and you have earned the praise of every good person by so doing. But the attempt will not succeed. People here are going their own new, bold ways—they are perhaps on their way to ruin, perhaps on their way to an astonishingly great future. Whatever you are trying to do, our times will not be held back from their appointment with ruin or triumph by the virtues of Benjamin Franklin or the enlightened spirit of Thomas Paine.

Whether ruin or triumph takes place, it will have to be brought about *by important, heroic men generated from the bowels of our own society,* or we shall have come to an end of our history. You are not going to save this republic from ruin or lead it to a great future with the spirits of Franklin or Paine, nor with the threatening shadows of Washington or Jefferson. This new, puzzling, chaotic time demands giants generated by this very time; men who, since they come from the midst of corruption, know what it is and go for its jugular.

In the midst of this time barren of spiritual greatness and civic virtue, go right ahead and warm your temperaments on the heroic figures of a better past—but do not expect that this cult will ever again become the cult of the people. Celebrate and you can be sure we will celebrate with you, but never forget that the past will never rescue the present, and that the people for this rescue must emerge out of the very epoch that must be saved from ruin.

Luther will no longer save the world from Jesuitism; the immortal Schiller will no longer return a consciousness of humanity to a depraved generation; it is not Benjamin Franklin who will lead this spendthrift, self-indulgent people back to civic simplicity—but *if* we are to be saved, then it will happen through our *own* efforts, through men who have experienced this corruption and have become great in *our* time.

So instead of a festival, deeds of great men once more; instead of remembrance of past greatness, the dawn of a new, better day; instead of laurel wreaths on the brows of *dead* busts, the sparkling eyes of *living* men, filled with freedom and virtue.

Mississippi Blätter, 20 January 1861

Legislature of Missouri

Jefferson City, 17 January 1861. When *Stevenson* of St. Louis* presented his excellent address on the basic constitutional position of the Republican party today, many secessionist members of the house sat as if on glowing coals. With my own ears I heard it discussed whether it would be advisable to prevent him from continuing to speak somehow, but finally the effort was dropped. Mr. Stevenson had not finished his speech at noon, so he resumed with full vigor after the break at 2 p.m. and pilloried Claiborne Fox Jackson and his entire fire-breathing ilk without mercy. I really do not believe that Stevenson has managed to draw many from the way of the unjust to the path of righteousness *in this house* with the speech, but it will have an important impact on public opinion when it appears in print, since the good sense of the people is still open to the truth in the last analysis, even though the majority of the legislators are corrupt and caught in the thrall of circumstances.

Your representative *John Sexton* declared openly yesterday in

*John D. Stevenson, a veteran Benton Democrat and ally of Frank Blair. JNP.

the house that he supported the "Union Men" who had organized themselves in the Court House in St. Louis last Saturday, and he claimed sole leadership over the movement.* In this matter, he said he probably differed from his St. Louis colleagues in the House of Representatives. In this last point he is doubtless correct, but it is also clear to me that he differs just as much with the almost unanimous views of *his own* constituents.

Perhaps the readers of this newspaper would be interested to know the place of origin of the state officials, senators, representatives, and subordinates in both branches of the legislature, down to the pages. A carefully compiled list shows that only 30 persons come from free states, specifically 8 from Pennsylvania, 6 from Ohio, 4 from New York, 3 from Germany, 3 from Ireland, and 1 each from Connecticut, New Hampshire, New Jersey, Massachusetts, Switzerland, and England, while 166 are arrivals from the slave states.

The members of the house were distributed in the following manner in a list that has come into our hands, according to origins:

Kentucky	39	Ohio	5
Tennessee	33	Pennsylvania	5
Virginia	22	New York	2
Missouri	15	New Hampshire	1
North Carolina	6	Massachusetts	1
Maryland	3	New Jersey	1
Delaware	1	Germany	3
Total Slave States	129	Ireland	2
[*sic;* should be 119]		England	1
		Total Free States	21

Among the members of the house there are persons of the following professions: 70 farmers, 26 lawyers, 9 merchants, 13 physicians, 2 newspaper editors, 3 factory owners, 3 mechanics, 2 goldsmiths, 1 shipbuilder, 1 tailor, and 1 contractor; by age, 7 are under 25 years of age, 12 between 25 and 30, 26 between 35 and 40, 24 between 40 and 45, and 21 over 50 years of age. (The totals are wrong in both of these tabulations, so there must be some small errors somewhere.)

---

*Sexton referred to a conditional Union meeting. JNP.

Mississippi Blätter, 20 January 1861

Legislature of Missouri

Jefferson City, 18 January. The amendment by Lacey that the house has attached to the convention bill was amended through the following motion by Senator Monroe:

> No act, ordinance, or resolution of the state convention shall be valid, nor shall any alteration or dissolution of the political relations between this state and the government of the United States or any other state take effect until a majority of the voters in the state shall have ratified the same through a referendum.

The amendment is in essential agreement with Lacey's amendment already adopted by the house, and the house approved it as well. The convention bill will now become law as soon as the governor signs it, which will naturally take place without delay.

The commissioner of the state of Mississippi, Mr. *Russell*, received permission to address both houses this evening in joint session, and he did so and delivered a fiery secessionist speech. He declared that the Union had been destroyed and that civil war had already begun. He called upon Missouri to join with the seceding states, since this was what its honor, peace, security, and welfare demanded. He painted the advantages that would accrue to the state in the brightest possible colors. The Democrats applauded vigorously, which was to be expected. (Does the legislature of Missouri have the right to allow itself to be officially harangued by a foreign emissary?)

Mississippi Blätter, 20 January 1861

Legislature of Missouri

Jefferson City, 19 January. Today a new "free Negro bill" was filed in the *House* that called for free Negroes who are convicted of a felony to be sold into slavery. The bill was rejected.

In the *Senate* the proposal to send a delegation to the consulting convention at Wheeling appears to have failed. *Goodlet* suggests in his substitute bill that representatives be sent to a convention of the border slave states in Baltimore. *Churchill* and *Johnson* are in favor of sending commissioners to Illinois.

The act of incorporation for the Mutual Assistance Society of St. Louis has been passed in the House.

Mississippi Blätter, 27 January 1861

Five Million

That is how much it is estimated that the state of Missouri will have to spend for defense and expeditionary costs if it declares for secession. We believe that this estimate is too low, particularly when we consider that Missouri is the most exposed of all the slave states because of its position, its borders, and its relationships. Bordered on three sides by free states, furthest extended into the North, Missouri would without a doubt have to withstand the greatest attacks of any. Montgomery and its forces would not be able to help on behalf of the Confederacy. Missouri would have to defend herself alone, and her western borders would have to be held by force. In the north lies Iowa. From that direction we hear that the feeling in Harrison and other Missouri counties bordering on Iowa is so strong that it is suspected that these counties will secede from Missouri and join Iowa if Missouri secedes from the Union. Even if these plans are doomed, as we believe, still it cannot be denied that they have the right to secede from the state at the same moment the state secedes from the Union. On the eastern border lies Illinois, a state that could cause Missouri a lot of trouble, and in whose power it stands to block the Mississippi at Cairo and thus cut St. Louis and the other river ports of Missouri off from the lower Mississippi, just as a war would cut us off from the upper Mississippi. Under these conditions it would be a serious consideration for St. Louis to secede from the rest of Missouri, and then confusion would be raised to the highest power.

If Missouri secedes, she would have to arm herself completely, and at least five million dollars would have to be raised for the war budget.

Where would this sum be found? At the moment Missouri declares for secession her public credit is dead. To float a public loan outside St. Louis would be impossible even under the best of circumstances. The state would be thrown exclusively on her own resources. To raise that much through emergency taxation would be every bit as impossible in these pressing times. What else would there be to do besides turning to the banks and wealthy men, as in South Carolina, and raising a "voluntary loan" through the use of direct or indirect pressure? And even this measure would only suffice for a short period in a long-term war. Open state bankruptcy, ruin of private property owners, emigration of many of the propertied residents, especially immigrants—in short, misery and want of all sorts would be the result of an ill-considered and treacherous withdrawal from the Union by this particular state.

And what would be the true motivation for such a damaging step? Perhaps the security of slave property? But who is not able to see that this property (which is endowed with understanding and its own will) becomes *ten times more insecure* on the day Missouri withdraws from the Union? The desire to secede does not come from fear for the security of slaveholding, nor from any of the other well-established complaints. In truth it rests on the private interests of a few persons who have the most to gain from the greatest disruption, and beyond that it rests on the "sympathy" of a portion of our population with their Southern cousins. But does such a sympathy, which is justified less through reason than through an unspecific feeling, have a prior claim on public support when another large part of the population inclines to the Northern population and its institutions? And when the dictates of reason and the clear, general interest of all citizens lie with the North as well? Even *if* all the slaveowners of Missouri had the will and interest to go with the South, which is not the case, should the *state* of Missouri declare itself that way *for that reason?* At the most there are twenty thousand slaveowners in Missouri, and together with their families they amount to about one hundred thousand persons total. The entire population of Missouri amounts to 1.2 million, so that the slaveowning interest amounts to *one-twelfth.* Should eleven-twelfths be ruled by the interests or preferences of one-twelfth? How does this square with our democratic institutions?

The slaveowning interest aside, what other interest or higher consideration would lead Missourians to cut themselves off from the old Union and exclude themselves from the neighboring states of Illinois, Iowa, and Kansas and to keep relations only with Arkansas? Not a single interest, and utterly no considerations. Humanity, loyalty, and justice, a hundred interests, all move us to keep our constitutional ties with the Northern states under all conditions. And this decision, we are certain, will be given *by the people* if it is ever given in a referendum the question, "Should this state secede under any circumstances?"

Anzeiger des Westens, 4 February 1861
(for Tuesday, 29 January 1861)

To All Steadfast Friends of the Union in This County!

Everyone will believe us when we say that we have never felt more the immensity of our responsibility than in the last few days. Have you thoroughly considered the situation of the Germans in St. Louis? Do you know the contributing factors through and through? Do you know how much a good and holy cause depends on you for its survival? Have you honestly asked yourself—and honestly answered—how much St. Louis, Missouri, and its adoptive citizens have to lose by leaving the Union? Have you decided to hold unconditionally with the Union as the only honest, intelligent, and decent path for a free man, and have you done this without consideration of party orders or party platforms or personal considerations, but solely as a result of the commands of conscience and of a knowledge of the best interests of this city and state, of your compatriots and of all citizens?

Our readers can believe every word when we say that we have considered these questions not simply in solitude but also together with the most dependable men from all classes and categories of society here, and that there are many other possible views that should perhaps be kept quiet in these troubled times, but that lead us to the same conclusion.

Within three days of the exit of the state of Missouri from the Union, there would not be a dozen respectable men in this city who would not mourn the loss of the Union, for which so many other people strive. The only people who promote disunion are unbearded youths, who have always played a disproportionate role in attacks on the Union, since they are themselves worthless and seek room for their wild thinking and striving in disorder and insecurity. Other than a handful of politicians disappointed by decades of defeat, they would constitute the total of the secession party. After barely three months had passed, an invincible party would form here to rewin the Union by all the weapons law or patriotism allows, while now men seek to do so only by the force of their wills.

What sort of person would not prefer to hold Missouri in the Union peacefully rather than allow it to withdraw and have to take it again by storm? No one doubts that if the Southern fools succeeded in their plans for Washington, the North would have to retake it—and what man with all five of his senses does not bless old General Scott for trying to hold on to something without violence that he would have to reconquer with streams of citizens' blood once lost?

Whoever believes in the Union should cling to it *now*, as one man, with all his spirit and bodily strength, with all his senses and abilities, with every muscle and nerve of his body. Keeping us in the Union will not cost us a hundredth of the effort it would take to bring us back into the Union once we have allowed ourselves to be forced out.

Citizens of St. Louis County, if you live a hundred years, you will never see days of greater responsibility for every one of you than those between now and the convention.

Say not that you have the right to vote on the results of the convention—do not say that or you are betrayed. Do not allow yourselves to elect halfway, lukewarm, two-faced, or entirely treasonous men to the convention out of pliability or indecision, since these men will not keep their promise to present their decisions to the people. Anyone who is traitor enough to sign a secession ordinance is traitor enough to cheat the people of its right to approve it. Why let yourself in for this danger? Elect men straightaway who will make known to the convention the full and unadulterated view of the people of this city, which is that they do not want to be separated from the Union, neither under this condition nor under that condition. Rest assured that such men would be a *power* in this convention.

And know what you have really done when you send fifteen unswerving Union men from this county. You not *only* have Missouri back in the Union, *but you have strengthened and preserved the bridge over which the South can return to the Union.* St. Louis was the city on which the eyes of both the North and South rested during the recent presidential election, and St. Louis is once again the city on which the eyes of patriots are directed from every corner of the Union. If St. Louis remains true to the Union, then the center is secure around which the conservative elements of the South may gather; if St. Louis is lost, then *we* will not give up hope for a recovery from the pestilential illness and a return to reason, but the thinly scattered Union elements in the whole South will be broken and humiliated when they see that the great city of a slave state that produced ten thousand Republican votes and twice sent one of the most free-thinking men in the entire land to Congress does not even have the power and courage to resist the advance of the cotton-knights of South Carolina.

You must therefore grasp how extremely important every vote in the next election is and how great the responsibility is in view of the importance of victory. Here in St. Louis there is not a single tailor or shoemaker, no shopkeeper or innkeeper, no merchant or manufacturer, no physician or lawyer, no average man or rich man, no worker or capitalist, who does not owe his entire past fortune to the Union and whose future prosperity does not depend on its preservation. St. Louis would be a ruin to end all ruins, Missouri would be a total desert, if the Union had not spread its wings over it. It is the Union that drew a population to this state and to this city—let the Union go and St. Louis is finished, and the only memory of this state will soon be its unpaid debts. Preserve this state in the Union and no one will dare to apply to *it* the word *treason*, and then we will have the right to arbitrate in the great struggle that now divides the land. For just as the two great systems of labor encounter one another on a large scale in the Union, so also they encounter one another within our state on a smaller scale. If Missouri decides to resolve this struggle peacefully by itself and without civil war, and if it sees its way to a better existence *within the Union alone* despite all of its supposed difficulties, then the bridge will have been built over which the South and the North will approach one another and join hands.

The entire dispute could certainly have been resolved by the politicians ages ago if the wit of these men had not been exhausted, their entire energy poured out, and the splendid capacities of their fellow citizens irritated and squandered by the thousands of local elections and detailed questions. Where all energy and argument, all purported patriotism and talent, are spent on a piddling mayor's race or a contest for a seat in Congress, where does one suddenly find the strength or enthusiasm to match the scale of danger when the well-being of every citizen, even the existence of the country, is in doubt? From this quarter very little help can be expected.

So in its hour of greatest need our country looks into the heart of every citizen, to the millions of loyal workers, ordinary men, men working their way up in the world by their own efforts, and our country places its destiny in *their* hands. *You* must save our homeland with your unsullied hearts, with your arms steeled by *honorable* labor—on you *alone* rests its sole, last hope! Speak out, as one man, and say that control over this city and this state belongs to *you*, not to this consciousless and accursed band of liars and office seekers, not to these unbearded boys and criminal semibarbarians, and never permit the slander to sully the pages of the history of this state: *Missouri, too, betrayed its mother, the Union!*

Mississippi Blätter, 24 February 1861

The Arsenal and Its Defenses. The Arsenal has now been garrisoned with five hundred men, behind whom a strong reserve force stands at Jefferson Barracks. The commander is Major Hagner, a very capable artillery officer. Second to him is Captain Lyon.* The infantry consists of six companies, each of seventy men; the remaining eighty men are artillerymen. All officers are enthusiastically in favor of the Union.

Captain Lyon, commander of the infantry, has distinguished himself since youth through bold deeds of war. Almost as soon as he left the Military Academy at West Point, he was sent to Florida, where he fought the Indians. Soon he was called from there to more honorable warfare, and he fought under Taylor and Scott in a large number of Mexican battles, at Vera Cruz, Cerro Gordo, Cortreras, Churubusquo, Molino del Rey, and before Mexico City itself. He was then sent to California, where he led difficult and successful campaigns against rebellious Indian tribes. If the secessionists give him the chance, they will certainly get an opportunity to feel his valiant hand.

Much has taken place quietly in the last few weeks to put the Arsenal buildings in a state of defense, and even without the bold support of the lower wards, which would be right at hand in case of attack,* Governor Jackson and General Frost would have a hard time getting anywhere with their Minute Men, should they be seized with the desire to try to take it.

The courtyard of the Arsenal is enclosed by a high stone wall, which is easily defended from the scaffolding recently erected behind it. Sentries keep watch, and one shot would call up the entire force. Each of the two gates is guarded by a 64-pound howitzer, protected by earthworks, and any column that would try to force entry would suffer certain death and ruin. The cannoneers who serve these guns are protected from shrapnel. Other cannon are

---

*Maj. Peter V. Hagner commanded the Arsenal, Nathaniel Lyon the men. As a brevet major, Hagner outranked Captain Lyon, but in his permanent rank of captain, he was the junior. He was also a less fervent Union man. JNP.

Nathaniel Lyon, 1818–1861, born in Connecticut, West Point class of 1841, served from 1854 to 1861 in Kansas and published antislavery articles in Manhattan, Kansas. He was assigned to the St. Louis Arsenal on 6 February 1861 for his brief ride to fame. He was an obsessive and suicidally brave leader, though those who came to know him in St. Louis thought him a thoroughly unpleasant man. Börnstein, who knew a bigot when he saw one, believed Lyon was a New Englander nativist to his fingertips. See *Dictionary of American Biography,* 6:534–35. SR.

*The lower (south side) wards were heavily German. JNP.

situated to control the railway causeways so as to make an attack from that quarter impossible, and others control the walls, so that they could destroy an enemy who has taken the walls.

Most of the weapons are in excellent condition, and men are hard at work making good any insufficiencies. Munitions are available in abundance. Most of the cannons are in condition for war use. Sandbags are ready to raise new bulwarks if needed. In short, one can say that the Arsenal has been put on a war footing.

Mississippi Blätter, 10 March 1861

German Immigration to Missouri. In Wisconsin newspapers we have found excerpts from the correspondence of a bureaucrat K. from Prussian Minden, and it tells us that a great emigration *to Missouri* is underway from various parts of Germany and Holland. He writes that permits have been issued to eight and ten families *a day* in the little administrative district of Minden, and that these families are taking their savings with them and heading for Missouri. This is largely the result of the efforts of our countryman *Friedrich Münch*, who made a tour of Germany in 1859 to agitate for immigration to this state.*

If the legislature were not doing everything it could to drive German immigrants away, we would probably be able to look forward to a very large immigration from Germany.

Anzeiger des Westens, 18 March 1861 (for Tuesday, 14 March 1861)*

A Whitewash for Missouri

is our state convention. The affair with the border terrorists and the baleful makeup of the last two legislatures have allowed the rest of the world to give up on Missouri. Outside people have become used to categorizing our state as the most reprehensible of all the

*Friedrich Münch's tour in 1859 was reported through Münch's columns in the *Mississippi Blätter* of summer 1859. He appears to have given special attention to recruiting experts in wine making. SR.

*The state convention, elected 18 February 1861, was made up largely of conditional Unionists, and its election was regarded as a setback for Jackson. SR.

slave states and our population as on the lowest level of decadence. Naturally, since "By their fruits they are known," so we can hardly complain when the staff of judgment is broken over us. And now this convention assembles, which shows not the slightest trace of the rowdy spirit, is in general so considerate and reasonable, and appears so thoroughly faithful to the Union that it is a genuine joy, even if it is a little pussyfooting, anxious, and wanting in energy. This, however, is the result of the fact that it is the first time the people have awakened and the first time the best men have not held themselves back. The legislature in Jefferson City, elected on 6 August of last year, and the convention in St. Louis, elected on 18 February, are like night and day. One is arrogance, arbitrariness, ignorance, and coarseness incarnate, the other respectability, goodwill, and complete dedication to the people and its interests! Hopefully the people as well as individual citizens will learn a lesson for all time from this.

Westliche Post, 25 March 1861
(for Wednesday, 20 March 1861)

All Important Missions Given Out

Carl Schurz Utterly Empty-Handed

The telegraph yesterday afternoon brought us the decision on the most important foreign missions. According to this, Schurz is definitely not going to Turin and Frémont has not received the French mission.* New Englanders are everywhere. They are all capable men, so nothing can be said against them individually. Since we have already said so much about the matter, we will satisfy ourselves with listing the names of the lucky ones: Minister in London: Charles Francis Adams of Massachusetts. Minister in Paris: William L. Dayton of New Jersey. Minister in Turin: George P. Marsh of Vermont. Minister in Constantinople: James Watson Webb of New York.

That is the end of the story. After Mr. Seward named his own son as undersecretary of state instead of Mr. Schurz, and after he sent

---

*Schurz's demand for a diplomatic post after Lincoln's inauguration was only the most visible symptom of disaffection with the new administration as far as Germans were concerned. They regarded the patronage they received as minimal, and they repeatedly spoke of a revival of the nativist side of the Republican coalition. SR.

Mr. Marsh to Italy instead of Schurz, now it is said that a bandage will yet be placed on the bleeding wound in the form of a German receiving an even higher office—*sure*. But only so long as Mr. Seward has nothing to say about it.

Anzeiger des Westens, 1 April 1861
(for Friday, 29 March 1861)

Mr. Carl Schurz Named Minister to Spain

Yesterday evening's telegraph brought the following very important decision:

New York, March 28

A special dispatch to the *Commercial* announces that the president has named Mr. Carl Schurz as minister to Spain in the place of Cassius M. Clay, who has volunteered to be transferred to Russia.

The special dispatch also announces that James S. Harvey, Washington correspondent for the *Philadelphia North American* and the *New York Tribune*, has been named minister to Portugal.

A second dispatch of 11 P.M. brings the confirmation by the Senate of Mr. Carl Schurz as minister in Madrid.

These dispatches dispel all the accusations of nativism against the Republican government with one blow. We do not doubt for a minute that these decisions come *directly* from Lincoln, and that they were done not only with the intention of giving deserved recognition to an extremely important man but also to make a definitive break with nativism.

So thanks, Mr. Lincoln, and rest assured that it took no less than this to placate the German element, which is always extremely touchy about its honor.

The Spanish mission is the most important one the president has in his gift, and Mr. Carl Schurz has received it.

Mississippi Blätter, 31 March 1861

The National Humiliation of the United States

Any child who has been in the United States for at least five years must have a lively memory of the grandiose rhetoric with which the people of the United States used to be regaled. The very same people who swore everlasting fealty to *Union and the Constitution* as recently as a year ago are now in the secessionist camp and do everything in their power to destroy that very same Union. Many also will surely recall a renowned gentleman who made a very great deal of noise in his time, but who now has vanished into thin air—we mean of course *Sir Manifest Destiny.* We no longer hear anything, neither in the North nor in the South, about this fearful Cyclops, who fixed the gaze of his single eye solidly on Cuba and who rested himself on the pillars of the Monroe Doctrine. Obviously he has emigrated, and it seems he has gone to—Spain!—scorned and downtrodden Spain, from which we have so long wanted to take the isle of Cuba. In the midst of the hubbub of secessionist madness, that old, talkative gentleman, *Manifest Destiny,* stretched himself out like a second Rip van Winkle to have a long sleep. The excessive pride of the nation has been broken, and normally this would be nothing to lament, but unfortunately some good has been lost with the bad, namely the pride and power of the nation in its dealings with foreign states.

Like vultures around a carcass, we shall soon see the mighty fleets of the European powers along our coasts ready to snap up every crumb that is fought over by North and South. When a nation is divided within itself, then neighbors are never lacking who are ready to assume their duties, and the destinies of Germany and Poland should be warning enough for all time against inner disputes.

What do we see already as a result of this crazy secession? The same Spaniards who trembled in fear of losing the Pearl of the Antilles for a decade have turned into conquerors, annexationists even, since the outbreak of treason in the United States. The Spanish flag has been raised over the island of Domingo, and a mighty fleet sails from Spain and Havana to take possession of the former empire of Soulouque.* In a word, the republic of the United States has forfeited its status as a great power in the eyes of the world as a result of the contemptible weakness or treason of Buchanan. A government that betrays itself in the way Buchanan's has deserves nothing better than contempt abroad, and this contempt eventually descends upon the entire people.

What are France, England, and Spain saying to themselves right

---

*In 1861, under pressure from Haiti and its own revolutionaries, the Dominican government invited Spain to take over its former colony. In 1865 the rebels drove the Spanish out. The new government requested annexation to the United States, but the United States Senate did not ratify the treaty. JNP.

now? Simply that the time has come to get as much American soil as possible. Earlier they would not have dared, since the United States had the sympathy of those nations' own subjects, even if the governments had been powerful enough to do what they wanted to do; now the unexampled cowardice of the Buchanan government has exhausted the last remnant of sympathy for America in the hearts of the European people, and the complex of North American states has been relegated to the same marginal status as the governments of Mexico, Costa Rica, and Paraguay.

But why should we complain? Not just the Buchanan government, but a large party in this country has always favored the proposition that the government should have *no* power whatsoever. It was demonstrated day after day that the president was powerless and had no choice but to give the reins to anarchy. Why should foreign powers respect a government that cannot acquire respect in its own land and that secretes the poison of despondency and pusillanimity in the heart of its own party, drop by drop?

They only waited for the appearance of the new government. The general opinion among European statesmen was that the Republican government would carry out the wishes of the people that brought it to power. They knew perfectly well that the government disposes of no large military power, but they also knew that here we have a system of popular rule and that a word from the newly elected president would stamp millions of armed men out of the earth. Now they see that they were wrong, and they are laughing; they are laughing at the democratic system and even more at the political lawyers who are studying how to run a government in Washington; they are laughing most of all at the fat morsels they can fish out of the troubled waters while the government in Washington preaches quietism and tries to divine the destiny of the land from the stars. In short, the secessionists have achieved their goal of ruining the reputation of the United States abroad as a great power. Unless the government of Mr. Lincoln or Mr. Chase* hurries up and changes its tune, we are very sorry for the freshly named emissaries to Europe who will soon be the laughingstock and kickball of all the other powers.

If only this cup of sorrow could pass by the great people of the North; if only the stupidity of the government were not so astonishing as to allow the whole proud structure to sink into the dust; if they were really so pitiful as to let themselves fall without daring to summon up the mighty powers that slumber in the North—then

*Secretary of the Treasury Salmon P. Chase, regarded by some as the strong man of the Lincoln administration. JNP.

the people, left to their own powers, must make the decision to remake their nation anew out of a new tempest and to obliterate through streams of blood the debits created by the cowardice of incapable men.

Anzeiger des Westens, 8 April 1861
(for Tuesday, 2 April 1861)

The Election Lost

We were beaten yesterday in the city elections, and it only remains to say why.*

Six weeks ago a ticket constructed on exactly the same basis, from the same elements, won by a majority of five thousand votes, and now it has been beaten by a majority of one thousand votes. How this change in public opinion was possible—this alone merits attention.

Between the election of 18 February and the election of 1 April falls the inauguration of the Republican government. The Democratic party had led the land to the brink of ruin—one hoped, and we know that even many of our political adversaries hoped, that the Republican administration would save both the country and its government. What happened instead? This government, through a perhaps excusable but still inexplicable and unjustifiable inactivity befitting a sleepwalker more than a government, has let the country just hang on the edge of ruin with neither aid nor counsel, waiting for some sort of miracle to pull things back into balance.

There is hardly an example in the whole of history to equal *this* policy for demoralizing both friend and foe. Thousands of its friends have declared that this government is not only not Republican, it is not even a government, and hundreds can be heard who have been so upset that they have withdrawn from political life altogether. Our adversaries mock us and say, If you cannot rescue the Union, then let *us* try. We want the Union, too, though differently formed than you do!

One party did not care much about holding the Union together if it could not be done its own way, and the other wanted to preserve it in a manner worthy of its creators' wishes, but *could not.*

*Democrat (not secessionist) Daniel Taylor defeated Republican O. D. Filley for mayor in April 1861—a surprising and shocking result for Republicans. Since its first city charter in 1823, St. Louis mayors had served one-year terms. JNP.

And so suddenly, or rather in the unheard-of short time of four weeks, all the limits of party and with them all party enthusiasm have been destroyed, while the central government goes on snuffing out all the newly revived excitement for the Union through its inexplicable incapacity.

The test of Union and secession, or rather unconditional dependence on the Union or veiled secession, was still at the top of the ticket, in the newspapers, and on the lips of the old party leaders—but it had disappeared from the hearts of the citizens, and the truly American response "I don't care a damn" completely overwhelmed this test. The Republicans, who were without a doubt unconditional Unionists but suddenly indifferent, turned to the Bell-Everett men, and the Democrats who were *supposedly* Unionists turned to them no less, but Republicanism and Democracy were nowhere to be found on the tickets or in the articles in newspapers dealing with the election; they were mixed together *pêle-mêle*, just as the political views and concepts were, and the tickets looked like it.

The good people were disappointed and lost their energy; the bad people began to present themselves as good because they felt their strength growing. Once principles had been abandoned and mere tactics and propaganda taken up, the position that supplies victory and true strength of purpose was abandoned and the former majority of this city fell into disarray due to the change of stance; it had already lost days before the election. Our adversaries, always conceded to be better managers, tacticians, and electioneers, quickly won the upper hand—for the mighty dam of principle that had always held them back no longer stood, and they have always been our superiors in electoral strategy and tactics.

Even the Germans started to become indifferent on occasion, even if they did not give way, *for as soon as an election is not waged on clear, unambiguous principles or using humane and noble elements, then its fate is in doubt.* This is their enviable privilege, but also their weakness in a land that has been ruled for over a quarter of a century in a more corrupt and unprincipled manner than any other country in the world.

In this manner we broke our very own legs and gave ourselves over as easy prey to our enemy. One single spark of life from the central government showing us that the executive branch stands with us and with our principles would have made us invincible. Its withdrawal from all positions dictates a similar policy for us—and just as this action dictates great troubles for all other places in the Union, so also it has harmed us in St. Louis.

So the work of a decade lies in ruins! Parties come and go, but the genius of mankind is immortal, and we flee to her flank to draw new strength from her breasts in our time of great need.

*   *   *

Still, the new municipal administration can expect us not to be an unreasonable opposition. We will give it full time for *a fair trial*. They promised to be true to the Union after the election, and they have thrift and a balanced budget as principles, so we shall see whether they keep their promises. If they do not keep them, the public will have given up on them before we raise a pen to give battle. We shall let them go their way in peace until they show prejudice against one part of the population or act unconscionably or waste money. If they reveal themselves to be what was feared, then we will battle them as we fought so many of the irresponsible acts of the earlier city government.

Anzeiger des Westens, 8 April 1861
(for Saturday, 6 April 1861)

We Have a Government

At least that is what at last appears from the dispatches of yesterday and the day before. We will leave it open whether it only *seems* so from this distance, since the new administration might have been planning policies in a new direction from the outset, but it appears that the Republican defeats in Cincinnati, St. Louis, and Cleveland *really* forced the government in a new direction. Our oracle here is the telegraph, and the New York newspapers that now are suddenly beating their drums appear to know no more than we do. We see ships fitted out, large bodies of troops gathered, but we do not know yet whither they are going or why. This much seems clear: the time of discussion about *which* side the government will take, the time of hesitation, is over, and in a few days the country will learn *that it has a government*.

Westliche Post, 10 April 1861

Arrest of Slaves in Chicago

Chicago, 3 April. A colored man named Harris, with his wife and two children, were arrested this morning on a warrant issued by United

States Commissioner Corkean. He was brought by special train to Springfield, where he will be heard tomorrow. The man was claimed as personal property by Mr. Patterson of St. Louis County, the wife and children by Mr. Vail of the same county; they had fled about three weeks ago. Since it was almost unknown that a warrant had been issued, the arrest took place with little difficulty. Once the matter became known, there was great excitement among the blacks. When the regular train was scheduled to depart, a great crowd gathered at the depot, since it was believed that the fugitive was on the train. Two or three shots were fired at the train; otherwise there was no disturbance of the peace.

Anzeiger des Westens, 19 April 1861
(for Tuesday, 16 April 1861)*

The Metropolitan Police and the Sunday Law

The Opera House Closed Down Yesterday Evening!

When many Germans worked and voted for the Taylor ticket during the last municipal election, the only excuse they could give when asked why was, "Oh well, we're tired of the Republican city government, we have *to have a change* for once." So now they are rid of the Republican city government under which we enjoyed four years of reasonable freedom and decent Sunday enjoyment such as was the envy of Germans in all other cities, and now we have our own sought-after "change."

Yesterday, on the first Sunday after the installation of the new police authority, which includes Mayor Taylor as a member, all saloons were closed, open-air musical performances and concerts were cancelled, and duly scheduled theatrical performances were blocked by force—even though no paragraph of state law bars theatrical performances or concerts or any other sort of entertainment, even though no municipal ordinances exist against them. The Opera House was forcefully closed at 7 P.M. by brutal and unlawful police measures.* We owe the public a simple, clear account of the course of events so that public opinion can decide on which side justice rests.

*The police bill, which transferred the appointment of the police board from the mayor to the governor, was passed in March. Republican mayor Filley was in office and was expected to be reelected. Union Democrat Taylor was preferred but not trusted by the governor. The new board president, John A. Brownlee, was an avowed secessionist. JNP.
*The St. Louis Opera House, opened in 1859 in the building of the closed Varieties-Theater, was Heinrich Börnstein's most ambitious cultural project in St. Louis. SR.

The director of the theater received no indication in the course of Saturday or Sunday that a performance could not take place. The director thus went ahead and sold tickets and reserved seats from a public kiosk, relying on the fact that there was no law against Sunday performances. This sale was not disturbed by the authorities, and only at 6 P.M., an hour before the box office was to open, Police Captain Rick arrived and announced to Mr. Börnstein that Mr. Brownlee had commanded *that no performance was to take place this evening.* Director Börnstein replied that such an order, which was not founded on any law, would cause painful losses to the owner and close the doors to over two thousand members of the public, and it would have to be given *in writing* and signed by a responsible official. Captain Rick left, and at five minutes before seven Police Chief James McDonough appeared and asked Mr. Börnstein not to perform. Mr. Börnstein replied that he knew his rights, that he had sold tickets for the performances and thus was duty bound to give the public a performance. If the police wanted to hinder the performance *by force* they could do it, since the power was in their hands; but Mr. Börnstein declared he would not be able to comply with this illegal order.

Mr. McDonough conceded that there was no such law, but argued that the new Metropolitan Police Law gave the commissioners the right to decree and enforce *any police rules they wished* if they held them to be necessary. Then a unit of police appeared in front of the theater, where the box office had already opened, and it blocked the public from entering. This naturally led to a crowd gathering in the street, and at 7:30 P.M. about two thousand persons had gathered in front of the theater. The mood of the crowd was foul, and the situation of the policemen standing at the doors had certainly grown precarious. Then Police Chief McDonough went to Mr. Börnstein again, who was in the office of the theater, and told him to inform the crowd that the performance would not take place. Mr. Börnstein refused to do this, since he *wanted* to perform; Mr. McDonough replied that he intended to seize the theater and presented the following written order:

St. Louis, 14 April 1861

By order of the Board of Police Commissioners I have taken control of Mr. Börnstein's theater on Market Street to prevent him from presenting a performance today, a Sunday.

Jas. McDonough
Police Chief

Since it had been demonstrated that might went before right and that Mr. Börnstein had no choice but to give in to force, Mr. Börnstein told the actors to get out of their costumes, and the lights were dowsed. At the request of the police chief, who was anxious about possible violence, Mr. Börnstein went to the front of the theater with the chief and made the following brief statement to the crowd:

Friends and Fellow Citizens!

The police chief has informed me that he has taken possession of the theater and will not permit a performance to take place, by order of the police commissioners. Since there is no law against theatrical performances on a Sunday, and since we were not informed in advance, I am very sorry that you have been expelled in this manner. I shall pursue my rights and demand compensation for the damages in court from the men who have forcefully interfered with the rights and affairs of citizens. (Stormy applause) I now ask you to return peacefully to your homes so we may show these gentlemen that the citizens of St. Louis are capable of ruling themselves without having a Metropolitan Police forced upon them. Good evening.

The crowd began to disperse, but as we write this, numerous groups of citizens, reinforced by late arrivals at the theater, have begun to gather in neighboring streets with an attitude to the Metropolitan Police that is less than friendly.

We have given special attention to this incident because it indicates the character of the new Metropolitan Police. According to the assertions of the police commissioners that they can *decree* any police rules they desire, all the liberties of the citizens have been utterly destroyed. These fellows, who have not been elected by the people but named by a secessionist governor, can regulate and tyrannize the citizens of St. Louis in any manner they wish; they can suppress the freedom of the press by taking by force any newspaper that displeases them, just as they took the Opera House last night, and by this means they could prevent the publication of newspapers; they could just as easily suppress the freedom of speech by taking possession of any assemblies that displease them, both preventing the people from exercising their freedom of assembly and speakers from making use of their freedom to speak. According to this doctrine, they could prevent citizens from taking walks on Sunday or even sneezing without the gracious permission of the police commissioners, if we follow the doctrine that they can *make* their own laws. The only question is how long the free citizens of St. Louis will tolerate such a regime of force. One thing is true, that if all innkeepers and owners of public facilities are handled in the manner of the director of the Opera House and Mr. Anton Niederwieser, it will not be nearly as easy for the police to subject free St. Louis to the yoke of the Sunday laws.

There is no tradition of regulation by prior restraint in the Amer-

ican republic such as there is in Russia or France, where the police
boldly intervene at will in the rights and affairs of citizens. Here
the police's function goes only so far as to arrest offenders of the law
and bring them before a judge, who then declares a penalty according to the prescribed laws. So we have no idea who gave the police
the right to push an audience *that had done nothing wrong* away
from a theater door or to throw men out of a saloon and dowse the
lights so the guests could not even find their hats on the way out. If
our lords the police commissioners have such powers, then no one in
St. Louis is secure in his person or property. There is no means of
defense against such a tyranny, other than insisting on one's
rights; anyone who shuts up and goes along without waiting for the
use of force sticks his own neck under the yoke, *and he deserves what
he gets.*

Anzeiger des Westens, 19 April 1861
(for Tuesday, 16 April 1861)*

The Scene at Tony's

   As early as Saturday evening a policeman let Mr. Tony know
quietly that his bar had to close at midnight. Since this decree of the
new Metropolitan Police had not been announced in any German
newspaper, as would have been the usual procedure, Tony paid no
attention to this tip and went on with business as usual. The number of customers grew around midnight, and among others Mr.
George R. Taylor, former president of the city council,* arrived in
the company of another gentleman he himself introduced to Tony
as His Excellency Claiborne F. Jackson, the governor of Missouri.
These gentlemen took their seats and tossed down a large amount
of German beverage until midnight was well past.
   About ten minutes after midnight several policemen appeared
and demanded once more that Tony shut his bar, since it was
Sunday. Tony told the policemen that *he* was not about to drive his

---

*This scene was played out at Tony's Tivoli, at Elm and Fourth, an establishment
owned by Mr. Anton (Tony) Niederwieser, soon to become a captain of Home Guards.
SR.

*G. R. Taylor was president of the Pacific Railroad. A native Virginian, he had
married into the Chouteau family and prospered in St. Louis. As the Democratic
nominee for mayor in 1859, he had lost to O. D. Filley. He was a shaky Unionist in
1861, a slaveholder with many friends in state Democratic circles. He was eventually
commissioned as colonel in the Union Army. JNP.

own customers out. If the policemen wanted to do it, they could come in and tell *these gentlemen* to leave first of all, and he pointed out Mr. Taylor and Governor Jackson. With the naming of their supreme leader the policemen shrank back, drank a few glasses of beer, and departed without making any further attempt to clear the bar.

Sunday morning at ten a policeman came to Tony's and told him he could continue to serve beer, but that playing pool had to stop. Tony once again refused to do the policeman's work for him. —Here were the pool tables, if he wished to drive the players away he could do it himself, but *Tony* would not do it.

In the evening (7 P.M.) police appeared once again, this time in force, and they drove the customers out and shut the bar. Several policemen were posted at the doors to make sure no one went in, and the police chief himself accompanied by three policemen closed the place down.

Governor Jackson was the important guest on Saturday at midnight, and the important guest at the moment of closure was former governor Stewart, so Tony's house was the scene of arbitrary police action in the presence of two governors, and so to the curses of life in the South, which we have long since learned to live with, are now added the curses of life in the narrow-minded North. Social life destroyed, an educational institution such as the theater closed—soon we shall lose the freedom of the press, and then, gentlemen, you will be able to say that both Austria and South Carolina will be at home in Missouri.

Anzeiger des Westens, 19 April 1861
(for Wednesday, 17 April 1861)

Not One Word More—Now Arms Will Decide

and if we could write bayonets, cannons, generals, and regiments instead of words, we would do it and place the whole legion under the command of our president.

There is only one duty for the citizens of this city, and that is obedience to the commands of the central government. The only source of rescue for the country is to support the legitimate government with might and energy.

Every question, every doubt has been swept away. The Fatherland calls us—we stand at its disposal. We wish to be ruled by law and not humiliated, conquered, and tyrannized by the mob rule of Montgomery or Charleston. We want to stand by the Union and not be led away into the Southland.

St. Louis has pronounced itself by a vast majority for the Union whenever the question of Union or secession has been posed to it openly. Very well, then, let us stand by this decision and hold this city in the Union, come what may.

The state has called a convention, and it, too, has declared its faithful loyalty to the Union by a great majority. Let us, therefore, keep not only the city but also the whole state in the Union.

Without any provocation, the Southerners have bombarded Fort Sumter. President Lincoln, as defender of the nation's trampled rights, has demanded an army of seventy-five thousand men from the states.

The Germans will make a major contribution to this army. We Germans of St. Louis know that we will not lag behind our brothers in the other states, and when the Union gives the call "To Arms!" and the stars and stripes are unfurled, then no German capable of bearing arms will fail to defend his hearth, his liberty, and his Fatherland.

Friends, do not beguile yourselves into thinking that mere words will resolve this struggle. Either the government in Washington will vindicate its authority and territory by force of arms or it will be ruined by force of arms. Whoever does not wish to be ground between two millstones should take one of the two sides. Have no doubt that the cause of justice and freedom is the stronger and that it shall win.

Anzeiger des Westens, 25 April 1861

Wire Dispatches

Jefferson City, 19 April, 8:30 P.M.

Fifteen cannon rounds were fired in honor of the secession of Virginia and one more for Governor Jackson. Great excitement prevails.

Special to the *Republican*
Boonville, 20 April

The largest rally in Boonville in ten years was held today. Seven hundred to eight hundred persons were present. A flag of the South with fifteen stars was raised—everyone is for immediate secession, Cooper County has only one will—for the South.

Independence, 20 April

The Santa Fe Mail arrived here today with news through the ninth. Business is bad. Reports from the mines are very good. Gold diggers come from all sides. The train of Majors and Russell, which was so long in the mountains, has finally arrived. Very early this morning the weapons and munitions at the arsenal in Liberty, Clay County, were given over on the demand of some citizens of the county. Thirteen hundred stands of weapons, ten to twelve cannon, and a great deal of powder was in the arsenal, and this materiel was distributed in Clay and neighboring counties. Some was brought to Independence.

Kansas City, 20 April

This morning Missourians took the United States Arsenal at Liberty and occupied it with a company of a hundred men.

Today a large secessionist rally was held here. Thousands from the surrounding counties in Missouri and Kansas were here. A pole 125 feet tall was raised with a secessionist flag hung on it, and the flag is also on many important buildings.

Leavenworth, Kansas, 20 April

Two thousand stands of weapons were distributed to the citizens of Leavenworth by the arsenal here, and the commander of the post took command of three hundred volunteers from the town to defend the arsenal. Preparations for all eventualities have been made. Otherwise all quiet.

St. Joseph, 20 April

Today the flag of secession was unfurled and carried through the streets by an armed company, and it was hung in the market square without trouble, but also without much enthusiasm. Great excitement. Dominant feeling is for the secession.

Mississippi Blätter, 21 April 1861

The Crisis

The Crisis was the title of a pamphlet Thomas Paine wrote in the midst of the noise of battle in the Revolution and by means of which he reawakened the sinking commitment of warriors for independence and filled their hearts with a sacred enthusiasm. It was a time "which tried men's souls": a struggle of seven years finally decided it in favor of independence and freedom. A few enlightened men who stood at the apex of the new philosophies of their own time laid the great and simple foundations on which this people would grow. These were the same principles as those of the French Revolution, the English Revolution, and any future revolution in Europe.

The fruitful lands of the new world and the appeal to all the oppressed and poor of old Europe quickly produced a constant, ever-growing procession of European immigration, which settled for the most part in the Northern states, where the climate of nature accommodated this immigration best of all. Every political upheaval in Europe had as a result a new, even greater hegira, and the revolt of 1848 and 1849 marked the highest point of this remarkable peaceful migration, which produced an unparalleled growth and increase of the Northern states.

But alongside this enormous increase of the whites crept soundlessly the increase of the blacks, the slaves in the Southern states. The invention of the cotton gin suddenly made the raising of cotton very profitable, and slavery, which Southerners regarded as an archaic institution doomed to disappear when they spoke of it in 1815, suddenly became a very profitable undertaking. The monetary profits of slaveowners quickly worked a complete reversal of the views of the Southern people, so that now slavery can be generally and unanimously praised there as a godly institution.

This relatively small number of men, accustomed to lead in the councils of the nation, insolent due to rapidly growing wealth, and trained by slaveholding to expect the immediate fulfillment of autonomous and despotic wishes, sought to preserve dominion over the North at all costs. Since 1819 and 1820 they were always certain of achieving their goal through the use of their ultimate weapon, the threat of division and civil war.

Their first definitive defeat was the election of Lincoln, and they moved at once to reach for civil war rather than give up dominion. It was clear to anyone capable of looking deeper that the system of slavery was in radical opposition to a truly democratic or republican government, and that sooner or later there had to be a clash between these material and human interests. Shortsighted politicians believed they had ended the danger when they got out of the way or made a diabolical pact with that ever-more-bloated monstrosity. Of course it did not help one bit. The opposing sides drew nearer to one another with the unswerving harshness of logic, and today the very existence of a system of popular government has been placed in question.

The question of slavery is no longer the first concern: it is only the basis, the starting point, of the party that wishes to overthrow the original system of the founders of the republic. In short, we have arrived at the second phase of the American Revolution, in which it will either recover the original principles of its foundation, or it will succumb to reactionary force; in other words, it will be decided in the eyes of the entire world whether this people will pursue its world-historical mission or whether it will sink into the ranks of decadent nations.

Many are only now learning that the development of this people is subject to precisely the same perils as all earlier peoples. Mighty Rome laid the foundations for its own decline when an overmighty and corrupt aristocracy took dominion for itself after the collapse of the free-soil party of the Gracchi. A victory of the two Gracchi would have reestablished a pure rule by the people, and it would have rescued the state from decline. The revolution in England, raised by the iron Cromwell, seemed to have been overcome for a time but preserved its essential content through the expulsion of James II, and at the same time it rescued the national greatness on foundations Cromwell had laid. Now we have our American 1688, when it is necessary to defend the basic principles by force of arms against an enemy the nation has nourished at its own breast.

With the victory of the Southerners the United States would become nothing more to the rest of the world than a South American or Asiatic colony—with the victory of the party of freedom, however, the names of Washington, Jefferson, etc., would gleam with renewed glory in the longing eyes of an enslaved mankind. With the party of freedom of this land stands or falls the holiest hopes of all self-sacrificing friends of the peoples of the entire earth; with the victory of the party of slavery the genius of freedom would snuff out his torch on the graves of the martyrs of freedom, and a fearsome time would commence such as that which followed the fall of the Roman Empire, when mankind had lost its faith in its own future and had forfeited its self-consciousness and pride.

Mississippi Blätter, 21 April 1861

Court Martial! Dreadful phrase! Who does not think at once of the scaffold of Arad or the moat at Vienna or Rastatt?—Could you believe it? And yet it is true, a court martial is taking place within our peaceful walls.

Major Schäfer has to appear before this kangaroo court, which smells of the noose, the gallows, lead, and blood, because he was so bold as to tell his former commander, "General" Frost, famed for bloodless duelling, that he could not serve under a traitor.*

The specifics of the indictment are (1) that Major Schäfer asserted that the general had permitted a portion of his command, the Minute Men, to raise a flag over their headquarters that represented treason against the legitimate government; (2) that Major Schäfer published the letter in which he offered his resignation before it was in the general's hands; and (3) that he accused his commander of other "infamous" untruths.

A fourth accusation was added to these three after the court martial had begun its session, which was that Major Schäfer had refused to recognize the right of "General" Frost to arrest him. Major Schäfer pleaded guilty to this last "crime," but "not guilty" to the others.

The court before which Major Schäfer now stands is made up of twelve persons, mostly declared and open cohorts of the "general" of the Minute Men, "Mr." Frost. Only eight of them were present, since the others seem to have been ashamed to attend. One of the leaders, or perhaps the leader, is a certain Shaler, major of the Minute Men. When he says "hmmm," the others follow in order, just as in the marvelous tale about the adventures of Hieronymus Jobs, the student of theology.

Yesterday "General" Frost and Major Wood were heard as witnesses for the prosecution. A motion to postpone proceedings to give the accused time to prepare a defense was denied, of course. Tomorrow the proceedings will resume. If Major Schäfer is convicted, which is inevitable under these circumstances, he can at least console himself with the fact that there is a higher court than a court martial in this country, *public opinion*, and it has already brought in a verdict against his accusers.

---

*The refusal of Governor Jackson to permit the recruiting of United States Volunteers requested by President Lincoln after the fall of Fort Sumter led to the resignation of a large number of officers from the Missouri State Guard, especially German officers. SR.

Anzeiger des Westens, 25 April 1861

Extra Session of the Legislature
Proclamation of Governor Jackson

A proclamation of the governor from Jefferson City, 22 April, of which a copy was obtained before this newspaper went to press, has called the legislature back into session in Jefferson City on 2 May "in order to act on measures and laws thoroughly to organize and finance the militia of this state and to raise the money to put the state in an adequate position of defense."*

*   *   *

The Militia of Missouri Called to Arms

An order of the adjutant general of Missouri has commanded the entire militia of Missouri to go into camps in their respective military districts and to remain there for six days. The quartermaster general will supply tents and camping gear.

The light battery and the cavalry squadron that were stationed on the Kansas border have been called to St. Louis to go under the command of General Frost.

Anzeiger des Westens, 2 May 1861 (for Friday, 26 April 1861)

The Armed Neutrality

of Kentucky and Missouri is so often mentioned in the same breath that there is a tendency to think of the states as twin sisters. This has always been the argument of the Half-Ways and Conditionals here, namely that we can always rest assured that Governor Jackson, a thoroughgoing secessionist, would behave like Governor Magoffin of Kentucky, since he would be much too sensible to upset matters as they stand. So far so good, and this comparison does seem a bit plausible at the start, but as events unfold the basic error of this argument starts to show. As the *Louisville Journal* shows us with utter clarity, the legislature would long since have met to pass

---

*The resulting measure financed the militia by seizure of the state public-school fund. Those involved understood that the "defense" was to be conducted against the United States. JNP.

a secession ordinance save for the threat of the banks to pull their money out of the state. Also we learn that the governor has prevented secessionist troops from marching to the South with the remark that there was plenty of work for them at home. Finally we see that this same governor carries on a secret correspondence with the rebel government in Montgomery and was asked by the so-called War Secretary Walker to provide a regiment of 640 men to go to Harper's Ferry to aid Virginia in its attack on Washington. Virginia was just as friendly to the Union as Kentucky until it was ready with its preparations for secession and war, and until it could declare openly for secession. Then it undertook to seize the Norfolk shipyards and Harper's Ferry to get weapons and war supplies. That has always been the policy of Jefferson Davis and the secessionists—lying, betrayal, and violence in a single breath. For that very reason do not allow yourself to be misled, but rather keep watch and arm yourself.

Mississippi Blätter, 28 April 1861

Court Martial, Conviction. The verdict of the court martial of Major Schäfer was announced in yesterday's *Republican*. It said, as expected, that he was "dismissed with disgrace." Mr. Schäfer is utterly indifferent to what people who are publicly pilloried by public opinion as traitors say about him. If they wish to cross sabers with him, they can come right down to the Arsenal with their Minute Boys.

Westliche Post, 1 May 1861*

Ceremony in the Arsenal

St. Louis, 27 April

Yesterday afternoon we had the good fortune of being ushered into the Arsenal along with the ladies who were to present a flag to

*On 23 April the enrollment and arming of the four regiments of United States Missouri Volunteers for three months service was begun at the United States Arsenal in defiance of the state government. Soon afterward twenty-one thousand sets of arms were sent to Alton by steamboat. A fifth regiment was signed up without advance authority from Washington, but did not enter active service until after the Camp Jackson raid. SR.

the Turner unit. The Turner companies were already drawn up in rows, along with Major Schüttner's battalion.* It was a strange, simple ceremony—without all the solemnity of something practiced ahead of time. The shy ladies stood with their flag opposite the battalion on the hill; the battalion marched in parade order to the sound of music around the ladies and formed once more in line. Then a color guard advanced from the ranks of Company A, led by Lieutenant Gollmer; Captain Lathrop accompanied it, and Mrs. Gempp presented the flag following a brief address. She was so overcome that she could not speak loudly enough. All those who stood there, not just the women but even strong men, had tears come to their eyes, despite the fact that no special fuss had been made. Strong feelings told each and every one of them that this flag, this staff with silk hung on it, was the symbol of the freedom of a great people, and the weaker part as well, the women, were filled with the patriotic hope that the men would defend this flag at all costs. When the columns marched along the wall we felt ourselves set back into the days of 1848 and 1849, and the dried-up milk of enthusiasm seemed in fact to flow again. If *these* masses of *this* people can just be brought to a molten flow, then a good metal shall be wrought worthy of a blade. At last, at last the Oden of enthusiasm has come among this people to make it a great band of brothers, and after its victory the world can say, "We offer a refuge and a homeland to all the oppressed and banned of the world."

Anzeiger des Westens, 1 May 1861

The Camp at the Arsenal. Yesterday morning we paid a visit to the Arsenal to seek out a few of our many friends who were now in the camp and to inform ourselves about the state of things. We are happy to be able to say that the morale of the volunteers could not be better. Their faith in their commander, Captain Lyon, is unlimited, and he earns it totally in view of his prudence and energy. Captain Lyon now commands without restriction, since General Harney and Major Hagner, who had limited his actions up until now, have been recalled,* and the new spirit that has become ob-

*Nicholas Schüttner (or Schittner), 1821–1868, was a carpenter manufacturing brick molds who organized his Schwarze Jäger company to counter the Minute Men. He became colonel of the Fourth Regiment, Missouri Volunteers, and served at Bird's Point in southeast Missouri. See Robert Julius Rombauer, *The Union Cause in St. Louis in 1861: An Historical Sketch* (St. Louis, 1909), 198. SR.

*General William S. Harney, commanding the Department of the West at St. Louis, had been summoned to Washington, primarily to answer questions about his con-

vious in all defensive institutions since then shows what a good thing that was.

Everyone is happy and healthy, and the most that the small discomforts and inconveniences can cause these gallant champions of the Union to do is to smile. Of course much was lacking in the first days, and we have to give credit to the fact that many of our compatriots who could not take up arms were able to contribute a great deal to the comfort and ease of the troops. Some few have already done their bit. Mr. Winkelmaier and Mr. Stählin each send a barrel of beer every day;* Tony, who has always had his heart in the right place, sent several cartons of cigars (it is well known that he has continued to pay the wages of two of his people who have joined the artillery. A splendid example!) A tobacco merchant has sent a supply of tobacco, etc. Anything can still happen, and we do not doubt that it will happen in excess.

Among the troops we saw a cheerful lad of thirteen or fourteen years of age who had run away from his father, a respected citizen, to sign up as a drummer boy. Today he had to give up his military career when his father came to take him home.

Several fortifications have been thrown up within the thirty-acre area of the Arsenal, which is surrounded by a high, strong wall. Now work will begin on the outer fortifications as well.

Yesterday afternoon an artillery company of Sigel's corps was moved to the Marine Hospital,* and the Schäfer battalion has occupied the heights near Concordia Park. It is said that a battery will be set up on Duncan's Island.

The total number of volunteers sworn in up until now cannot be much more than two thousand. Sigel's corps now has a full seven companies, including two artillery companies. Yesterday afternoon a company made up entirely of Americans entered the camp, commanded by Frank Manter, president of the last Republican town council. Carondelet has already sent its company, and a second, under the command of Henry Miller, a member of the legis-

---

ciliatory attitude toward the recalcitrant state authorities. Frank Blair, who had directed a stream of complaints about Harney to Washington, saw the general's absence as an opportunity for decisive action. Harney had not been "recalled" at this point. JNP.

*Winkelmaier and Stählin, brewers, were typical of their profession for being ardent Unionists. Julius Winkelmaier and George Schiffer were brewers on Market Street between Seventeenth and Eighteenth. Stählin and Halm were the owners of the Phoenix Brewery, Lafayette at Second Carondelet Avenue. See St. Louis Directory, 1860. SR.

*The Marine Hospital stood between Marine Avenue and Second, south of Miami. See Compton and Dry, Pictorial St. Louis, plate 12. SR.

lature, will soon be full. A company has also been promised from Ste. Genevieve. So St. Louis does not stand entirely alone in Missouri!

By the end of the week there will probably be very little left lacking of the four regiments Missouri has been allotted, and then the main energy will go into creating a strong and competent Home Guard, for which the basis has already been laid.

St. Louis, 28 April

Westliche Post, 1 May 1861

The New Direction in the Spirit of the Nation

What we have long predicted along with others has at last come to pass. The North has awakened from its slumber; the earth shakes under the tread of its legions, and the South trembles. The youth of the land streams to the flag in its enthusiasm; the spade and plow, the hammer and the ell are thrown aside by all who feel strong enough to carry a weapon. The two sides, which have contested for so long under false colors in the halls of legislatures and in the Capitol, have stepped into the open field to fight with weapons what could not be settled with arguments. The lovely speeches of our politicians are now a thing of the past; so also are the tricks and deals that were fixed by those worthless people who worshiped the dollar alone. Suddenly a new race arises like a phoenix from the general conflagration, and our workaday politicians sink into the oblivion they deserve. War will naturally make a great rent in our current relations; much personal misfortune, much suffering and tribulation will follow from it, but the great goal of mankind—the demand for freedom—will rise ever more glorious and flow like gold in the heat of the fire of battle.

War is often gruesome and destructive, but no more so than the purifying storm and the welding lightning, which strikes its victims with all the necessity of nature. War is also a school, a strict educational institution from which the right men emerge. Long peace promotes the lower, petty passions of men, while the perils of war bring to life noble feelings of self-sacrifice, valor, and magnanimity toward the conquered and the prisoner. A war, even a short one, will give this land a youth that is not too precious to be bought even with the greatest sacrifices; a generous, patriotic band of men who will in time spurn the temptations that once victimized them; a class of men who shall serve the nation for its own sake and not for the sake of profit; sworn enemy of all baseness and corruption that now infests society, a poison that will effectively purge poison.

The perils foreseen by pessimists, those of a standing army, a rule by dictators, and military rule, are a chimera whose pointlessness is easily shown by the character and grandiose scale of this land. So let us get to it and clean this Augean stable so that freedom can prosper in purer air.

Westliche Post, 1 May 1861

A Secessionist Demonstration That Came to Grief. Yesterday evening about 7 P.M. a red-haired son of the Emerald Isle showed himself at the corner of Fourth and Elm with a rectangular lantern with only one legible pane, on which could be read: "Shall the majority be ruled by the Dutch?" —Some German boys, who seem to have already followed him for a while, tore the lantern from his hand and stomped it in the dust. Pat showed little desire to fight, but after a few pushes and blows he took flight to the merriment of the crowd of several hundred that had rapidly gathered.

Anzeiger des Westens, 9 May 1861
(for Thursday, 2 May 1861)

The Arming of the Home Guards

continued along its sure course yesterday.* In the morning it was the turn of the contingents of the third, fourth, and fifth wards. The wards marched in a force of about thirteen hundred men to the Arsenal, including three companies of Americans and one French company, with the rest naturally all Germans. In the center of this seemingly endless procession was the banner company of Captain Tony Niederwieser with its imposing white-haired flagbearer D. Krebs, the father of the pastor, who marched alongside him shoulder to shoulder. The chief decoration of the procession was the Turner Zouave Company in the vanguard in its extremely impressive and comfortable uniforms. After all of the companies were mustered, sworn in, and armed, which took about four hours, they formed up while the Sigel Regiment began its regular evening

*The arming of the Home Guards is described in Rombauer, *The Union Cause*, 219–21. SR.

parade, which made an extremely fine show. Before the Home Guards of the three central wards marched out, that of the seventh and eighth under Colonel B. Gratz Brown* marched in, a good eleven hundred men strong. As their muster began, the first unit turned toward the city with flag flying, to the tune of the music of Böhm's marching band. It returned to its headquarters at the Turner Hall, where the forest of shining bayonets excited great enthusiasm. It was late in the evening before the seventh and eighth wards were armed, and then these made their return march through the city to rousing music. A grand, proud future now unfolds before us.

Westliche Post, 8 May 1861

(Correspondence of the *Westliche Post*)

Lexington, Missouri, 3 May 1861

Dear sirs,

As soon as a pro-Union meeting was announced yesterday, you could see the secessionists getting their heads together. Some rowdies just returned from Pike's Peak showed up as if they had been summoned, and whatever the leading local louts had not dared to do, namely to break up the pro-Union rally at all costs, was undertaken by these sneak-thieves in exchange for some whiskey and a good payoff. In order to strike fear in the pro-Union element in advance and to keep people away from the meeting, a fight was picked as early as 4 P.M. with one of the most peaceful citizens of the town, Mr. Chr. Schäfermeier, a German, and two shots were fired at him. Mr. Schäfermeier escaped unhurt, while an attacker shot one of his own cohorts through the arm. That evening, despite all of this, and despite various other efforts to discourage them, the pro-Union meeting took place with over five hundred people present to hear brave orators such as W. G. Field speak to continuous applause. Suddenly a band of thugs armed to the teeth broke in, planted themselves in front of the podium, and raised a ruckus while waving slingshots, clubs, and revolvers, so that order broke down and the speakers could not be heard. Then the leader of the rascals, Charles Martin—the very same person who had fired at

---

*Benjamin Gratz Brown, 1826–1885, one of the earliest open opponents of slavery outside the German community in Missouri, would serve as Missouri's United States senator from 1863 to 1867 and as governor from 1871 to 1873. See *Dictionary of American Biography*, 3:105–7. SR.

Schäfermeier—charged the podium to seize the Union flag. Mr. Nic. Haerle, a German, snatched it away from him with a "Hurrah for the Union" and fell at once, stricken by a bullet and several balls from slingshots. Haerle, who had only been stunned for a moment when the bullet had pierced the flesh of his thigh, quickly arose and left the hall with his flag, shouting "Hurrah for the Union" in the face of the curs who pointed their revolvers at him. The "brave," cowed pro-Union people had meanwhile fled through windows and doors, and the meeting was well and truly adjourned. I am ashamed to confess to you that it took at the most fifteen or twenty rowdies to disperse five hundred pro-Union people. A kingdom for ten pro-Union rowdies and Lexington is ours! Could anyone send us French Louis?

Right now all hatred is concentrated on the "Dutch," and they will soon receive the blessings of mob law. Many have already made themselves ready to depart. At the moment the secessionists have gathered in the Arkana Hall, and many Germans are expected to be forced to leave—if nothing worse happens to them. The sword of Damocles hangs over everyone's head. Day of Reckoning, can you be far off?

Westliche Post, 8 May 1861 (for Friday, 3 May 1861)

Citizens of the Free States!

Placed on an exposed bastion of freedom in the current struggle to uphold the constitution of our land, in obedience to the call of our president, we are undertaking to organize volunteer regiments for the service of the United States in Missouri. Living in a state whose supreme magistrate has denied obedience to the federal government and from whom not the slightest cooperation to aid the federal government can be expected, we, the Missouri Volunteers, are relying utterly on the sympathy of the free states, which have risen as one man to preserve the constitution of our country, to supply the pecuniary means to raise the first and most necessary supplies for our volunteers. Many of these volunteers are poor and lack the means to pay for basic clothing, uniforms, etc., out of their own pockets, since they can only expect to be paid at the expiration of their three months of service. So we appeal to the sympathy of friendly fellow citizens in the free states, and we live in the hope and conviction that this support shall not be denied us, just as needy fighters for the good cause of our common Fatherland are not neglected in their own areas. Relying on this support, we shall strain every nerve to maintain the authority of our federal government against every treachery in this distant and important outpost of the West, and with the most of our strength we shall work to accomplish quickly what all patriots and friends of the Constitution desire, which is that the rebellion be dashed to the earth forever, and that the triumph of the cause of justice and freedom will be secured against rebellion for all time.

Governor G. Körner, Belleville,* has agreed to receive any donations for the purposes described and to forward them to us.

The Volunteer Regiments of the State of Missouri:

Frank P. Blair	Colonel, 1st Reg., M. V.
Henry Börnstein	Colonel, 2nd Reg., M. V.
F. Sigel	Colonel, 3rd Reg., M. V.
Schüttner	Colonel, 4th Reg., M. V.

N. B. All Unionist newspapers are asked to print this appeal.

Westliche Post, 8 May 1861

Legislature of Missouri

At the session of the *house* of 3 May a long debate took place during the election of a speaker pro tempore, which ended with the election of *Harris* of Marion with forty-eight votes against Colonel *Boyd*, a Union man.

In the course of this debate, Mr. Vest,* the leader of the secessionists, spoke in such a way as to shed some light on the plans of his party.

He said that the curse of the last session had been the squandering of so much precious time to so little purpose through the "verbal diarrhea" of the members, and that this had led to a neglect of the larger interests of the land. The crisis was such that there was no time to waste with useless debates. He wanted to express himself as

*Gustav Körner was, in fact, quite surprised to find that he had been named to receive donations for Missouri: "Of course, I could not refuse. But it gave me a great deal of trouble." See Gustave Koerner, *Memoirs of Gustave Koerner, 1809–1896*, ed. Thomas J. McCormack (Cedar Rapids, Ia.: Torch, 1909), 2:148. SR.

*George Graham Vest, of Boonville and later Sedalia, served in both the Confederate army and the Confederate congress during the Civil War. He was a United States senator from Missouri from 1879 to 1903. JNP.

briefly as possible. The greatest crisis had come, "the writing of the Black-Republican, nigger-loving United States is now visible on the wall." We should act at once to put aside party and act for the good of the state. *Missouri does not need a dis-Union ordinance. It is in fact already out of the Union.* Virginia is out, thank God! North Carolina and Tennessee soon will be. *None of those states had to pass secession ordinances.* During the last session he had tried to make these facts clear to the house. Lincoln had already taken twenty-one thousand sets of arms out of the state. He wanted to say to the house that Lincoln does not want to allow Missouri to stay out of the Union. It will be forced out by him or must become a degraded appanage. Let this house get right down to work and arm the state, if it can be done. *Let us march to meet these Black-Republican nigger-loving nigger-stealing hordes now descending upon us.*

Since Mr. Vest spoke last of all, just before the vote for president pro tempore, no one could answer him in the manner he deserved. But from his words we can see sufficiently what Governor Jackson and his secessionist supporters take to be "armed neutrality." They see no need for a secession ordinance, and they desire *that neither the people nor the state convention be polled on secession, but rather that the governor and his aides should arbitrarily declare the state seceded and join it to the Southern Confederacy.*

They only delay doing this until the legislature grants weapons and money. The chief power of the legislature is to *deny* this; if it had already done this, it would no longer be asked to do anything. All members of the legislature loyal to the Union desiring to protect their compatriots from ruin and civil war should join together and deny the governor what he wants—the secession of the state from the Union, as he has shown again in his latest messages to the legislature—by granting him neither men nor weapons nor money. No reasonable man can doubt what he would do once he got them. It is inconceivable that anyone who says he is for the Union would support arming the state under this governor. In this manner General *Price* proclaimed at the same session in which Vest made his revelations, "In the armament of the state he would go as far as any member of the house," and yet he also declared his unaltered loyalty to the Union. Is this not like selling a weapon to a robber and placing it in his hand even though I am convinced he will only use it to attack me?

This was the last public session of the house. From now on they will proceed in secret as a result of Vest's motion. General Price opposed this motion in vain. The Speaker decided that the debate on the motion should take place in a secret session with closed doors, and then the house was cleared of observers.

It is believed that the secret sessions will last three, four, or more days. Doubtless the secessionist leader wants to arrange his revolutionary measures in these sessions so that everything will be absolutely ready to carry out secession without an ordinance. Instead of receiving their instructions from the people, they would rather command what they want. Worse than Russia!

On the afternoon of 3 May the question of closed sessions was debated in the *senate* as well. Contrary to expectations, the motion was opposed, but it passed. All members of both houses have sworn to keep the proceedings of these closed sessions secret.

Westliche Post, 8 May 1861

The Flag of the Third Regiment

St. Louis, 4 May

The Third Regiment under Sigel* now has a flag under which it will know how to fight—and woe to him who does not do so. The time of *men* has now come, the time of honorable men who want to give their drop of blood for the Fatherland if the Fatherland needs it. —The presentation of the flag to the Third Regiment took place yesterday in the Arsenal. An enormous number of people got in somehow, despite the rules about passes. Most of them were ladies, of course, since they can enter without passes. Unfortunately there were also a large number of children along. If a father has a young comrade, say of eight or ten, then he should bring him along so he

---

*Franz Sigel (1824–1902), colonel of the Third Regiment, was often spoken of as "General" Sigel because of the rank he had held as commander of the revolutionary army in Baden in 1849. Due to his political radicalism, his strong involvement in the Turner movement, and his extensive writings on military theory and practice, Sigel was lionized by the German press as some sort of military genius whose mission was to show the Americans how wars were fought. He had come to St. Louis to teach mathematics at the Deutsches Institut, and he was deeply involved in secretly training the Turner Society for armed defense in 1860–1861. He was closely allied with the radical Germans in New York, and he declined the offer of a regiment in New York in April 1861. His actual record in combat was very mixed, but he became a symbol of German participation in the war effort. He named his regiment "Lyons Fahnenwacht" (Lyon's Color Guard) in defiance of the American custom of using only English titles for militia units. SR.

can always remember seeing his father bearing arms once, but we do not have any idea what small, crying children are doing in such a place.

It almost seemed as if the whole brotherhood of humbuggery had been called up, and that the Arsenal had become a playground for little children and their nannies. We would like to recommend to the commandant never again to permit such a visit under any circumstances, for it is impossible to instill military discipline when the Arsenal is turned into a game of hide-and-go-seek.

But back to the festivities! The ladies' flag earned universal admiration from all sides. It was the usual flag of the United States in double silk, with the stars embroidered in silver, and among the stripes were the words:

III. Regiment

MISSOURI VOLUNTEERS

Lyon's Fahnenwacht

At 1 p.m. the ladies were invited to present their flag, and after the Sigel Regiment had formed itself in rank and file, Miss Josephine Weigel delivered the flag to the commander, while she delivered the following words to the general, spoken in a clear voice:

> General Sigel!
> It is a great honor for us to present you with this flag, made by German women and maidens, for your regiment.
> Germans can bear themselves with pride since men and youths stream to you as to no other to protect their adopted Fatherland against the most shameful and disgraceful treason, in keeping with their oath of fidelity.
> In keeping with old German custom, we women do not wish to remain mere onlookers when our men have dedicated themselves with joyful courage to the service of the Fatherland; so far as it is in our power, we too wish to take part in the struggle for freedom and fan the fire of enthusiasm into bright flames.
> Shame and disgrace to the German man who does not offer everything to the Fatherland in its hour of peril.
> Receive this flag, my general! Let it unfurl and wave when it leads a victorious path for freedom, so that it can be cited in the history books: the flag of the Third Regiment, Lyon's Fahnenwacht, cut a path for freedom through the poisonous mists and announced the rebirth of a united, great, free Fatherland.

As the flag was handed over, the cannons on the river thundered a greeting. General Sigel answered in English, and very well; when he grasped the flag and unfurled it, the cannons saluted; then he expressed in simple words the convictions for which so many had sacrificed for half a generation and would continue to do so even longer. He declared that he hoped his men would never desert this flag save through death. After Sigel, Captain Lyon said a few excited words, both complimentary to the Germans and an honor to himself, since he demonstrated that he is an enthusiastic friend of freedom—one of those modest men who only step forward when the Fatherland is in peril.

When Captain Lyon had spoken, the color guard took the flag to a nearby hill, and the entire regiment lined up before it; Mr. Scherff then sang the song "Die Fahnenwacht" in a powerful voice with good delivery. The many onlookers forgot their clapping and shouts and stood in utter silence. Everyone marveled that such a regiment could be brought into being in fewer than fourteen days, for Sigel's Regiment has almost entirely new companies, since the Turner companies A, B, and C are in the F. P. Blair Regiment.

Anzeiger des Westens, 9 May 1861 (for Tuesday, 7 May 1861)

From Jefferson City

From this, the most obscure of all the spots under the sun, we hear the most marvelous things. Since sessions are secret, and since this brood does everything as secretively as if it had to shun the light of day, we learn everything we know through a sort of inspiration; our readers can judge how inspired are the specters that whisper to us by the fact that they gave us the governor's message twelve hours before it was presented to the legislature.

First of all we learn that the political doctrine of the majority of the legislature is that Missouri has already left the Union. Lincoln's declaration of war and the governor's reply to it are tantamount to withdrawal. Further, Lincoln has expressly recognized the separation of Missouri by the measure "That he caused weapons that belonged to Missouri by force of law to be taken from Missouri to Illinois." This doctrine springs directly from the brain of the denizen of a madhouse, with whom reason is futile and for whom other methods of cooling the inflammation of his brain are necessary.

And now to their plans:

1. The governor has presented the correspondence betwen Cap-

tain Lyon and the Metropolitan Police here to the legislature and demanded its intervention.

2. He has asked the legislature to place a military force opposite Cairo to prevent ships taking supplies to the South from being hindered by United States troops.

3. He intends to give an order to the Metropolitan Police here to hinder the issuing of weapons from the United States Arsenal to states friendly to the Union.

This last measure reminds us of the peasant who locked the barn door after the cows had been stolen. Still, the governor will have a great deal of trouble hanging a lock on this barn door by himself after the iron cows have vanished! Might helps right, that is how it is and that is how it must be.

Finally, they even want to expel Captains Miller and Cavender of Frank P. Blair's Regiment from the house, whose members they are, because they have placed themselves under their Fatherland's flag.

All of this illustrates the doctrine that Missouri is already out of the Union. Still it is a good thing that there is no secession ordinance in the statute books. Then they will not have to pass any *expunging resolutions*. We shall *now* see where they shall find the money and men to uphold this new doctrine.

If secession cuts as poor a figure everywhere else as it does in Missouri, then it would be a threefold embarrassment for the government of the United States if it cannot finish the whole swindle in three weeks.

Westliche Post, 8 May 1861

Patriotism in Missouri

The enthusiasm for the Union, even in the *slave state* of Missouri, often shows itself in an extremely naive, touching fashion. An example of this came to us yesterday in the form of a letter that a respected local wholesaler received from one of the counties of Missouri, which reads roughly as follows:

Dear friend,

    The bearer of this letter, ———, is my nephew, the only son of my sister, just eighteen years of age; he has decided to join the struggle for freedom and believes that St. Louis is the place where he can best do his duty. I commend this young man to you as if he were your own brother; he is as dear to me as my own son . . .

We are seeing things like this every day. On the evening of the day before yesterday, for example, some six young fellows were camping in the Turner Hall, none of them more than eighteen, none of them with another place to go, or perhaps none of them wanted to be any other place, and they slept there under the watch of adults. These poor youngsters were bedded down on the hard floor, but each possessed the joy of a youthful commitment, each was filled with the most splendid longing that could occupy the heart of a youth of eighteen, enthusiasm for freedom.

Westliche Post, 15 May 1861

Rumor of a Campaign Against Jefferson City

Union People Driven Out of Several Counties

(Correspondence of the *Westliche Post*)

Jefferson City, 7 May 1861

Our town was greatly agitated late yesterday evening, and the secessionists both inside and outside the legislature trembled at the rampant rumor that Frank Blair was on his way with eight hundred to one thousand soldiers to crush the head of the entire secessionist movement. It is true that they would be entirely defenseless here, and there would have been no thought of resistance.

Little or nothing can be learned of the doings of the legislature, at least as far as the all-absorbing political questions go, since all discussions take place in closed sessions. It is only known that every day an attempt is made to open the debates to the public; it hardly seems likely that this will actually happen. Our members of the legislature keep secrets even more strictly than they are obligated to do.

News has come from several neighboring counties such as Moniteau, Benton, and others that Union people have been chased from house and land where they have not united and defended themselves. There is as little respect now for property as there usually is for life.

In all these matters the governor has either done nothing or has indirectly indicated his approval. It is impossible to say what will happen if no strong power intervenes. If this does not happen, then we are on our way to total anarchy.

Westliche Post, 15 May 1861

Legislature of Missouri

Jefferson City, 8 May. The house discussed the militia bill today in a closed session.

In the senate a joint resolution was passed unanimously today *suspending the distribution of the school fund.*

Senator *Churchill* of St. Louis made a long speech in the Senate *recommending that all available money be used to arm the state, even the interest fund*—so that the interest on the state debt would not be paid in July; in other words the *state would be declared bankrupt.* This is the way traitors deal with the state's funds to realize their treachery, to compel the state to secede!

Finally, *both houses* have passed bills authorizing Governor Jackson to extend the "practice camps" beyond the required six days— probably for as long as the governor wants it.

In this manner, the governor and the majority of the legislature, which have broken faith with the Union, dispose of state funds collected for entirely different purposes in order to hand the people who elected them over to the hated Southern Confederacy and then bind the people in chains.

How long will the sovereign people endure such contempt from its own servants?

Anzeiger des Westens, 9 May 1861
(for Wednesday, 8 May 1861)

Come on, now, Friends of the Union

both here and all over the country—bring the people the good news that this beautiful, great, populous city of St. Louis *is secure for the Union from this moment on and remains solidly in the Union* and that no Governor Jackson, no legislature, no Minute Men or traitors, however they come or however many there are, can rip this city out of the Union. *Eight thousand* bayonets, borne by brave, loyal Missourians, are the bodyguard of the Union in St. Louis, and ten thousand houses, fortresses of patriotic citizens, will have to be stormed one after another to drive the Union out of St. Louis.

We were beaten in the last election—it could not have been any other way: the government had done nothing for the Union, so how could it expect *us* to do something for it. But as soon as the traitors showed themselves openly, the citizens of this loyal, free-spirited town rose up and organized an army of warriors to protect the property of the United States such as no other town of equal size in the whole country has formed. Here there sits a secessionist mayor, freshly elected by a majority of eight thousand votes; here rules a secessionist police appointed by the governor* . . . and under their very eyes the entire city arises and stands armored and weaponed like a giant against their treason.

The glory belongs to you, our German compatriots; you were the first to declare yourselves for the Union with your enthusiasm and your whole might. You were cool enough when the flag of betrayal first fluttered over the Minute Men's headquarters. The feelings of all were injured; you felt yourselves shamed and humiliated! You put up with it until the moment your patience was taken to mean cowardice! You took your time, and *now* you can gaze on the tattered rags with a pitying smile.

Keep your blood cool even now, as you march out in full regiments under the Union flag—for the strong should be calm, and you are not dealing with *enemies* but rather with confused, misled *fellow citizens*.

Thousands of native-born fellow citizens have stood at your side in the last few days, and if the central government holds to the right course, which it seems to be doing, secession and treason will soon be but a memory, and the sooner it is over the better it will be for the peace and well-being of this country.

The Union power of St. Louis has now been organized, and it only remains to keep it as it is; do not fight with one another, but consider that only unity makes you strong. More than anything else, you must keep your faith in the Union and in freedom, and find no place for doubt in them. Whoever doubts is already half a traitor, whoever is not entirely for you should be seen as entirely against you. For freedom and the Union, for the preservation of German honor and manhood—under these mottos only victory is possible and defeat is unthinkable.

*Mayor Taylor, as is pointed out above, was not a secessionist—the police board majority was. JNP.

Westliche Post, 8 May 1861

*The Rising of the People**

The uprising of the people in the Northern states is one of the most impressive events since the so-called Wars of Liberation dashed Napoleon's waning power in the dust on the fields of Leipzig.* It is a phenomenon on which future historians will dwell when they wish to show how a young and great people gone astray due to an environment too bountiful for its own good is suddenly awakened from its slumber and shows its better, nobler nature; how a people of peaceful farmers and traders suddenly stamped armies out of the earth; and how the ranks were not ample enough to hold all the volunteers who wanted to join. They will not neglect to tell stories unimportant in themselves but which define the spirit that ran through the masses; they will tell, for example, how hundreds of women sent their men to join while saying that they were "man enough" to support their own families; they will not forget the volunteers from Illinois who came home weeping because they had been rejected as not needed, and who came at once to the Arsenal in St. Louis; they will not forget those whose hearts burned to join in the holy struggle, but who had to work for the good cause in other ways, with the pen or with other peaceful tools.

This period will be called the *second American Revolution.* It will only be able to turn the great principles enunciated in the first revolution into reality after that gang is exterminated that has been bold enough to describe the Declaration of Independence and the Bill of Rights as "glittering generalities." This revolution will proclaim its message in thunder, once the mighty armed hordes of the North have spoken in deeds that *here* is the homeland of the oppressed, banned, and poor of all nations; that *here* the words "Liberty, Justice, Humanity" are no empty sounding brass or tinkling cymbal but realities. Only *then,* after this great victory over the 350,000 slaveowners, can the poor whites of the South, the "white trash," breathe easily and really enjoy their civil rights.

Someone who stands at the base of a great mountain cannot

Der Volksturm, the title of this article, at this time had a clear association with the Wars of Liberation against Napoleon I, 1812–1814. The literal meaning is "people's storm," and it is the term used for the total levy of all forces in a community to repel invaders. SR.

*The Battle of Leipzig, the so-called Battle of the Nations on 14–18 October 1813, was the final major confrontation between German forces and Napoleon I. The role of popular *Freikorps* units in the campaign led to a conviction that the victory over Napoleon had been the work of the people rather than of the German princes. SR.

evaluate its height, and someone who lives in the middle of great events normally underestimates their importance. *The present people's revolution is greater and more momentous than 1776.* With their victory all the hopes of free men in America and the entire world either stand or fall. Since the start of the century this land was the pillar of fire showing the wretched of the earth to a new homeland; for seventy years this republic has been the holy spark of hope in the hearts of the patriots of Europe, the Oriflamme never quenched that ever revived the peoples over there to struggle against their oppressors. If this republic falls, then there would be a great cry of despair that would echo its rage through the whole of mankind; it would be the cry of despair to the god of history, and a cry of rage against the cowardly race, against *us*, for letting the holy banner of freedom fall to the earth.

America and its people are the vanguard of the great mission of the nineteenth century. On its flags are written the magic formula of the future, which is "Liberty and Fraternity for all Free Peoples." Not just the destiny of centuries but also the destiny of millennia depend upon this struggle. The whole European world is on the brink of casting off its old chains through an elemental upheaval. Just as the American Revolution of 1776 preceded the French Revolution of 1789 by only a short interval, in the same way the logic of history demands that our second revolution will go before a confirmation of the earlier European revolution by only a brief space of time. The ocean is now spanned by steamships, and we are no longer a people cut off from the rest of the world, but rather a great and powerful member of the cultured peoples of mankind, combining in ourselves in a happy way the elements of the old English, German, and Romance races. If we win—and we *will*, we *must* win—then soon the cry of jubilation of the liberated nations of Europe will echo across the ocean, greeting us as saviors and brothers. If we lose, if we are so miserable as to bring this fate upon us, then the curse of all the oppressed peoples of the world, the curse of world history will be piled on our race.

So every hand to a weapon, every arm that still has strength raised to strike a blow against the traitors, and every head that can think, every pen that can write—everything has been called into service for the holy war to restore freedom, the republic, the unshakable rock of hope for mankind. Good luck!*

' **Glück auf!* is a miner's greeting, also used by the Turners. SR.

IV.

The Missouri Putsch

May–June 1861

"... Many screamed furiously, 'Hurrah for Jefferson Davis! Our day will yet come!' Officers broke their sabers before they could be taken from them, drummers stomped in their drums, soldiers worked out their wrath on their own mess kits."

Westliche Post, 15 May 1861

Westliche Post, 15 May 1861*

How Our Situation in St. Louis Is Seen

has been shown in very striking fashion yesterday. After Governor Jackson and the legislature of Missouri openly worked for a proclamation of secession, after they have seized all available state funds in order to arm, after—as the Atlanta *Commonwealth* has revealed—the governor sent a representative to President Davis in Montgomery to ask for help in taking the St. Louis Arsenal, after cannons from Fort Sumter were shipped to Memphis and on to an unknown destination, probably to be used against our Arsenal, and after the armed Unionists and the armed secessionists stood opposed to one another in armed camps, suddenly a heavily loaded ship, the *J.C. Swon*, arrives, probably from Memphis, bearing the secessionist flag. The ship had to pass Cairo, where five thousand Union troops lie, and yet no effort was made to halt it. The commander there probably did not know all the circumstances, and he is probably not to be blamed. Perhaps he did not know the importance of the matter, or did not act because his orders from Washington were to allow no ship with weapons or military supplies to go *down* the river toward secessionist or doubtful states: such a combina-

---

*Camp Jackson, located in Lindell's Grove near Olive Street at Grand on St. Louis's city limits, was one of the training camps for the Missouri State Guard set up in early May. By the time it was assembled, the original goal of taking the United States Arsenal had been made impossible by the arming of Unionists in the city and the placing of defensive forces on the heights around the Arsenal. Unionist Volunteers were stiffened by small units of regular troops under Lyon. SR.

205

tion of words in the order would have been most unfortunate. Is this a country where nothing happens in time of war unless there are special instructions from Washington? Then things are even worse off here than with the Imperial Austrian Military High Command in Vienna.

After the *Swon* had gone further up the river, it had to pass Jefferson Barracks and the Arsenal before it reached our city. Both places have strong federal garrisons. The ship passed without any disturbance. The *Swon* only raised the secessionist flag once it had passed the dangerous points and had arrived at the city. No one is to blame for letting it pass. But the fact that, despite repeated notification to competent authorities, the weapons were unloaded unmolested and brought to Lindell's Grove without any camouflage and without being seized—that tells us something! Why did the United States marshal do nothing? Why did he not call up the *posse comitatus* once he had an inkling of what was going on, and take these more than suspicious weapons?*

Troops are being trained and armed as best can be done, and yet at the same time they allow the opponent they are arming against to receive a fresh supply of weapons!

Figure that out if you can!

Westliche Post, 15 May 1861

The Events of the Past Week

The week just past was so rich in exciting events that it will ever retain a historic importance for St. Louis and Missouri and in the history of the country. The battle has not yet been fought to its conclusion; the billows of the tempest move now one way, now another, but the end cannot now be in doubt, even if many victims will still have to fall. The brave man who has lived through this time of upset and danger, who has endured its tensions, will later be able to swell with pride when he tells his children, "I too bore arms in this struggle."

For the comprehension of the reader living away from St. Louis, we will give the events in outline as they developed from the start of the week just past.

After long hesitation, after long disappointment, the order final-

---

*Lyon and Blair did not interfere with the shipment because they wanted to seize it later at Camp Jackson, when the responsibility for it could be firmly fixed. JNP.

ly came from Washington to arm the citizens of St. Louis. Last Tuesday the militia of the first and second wards went to the Arsenal in keeping with this order, where they were sworn in and received weapons. On Wednesday the regiment of the third, fourth, and fifth wards received its weapons, and on the evening of the same day the regiment of the seventh and eighth wards did the same. So the citizens were supplied with about thirty-five hundred weapons, and it was clear that this fact alone whipped the secessionists into a fury. Few dreamed what would happen next, since until now no one was used to energetic action on the part of the central government.

On Thursday most of the armed Home Guards were gathered in their headquarters and remained there until midnight. A heavy rain that fell from eight or nine o'clock on probably delayed the expedition until the next day.

On Friday morning at ten o'clock, they were called together once more and remained in their quarters until about 2:30, when the news spread like lightning through the city that Captain Lyon's four regiments were on their way with ten cannons to the camp in Lindell's Grove. When a division of that force passed by the Turner's Hall and our people saw that, at long last, after waiting, after long impatience, a decisive step was in fact being taken, there was a scene inside the hall that was beyond description. First, everyone rushed to the windows in wild haste, not from worry but from joyous curiosity; officers ran around in the crowd with drawn sabers trying to bring them back and form them in rows. When it was known for certain that a blow was being directed against the camp, the mass in the hall gave a great shout of jubilation, so that the whole building shook. We saw old men weeping tears of joy, and everyone gripped his weapon tightly. We saw few scenes of this sort in 1848 or 1849, either in Paris or in the Baden-Palatine Revolution. It was one of those splendid moments when emotion glowing deep in the heart of the masses suddenly breaks into wild flames.

The Home Guards of the first and second wards came right behind the Volunteers; after them came those from the Turner's Hall, and last of all came the division from the third ward.

Westliche Post, 15 May 1861

St. Louis, 11 May

Victory for Union Troops!

———

*The Secessionist Camp Near St. Louis Taken by
United States Troops!*

———

*Secessionists Surrender Unconditionally and
Taken Prisoner!*

———

14 Dead and Many Wounded!

———

Only a Few United States Troops Wounded

———

Some of the Prisoners Already Released

———

Yesterday a decisive crisis that had become unavoidable was resolved in St. Louis. The two hostile camps pressed toward a decision. This would have taken place even if the dispute over the weapons owned by the United States, whose return had been refused by the state troops at Camp Jackson, had not provided an excuse.

The plan for the occupation of the enemy camp was carried out with great care by the commander of the United States troops, and the whole affair would probably have ended without bloodshed if a treacherous shot from the crowd had not precipitated the fire of the United States troops, which led to the pitiable killing and wounding of a number of people, mostly innocent bystanders.

The immediate result of this incident, of the defeat the secessionist party of Missouri has endured, is clear. *St. Louis is now an indubitable Union city, despite the doubtful mayor and city council, despite the governor's police and the secessionist legislature and state administration.* The further result will be that Union men in all of Missouri will gain new courage and the secession party will let up on its persecutions for a while, since they can see that they will otherwise be dealt with, even in the countryside. It is impossible to say what influence yesterday's events will have on the whole war.

All Union men, not just in St. Louis but in the whole Union, owe the deepest thanks to all of the United States troops, and particularly to their leaders.

Here we will give a preliminary account of the happenings in detail, insofar as they can be known in the reigning tumult and the confused details of the accounts. There will be some inaccuracies, which will be supplemented and eventually corrected by more complete accounts tomorrow.

Since the day before yesterday, negotiations had been going on between commander Lyon and General Frost over the delivery of United States guns that the state troops had been loaned when they were ordered to the Kansas border last fall. General Frost expressly refused delivery, and so commander Lyon decided to take by force the United States property that had been openly refused him.

As early as the day before yesterday the Home Guards had been called to their quarters, which were occupied by large contingents all through the night. Yesterday morning at ten they were gathered again, and they waited patiently for something to happen.

Finally, yesterday afternoon between two and three the news spread with the speed of lightning through the city that United States troops were marching on the secessionist encampment called "Camp Jackson" at the city limits in Lindell's Grove. We rushed there at once and established that the rumor had substance. The Union troops were marching toward that place in long rows, each regiment supplied with a number of well-rigged field pieces.

Sigel's regiment drew down Olive Street and surrounded the enemy camp from the northeast. Schüttner's regiment came down Market Street and posted itself on the southeast. The regiments of Börnstein and Blair held the enemy to the northwest, west, and southwest. Large units of Home Guards were held in the city. Secessionist Home Guards who had been mustered in the city came out to help their brothers, but they arrived too late and had to turn back. Quite a number of officers and soldiers who happened to be on leave in the city found themselves cut off and thus had the good fortune not to share the fate of their comrades.

The disposition of forces was such that there was no chance for a defense of the secessionist camp, which hardly held a thousand men at the time. It was entirely enclosed on all sides and completely covered by advantageously placed field guns.

At first there were negotiations, which went on for about an hour.

We are not yet in a position to relate any details about this, but we believe that the following account is close to the truth.

When General Frost saw that he was surrounded by superior force, he offered to deliver the guns that had first been demanded of him, but the commander of the Union troops would no longer be satisfied with that. He demanded that the secessionists surrender *unconditionally* and commit themselves never again to bear arms against the United States.

After some hesitation, these conditions were accepted and the white flag was raised over the camp. The militiamen stacked their weapons, surrendered sidearms, cannon, tents, etc., a watch was set over them, and they had to form up in rank and file without weapons.

The rage of the conquered was unbounded in some cases. Many wept, others blasphemed and cursed, many screamed furiously, "Hurrah for Jefferson Davis! Our day will yet come!" Officers broke their sabers before they could be taken from them, drummers stomped in their drums, soldiers worked out their wrath on their own mess kits, etc.

An enormous crowd had gathered around this martial show in order to take it all in. After a while the press grew so great that it was impossible for the soldiers to keep the crowd back despite the greatest efforts. Again and again it pressed forward and would not be held back by pleas or threats.

Now the victors formed files in order to gather the conquered between them and escort them back to the city as captives. In front went a band that played "The Star Spangled Banner," and then came the captives, escorted by two regiments of volunteers and a unit of regulars. At their head rode General Frost and his staff, all disarmed, then the First and Second Regiment of state troops, and lastly our brave German soldiers who had gone along on the Kansas campaign. We were truly sorry to see these men in such a situation, since they were mostly Unionist in their sympathies.

The vanguard of this column began to be insulted by some secessionists before it had gone too far, and some soldiers were so upset that they fired their weapons, admittedly over the heads of the onlookers. As soon as the commander heard of this, he had the weapons inspected and the guilty arrested.

At the point where the captives left the camp a grassy area runs along the northern side of Olive Street, which rises gradually to a hill; on the south side is Lindell's Grove, which is bordered by an escarpment about three feet high topped by a board fence along the road.

At the moment when the last captive turned into the road along with the escort, a revolver shot came from the crowd, accompanied by several flying rocks. The fire was returned at once. Again shots came from the crowd, and several captives pulled revolvers they had hidden in their clothing, and some tried to use the confusion to escape; then followed a platoon volley by the troops, and in the excitement the fire probably spread more rapidly than the officer giving the command wished.

There is hardly any other possibility than that the whole thing was planned by a misled gang of secessionists to precipitate bloodshed and to excite hostility against the Unionists among the people.

This reporter stood perhaps seventy or eighty paces from the place where the first shot was fired, and I can vouch for the course of events as told here. Before anyone could do anything, the fire had spread to where we stood. Bullets whined to our left and right. Right next to us a man fell dead. A second man not far from him had his knee shattered.

As soon as the shooting stopped, we went to look at the field where the dead and wounded lay. It presented us with a heartrending sight: wherever the eye moved there were dead and wounded. We counted fourteen who were killed outright, and a good forty were wounded, some seriously. There were women and children among the dead and wounded, and we were convinced that there were more Unionists among the victims than secessionists, since in general Union sentiment was more prevalent than sympathy with the rebels. On the military side three soldiers of the Second (Börnstein) Regiment and Captain Blandowsky of the Third (Sigel) Regiment were wounded. One volunteer of Company H of the Sigel Regiment was killed, and Nicolaus Knobloch of the regulars.

Those responsible for the blood that flowed were the fanatics who made this cowardly attack on quietly marching troops from the middle of a peaceful and unarmed crowd, as if from behind a shield. But however it was, this sad final act cast a dark veil over an otherwise glorious day.

The military column with the captives proceeded through the city and down to the Arsenal after a brief halt and without any further disturbances. The applause from the people in the lower part of the city was unbounded, for they had not yet heard of the bloody turn of events. The captives were kept for the night in the Arsenal. Some suspect civilians who had been found in the camp, among them the notorious Captain Grimsley, as well as some militiamen who represented themselves as Unionists, were set free.

When the news of the aforementioned bloody developments spread through the city, there was an indescribable uproar. The fury of both open and secret secessionists was enormous, as one might have expected. The printing shops of the Republican newspapers were threatened by the mob, and bloody revenge was sworn against the Unionists. In the end cold calculation won out, and they decided to keep quiet and delay their revenge until later, which was a result of their knowledge of their own weakness. It is not to be forgotten that among the orators who appeared at the Court House alongside Dick Barret was Uriel Wright, who had earlier made such lovely Union speeches, and who only yesterday openly declared himself a secessionist.*

In order to repress any disturbances of the peace, a large group of the Home Guards was kept at their posts through the night.

The Sigel and Schüttner Regiments, together with a unit of regulars, camped the night in the secessionist camp, where the captured war materiel was kept.

Westliche Post, 15 May 1861

How the News from St. Louis Was Received in Jefferson City

Jefferson City, 11 May. The news of the surrender of Camp Jackson arrived here between five and six o'clock and excited great agitation. The telegram was read out in the House of Representatives, and the *militia bill* then being discussed was *passed* in fifteen minutes, sent to the Senate, and passed there as well. Both houses adjourned from 6 to 7:30 P.M. In the meantime large crowds gathered in the street to discuss the news, and most came to the conclusion that it could not be true. Soon a second telegram arrived, which said that the battery of the Southwest Expedition had been demanded and handed over, which more people believed. The governor seized the telegraph before more news arrived, and no one could send telegrams either to or from St. Louis.

When the two houses assembled, they remained in closed session until 9:30. Shortly after eight a locomotive with a number of soldiers and powder kegs was sent in the direction of St. Louis, and it was rumored at the time that this was to blow up the bridge across the Osage River. The rumor had spread that two thousand men

*Ex-Congressman Richard Barret, a proslavery Ultra, and attorney Uriel Wright, who had been elected to the state convention as a Unionist. JNP.

were already underway to Jefferson City. Shortly after midnight the bells rang and the members of the legislature were called back into session. There was a powerful storm, which lasted two or three hours. When both houses had reassembled, they stayed in closed session until 3:30. The reason for this night session was a dispatch that said two thousand men had been sent from St. Louis to Jefferson City at 11 P.M. But before the two houses adjourned it became known that the Osage bridge had been burned, and so they felt they could be calmer, since even if the troops were underway they could not arrive before adequate preparations could be made. As a result of that news, twelve thousand kegs of powder were loaded on wagons and sent into the countryside, and the state treasury was also sent to a safer place.

Today people remained uncertain about the true state of affairs until after three o'clock. Many streamed in from the countryside, and anyone who swore an oath to the state received a weapon from the Capitol. A militia company was also organized. Today the legislature took only two important actions before adjourning until Monday. These important acts consisted first of expanding the authority of Mr. Brownlee (president of the police commissioners) in such a way as to give him total control over St. Louis, and second of granting the governor the greatest possible powers to suppress riots and insurrections of all sorts in the state.

The mail arrived from St. Louis two hours later than usual. This was a result of delays due to the partially destroyed Osage bridge. Only one span of the bridge had actually been burned down.

Many citizens enlisted during the day today as Home Guards, and it is believed that several hundred troops will come in from the countryside as a result of a special call by the governor.

The governor has suspended his control of the telegraph, and telegrams may be sent as usual.

Westliche Post, 15 May 1861

The Situation in St. Louis

St. Louis, 12 May

Yesterday was even more disturbed and almost as bloody as the day that preceded it. Already in the morning threatening crowds gathered in various places on the streets, and they soon began harassing individual members of the newly enlisted United States troops and Home Guards, wounding several, some probably fatally. This rioting and mishandling of totally peaceful citizens provoked the mayor's proclamation, which is printed in another column. The attitude of the anti-Union crowds remained threatening, and their agitation grew to the highest degree when the Home Guards of the ninth and tenth wards marched through the streets back to their wards after having received their weapons at the Arsenal in the afternoon. In our part of the city they were greeted in a friendly manner, but when they turned from Second Street up Walnut Street and marched on to Seventh Street, they were cursed by dense mobs, threatened with knives, and here and there pelted with stones. The troops, though they had been such a short time in service, kept perfect order. They were about a thousand men, armed with loaded rifles or muskets, and they would have had an easy time scattering the mob by force, but they hesitated to shed the blood of citizens and preferred to endure the worst abuse and even attacks. It did not take long, since at the corner of Walnut and Fifth Street, and then at Seventh Street, revolver shots were fired at the last soldiers in the column; shots were supposedly even fired from the windows of houses. Several soldiers fell. Now it was necessary to use weapons in self-defense. The ranks faced about and fired several times into the crowd, which dispersed. Three Home Guards fell, and six or seven in the crowd were killed and a number wounded. The Home Guards of the ninth and tenth wards continued marching back to their district with little further trouble.

It was expected that the Home Guards of the first and second wards, around two thousand strong, would come up when they heard of the attack on their comrades. This did not happen.

In the meantime, General Harney had taken command of all United States troops, including the Home Guards, as commander of the Military District, and it was rumored by the secessionists that he is of a different mind than Mr. Lyon, the previous commander, in the handling of local affairs.* We have the reason and the right to expect that General Harney will provide just as effective protection for citizens loyal to the Union as did Captain Lyon. The release of the prisoners of Camp Jackson, which took place after the incident on Seventh Street, supposedly on General Harney's order, is a matter of great concern for peaceful citizens—particularly in this agitated time. It is to be hoped that this act will be accompanied by other measures that will see that harm does not result.

*Harney's return was on the evening of 11 May, and he at once issued a proclamation appealing for calm and expressing distress over the bloodshed. SR.

After the street skirmish already described, it was quiet for a short while, but soon after 7 P.M. great crowds began gathering in the area of the police precinct on Chestnut Street, and mob violence threatened this area later in the evening and into the night. We can only hope that sufficient military measures will be taken to cow any who would consider carrying out these threats, and that in the last instance the troops would hinder such acts with force.

In the course of the day it became almost universal opinion that martial law would have to be declared in order to restore peace in the city. If this view is correct, as we believe, then the authorities should not hesitate to act.

The depots of the Pacific and the Iron Mountain railways were occupied by United States troops in the course of the day. On the Pacific Railway, the bridge over the Osage is said to have been damaged by order of the governor. We do not know whether communications with Jefferson City have been completely broken. We did not receive expected dispatches from there yesterday evening.

The rumor that had spread widely in the course of the day yesterday, that three thousand Illinois troops had arrived in Illinoistown across from St. Louis to protect St. Louis, is totally without basis in fact. A small unit of unarmed men went from Illinoistown to Belleville—that is the only truth in the story. Other unfounded rumors have made the rounds, as often happens in troubled times.

The following account gives further details about the incidents yesterday:

*　　*　　*

Yesterday was a terrible day for St. Louis, which no one who lived through it will ever forget.

Agitated crowds began gathering on street corners as soon as the early morning hours. From time to time speakers appeared who made every effort to blow the wrath of the secessionist portion of the population into bright flames over the events of the day before yesterday.

Wherever individual members of the Home Guards were seen and recognized by the mob there was a chase. They were pursued with clubs, stones, and pistol shots, and many escaped death only by a miracle. Union people were most endangered in the fifth, sixth, and seventh wards. Many did not dare to open for business that day, and others closed early.

The Home Guards of the central wards were kept at their posts from early in the day, and only a few received permission to take care of urgent business.

It is impossible to claim to be complete in describing the events that morning, since descriptions have only come to us in a disjointed form. There were some severe wounds, but we have not heard for certain that anyone was mortally wounded.

After noon it was learned that General Harney had arrived from Washington, and in the evening he took command of the troops in the Arsenal.

We expected a proclamation of martial law from hour to hour, and every peaceful and orderly citizen longed for it, but it did not happen. All that did happen was that the mayor proclaimed that all saloonkeepers close their houses until things had calmed down. This was hardly necessary, since most saloons were already closed.

General Frost, who had been released on parole the night before, published a proclamation of sorts that beseeched his partisans to keep quiet lest the Home Guards of the first and second wards be moved to march into the upper part of the city.

In the meantime the rabble had become continually more dangerous, since wealthy secessionists had endowed them richly with revolvers and Bowie knives and encouraged them to every sort of violence.

At about three a general muster was called in the lower wards, and the Home Guards streamed to their quarters. At South Market a company had stood in arms as early as noon.

In the middle of the day a relative calm reigned because citizens generally recognized as Unionists were staying off the street. But this was only the quiet before the storm. In the evening at about six o'clock when the Home Guards of the ninth and tenth wards, who had been armed at the Arsenal, marched back to their quarters through the city streets a thousand strong, a storm broke that was almost as terrifying and bloody as on the day before.

As these troops marched up Walnut Street to Seventh Street, they were pursued by a raging mob with curses, threats, and thrown rocks. They bore these afflictions in a manner that would have done credit to veterans. But when a large number of pistol shots were fired at them between Fifth and Sixth streets, they felt compelled to use their weapons.

We know from eyewitnesses that a well-dressed gentleman carefully opened the window of a house and painstakingly aimed and fired into the ranks of the citizen-soldiers. A number of rowdies hid themselves in the entry of a church and fired from there with revolvers. These are facts we can guarantee.

Two or three soldiers fell to the earth dead. Now the last ranks turned about and fired on their attackers. A number of these—it was not clear last evening how many they were—fell to the ground mortally wounded. The rest dispersed in all directions.

The troops continued their march, though they were attacked several more times, especially at Biddle Street, but it is not known whether there were any injuries.

Walnut Street, where the main attack took place, was an awful sight. We saw two Home Guards who had obviously been shot through the head at close range. The bullet had hit one of them in the back of the head so that his brains were splattered all around, and the other had been shot through the temple. We could not learn the names of those killed.

In the meantime the officers of the imprisoned secessionists captured the day before yesterday were released in the afternoon, and in the evening the common soldiers were released, and their appearance before the Courthouse among the rabble gathered there called forth general jubilation.

In the evening pickets of the Home Guard held many points in the city, and the humid stillness ruled—we cannot say quiet, since everyone waited in almost feverish expectation for what the next hour or the next day would bring.

Westliche Post, 22 May 1861

Warrensburg, Johnson County, Missouri

12 May 1861

Our peaceful town was first thrown into excitement only a few days ago through a sudden burst of activity on the part of the secessionists. They commenced buying all sorts of weapons, munitions, and powder that they could get, with the acknowledged goal of isolating the Unionists. Another of their maneuvers consisted of buying out the Unionist newspaper here, which had worked long and hard for the good cause, and turning it into a secessionist newspaper. So now our little town has two secessionist newspapers, and the voice of Union men cannot be heard in the press at all. Both newspapers immediately set to work fanning the flames of resentment into a blaze, to win people for secession through the use of rumors and lies of every sort.

It is obvious that the arming is aimed against St. Louis in the first instance, where they say that the Arsenal must be taken. At least a company is soon to be sent out of Johnson County to Jefferson City in order to strengthen the governor's army. Incidentally, our county has been less fanaticized than many neighboring ones until now; but it will be pulled along with the current unless a powerful blow is struck against the secession movement. There have as yet been no forceful expulsions.

Westliche Post, 15 May 1861

St. Louis, 13 May

The peace was not disturbed again yesterday. We still harbor the hope that the scandalous scenes of tumult of the last two days will not be repeated again, though many families left town the day before yesterday, but particularly yesterday, out of fear of further disturbances of the peace. These were thought to include many secessionists and their families, who did not flee into the Confederate states but into the free states, the best proof possible that even they know that their persons and property are much safer there than among their own cohorts.

The proclamations of General Harney and the stationing of regular United States troops with artillery yesterday did a great deal to obtain external tranquility; no one doubts the intention of the general to keep his promises, made on his honor as a soldier, to keep the public peace. It is a further assurance to the citizens of St. Louis that General Harney has determined, after a closer investigation of his instructions, that he *does not* have the power to alter the assignments of the Home Guards. Yesterday, before the proclamation appeared, the rumor was making the rounds that the Home Guards would be disbanded or at least transferred to the Arsenal or out of the city entirely. If such a measure had been carried out, we have no doubt that a serious conflict would have been stirred up. This brave band of men, which has done the heaviest service in these days at great cost, has been continuously cursed by the secessionist rabble, and once it has risked and lost lives and blood it would not have allowed itself to be disarmed and scattered. That much is certain. These are no hirelings or time-servers but men who have taken arms out of patriotism, love of Union and freedom, and they have earned the thanks of their fellow citizens, the thanks of every upright freethinking man in their new Fatherland. So the Home

Guardsmen will keep their weapons and stand ready to defend their fellow citizens. It is certainly proper that they have been relieved of the burden of most duties by regular troops, since they have stood under arms both night and day for three of four days with hardly an interruption.

As ready as we are to recognize that there is much that is good and proper in Mr. Harney's proclamation and orders, as far as they can be known, still we cannot help marveling that this general of the Union army *has failed to utter even a word about the Union* in his proclamation. It is certainly the general's duty to keep order in St. Louis and in his entire district, but it could never be the sort of order a secessionist state would wish; it is certainly his duty to support the officials of the state and city in the present circumstances, but *only when* these officials are true to the Union, and in the same way it is *his duty to fight them* when they oppose the Union.

Under the present circumstances it would be obvious for General Harney to express himself in this direction, even if only with a few words. We are very sorry that he has not done this, and we hope that he will make this lack good at the first proper opportunity. In times such as these the first and indispensable quality of an effective control of the situation is the strongly held conviction of the military commander. It would be all that much easier for Mr. Harney to make a statement of this sort in his proclamation, and thus condition what he said about cooperation with the authorities, because he has recently made a public statement in writing witnessing to his loyalty to his country.

As we said before, we trust that tranquility is returning to our city, and this despite the rumors that have been making the rounds. Some of these rumors are of the most extravagant and absurd sort. Yesterday, for example, Americans were concerned that the Home Guards, who are mostly German residents with property and families, were planning to attack their American fellow citizens last night, burning and murdering. The secessionists are spreading these sorts of stupid rumors, of course, to turn a political struggle into a battle between ethnic groups so they can gain a few more adherents among the native Americans. To such people all means are proper, and we are not surprised to see them using such absurdities, but it is astounding that otherwise honorable Americans who are not secessionists could be moved by such fairy tales. It is as if the German citizens did not already have as much to lose from anarchy as the Americans! As if the Germans, without exception, did not have to earn their bread honorably, mostly through hard labor! The rabble, which is made up of work-shy, unemployed, lounging, quarreling, fighting tramps, is not found among German Unionists but on the other side. This rabble, and some of their more eminent comrades, have fired on marching soldiers from their windows—it is they who have called up this violent disorder; not the Unionists, least of all the German Home Guards.

Westliche Post, 15 May 1861

Quickly and Decisively Done!

In times such as these, that is what always settles everything. Under the circumstances that presently prevail in the border slave states, it is actually madness for one side to observe the ordinary rules of peace while the other side does exactly what it wishes. So Unionists, especially Germans, have been driven from their houses and farms in many counties of Missouri (several examples appear again in today's edition among our letters), and they are happy to escape with their lives. Are they not supposed to take any measures in common when they cannot stay where they are living because the state authorities have sold them out and have been unready to provide them with any help whatsoever? We believe that our harried fellow citizens hesitate to take the proper measures because they are concerned with legality. Yet if they protect themselves by any means available, they are only practicing self-defense, *legally permitted self-defense.*

But it is even more surprising that the federal administration has *so completely and utterly abandoned* those friendly citizens who are ready to defend *it* by all means. Here we will not speak of the obligation of honor the administration owes. But does not the administration comprehend that it brings untold damage upon itself as a result of its indirection and inaction? What is a person to say about a government so weak and indecisive, yet so absurdly legalistic? Every day the newspapers promise that troops will be sent to Missouri to protect against the violence of the secessionists. But *it does not happen.* Does no one realize that *every single day*, I would say *every hour*, is of the greatest importance? Are they going to arrive too late, as at Fort Sumter?

Do not think that we are just talking about ourselves; we in St. Louis can protect ourselves; but this is not the case with the scattered Unionists in the counties of Missouri. These men would have received considerable protection if only a few thousand militiamen had been moved here from other states to make patrols in those areas of the countryside where the secessionists are bold enough to raise their heads.

Once again we ask: why cannot Illinois troops not needed in Cairo be stationed here just as well as in Springfield and Alton? If they are not all well trained, then they can be drilled just as well here as there. Our enemy is even more poorly trained and yet less destined to be soldiers; they do not fence according to the manual, but they strike anyway. They strike! A poor soldier who strikes and shoots is still better than a good soldier who neither strikes nor shoots but stands there like a doll. The government is acting as if time—*time*, which is everything in a revolution!—has no value whatsoever. So once again:

Quickly and decisively done!

Westliche Post, 15 May 1861

The Situation of Missouri

The five hundred Unionists of Lexington, Missouri, who allowed themselves to be put to flight by twenty secessionist rowdies deserve ridicule and disdain, but are the Unionists as a whole in Missouri doing anything differently when they allow themselves to be driven out of the Union by their governor and the 160 delegates in the legislature? The governor and the legislature lose their official character when they oppose the legitimate power of the Union and make themselves into enemies of the Union. The people have elected them to administer the state *under the federal government* and to grant it laws under the United States Constitution and in agreement with federal laws. When they misuse their offices so that they turn the mandate they received from the people into its opposite, which is what they do when they use all the power and the influence they have to overthrow the United States Constitution, shatter the federation, sunder the state from right and law, and make themselves into *lords* over the people who elected them as servants, then they are simply private persons no better than the twenty rowdies in Lexington—save that they are incomparably worse, more dangerous and more threatening. If this is so, then are not *all* the Unionists in Missouri to be compared with those five hundred Unionists in Lexington, driven out of their own hall by twenty filthy curs?

The St. Louisans have ten thousand men under arms. The secessionist governor has barely two thousand in his camp. If these facts are examined carefully, it appears that on the average the Union faction has *five times* the strength of the secessionists in all counties. Despite this, Unionists have been chased away and mishandled while the so-called state government looks on quietly. Is not this the most repellent terrorism, that of a minority? How long will the loyal citizens of Missouri put up with being terrorized by a minority and being mishandled by a pack of rebel upstarts?

It is to be hoped that the citizens of St. Louis will not fall into the error of believing that their city, their persons, and their property are secure and the good cause sufficiently well served now that they have the upper hand in the city itself. There can be no return to a secure order, no trust in the stability of things until *the state of Missouri* has been secured for the Union. For that purpose a dependable executive and legislature are absolutely necessary. As long as Governor Claiborne Jackson is at the rudder, peace and security cannot return, neither in the city of St. Louis nor in Missouri in general. The same must be said of the majority of the legislature that now rules the state from Jefferson City. Should a gross miscarriage of one gubernatorial election mean that the people must subject themselves to the arbitrary will of such a governor for the duration of his term in office? Can he overthrow the constitution of the state through his minions, treacherously abstain from performing his federal duties while rebuking the highest federal official, and arm himself all but openly to wage war against the Union and to conspire with the armed enemies of the national government?

And all of this takes place against the legally proclaimed will of the people of Missouri in the state convention!

The governor renounces and reviles the power of the federal government! He allows citizens loyal to the Union to be persecuted and expelled from those places where the rebels momentarily have the upper hand! He requisitions troops and money to come to the aid of the cotton states under the mask of an "armed neutrality." How long will the people loyal to the Union watch these doings without telling him to halt? Will it wait until the governor has so increased his power that he can allow the mask to fall completely off and reveal himself an open enemy? At the moment the Union faction is the stronger—thanks to the manly action of the citizens of St. Louis!—stronger, more numerous and better armed. Where is the guarantee that it will stay that way if the enemy within is given time to gather all of his resources and to bring more and more parts of the state into his unconditional power through terrorism, seduction, and other means?

In the meantime the legislature brews treason behind closed doors. Its sole activity is to gather men and money to come to the aid of secession. The sooner that is stopped the better. It would have enough trouble performing this difficult task under the best of circumstances, but it would be better still not to let it try. An enemy who constantly works toward a particular goal is always dangerous, and all the more so when he is clothed with the appearance of legal authority.

Nothing remains but to meet unjust force with force, and every effort must be made to apply it at the precise moment when it can be done with the greatest success. If we can get rid of our current governor, then we will be doing more for the Union than anything else in our power. Claiborne Fox Jackson is the evil genius who keeps Missouri out of the Union and leads the whole state and particularly the city of St. Louis to its ruin.

If we feel ourselves completely strong in defense, then when things are such as they are for us now we must go over to the offensive—*it must be done at once;* otherwise we will lose ground without a doubt.

Westliche Post, 15 May 1861

The Officers of Camp Jackson

have published a defense of their actions in yesterday's *Journal* over the signatures of *Frost, Bowen, Wall,* and *Voorhies,* and they have shifted the major share of the blame for the surrender of the camp to the state government.

They said that a withdrawal or an attempt at defense would have been nothing less than suicide. They had a strength of a good eight hundred men, but they had neither adequate weapons nor ammunition. More than half of their Second Regiment and many of their First Regiment had neither percussion caps nor cartridges, and many of their muskets would not have been able to use what cartridges there were. As officers they had pressed the state for six months to get necessary supplies; how they were treated can be seen from the fact that they have still not received any money for the last expedition to the Southwest. They had to serve without compensation and without reimbursement of expenditures.

Then they passed to a description of the fearful destiny that would have been the lot of the residents of St. Louis if they had defended themselves. "The horde with which they would have had to deal" was of such a sort that if these gentlemen officers had offered any pretext, they "would have plundered the city and murdered the unarmed citizens without regard for either age or sex!" (These largely German citizens of St. Louis are supposed to plunder their own city and massacre everyone—worse than Huns or Vandals!—a colossal thought!) They themselves were of course unconcerned about their own fate.

But if they had withdrawn to draw the conflict away from the city, which many held to be the best idea, there was concern that they had neither rations nor transport, nor would they have had any credit.

Anzeiger des Westens, 16 May 1861*

*The Irish, the Germans, the Union, and
Our Lord the Archbishop*

A silly, tasteless news item that a local reporter in this office happened to write down, inspired by what spiritual medium God only knows, unfortunately escaped our control and was printed in the local news columns and thus reached the public. This item has elicited all sorts of discussion, and within three days of its publication it has led to a pastoral letter by the archbishop, Peter Richard Kenrick.

This news item reported that priests had been illustrating to their flocks the view that the rebellion in the Union was chiefly a German concern and that Catholics were to abstain from associating themselves with Germans by urging prayers to the patron saint of Ireland to grant them greater aid than had been the case at Camp Jackson, and also to protect them during the impending uprising against the Germans.

In the next number of the *Anzeiger* we were happy to confirm the

*The anticlericalism of both the *Anzeiger* and the *Westliche Post* was always complicated by their often-patronizing attitude toward the Irish, the Germans' chief rivals. In St. Louis the Irish had been intensely courted by the secessionists, and they held important positions in the Minute Men units. SR.

facts as reported, but we ignored the excessively tasteless and childish comments of another newspaper, which was willing to lend its columns to the following analysis:

> That he is all the more inclined to see this story as groundless because up until now the Catholic Church has regarded the country's troubles with great forbearance, and also because St. Louis would be the very worst place openly to raise the banner of treason. Also he agreed with the position of the Church up until now, and he would not fall into a ditch by accepting the Church's responsibility for the crimes of a bunch of drunken Irish rowdies unless clear evidence of complicity were presented.

Yesterday the archbishop himself spoke out in the following pastoral letter to the faithful:

> To the Roman Catholics of St. Louis:
> Beloved Brethren:
> The regrettable events that have recently taken place urge me to renew the appeal I made to you on an earlier occasion and to remind you that the great principles of our religion are the sole efficacious means of stilling the reigning distress. A Christian is never justified in forgetting the prescriptions of general love that the Son of God imposed and practiced through His teaching and example. Do not listen to the urgings of wrath but purge from your consciences and good hearts every feeling that cannot be reconciled with the duty both reason and religion command. You cannot hope to find a remedy for the evil that now strikes this community, and that has brought so much unhappiness and loss to individuals, in the excitement of the moment.
> Remember that any attacks on individuals or groups of persons that are not recognized by the law and that lead to loss of life are murder. Everyone who takes part in such an attack is guilty, no matter how strong or bitter the provocation. Remember that under the influence of such unholy feelings the innocent are mingled with the guilty, or at least those we hold to be guilty.
> A solid reliance on ruling Providence, a humble subjection to His will, which has brought this chastisement upon us for our improvement to remind us of our dependence, and a noble renunciation of all feelings that are not consonant with the brotherly love that is especially proper for the inhabitants of a city, will do more for the restoration of public peace and the maintenance of order than the urgings to revenge, which will make the evils of our situation worse and more oppressive.
> My beloved, love one another, for love comes from God. Everyone who loves is born of God and knows God. He who does not love does not know God, for God is love. (I John 4:7–8)

Let us see how this pastoral letter compares with the words of Archbishop Purcell in Cincinnati and Archbishop Hughes in New York.

Here speaks the prelate of New York:

Catholics,

Even though longing for peace, if it be granted by God's Providence, still I can say that since I became a citizen I have only had one country. Since then I have never seen my duties as a citizen any differently. The government of the United States was represented then as now by a national flag, which was popularly known as the "Stars and Stripes." This has been my flag, and it will remain my flag until the end. I believe it is destined to flutter in the breeze wherever the sea billows, in the soft zephyrs of many distant shores, just as I have seen it wave in foreign lands, forming in strangely attractive lines of beauty. May it live and ever unfold in beautiful waves at home and abroad for a thousand years and as long beyond as heaven allows, free and without terror.

And the archbishop of Chicago, who has declared himself openly and freely for the Union!

And Archbishop Purcell of Cincinnati, who declared that he prayed to Mother Mary to crush the head of the secessionist serpent!

Let us add to these explanations the fact that one hundred Irish joined the Union troops in the Arsenal last Monday, and that since then about two hundred more have come in, and that even before Camp Jackson, Irish had entered the Volunteer companies, among them several Irish former officers of the Missouri Militia.

This is how we see our situation. Most of all, the fact is instantly obvious that the Germans needed no priestly intervention to join the Union regiments. The Fatherland, the Union, the president of the United States called them, and they needed no other call, no apostolic sanction.

In the North, particularly in the free states where one would expect a unanimous opinion for the Union, the archbishops rapidly took stands for the Union in the most enthusiastic terms, and the *Anzeiger* gave them full credit, to the scorn of the hyper-Catholic newspapers.

That was where the relations of force stood, and the clergy had no power to take a different stand. But despite the fact that the clergy only did what it *had* to do, still we think it is worth recognizing that they acknowledged this power *so early* and with such *energetic words*. Further, they made it clear to the Irish that they were not just talking about another Democratic ticket but about survival or ruin, and that the Irish had to do their duty like other men or go to destruction as traitors.

We know this clergyman. In the space of a single year he has turned himself inside out like a glove to be on the winning side, whenever he saw which way things were going. We have seen him grovel before Louis Philippe; a few days after the February Revolution he blessed republican trees of liberty, and we have even heard him preach communist sermons in all manner of churches; we then saw him surrender to Louis Bonaparte, and we heard him call this greatest of all despots the most beloved son of the Church. We are never surprised to see this clergyman on the *winning side*.

The bishops in the seceding states are silent. We believe that all their interests lie with the Union and that the Southern Confederacy does not have a chance, so it cannot be of any use to them. But they have kept their thoughts to themselves and have preferred to abstain and not to become martyrs for the Union. For prudence has won out over their political loyalty, and we have not heard that they have done anything to ally with the prevailing power as is the case here.

In Missouri the matter was in doubt. Here the pendulum swung for a while between Union and secession. Where did the archbishop stand in that period? We expected him to speak out from day to day. At the very moment when the Union flag flew from the towers of Northern cathedrals, and bishops declared that the head of the serpent of secession had to be crushed, here there was not a whisper save for dubious and unverified rumors about the archbishop's sympathies. No one was able to say anything for sure, and the Irish, who have rushed to arms in the North in the full flame of patriotic excitement because their archbishops showed them the *right* way, hesitated and swung back and forth here in St. Louis. Even at the time of the election for the convention, as well as during the latest election, they went along with the fabricators of the Democratic ticket and the haters of Germans as if it were a matter of another scramble for public office or to satisfy the ambitions of the crooked politicians of Chestnut Street.

Finally, after civil war broke out, after the irrepressible conflict had its bloody consequences, our lord the archbishop wants to step forward with a bunch of commonplaces about reconciliation, and even now he says not one word in favor of the Union, not even one word of reproval against the traitors.

Not that we are not thankful for these commonplaces—no, we commend him for them. Not that we doubt his personal loyalty to the Union, for we *know* from his most intimate friends that he is a Union man and would disavow the *Western Banner* if it declared for secession. Not that we think there are *no* grounds for avoiding taking a stand—no, on the contrary, his view that an open stand for the Union would endanger Catholics scattered all over the state is worth considering, but only worth considering and not worth acting accordingly.

It appears that the archbishop has been waiting to see which way the pendulum will swing—and for that reason he has been holding the Irish back *so that they can grab onto the winning side after the fact.* If a declaration from the archbishop here had appeared at the same time as the pastoral letters of the Northern prelates, and if the cathedral had displayed the flag as prominently as does the Customs House, then a civil war would have been impossible in this city, because we all would have been on *one* side. We would have been exactly like Illinois; not one drop of blood would have been shed, and even the old hostility between Germans and Irish would have been soothed—perhaps dissolved forever—by the balsam of love of country, here as in all the free states.

Only twenty-four hours ago we were deep inside Illinois. There we saw Germans and Irishmen serving together in the same regiments and getting along peacefully with one another. We saw them sitting together at inn tables, and not a single bitter word was exchanged—yes, it is with the greatest justification that people say that this great struggle for the Union has expelled all the nastiness of ethnic conflict.

But what do we see here? The question of life and death for the Union is transformed into an ethnic feud. Why? Because the Irish have not entered the ranks of the Unionists fast enough, and a miserable little clan of secessionists still counts on exploiting their hostility against the Germans.

The archbishop must feel this, he must know this, and no one can absolve him of his responsibility.

For even we have never doubted for a second that the Irish are as Unionist here as they are everywhere else. But unfortunately they have been raised to go to their priests for a sentence of absolution. This sentence of absolution has unfortunately only been given just now, not directly from the heart as it would have been if it had come immediately after Lincoln's proclamation. We know the Germans would have been happy to have them fighting at their side, for the whole world knows what fine soldiers they are. We do not even need to think of Montgomery or the blood flowing in Jackson's veins, or the Irish regiments in Mexico, since even the English recognize them as the very best fighting troops, and Wellington, Wellesley, and other great generals have spread their military fame far and wide.

They are good Union men and brave soldiers—we wish we could also say that they are brave fighters for the good cause. If the archbishop had spoken out at the right moment, the fame of the first passage of arms for the Union would not have been darkened by the useless shedding of blood, and today millions would think of it as one of the finest days in the history of this struggle without a lingering aroma of bitterness.

All right then, Irishmen of Missouri! Even without the direct, express, enthusiastic words of your ecclesiastical shepherd you know what he thinks and where he stands, and after his epistle of reconciliation you have the material to see that he stands where he should. Give us a hand in the struggle for justice, liberty, and the Union, and rest assured that you will never find more loyal, more stalwart brothers in arms than Union troops of German-American blood.

But you, archbishop, should fill up the last three regiments Mr. Lincoln still needs and demands from Missouri, fill them up with Irishmen at once, as soon as you raise the star-spangled banner on the tower of the cathedral—this would be a noble payment for pardon for the time you allowed to pass without acting.

Anzeiger des Westens, 23 May 1861 (for Friday, 17 May 1861)

Security Measures for the City, Decided Upon
and Carried Out by the United States Military Department
on 16 May 1861

Once the government had received unambiguous proof that the prisoners released from the Arsenal had organized themselves in the interior of the state, that caches of weapons were being found in the city, and that irresponsible persons were secretly bringing weapons in, it was decided to occupy all approaches into the city to prevent the traitors from gathering in sufficient force to disturb the tranquility of the loyal citizens of this city.

General Lyon gave the order to move out on Wednesday evening at 6 p.m., and the men received their orders at 9 p.m. so that no one could pass information on the marching route to civilians in advance. Part of the night was passed in breaking up the kitchens and in packing, and after a short rest, reveille was sounded at 3 a.m.; at 3:45 the regiments were in marching order, and at precisely 4 a.m. Colonel Börnstein's regiment marched out, at 5 a.m. the Sigel Regiment, and at 6 a.m. the Blair Regiment. The departures were staggered due to the unequal distances to be marched.

The Börnstein Regiment, consisting of the rifle battalion under Major Osterhaus* as vanguard, followed by the battalions of Lieutenant Colonel Schäfer and Major Laibold* with four cannons under the command of Major Backhoff,* along with one powder wagon and sixteen wagons of baggage, marched out of the Arsenal up Second Street all the way to Broadway, then into O'Fallon, then up this street in the direction of the water works, which were militarily occupied by two companies and two cannons while the camp of the first battalion was set up on the north side of the reservoir.

The water works lie fifty feet higher than the highest point in St. Louis proper, so that they dominate both the city and the surrounding area beyond. Colonel Börnstein's headquarters are in the workshouse of the reservoir, and the second battalion (Major Laibold) has its camp at the intersection of Natural Bridge (St. Charles) Plank Road and Kossuth Street, while the rifle battalion under Major Osterhaus camps on the heights between Hyde Park and Bremen Avenue, dominating the North Missouri Rail Road and the river with two cannons. The Sigel Regiment marched up Chouteau Avenue, then turned off right and took a position to the south of Neuer's soap factory in Rock Springs directly alongside the Pacific Railroad, which runs through the camp. The regiment controls the St. Charles, Manchester, and Pacific railways from that position, using two cannons and two mortars. Yesterday Colonel Blair's regiment took possession of the island opposite the Arsenal, where there is now a sufficient number of troops and guns to check any ship coming from downstream. In the same way the Iron Mountain Railroad, which passes through the Arsenal, is under the control of United States troops. A detachment of Colonel Blair's regiment also occupies Gravois Road, which leads to the southern counties. So by these means St. Louis is surrounded by a barrier of bayonets and cannons that makes it impossible for armed bands

*Peter Joseph Osterhaus (1823–1917) was a former Prussian militia officer who emigrated to America in 1849 and worked as a merchant in Illinois before moving to St. Louis in 1851. He joined the Second Regiment, Missouri Volunteers, as a private, was elected a major, then became colonel of the Twelfth Missouri Regiment, and in the end a major general under Sherman. After the war, "Peterjoe" Osterhaus served as military governor of Mississippi and United States consul in Lyons and Mannheim before retiring in Germany. See Kaufmann, *Deutschen im Bürgerkrieg*, 445–49. SR.

*Maj. Bernhardt Laibold, a sergeant in Germany, succeeded Friedrich Schäfer as colonel of the Second Missouri Regiment and served as a brigade commander at Chickamauga. See Kaufmann, *Deutschen im Bürgerkrieg*, 524–25. SR.

*Major Johann Backhoff had participated in the mutiny of the Baden Army at Rastatt in 1849 and served Gen. Franz Sigel there as well as in Missouri. Kaufmann, *Deutschen im Bürgerkrieg*, 480. SR.

from the interior of the state to advance against St. Louis or for large amounts of weapons to be smuggled in. These troops will establish peace and order in the suburbs, where acts of violence are still taking place, and together with the Home Guards and United States Army units in the city, they can gradually clear the community of open or covert Minute Men, armed or plotting secessionists, and other suspicious elements. The peaceful citizen and the dependable Union man has not the least to fear from these measures.

The commanders at the various posts will carry out their orders in a humane and tolerant manner, but they will also act without hesitation against rowdies who insult or attack United States troops who are carrying out their duties, or those who endanger the personal security and property of peaceful citizens.

The Arsenal, with two thousand men and numerous cannons, stands as ever under the command of the dashing General Lyon, and the Marine Hospital is occupied by a portion of the Blair Regiment until the new Fifth Regiment under Colonel Salomon is ready to come out of the Arsenal.

Two steamboats have been chartered by the United States government, and they lie ready for instant service at the foot of the Arsenal with steam in their boilers at all times, so every effort has been made to establish tranquility, order, peace, security, the authority of the United States government, and the respect for its laws. All good citizens and Union men can feel totally secure, and the secessionist will receive the same protection and security if he abstains from attempting disruption or uprising.

Political opinions are free, but traitorous actions will be suppressed.

Since St. Louis has finally been completely pacified and secured for the Union, time has now come to purge the entire state of Missouri of its traitors and energetically to combat the persecution of good Union men by secessionist mobs.

Anzeiger des Westens, 23 May 1861 (for Friday, 17 May 1861)

Two More Regiments—No, Four

The first brigade of Missouri Volunteers, consisting of four regiments, was joined yesterday by a fifth regiment, and yet another organized today. The new regiment of Colonel Salomon is also almost entirely German. Even before it had been completed, a sixth had begun to form that was predominantly Irish; four companies are already full. And that is as it should be. The Irish are the last people who should abstain from a war for the Union. Once they have completed one regiment, more will follow, and there is room for a seventh and an eighth, for the War Department has assigned four of the new regiments mustered for three years to the state of Missouri. Since Missouri was so quick to fill its first four three-month regiments, and a fifth besides, then it will have no problem raising four three-year regiments.* Anyone who signs up will want to serve until the end of the war; there are experienced German soldiers here, young and enthusiastic people, and now with almost all the Irish on our side under General Lyon's command, the war will have a happy conclusion.

Westliche Post, 22 May 1861

Another Secessionist Nest Destroyed

St. Louis, 17 May 1861

Yesterday morning two companies of the Blair Regiment departed on a secret mission on the Iron Mountain Railway. Through the whole day the mission remained secret, and only in the evening was its purpose learned. The soldiers had been sent to Potosi in Washington County to destroy a secessionist camp that was in the process of formation there. The mission was a complete success. The brave knights of the secession, over two hundred in number, put down their weapons without firing a shot, and the Unionists returned to the city laden with booty. This consisted of a quantity of weapons, thirty horses, and two wagonloads of lead.

Some of the secessionists ran away on the approach of the Union troops, the others had to swear never again to bear arms against the United States, and fifteen daring youths who refused to do this were brought to the Arsenal as prisoners. A secessionist banner was captured, torn to pieces, and divided among the victors as a souvenir.

---

*The three-month enlistments covered the forces raised in April 1861, which led to units falling apart in the third week of July just as the situation in southwest Missouri grew critical. Units enlisted later in the spring were usually obligated for three years. SR.

General Harney finally seems to want to get serious with the secessionist tyrants in the countryside, and soon the persecuted Unionists will feel his protecting hand.

Westliche Post, 19 May 1861

The Pacification of Missouri

Two things are needed for the pacification of the utterly anarchic situation found in many of the counties: (1) military repression of the secessionist bands, which have arrogated to themselves public authority in many places and persecute, mishandle, and expel those citizens faithful to the Union, and (2) the reorganization of our domestic legal institutions, which have been thrown into utter confusion by the actions of the current legislature and the governor, so that the citizens can no longer know what the law of the state is, since the federal authorities themselves have declared some of these acts of legislation to be null and void.

We believe that these two measures are seen to be necessary by all law-abiding citizens. Order and security for life and property must be restored at all costs. This is the first demand. Experience has shown unmistakably that the executive of the state either cannot or will not do enough. The governor has declared in the crassest manner possible that he does not wish to carry out his duties to the Union, and he has acted accordingly, and it is indisputable that the executive officers of a large number of towns and counties in this state are cooperating with the governor against the federal government, and it is just as obvious that others are too weak to hold the secessionist rabble in check.

In such a situation the federal authorities have the unavoidable responsibility to extend complete protection to the citizens of the Union who do not wish to be restrained by force from doing their duty, and further they should punish attacks on their rights, whether by state authorities or by more or less organized mobs, and to make repetition of these attacks impossible. In the present circumstances, this cannot be done without military force.

If this use of military force is to be applied in the most rapid manner possible, a coordinated operation embracing the entire state is mandatory. A systematic plan of campaign must be drawn up covering the state generally. It appears to us that two preconditions are necessary, which are *unity in command* and a militarily trained *general staff*. It is not certain that these two conditions exist yet. The War Department has recently organized a new command district for the states of Ohio, Indiana, and Illinois. Missouri, as part of the Western Military District, stands under the command of General Harney, but many doubt whether he has the unlimited authority to command Volunteers as well, and in fact it occasionally appears that their commanders are operating on their own. We say it "appears" now and then, since Harney's name is not even mentioned in some operations, and announcements are made that are written as if they rest on no authority below the very pinnacle of the federal government. We can hardly believe that this is so. We assume that the chief of the Western Military District also has command of all United States troops in Missouri.

What about a general staff? In European armies a fully organized general staff is a prime requirement for a supreme command. The chief of general staff is the first technical adviser of the general and often more than that—he is often the true originator of plans for campaigns and battles, and the general only carries these plans out. Under him stands the adjutant general's staff, the quartermaster general's staff, commissary officials, and superior medical authorities. The adjutants on the staff are drawn mostly from the technical services for various types of weapons. Here these vital armatures of a good army leadership do not yet appear to have the necessary training. Since American troops are not poised against a foreign enemy, they never seem to have felt that a more sophisticated organization was needed. But the army should indeed be organized at the highest level. Nothing strengthens the trust of one's own troops or stirs more respect in the enemy than a superlative organization of leadership, and where it exists it should not be kept hidden but allowed to show itself in the daylight. Then everyone knows what he has to deal with in this or that situation, and the whole body of troops gains that stature, influence, and effectiveness that is in fact the essence of an army.

If these conditions exist, then there has to be a complete, well-thought-through, and coordinated plan of operations. We do not believe that the state can be pacified without the execution of such a plan. It will not suffice to keep the peace if all that is done is to expel or disarm the secessionist bands first in this place and then another, starting with places close at hand or where serious violence has occurred. It will be necessary to occupy certain important points in order to clear the land in a small area around with flying columns, wherever it seems necessary, but the whole population of the district controlled from this point will have to be overseen continuously. Four or five such military central points should be enough. The occupation of the railways alone will not suffice.

These operations, which appear to be necessary for securing and pacifying Missouri, could probably not be carried out by the United States military force currently in the state. But if the federal government recognized its strict commitment to protect citizens as it has proclaimed, then they *must* raise the forces necessary to achieve this goal. The Washington government will not hesitate, one hopes, to station troops from one state in another state that requires more help. We will no longer rely on the childish tendency to think of the situation in nonmilitary terms. This being the case, we return to the question already posed many times: why are a few thousand of the United States troops in Illinois not brought into Missouri? Why cannot troops stationed in Quincy, Caseyville, Belleville, etc., stand just as easily in Hannibal and St. Louis? They are not needed to defend Illinois, and they would be as good reserves in St. Louis as in Belleville, and they would do a great service by freeing a large portion of the troops stationed in St. Louis for the pacification of the rural districts in Missouri.

Today we want to conclude these general remarks on measures for the first phase of pacification by saying that we are convinced that even a momentary suspension of secessionist violence is no justification for hesitating to occupy the chief centers of the secessionist bonfire with military force. The chief culprits must come to feel the force of the federal government to be strong and effective here, or they will soon be right back after lying low for a while.

As far as the second phase of pacification, the reorganization of our legal institutions, is concerned, we want to abstain from a thorough review and simply say that we think the best and most efficient means of returning to a generally recognized basis of law would be *to declare null and void all the acts of the latest legislature.* The current legislature has betrayed the trust of the people in the most flagrant manner and acted in a treasonous way toward the federal government, so that any law from such bogus representatives lacks the respect a law should have. All of those acts would be regarded with the greatest suspicion by the people if they were allowed to stand. If there is a bit of good grain among the chaff and dirt of these acts, then let them pick it out and reactivate it in the form of a new law. But they should not leave one stone on another of the traitorous secessionist legislation.

Anzeiger des Westens, 23 May 1861
(for Wednesday, 22 May 1861)*

Important, but Very Obscure

A Compromise Between the Commanders of the United States and
State Military Forces

St. Louis, 21 May 1861

The undersigned, officers of the United States government, and of the
government of the state of Missouri, for the purpose of removing mis-
apprehensions and allaying public excitement, deem it proper to declare
publicly, that they have, this day, had a personal interview in this city, in
which it has been mutually understood, without the semblance of dis-
sent on either part, that each of them has no other than a common object,
equally interesting and important to every citizen of Missouri—that of
restoring peace and good order to the people of the state, in subordina-
tion to the laws of the general and of the state governments.

It being thus understood, there seems no reason why every citizen
should not confide in the proper officers of the general and state governments to restore quiet; and, as the best means of offering no counterin-
fluences, we mutually recommend to all persons to respect each other's
rights throughout the state, making no attempt to exercise unautho-
rized powers, as it is the determination of the proper authorities to
suppress all unlawful proceedings, which can only disturb the public
peace.

General Price having by commission full authority over the militia of
the state of Missouri, undertakes, with the sanction of the governor of
the state, already declared, to direct the whole power of the state officers
to maintain order within the state among the people thereof; and General Harney declares that this object being thus assumed, he can have no
occasion, as he has no wish, to make military movements which might
otherwise create excitement and jealousies which he most earnestly
desires to avoid.

We, the undersigned, do therefore mutually enjoin upon the people of
the state to attend to their civil business, of whatsoever sort it may be;
and it is to be hoped that the unquiet elements, which have threatened so
seriously to disturb the public peace, may soon subside, and be remembered only to be deplored.

Sterling Price   Wm. S. Harney
Maj. Gen. Mo. S. G.   Brig. Gen. Command'g

*The original text of the first four paragraphs is from the *Missouri Republican,* 22
May 1861. This pact is the notorious "Price-Harney agreement," which the *Anzeiger*
took an understandably dim view of, but which was welcomed by conditional Unionists as a peace-keeping device. In Frank Blair's view, it merely authenticated Harney as a dupe of secessionists. Having surrendered vital federal sovereignty, Harney's days were numbered. James Yeatman and Hamilton Gamble conferred in
Washington with General Scott in an attempt to persuade the administration that
Harney was on the right course, but Lincoln left the decision to Blair. Ironically,
the Price-Harney agreement also strengthened Jefferson Davis's view that Jackson
and Price could not be trusted. JNP.

The whole thing is very diplomatically phrased, and one gets the impression of a soldier being led around by the nose by a diplomat. Certainly the *State Journal** is not at all pleased, since in the last analysis all the concessions were made by Mr. Price, concessions that can be read to say that he not only has to keep peace and order in the state, but even that he has to send his soldiers back to their civilian occupations. But everything is still too obscure, and since we never expect anything good to come out of Jefferson City, we cannot avoid the thought that the whole thing is intended to prevent General Harney from taking the military initiative and to win time. Further, we have hopes, based on the decisiveness he has recently shown, that Harney will break the convention the moment he hears of the mistreatment of one friend of the Union in the interior of the state—or the first muster of the State Guard or other measures to take up arms. If the state lacks the force, he is supposed to loan weapons to the state! General Harney has more than enough for him, or perhaps Governor Jackson has already abdicated all his powers to ex-Governor Price? This is not entirely impossible, since Price is only supposed to have come to Harney as a result of a threatening letter, and the result was that the state official appeared before a United States general as a supplicant.

*   *   *

Our German Fellow-Citizens

will find an agreement between United States Brigadier General Harney and Maj. Gen. Sterling Price in another part of this newspaper.

At first glance it makes a very negative impression—we will not deny it—on all loyal friends of the Union, since as far as form and content go it is one of those acts that depresses rather than encourages the spirit and enthusiasm of *recognized true friends* and gives enemies new faith in their success in the end. This obsession for endless writing and proclaiming is an evil in its own right, and where there are no generally accepted guidelines for drawing these things up, and where generals start playing diplomat and flail away with pens rather than daggers, then the proclamations are twice as badly conceived as otherwise would have been the case.

The agreement between the two generals gave the impression to many of our friends that the federal authority was falling back

---

*The *State Journal*, or the *Daily Missouri State Journal*, was published 11 March to 11 July 1861, when it was suppressed for secessionist sympathies. See Winifred Gregory, *American Newspapers, 1821–1936* (New York, 1937; reprint, New York: Kraus, 1967), 371. SR.

before the traitors and making concessions to them. And yet this impression is largely the result of inept phrasing. We *know* that Claiborne Fox Jackson was approaching as a supplicant; we *know* that he has had to promise to keep law and order in the interior of the state and that he has pulled back from all his senseless positions; we *know* that General Harney made this agreement *only in order to get these formal assurances,* and that he is strong and decisive enough to maintain the authority of the United States and the security of threatened pro-Union citizens in the interior of the state if the trouble now going on in violation of this agreement does not stop.

We confirm that totally, but we are sorry that it was not registered very clearly in the agreement. All of the various measures specious speculation has already projected on this agreement, such as disarming the Home Guard and the Volunteers and whatever else would inevitably follow, would fall away by its own weight; in the next few days acts in the federal capital will show how utterly serious the federal government is about holding this state solidly and inseparably in the Union.

It is certainly obvious that this agreement with Claiborne Fox Jackson has taken place without *our* approval. It is wholly a product of the American political style, not of the European revolutionary style. *Everything* in this country is done this way, and the German manner of getting things done is in for many more disappointments yet in this struggle.

A German cannot imagine how General Harney can declare the whole military bill unconstitutional and despotic and then turn around and negotiate with a general set up by that very bill. An American does not find it the least bit odd.

A German thinks that the whole right in this matter lies with the Union and none with the secessionists and neutrals. For that reason, since in this case might aids right, he thinks that rapid, bold, and direct action is called for to assert justice. An American prefers to avoid force by hesitating for a moment and taking another look, hoping always to achieve a peaceful settlement up until the last possible instant, and he does not like to settle anything rapidly or definitively. The state demands peace; the most disloyal of the disloyal, Claiborne Fox Jackson, wants to make peace; so long as he keeps his word we will accept peace from his hands.

That is how it has come to pass that the Germans have declared the secessionists their enemies *once and for all,* and yet some of their best and most loyal friends among the native-born see the matter differently and want to resolve the matter differently, and so they are seen by the Germans as enemies or duplicitous, despite the best intentions.

We have long expected that some day the German style of operation would separate itself from the American style over some important matter. The way the two peoples think, their education and historical experience, are too different for it to be any other way. Except that good faith and trust *have* to see us over these shoals, and even if on the whole we achieve only half as much together with our American fellow citizens than German enthusiasts for freedom expected at the outset of this struggle, still it shall have been worth the greatest sacrifices.

P.S. The many denunciations of the agreement between the two sides appear to have moved General Harney to issue a further proclamation yesterday evening. We were told that we would certainly receive it in time to be printed, but about midnight it had reached neither us nor the *Missouri Democrat*. Perhaps *only* the *Missouri Republican* will get it!

In any case the specific points were indeed settled by the two generals, for we were shown a telegram to an Eastern newspaper yesterday evening in which the following points were described as settled:

(1) Protection of all citizens by state authorities, regardless of their political beliefs.

(2) United States troops may only extend their protection if asked to do so by state authorities.

(3) The State Guard called together by the governor is to be dissolved.

We have not checked how well the writer of this telegram was informed.

Anzeiger des Westens, 23 May 1861
(for Tuesday, 21 May 1861)

Before and After 1848

It is generally known that the year 1848 still causes *European* despots indigestion, but we would hardly have expected it to sit like a cobblestone in the belly of the despots here as well.

Listen, friends, to what the *Missouri Republican*, our city despot, said yesterday. We shall give it to you in an epitome comprehensible to anyone:

The Germans who came here before 1848 were a happy, dumb race of feedbags. They came here because they had heard that there was enough cornbread and bacon, while all they got to eat in Germany was an old leather sole for beefsteak every two weeks. They were not interested in politics, they allowed themselves to be pushed around by the native-born, and they were royally pleased when one of their top goats got a job in the night watch once in a while. If they had enough to eat and no one actually bit them on the throat, they were as happy as sparrows in a seed barrel—and a peace reigned between the Germans and the native-born that was like that in Paradise before Eve bit the apple.

Then the year 1848 snowed on us an entirely new sort of German. Pure desperate wreckers! Pure Robespierres, Dantons, St. Justs! Pure red republicans! People rotten from the ground up, red all the way through to their kidneys, who could convince themselves that they were every bit as good as any other American as soon as they were citizens, with the same rights and the same duties as those the United States Constitution granted every other citizen; they made an equal claim on all offices, and they asserted they had the same justification and understanding to judge the laws of the land as the native-born.

When that got started our tranquility was done for. Soon a scarlet-red speaker would start to give addresses of this sort:

"Germans, keep together, since otherwise the others will mistreat you.

"Germans, pay close attention to the politics here, since otherwise they will cheat you coming and going.

"Germans, become landowners and craftsmen and taxpayers as much as all the others—and demand participation in everything that is going on.

"Hold meetings, read your own newspapers, debate public matters, and let people know you are there when the offices are handed out.

"Preserve your language, for that is your greatest treasure; it is your very own identity in speaking and writing. Set up your own schools, your own places of entertainment, your own theater—do not cast aside your German identity without a thought—you have nothing better for which to exchange it."

These reds and Forty-eighters are to blame for everything.

Roughly so much for the *Missouri Republican*. But for what are the Germans to blame?

That the South has declared war on the United States?

That Claiborne Fox Jackson has tried to chain *this* state and *this* city, with sixty thousand Germans in it, to the South?

No. But they are to blame for the fact that Claiborne Fox Jackson's traitorous little game did not succeed and that salt has been poured into the *Missouri Republican's* secessionist soup.*

The salt really is in the soup now, and the *Missouri Republican* is glugging it down with an indescribable grimace. But he never shall

---

*Despite the *Republican's* anti-German, antiemancipation venom, it did not support secession. Although he had been with the state guard at Camp Jackson, John Knapp emerged eventually as a Union army officer. JNP.

admit to the Forty-eighters that the soup disgusts him. Of course he has no means at hand for revenge, so he cries out in his anguish:

"Oh, if only we had our happy, antediluvian feedbags back, who never made a splash, then Missouri would be ours!"

*   *   *

We have looked at the Germans around us here in St. Louis, and we have not been able to verify the distinction the *Missouri Republican* has made. Once in a while we can find a sleepyhead or even a mummy, sometimes a petrified pigtail, even occasionally a German secessionist misled by incomprehension or subservience—and on the whole it is indeed the *younger* Germans, who came after 1848, who have joined the Union regiments—but out of sixty thousand Germans in this city there are not even sixty hairbags, mummies, nightcaps, or secessionists to be found, so it seems to us impossible to separate the Forty-eighters from the pre-Forty-eighters. On the contrary, all are of one heart and one soul; all of them have utterly forgotten that they are Germans, and they have flocked to the flag of their Fatherland as good, patriotic Americans. This is the *American* 1848—let us hope that it will give the enemies of the Union indigestion permanently!

Anzeiger des Westens, 23 May 1861
(for Wednesday, 22 May 1861)

In Jefferson City

the situation has grown rather unpleasant in the course of the last few days. The governor and the lieutenant governor have been abandoned by every decent man. They are surrounded only by a lawless mob over which they themselves have no control. Without money, without weapons, without any moral force—what are they to do! We also hear that Claiborne Fox Jackson and Reynolds are ready to resign if they can escape trial for treason! Who could promise such a thing? If we consider the situation together with the agreement between the two generals, then the agreement takes on a different appearance. We shall soon see how it all turns out.

*   *   *

From Jefferson City

Passengers arriving here Monday night said that there were 3,300 state troops in Jefferson City.

On Monday a company of 42 men arrived from Warrensburg, and it marched through Jefferson City with continuous hurrahs for Jefferson Davis, flying the flag of secession.

They were most warmly received by Governor Jackson.

The population of the state beyond the Osage River is in continuous agitation due to the undisciplined and irresponsible hordes that are marching about and mustering as state troops.

Westliche Post, 22 May 1861

From Lexington, Missouri

came two refugee Germans who had left on Tuesday afternoon on the steamer *Thos. Tult.* Six Germans and several refugee Americans came with this boat, which unloaded four iron six-pounder cannons (stolen from the Liberty Arsenal) at Jefferson City.

Our witnesses described the situation in Lexington as one of thorough terrorism. The rowdies, led by the sons of some wealthy citizens, rule the town, and the mayor, who is a fanatical secessionist, supports them. No decent person dares set foot on the streets after dark. A vigilance committee has unlimited rule and oversees persecution and other activities. The news of the tenth of May from St. Louis caused great embitterment. On Sunday the Turner's Hall was searched, since it was believed that the Turners had received weapons from St. Louis. People are very suspicious of the Turners, and all but a few have left town. Still, all "damned Dutch" are threatened hourly with hanging. A black list has been drawn up with twenty-four names, including the Kreutzdorn brothers, respected merchants. On Monday at noon, ten of those on the list were notified that they had twenty-four hours to get out of town or be hanged. With the exception of Mr. Haerle, who was wounded at the last Union rally when he rescued the Union flag, these ten were all pure Americans. All of them left town. Mr. Haerle went to Hamilton on the Hannibal–St. Joseph Railroad, leaving all of his property behind. Beyond these, everyone who would not enter the governor's militia or swear an oath to the governor has been threatened with mob violence, which has caused many who were not on the black list to leave town. Certainly a good three hundred persons have fled Lexington, mostly Germans, and as many Germans have left as could get out.

Two badly organized and armed, undrilled secessionist companies are in Lexington, and as of Tuesday no militiamen had been sent to Jefferson City.

Despite all that, our witnesses assure us that the Union men are the majority in Lexington, but that they are mostly unarmed and lack the courage to act. Still, if they could receive support from outside, many of them would join the Union forces. They believe that it would be easy to suppress the secessionist movement in Lexington with a hundred Union troops.

The slaveowners, particularly the larger ones who hold many slaves, are not for the secession in Lafayette County, since they would be less assured of their living property under the secession than now is the case. But now they can do nothing against the mounting fanaticism. The mass of the rowdies who rule, or rather the few intriguing politicians and ambitious young men who rule through them, own neither slaves nor anything else, and they are simply using the confusion to make things easy for themselves. They charge around the town, visit the inns and saloons without paying, and act like occupying barbarians. They have given no evidence of any real courage. One hopes that General Harney will soon give them a chance.

Westliche Post, 22 May 1861

A Gain

This is a poor time for calm editorials, moral reflections, even for objectivity. It is a time that has reached for the final argument: action, or perhaps it is better to say, force. The madness of our enemy has forced all patriots to seize this final tool, and we have not done badly. In the moment of calm we are enjoying now, we have suddenly realized that something very good has taken place. The call to arms has suddenly pulled together the Americans of our party and the Germans of all classes and brought them to a single level, into a sort of cooperation. Americans and Germans have come to know and to understand each other better, and among the Germans themselves the barriers of class that had been erected out of narrowness or small-bore hatred have fallen. In the ranks of the people's army the lawyer stands shoulder to shoulder with the laborer, the writer next to the brewer, the "Green" next to the "Gray."* The old cheap labels, such as *Latin* or *snob* or *fatso*, have

---

Grays and *Greens* were terms used by Germans to describe Germans of the various generations in America. A *Gray* was someone who had emigrated before 1848, a *Green* someone who had come over after the 1848 revolution and thus could claim to be a Forty-eighter, even if only *honoris causa*. SR.

been completely forgotten under the powerful force of the patriotic movement. Everyone feels himself to be an equal among equals, each carries his musket as well as the other, and all are proud to share in the common danger. We can admit with pride that our wildest expectations have been exceeded by the conduct of German citizens in the latest eventful days. There was no hesitation to be seen, no "hunkering down," in short, nothing of what we call the Philistine. To be sure we should not praise the day until evening comes, and praises and self-congratulation do not suit the iron seriousness of this time. But we can say this much: every good patriot, every good German, has reason to be satisfied with what has happened so far and to harbor the best hopes for the future. The Germans of the City of St. Louis will come out of this vital struggle a purged people, a better people, purified of its lower characteristics of lust for mere profit, capable now of sacrificing for its neighbors and partisans, a band of brothers.

Westliche Post, 29 May 1861

Jefferson City, 25 May. At three o'clock yesterday a large flag of the Confederate States was raised once more in front of the governor's house; this flag had been raised earlier by members of the legislature, and it is waving right now as I write this. The troops were told they would be discharged, and the governor received them company by company at his front door. He told them that they had been called up to defend the capital, but that this was no longer necessary, and that they could go home, but they were told to hold themselves in readiness to come at the first call. The taking of Camp Jackson and the murder of innocent women and children had not yet been avenged, but *the time shall come when they shall rise up in full force and smite their enemies to the ground.*

This is the peaceful, conciliatory tone that reigns with the governor and his comrades.

Most of the troops departed today, to the great relief of the residents. Only yesterday a German citizen of this town was attacked by two secessionists from Clay County and badly cut up by knives. He had given no cause for the dispute, nor any other provocation other than the fact that he was German. The culprits were arrested and are now languishing in jail.

The United States postal agent on the Pacific Railway, Mr. Joel, was once again in peril of his life in *Sedalia*, the railhead, when a bandit tried to stab him in the back with a large slaughtering knife. A Mr. Cameron, a wood merchant of Sedalia, came and rescued him, but he was pursued in turn by a secessionist gang and barely managed to save himself by flight. The same gang ripped apart an inn managed by a German by the name of *Tisch*, and they did the same in the Südwest-Saloon, where the host is also German. There was no pretext for these abuses save that the victims were Germans.

Here are a few samples of how the *Missouri Press* has received the agreement between Price and Harney:

The Warsaw *Democrat* says, "We have read the agreement with care and have come to the conclusion that it will come to nothing. Harney says nothing to cover up the recent acts of violence by Lincoln's military in St. Louis and elsewhere in the state, and we suspect that he takes them to have been legal. We hope that the agreement between these gentlemen will have the effect in any case *of giving our state a little time to arm and defend itself.*"

The Lexington *Expositor:* "And this man Harney dares to come here like a dictator and tell us that the law for the arming of the state is unconstitutional and does not need to be observed. But it will be observed, despite everything he and his master try to do, and later when Missouri decides to leave the Union, woe to him who tries to get in the way! Let Harney look out if he tries to subject the state of Missouri to his will. There are strong hands and strong hearts in every township in the state, and an invading enemy would fall as quickly before 'native' rifles, revolvers, and Bowie knives as would be the case with better weapons."

The Canton *Reporter:* "Up until now we have proven ourselves to be a brave, chivalric people, but how are things today? Bound hand and foot, we have been compelled to be subjected to the curses of an armed mob, to kneel before an abolitionist dictator and beg the mercy of a military despot without resisting the injury to our rights and liberties."

The Chillicothe *Chronicle:* "General Harney, the military dictator, has ordered Governor Jackson to disband the troops concentrated in the capital. Is that not the highest degree of impudence? Perhaps Governor Jackson feels it necessary to guard the *state treasury* and the state arsenal against Lincoln's mercenaries. Has it come to this, that a governor of a state no longer has the right to call out the militia to protect public property without some military bigmouth and braggart ordering him to disband it? Is the state of Missouri going to submit to him and thus degrade itself before the entire world? Never! There might be some cowardly hands who are ready to make such a sacrifice of the honor and rights of the state, but no one with his heart in the right place would ever agree that Missouri should have a military dictator over it. Harney's order to Governor Jackson to send the militia home from the capital is an unheard-of abuse of powers. The governor will, we hope, treat the order with the *quiet contempt* it deserves, and if any attempt is made to drive away the state militia, then he will make a last stand, and thousands from all over the state will rush thither and support the governor."

The governor has obviously taken care to send the State Guards away from Jefferson City but not to disband them, and there is no prospect either of a lasting peace or of an unconditional recognition of the federal government.

Westliche Post, 29 May 1861

Captain Blandowsky Is Dead

Today we have a sorrowful message to give our readers: yesterday afternoon at 3:30 Captain Blandowsky died of the amputation made necessary by his wounding at Camp Jackson. The good cause has thus endured a loss that will be hard to make good, since he was without doubt one of the best officers of the federal army here. His comrades and his many friends will long rue his premature loss, brought about by a sniper's bullet. But it has ever been the fashion of war that the bravest and best are chosen as the first victims, just as in old times,

For Patroclus is buried
And Thersites returns from battle!

The Burial of Captain Blandowsky

Yesterday morning was the burial of Captain Blandowsky. The ceremony was grand and impressive, and it certainly left a lasting mark on all who participated.

At 8 A.M. Companies A and B of the Sigel Regiment, and Company C, which the departed had commanded, marched to the Samaritan Hospital, where he had died. Twelve men from the other companies of the regiment accompanied them as a funerary guard.

Near the Samaritan Hospital, Company D of the Börnstein Regiment joined the procession, along with all the officers of the regiment.

Companies A, B, and C of the Blair Regiment, the Zouave Company, and Company C of the Third Home Guard Regiment assembled in the Turner Hall. They were joined by eight Turners wearing the Turner uniform and carrying the flag of the Turner society, passing down Market Street, Fourth Street, and Franklin Avenue to the place of assembly.

From there the funerary procession moved to Picket's Cemetery.

The procession, by order of Colonel Sigel, was to have the following rules:

The body will be accompanied by Company C, First Battalion, Captain Strodtmann.

Company F, under the command of First Lieutenant Busche, will follow the coffin.

The commissioned officers of the regiment, save one for each company and those officers in service at the time, will also follow the coffin.

A sergeant, a corporal, and ten privates from each company are allowed to participate in the ceremonies without weapons.

Company A, Rifle Battalion, under the command of Captain Albert, will serve as the rear guard of the procession.

Following is the order of the procession:

1. Two pieces of field artillery
2. The funerary escort
3. The band
4. The coffin
5. Company C (Blandowsky), Third Regiment
6. Relatives of the departed
7. Officers of the United States Army, officers of Volunteers and of Home Guard
8. The Turner Society
9. Officers of the Third Regiment
10. Rear guard of Captain Albert, Company A, Rifle Battalion
11. Carriages

In this order the procession passed to the cemetery to the strain of funerary dirges. At the grave Captain Hohlfeld* read out a biography of the departed; the notary Krebs gave a truly masterful speech. Everyone knew that each word sprang from a full heart, the words went directly to the heart, and tears welled up in many an eye. He specifically reminded his listeners that the first victims in this war had been brought down by cowardly assassins, and we are convinced that many quiet but earnest oaths of revenge against the cowardly snipers flitted toward heaven from this open grave.

*Dr. Johann Hohlfeld, also known as John F. Hohlfield, would have a moving obituary after his death of wounds suffered at Wilson's Creek in August. In 1860 he lived on the north side of Carondelet Avenue near Capitol. He was the second lieutenant of Company F, Third Regiment, Missouri Volunteers, under Captain Blandowsky. He would be captain of that company when he was wounded at Wilson's Creek. See *St. Louis Directory;* Rombauer, *Union Cause,* 389. SR.

We will not say more about the contents of this speech, since a mutilated excerpt would never be able to give an idea of its powerful impact.

Then the coffin was lowered into the ground, and the funerary procession headed home after the usual three volleys had been fired over the freshly covered grave.

Westliche Post, 29 May 1861

The Military Honors for Captain Blandowsky

There certainly has never been such a funerary procession as that which passed through the streets of St. Louis yesterday, not in the entire history of the city. Never had anyone ever seen so many soldiers or such good ones. The quiet procession of about twenty-five hundred persons marching in parade to the beat of muffled drums and funerary airs made an irresistible impact on friend and foe alike. We ourselves, a private in the Home Guard, were moved as the regiment marched down Franklin Street with the coffin, and the bearded, solemn faces showed a strangely earnest spirit. We were particularly struck by the companies that followed the coffin, which carried no weapons, and most of them had crossed their arms. These unarmed men, aware of their own strength and of the aid of their brethren, these athletes glowed as if they had already fought ten battles.

The writer of this was in the procession, and he has never seen a more powerful expression on the face of the masses. It was as if every tongue were stilled by a magic spell, and even when a small child gave a cry of surprise there was at once a command for him to be quiet. Men poured out of their shops, and we saw many a face without tears, but with the muscles twitching with an emotion we could not describe. At first it was joy and surprise at the great procession, then agitation, sorrow, scorn, rage, and pride. Let everyone get out of this what he can.

It was good that our dead captain was buried so splendidly. This day of peace was worth more for freedom than all of the days of terror and killing that went before.

Westliche Post, 29 May 1861

Missouri

From Scotland County, from which a large group of Unionists was expelled recently, we received a letter dated 21 May saying that two Unionist rallies were held, one in the northeastern and one in the southwestern parts of the county. The people declared itself against secession and for the Union by a great majority. Best of all, however, was the fact that resolutions were passed demanding the *resignation* of the governor, the lieutenant governor, and the convention delegate of the district, *Henry M. Gorin,* because of sympathy with secession.

In Stockton, Cedar County, in the southwestern quarter of Missouri, United States Senator Judge Johnson recently gave a rabidly secessionist speech. Among other things, he said, "The honor and security of Missouri demands the quickest possible association with the Southern Confederacy. We should not so humble ourselves as to allow things to stay at armed neutrality. *Not* to be a secessionist means to be a contemptible defender of Negro equality, and if such a person were in this gathering, I wish he would raise his head high so I could take a photograph of him and write underneath, 'A man with a white skin but a nigger-heart!' " The citizens of Cedar County had always supported him and helped him to achieve the second-highest office the people could bestow. Now they would continue to support him in freeing the state from black Republicanism. "Place your hand on your heart and vote for a secession ordinance. I know that you are not in favor of holding woolly haired, thick-lipped, ivory-toothed niggers to be your equals. Don't take the position of a 'politic-Orr,' no, never!"* And in this style he went on and on. —If anyone ever believed he would gain anything by replacing Senator Green, then he was most mistaken.* Johnson is Green multiplied by ten. He still says that anyone who voted for Orr committed a mortal sin that he could not beg God to forgive, and that Governor Jackson has earned "the admiration of every friend

*Sample Orr had been the Constitutional Union candidate for governor in 1860. See B. B. Lightfoot, "Nobody's Nominee: Sample Orr and the Election of 1860," *MHR* 60 (1965/1966): 127–48. SR.

*Senator James S. Green of Louisiana, Missouri, a vociferous secessionist, had resigned from the Senate after Lincoln called for volunteers to suppress rebellion. Inexplicably, Green went into seclusion at home and did not surface again during the war—a bitter disappointment to his friends. JNP.

of his country" through his powerful patriotic refusal to carry out Lincoln's requisition.

This powerful speech was received with great enthusiasm by secessionists, but with just as much hostility by the Unionists, to whom he apologized afterwards by saying he did not wish to insult anyone personally.

There is general agitation in the southwest of the state, and the Unionists live in fear of the secessionists. Every day hundreds are leaving the state. Last week twenty-five families left Stockton, along with seventy-five from Spring River. All are going to the free states.

Westliche Post, 29 May 1861

The Home Guards

A long article in the *Republican* published Sunday and yesterday declares in a defamatory manner that there have been daily incidents in which the Home Guards insult peaceful citizens—both men and women—without provocation, and that it is necessary to bring this militia under better discipline. We would ordinarily treat these outbursts as we do similar statements in that hate-sheet, namely by passing over them with silent contempt, but we see this as the opening move for a public *demand that the Home Guard be disbanded.* It is certainly well known that delegations of so-called "respected" citizens of St. Louis have been sent to Washington to lobby for this disbanding with the administration. This delegation is supposed to have received an encouraging response, even if this was anything but outright agreement. We would have regarded such a response as impossible even a week ago, but since General Harney's agreement and the publication of Mr. Gibson's letter, which says that the government of Missouri would not be compelled to take sides in the coming battle, we have to hold anything to be possible—we say this so that the Home Guards will know their situation and be able to counter the plots being hatched against them.

Westliche Post, 5 June 1861

Incompetence or Treason

In times of peril and revolution, out of whose crushing waves the solid forms of a coherent, reformed state system will emerge like a rock only with time, it is not possible to make a sharp distinction between the incompetence of impotent and cowardly moderation and premeditated treason, since the results of stupidity and faint-heartedness are usually even worse than those of direct treason. This bitter experience of history should serve as a warning to those silly people who let themselves be blown along by the storms of current events while they hold positions of trust, for soon the very same storm will blow them away.

Whatever local problems are being discussed, we have seen it repeated for the tenth and the hundredth time that until now the United States government has neglected its duty to the Union people of Missouri in the most contemptible and irresponsible manner. Even if a policy of delay is right and expedient in the case of the states that have withdrawn, in the case of the border states it is injurious and nothing less than a cowardly betrayal of one's own friends. How do things stand right now, both here and in the entire state?

After lengthy pressing and begging, the citizens at last received their weapons; soon after this there was the promenade to Camp Jackson, and it seems since then almost as if the government in Washington has been shocked at its own boldness and has let dear God and General Harney rule once more. While the friends of the Union have been driven from all parts of the state with a beastliness that was hardly experienced under the Sepoys, our philosopher-General Harney concludes a peace treaty with General Price, which is to say that while the knife of the secessionists is at the throat of the Union people in the entire state, the general allows himself to agree to a treaty that has hit all the patriots in the land like a thunderbolt out of the blue.

The camp in Jefferson City is to be disbanded; but it is clear enough from our correspondence today from Lexington that the border ruffians have simply changed their tactics. What should anyone think under these circumstances of a government to which a loyal people has made every possible sacrifice?

It is traitors or fools who care for Missouri in Washington?

Has the general government contributed one cent from its bag of patriotic contributions to promote the good cause?

It is true that the weapons and munitions are here, but all other supplies are lacking; the physicians of the regiments do not even have essential medicines, and if it were not for voluntary contributions our regiments would have had to sleep on straw or beg in the streets even as defenders of the Union!

Are those in Washington who bring this to pass traitors or fools?

It has even been reported that a delegation of "respectable" dishrags has been in Washington, and that Mr. Bates was supposed to have given them a not-unfavorable answer. While the gentlemen in Washington gave satisfactory answers to these covert enemies, these tools of the *Missouri Republican* and of secessionists in general, or even promise them the disarmament of the Home Guard, which we can hardly believe, Jackson brazenly raises the secessionist flag before his house in Jefferson City once more, and a small army gathers in Lexington with the open intent of slitting the throats of all friends of freedom. At the same moment the government in Washington clings to its almighty indifference! The best men we have to defend the Union are being double-crossed and injured in their activities by this dishrag-clique, these so-called men of peace, who try to make war just so many words. It seems that they rely more on the counsel of covert peace-secessionists than on that of representatives of their own party in Washington.

The government carries a fearful responsibility in this matter. If the Union men of Missouri and St. Louis are defeated, exiled, and massacred due to the measureless failures of Washington, then the baleful finger of world history will mark out Washington, where these traitors or fools sat who let their friends fall before they fell themselves in their turn!

Westliche Post, 5 June 1861

Remarkable Disclosures about Our Situation

Bit by bit the clouds that shrouded the pact between Messrs. Harney and Price are rising. A correspondent writes a few things from St. Louis to the *Chicago Tribune* that we did not know here or could not yet say. It appears that General Price came here with the goal of saving himself and Governor Jackson from the penalty of treason through a compromise; even General Harney believed at first that Governor Jackson would have to resign. On the Tuesday after the surrender of Camp Jackson, some self-appointed so-called Uniønist dishrags led by Wayman Crow* came to General Harney, and they succeeded in getting him to drop the demand for Jackson's resignation and even to show stubborn opposition to Messrs. Samuel T. Glover and Thomas T. Gantt, who had come to protest any pact with the rebels, so that these gentlemen were moved to take their leave of the General of Peace with some hard words. General Price managed to get Governor Jackson out of a tough spot through this pact, and without compromising himself. As the matter stands now, the covert secessionists, led by the *Republican*, have a better hearing with General Harney than the upright Union men. This is the case with Wayman Crow, one of the people who supported the conditional secessionist ticket in the election for the state convention; he openly declared that when it came to a decision, Missouri would have to go with the South; this is a man whose three business partners are all openly declared secessionists—and such people are General Harney's advisors.

On the day of the capture of Camp Jackson, a meeting took place in the office of Mayor Taylor, made up, sad to say, of men such as Robert Campbell, James C. Yeatman, Hamilton R. Gamble, Captain Eaton, Henry G. Turner, and former mayor King.* The conclusion of this self-appointed assembly was that Captain Lyon should be removed from his post, and all steps were set in motion to realize this goal.

Hamilton R. Gamble, a Union delegate from St. Louis in the recent state convention, and James C. Yeatman, a merchant with decided Southern sympathies, were sent to Washington as commissioners to depose the offending Captain Lyon. They set off at once for Washington to present the matter to General Scott before the friends of Lyon could learn of their actions and protest them. Fortunately, Capt. James B. Eads and Franklin A. Dick were in Washing-

*Wayman Crow, president of Crow, Hargadine, and Walker, headed the city's largest wholesale firm. He was a founder of Washington University, a member of the public school board, and a leading civic activist generally. Much older than Blair's Yankee merchants, with strong ties to elite Southern and Creole families, Crow believed with other conditionalists that war could be averted in Missouri. Gantt and Glover, both attorneys, were hard-nosed Blair men. The "conditional secessionists" referred to by the partisan editor were Unionists. Naive about the prospects for peace and Governor Jackson's intentions they were, secessionists they were not. JNP.

*Robert Campbell, a long-time Benton Democrat, was the venerable dean of the fur traders, whose home on Lucas Place (now Locust) is still one of the city's historical treasures. Like Yeatman, Gamble, and King, Campbell was merely a conciliatory Unionist. Turner, a banker with business and family ties with James H. Lucas, and the old Creole families as well, may have been a covert secessionist, but if so, his views remained covert. JNP.

ton and opposed these dishrags.* The result was that Captain Lyon was named a brigadier general.

From these disclosures we can see with what brazenness the secessionists maneuver. They continually operate through intermediaries who wear the masks of Union men or "conservative respectable patriots" and cripple the strength of the government as soon as it wants to strike a blow. It is high time that a swift end was made to this two-faced, dangerous, and treacherous game.

Anzeiger des Westens, 13 June 1861
(for Wednesday, 12 June 1861)*

The Meeting

between Gov. Claiborne Fox Jackson and Sterling Price on the one side and General Lyon, Colonel Blair, and Horace Connell on the other side was an absolute failure insofar as no agreement could be reached on any points.

Several days ago, Thomas T. Gantt went to General Lyon and arranged this meeting. General Lyon issued passes of safe conduct for their visit to St. Louis, and on their arrival here he invited them to come to the Arsenal to confer with him. Governor Jackson rejected this and suggested the Planter's House as a place for the meeting, to which General Lyon agreed in order to show his good faith. The meeting lasted four hours. Governor Jackson opened the negotiations with several commonplaces on peace, then fell silent for the remainder of the meeting and used General Price for his mouthpiece.

General Price demanded the disbanding of the Home Guard in the entire state as a condition for an agreement, and he insisted that no United States troops be allowed to occupy or pass through the state.

If these conditions were met, all state troops would be disbanded and peace established. He asserted that he had strictly observed

*James B. Eads, a self-taught engineer, and Franklin Dick were unconditionalists. Eads built the Union's ironclad gunboats during the war at the Nelson-Eads shipyards on the south side. JNP.

*General Harney was replaced on 30 May 1861, but the Harney-Price agreement continued to be observed until the Planter's House Conference on 11 June. The account here neglects to repeat Lyon's statement that he would rather see every man, woman, and child in Missouri dead and buried than to allow the authority of the federal government to be diminished. SR.

the agreement with General Harney up to that time and had not altered so much as one iota.

General Lyon responded in his usual decisive manner that he could not agree. In his second proclamation General Harney had declared the militia law* to be unconstitutional and had insisted that it not be carried out—but despite this the governor had organized the militia, and Lyon was sure that if he did not occupy the state there would be covert if not open reinforcement of troops hostile to the United States, all agreements to the contrary. Further, he believed that the governor would not resist any invasion by enemy troops across the border with Arkansas.

The discussion grew very animated at that point, until Governor Jackson moved they continue the discussion through an exchange of correspondence. General Lyon rejected this out of hand, since it would not solve the problems discussed here and would even prove injurious to the interests of the United States.

The gathering broke up without settling anything, and the gentlemen from Jefferson City departed our city by an evening train.

It is likely that there will be a proclamation from the governor in Jefferson City that will call for resistance to the United States troops, even if in a veiled manner, while the federal troops themselves will take measures to protect the exposed Home Guard and faithful Union men.

Anzeiger des Westens, 20 June 1861
(for Friday, 14 June 1861)*

The Declaration of War

against the United States government by the rebel Jackson in the article immediately before this bears the stamp of its lies and treason so clearly on its forehead that any additional word of comment seems a luxury. Even the *State Journal*, which still seems to be happy about the burning of the bridges, was silent in the presence of this enormity. A column and a half was fiddled away with nonsense, but not one word was expended in favor of the proclamation. And yet the lies of the proclamation are nothing more nor less

*The "military bill" adopted by the legislature after Camp Jackson had authorized the governor to mobilize and expand the State Guard to fifty thousand men. JNP.
*This article follows a translation of the declaration by Gov. Claiborne Fox Jackson proclaiming defiance against federal authority in the state of Missouri. SR.

than the lies of the *State Journal*. The passage on the meeting with Lyon is almost word for word from the *Journal*, save that a few unimportant things have been added. Everyone knows better than this, since the governor refuses to commit a description of the negotiations to paper and release it to the public, obviously on the grounds that he would not be able to get away with his lies. But that has no effect on his old-fashioned nullification theory, according to which the citizens need not trouble themselves about the government in Washington, since they owe their first allegiance to their state whenever the governor decides for usurpation and a military despotism. So before he preaches crusade against this administration he mentions that General Lyon spoke of *"loyal subjects"* and that he threatened Missouri with the fate of Maryland—both damned lies, though no one in Baltimore or the whole of Maryland, not even Police Chief Kane or Mr. McLane, deserves the rope as richly as Governor Jackson. And to speak of subjects would more befit a despotic nature such as that of *canaille*-Jackson than that of General Lyon, who has preserved the pride of a citizen and a Republican together with the nature of a soldier. But having said this he lifts his voice and cries, "Arise, ye fifty thousand, to expel these invaders with disgrace." Invaders? That must mean the citizens who have declared themselves ready to stand by the Union, for beyond them there are no United States troops on Missouri soil.* Will the citizens of Missouri arise for this purpose? That would be laughable, since most of them are friends of the Union, so much so that any secessionist effort in any locality is defeated as soon as things get serious. General Lyon has not waited for Jackson the Fox to throw down his gauntlet, since he knows him from long experience. Even when he is scared to death, Mr. Jackson still thinks he can bluff the United States. But the United States only requires him to serve as crown witness against himself through a proclamation, and then it will do everything necessary to bring him to the gallows he deserves. The shamelessness of his defying the president and of his ordering the State Militia into camps are as nothing compared with this proclamation of open opposition to the federal authority, to a bloody rising against the highest government of the country. He does not even have to confess that Missouri still belongs to the Union to brand himself a traitor. The only question now is whether his legs are long enough to get him safely away from Lyon. Hardly a thousand men could be found in all of

---

*Except for five hundred or more regulars at the Arsenal and Blair's ten thousand Missouri Volunteers who had been sworn into the federal service, far more troops than Jackson had. JNP.

Missouri who would intervene with the president on his behalf to gain him mercy.

Anzeiger des Westens, 20 June 1861
(for Friday, 14 June 1861)

The commencement of troop movements for the occupation of the state of Missouri was continued and completed yesterday. The two government steamers *Iatan* and *J. C. Swon* took the First Regiment and regulars, along with the brigade staff, in this order: on the *Iatan* was the left wing of the Blair Regiment under the command of Lieutenant Colonel Andrews, along with a section of Captain Potter's light field artillery and two companies of regulars under Captain Lathrop as escort. The *J. C. Swon* brought the right wing of the regiment along with Colonel Blair himself, his staff and band, *General Lyon* and his brigade staff, and yet another section of Captain Potter's light artillery and provisions. In all fifteen hundred men, four field pieces, and a howitzer—both steamers left the Arsenal at midday, one immediately after the other.

At 5 P.M. Col. Franz Sigel with staff and band formed with seven companies of "Lyoner Fahnenwacht" and marched to the depot of the Pacific Railway, joining five companies under Lieutenant Colonel Hassendeubel.* These were also joined by the pioneer company. A company cf volunteer artillery under Major Backhoff with two guns, two howitzers, and eighty-five men was formed with the remnant of the Sigel Regiment.

In the evening the Börnstein Regiment came up from Jefferson Barracks to the Arsenal to follow two companies with baggage that had gone ahead to Hermann by train the previous night, and they set out nine hundred men strong at 9 A.M. today to meet the steamer *City of Louisiana.**

---

*Franz Hassendeubel, 1817–1863, was born in the Palatinate and emigrated to America in 1842. He served as an artillery officer in the Mexican War, and in April 1861 he was lieutenant colonel under Franz Sigel in the Third Missouri Regiment. He built a series of ten forts around St. Louis for General Frémont in autumn 1861. He was regarded as a brilliant engineer and was promoted to brigadier general in 1863. He was wounded before Vicksburg and died on 17 July 1863. See Kaufmann, *Deutschen in Bürgerkrieg*, 508; State Historical Society of Missouri, Vertical File, for Hassendeubel service record abstract. SR.

*The *City of Louisiana* was the steamboat that brought Börnstein's Second Missouri Regiment from Hermann to Jefferson City; Börnstein mentions it in his memoirs. SR.

Anzeiger des Westens, 20 June 1861

A State of War

Missouri, 14 June 1861

has now been declared for Missouri, and all that is left for us is to take up with courage the struggle that has been forced upon us. Those citizens loyal to the Union have injured no one, have spoken not one word of challenge, and have only asked to be able to fulfill their sworn obligations and to pursue their peaceful activities in keeping with the rights guaranteed them. Others want to compel them to participate in treason and rebellion in order to drag themselves and their entire state into ruin; no one would willingly do this at any price.

While the Germans, with very few exceptions, are ready and willing to do their duty, since they are naturally immune to infection by Southern sympathies, many of the Americans have been torn apart, with their interests pulling them one way and their sympathies the other. This situation must end now, since even the native-born must decide either to join with the Germans against Jackson's gang or openly enlist in the rebel army. Already the names of those liable for military service have been posted and the notorious militia law has been put in operation.

There is no time to be lost in forming a Home Guard everywhere one is possible, so that by arming and exercising, the masses of the people can come to repress the threats and protests coming from a few. Everywhere it is clear that only the greatest determination will do any good, but that it really does make a difference. Wherever a Home Guard has been established, there is peace, and even threats have been stilled. We have to know who is our enemy and who is our friend, and in the long run a decision on this is better than having tensions continue indefinitely. Missouri has been sold to Jefferson Davis without a doubt; we should see that this despicable transaction is never carried through and that it brings the seller no greater profit than a rope. They seem to want to bring Virginia's misery on Missouri; it is high, high time to shut these troublemakers down—we should have done it long ago.

I hear that the governor had the bridges over the Gasconade and Osage burned yesterday. Is there no law against criminal arson? Yet no *enemy* was on the march, since the federal government is the *friend* of every state in the Union, Missouri included, and of all citizens who do their duty. Only a fool would dispute the right of the

federal government to occupy militarily every foot of federal territory in case of war or rebellion. Is that not what happened during
the Mormon War?

Rest assured, my countrymen, that the traitors have a troubled
conscience, but they have all that much more respect for the loaded
muskets of the united Unionists; let it be "one arm, one sword, one
will."

Far West [Friedrich Münch]

Anzeiger des Westens, 20 June 1861
(for Saturday, 15 June 1861)

Progress of the Missouri Campaign

The governor and officials of the state have fled Jefferson City,
and the archives have been taken in the greatest haste to Arrow
Rock in the governor's own county, Saline. And they are even
robbers and arsonists! In order to facilitate their departure from
Jefferson City on the following day, the place was rendered as
inaccessible as possible by burning down the two railway bridges
over the Gasconade and Osage. It appears that the governor has let
it be known that he will dig in at Arrow Rock and meet the federal
troops face to face there. That would be even better than we had
hoped. There are supposed to be no state troops left in Jefferson
City, and we should imagine that no one wants to be a martyr for a
burned-out governor.

On the other hand the *J. C. Swon* with the general and Col. Frank
Blair ran aground and could not get loose during the night. Yesterday the *D. A. January* went to her aid.

Latest: The *Swon* lay for five hours before it was pulled loose by
the *D. A. January* and arrived at Hermann to great jubilation at
3:30 P.M. yesterday. It left after a stop of half an hour.

The command of Colonel Börnstein arrived safely in Hermann at
6 P.M. on the Pacific Railway, also to a jubilation that would have
been suitable for liberators. The *D. A. January* was being awaited
until 9 P.M. to take the regiment upstream.

We have no news on the Sigel Regiment, but there are rumors
that it is already close to Jefferson City.

Mississippi Blätter, 16 June 1861

Support the Families of Our Freedom-Fighters

An unsolicited article reached us sent from Highland, Illinois, which complains that "Jesuit Missionaries" are collecting money there, and that Swiss and Germans there are actually supporting "this sort of swindle." We are unable to publish the note in our newspaper due to the form it took, but we want to report what is going on and to say how much we agree with the opinion of our contributor—the very idea that at this very moment when every resource is needed for the struggle for right and freedom anyone would willingly fill the purses of the Jesuits deserves a double and a triple rebuke!

Anzeiger des Westens, 20 June 1861
(for Sunday, 16 June 1861)

Lyon in Jefferson City

The Capitol of Missouri in the Hands of the United States

The events in the interior of the state have developed much more rapidly than anyone could have expected. Yesterday at noon a special dispatch came from Jefferson City saying that the steamer *Iatan* had arrived in Jefferson City at about 2 P.M. carrying General Lyon, the left wing of the Blair Regiment, and a company of artillery. They went at once to the landing by the penitentiary, which was taken in good order. They were greeted by a great number of local citizens, led by Gen. *Thomas L. Price.** From there the battalion marched the length of the town and occupied the Capitol Hill. A Mr. W. H. Lusk was the lucky one to raise the stars and stripes for the first time.

No secessionist demonstrations were attempted, let alone any acts of resistance. On the contrary, people wanted to crowd around the troops and bless them for deliverance. The *J. C. Swon* with Colonel Blair arrived with the rest of his regiment just as the first troops occupied Capitol Hill.

We have no further news of Börnstein's regiment, which only

---

*The same Thomas L. Price who was reported by the *Anzeiger* as traducing the Germans for voting Republican a few weeks earlier. JNP.

arrived the next morning from Hermann on the *City of Louisiana* and the Washington ferry.

Colonel Sigel has arrived in Rolla, the railhead of the Southwestern Railroad, with a portion of his regiment. The train stopped about half a mile before the station, and then the troops formed into battle order to march on the place. Here as well the flag of secession was pulled down and the stars and stripes raised with as much festivity as at the Capitol. A state militia unit of 180 men, which had made loud threats when they first arrived, fell over themselves fleeing and were nowhere to be found. The citizens remaining seem to be the most enthusiastic Union people in the world.

Since his route of escape seemed to be closing, Governor Jackson is said to have escaped his redoubt in Boonville, whither he has precipitously fled from Jefferson City, and he was on his way to Arkansas with an escort of 120 men before dawn yesterday.

In the meantime eight more Illinois regiments were gathered two hours away from St. Louis, four in Caseyville and four in Belleville, although there was no news from Belleville until yesterday. Four regiments are supposed to be on their way to Quincy.

So our state can rest assured that it will stay in the Union. And now the convention can gather once again to fill the vacancy in the executive branch. It should have been done long ago, but better late than never. It is impossible to proceed in an utterly revolutionary way here, so Jackson and Reynolds have to be removed by constitutional means. It is a matter of indifference to us whether the convention meets in St. Louis or Jefferson City so long as it meets under the star-spangled banner!

Mississippi Blätter, 16 June 1861

Triumph of Our Army of Freedom

Yesterday was a day of anxious, tense expectation, since we were unable to get any news through the entire day from our brave brothers who had sallied forth to stomp on the head of the serpent of rebellion. Even the afternoon newspapers breathed not a syllable, and the usual scattering of false rumors was lacking. At last, at about six, an extra of the *Democrat* appeared that caused widespread jubilation. The sum of the news can be gathered in a few short sentences:

Jefferson City Occupied Without a Shot

Gen. Sigel Has Occupied Rolla, Terminus of the Southwest Railway, Without Battle

Governor Jackson Has Fled from Boonville to Arkansas

So already the specter of rebellion has dissolved into smoke, and it hardly seems likely that the border snipers of the West will ever dare to put up serious resistance to our army of liberation.

But back to the events. Sigel's corps, in the person of his Lieutenant Colonel Hassendeubel, set out first of all last Wednesday with five companies and attached artillery on the Pacific Railway. One unit continued from Franklin on the Southwest Railway, another went to the Gasconade bridge to put it back into use. On Thursday evening Sigel himself followed with the rest of his regiment, and at midday on Friday the First Regiment with General Lyon and Colonel Blair went up the river on the boats *Swon* and *Iatan*.

As early as 1 P.M. on Friday the fourteenth, Sigel entered Rolla, the terminus of the Southwest Railway, leading a part of his regiment. The soldiers got off the train half a mile before the town and marched northward, with the vanguard under the command of W. Pretorius, Sigel's ordnance officer. The secessionist flag in the town was torn down and stomped in the dust, and the star-spangled banner was raised in its place to the great jubilation of the people.

The state militia unit that was there, about 180 strong, suddenly vanished in a cloud of dust when it heard that the defenders of the Union were on their way. The citizens of the place who remained declared themselves to be solidly for the Union.

Symptomatic of the spirit of the secession is a story that is told locally. One old farmer bragged aloud that he could chop down five or ten damned Unionists, but then someone pointed out the approaching Union troops. He let out a shriek of terror and vanished in "double quick time," leaving a cloud of dust behind him.

Just as General Sigel was occupying the route to the Southwest, the two ships proceeded up the Missouri without opposition and arrived below Jefferson City about 2 o'clock. The steamer *Iatan*, commanded by General Lyon, was the first, landing below the prison. The first to land was the company of regulars, the Artillery Company F under Captain Totten. The regulars marched up the road past the prison in quick-step, occupying the heights opposite, where the secessionist Alfred McLoy lives. General Lyon and his staff followed this company; then came the volunteers under Lieutenant Colonel Andrews; Company G, Captain Cavender; F,

Captain Graetz; E, Captain Cole; D, Captain Richarts; and C, Captain Stone. They marched through the town to the Capitol, to the cheering of the populace, and W. H. Lusk was the chosen one who raised the star-spangled banner once more on the dome of that imposing structure, to the accompaniment of loud hurrahs.

The secessionists were nowhere to be seen. The *Swon* arrived when the Capitol had already been taken. The demonstration of utter joy in the streets was said to be very moving. We can easily imagine that, since three-quarters of the town is German, and they have suffered under a reign of terror. Women wept profuse tears of joy and men shouted their throats raw. Jackson is supposed to have arrived in Boonville on Friday at 8 P.M., with a bodyguard of 120 men. He is said to have left Boonville for Arkansas. This last assertion has still not been confirmed.*

This would be the end of the first act of the civil war in Missouri!

---

*The battle of Boonville, 17 June 1861, was a quick action by Lyon against a small force directly commanded by Governor Jackson. Jackson fled to the south. Thomas Snead, Jackson's aide-de-camp, remarks, "From a military standpoint the affair at Boonville was a very insignificant thing, but it did in fact deal a stunning blow to the Southern-rights men in Missouri, and one which weakened the Confederacy during all of its brief existence." Robert Underwood Johnson and Clarence Clough Buel, eds., *Battles and Leaders of the Civil War* (New York, 1887), 267–68. SR.

V.

Beyond Heroism
June 1861–March 1862

"... Give a cheer for the men on whom our hopes for a happy future
rest. Long live Frémont! Long live Sigel!"

Mrs. Doehn, *Anzeiger des Westens*, 28 August 1861

"For us Germans, emancipation is a matter of life and death. If
Missouri remains a slave state, then we will not remain here
any longer. No one is fooled about that."

Anzeiger des Westens, 3 March 1862

Anzeiger des Westens, 20 June 1861
(for Wednesday, 19 June 1861)

The Jackson Revolt

Henceforth we shall use this title for all events and documents
concerning the military occupation of Missouri by federal troops
and the struggle against the rebel governor and his cohorts.
We begin with the

Proclamation of Colonel Börnstein

of the Second Regiment, decreed in his capacity as commandant of
Jefferson City and Cole County.*

Jefferson City, 17 June

To the Citizens of Cole and Neighboring Counties!
Fellow citizens: I have been named by the commanding general to be
commandant of this place, and I shall exercise my authority in Cole
County and neighboring counties to protect the peace and tranquility of
all citizens and to assist the civil authorities in upholding the government and the Union and in carrying out the constitutional laws of the
land.

*Heinrich Börnstein at Jefferson City was serving simply as district military com-
mandant, in no sense as acting governor. He makes this quite clear in his memoirs.
Börnstein eventually had his wife come out to join him in the Governor's Mansion,
and he remembered the weeks spent there as among the most pleasant in his life.
See Börnstein, *Fünfundsiebzig Jahre*, 2:312–26. SR.

265

Through the precipitous flight of Governor Claiborne Fox Jackson and others you have been left without state officials—without a government. This state of things could have led to lawlessness and anarchy and all the evils that flow from such a situation. It has been deemed necessary to supply this want by naming a commandant of this place to keep watch over this town and its surroundings. I therefore demand that the officials of this town and county continue in the practice of their official duties, and I declare myself ready to assist them in carrying out the constitutional laws of this country. I do not desire to involve myself in their official business, nor do I intend to meddle in the private affairs of citizens. Your personal security will be guaranteed. Your property will be respected; your slave property will not be touched by any part of my command, nor shall any slave be allowed to come to my lines without written permission from his master; despite the fact that we live in times of war, I will still try to carry out my instructions with moderation and clemency, but at the same time I shall not tolerate the slightest attempt to destroy the Union and its government, nor shall I approve any sort of illegal activity; and I shall pursue all traitors and their partisans, aides or cohorts, and deliver them to the proper authorities.

I call on all friends of the Union as well as all good citizens to form Home Guard companies for the protection of the Union, to arm themselves, and to train. I shall see that you receive training from my officers, so far as possible, and I shall contribute to your military organization with all my strength. Any citizen who has business to transact with the commandant of this place or who has complaints can enter my headquarters from 10 A.M. to noon. My soldiers will observe the strictest discipline, and I hope that the support of all good citizens will make it possible for me to keep this town and its region in complete peace and order and shield you from the terrors and devastation of this war.

Henry Börnstein
Colonel commanding the Second
Regiment, Missouri Volunteers
Regional Commandant
Headquarters, The Capitol
Jefferson City, 17 June 1861

Anzeiger des Westens, 27 June 1861
(for Sunday, 23 June 1861)

The Activities of Colonel Börnstein

Documents of Current History

What Is High Treason?

Our readers have certainly seen the documents published yesterday demonstrating in the most concrete manner possible the high treason of a whole series of highly placed persons in our common-wealth: high treason, in fact, which goes back long before the Camp Jackson affair. As early as the start of April they were thinking about a coup, particularly the capture of the United States Arsenal and the Subtreasury of the United States. An intense effort was also made to raise half a million dollars promised the state by various banks here. It is remarkable that a letter from Claiborne Fox Jackson appears with the date of 9 May to Mr. Sterling Price, not yet a major general, asking him to collect the money so it could be stowed away in nests in Boonville, Arrow Rock, Brunswick, etc., as well as in the hands of the president of the State Bank, Robert A. Barnes. But it is well known that the banks were all warned of the treasonous plans of the governor by the *Democrat* and knew well enough not to loan money to the governor at the instant he was planning to separate from the Union; the president of the bank himself is aware of this when he says that the governor would like to have the money quickly so it would not fall into Blair's hands or so that Blair would not demand an accounting. Would that not be giving *aid and comfort* to the rebels and enemies of our country? Is this not high treason in the classic form?

It is possible to hold a strict view of high treason and strongly to believe that one undergoes the penalty for high treason only when he gives aid and comfort to someone bearing arms against the government and the country, but one can do nothing but call sup-porting the enemy with money high treason. His business for the State Bank brought General Price here precisely at the time of the Camp Jackson affair, which provided him with an explanation for his treasonable activities after the fact. The blood of citizens that flowed and the acts of aggression carried out against the state helped to explain why the best Union man of them all (almost better than Uriel Wright) abandoned his federal government. How lucky that it happened just then, for that was just what it took to terrify the banks into refusing to pay the money to the governor's agent.*

If the discovery of these documents finally succeeds in exposing the conspirators of rebellion and their cohorts as bad examples, then special thanks are due to those who brought these devastating proofs to the light of day. The main contributors to this are our troops, who beat the enemy at Boonville and then occupied Camp

---

*Since the Bank of the State of Missouri was jointly owned and controlled by the state and private investors, with half of the directors plus one elected by the legislature, the officers of the bank were usually responsive to state pressure. The "best Union man of all" was of course Sterling Price, whose Unionism had been short-lived. Uriel Wright of St. Louis had also recanted his Unionism. JNP.

Vest. Then thanks are due to Colonel Börnstein, who has taken it upon himself as his first duty as commandant in Jefferson City to keep the peace and show treason the door.

Since Governor Jackson left here on the twelfth, returning here only to issue his war proclamation on the fourteenth before departing from Jefferson City even before General Lyon had a chance to set out, and since he had destroyed a great deal of property to be left behind, the prisoners of the state penitentiary naturally figured they were entitled to break out, since they were strong enough to do so. A certain Mr. Worthington wrote the governor saying that the state government was able to settle its own bankruptcy through a special regulation of debts, and in the same way it could solve many problems simply by opening the prisons. So the prisoners set about breaking out. Governor Jackson could not have cared less. —But Colonel Börnstein set about at once to solve the problem. As remarkable as it seems, we must believe it when we are told that Colonel Börnstein's rule is as popular here as the civilian administration of Jackson was unpopular and hated.

He achieved his first results, however, when he searched the Governor's Mansion and found bundles of treasonous correspondence, including Barnes's letter and all the others printed yesterday, which we printed from a transcript of the originals prepared by a friend participating in the investigation.

Mississippi Blätter, 2 July 1861*

The Ancient Antagonism

The struggle that is now bursting forth between the peoples of the North and of the South certainly has as its first palpable cause the dispute over slavery. It is also true that both the people of the North and the people of the South are gathered out of fragments from all the nations of the earth, and that up until now they have been combined in a ramshackle fashion. There are Germans, English, French, Irish, etc., both in the North and in the South; there have been and are haters of foreigners among the natives of both regions, and in both the North and the South we find a small band of

*Attempts to explain sectional hostilities in the United States often gave rise to macrohistorical interpretations of the sort popular with nineteenth-century intellectuals. This is a racist interpretation with several large factual flaws, not the least of which is the fact that the Normans were of Scandinavian rather than Romance background. SR.

enlightened men who stand at the commanding heights of their times, who understand the mission of their century and their people, and who know how to carry out that mission. At first glance it would appear that since both parts are so similarly composed, a uniform opinion should rule both in the warm and the cold climates. That has never been the case, and now at last the long-smoldering hostilities of blood, outlook, and style of life have burst into bright flames. Now everyone says that slavery is to blame for this struggle, and at one level this is true enough. But how did it come about that it was precisely the denizens of the Southern regions who held onto slavery with such determination, while the Northern peoples shook it off after having been accustomed to it for a long time?

The fact is that the native, or at least the long-term, population of both parts has retained characteristic differences despite foreign immigration, and that these distinctions have marked the entire nature of the people in North and South. These characteristic antagonisms have in fact in some cases been reinforced and sharpened by immigration. The German, born in a temperate zone, has preferred to seek out the corresponding climate of the Northern states in order to find himself a home under the rays of a gentler sun. The southern Frenchman, the Spaniard, and the Mexican of Spanish descent feels himself more at home in the sunny South, since it suits him better.*

The Anglo-Saxon puritan with blond hair chose the inhospitable coast of Massachusetts two and a half centuries ago, while the Norman cavalier with the black locks of a southern European went to Maryland and South Carolina to live with his kind under a warmer sun. So in this struggle we are seeing once again revealed that remarkable law of world history, precisely the eternal opposition and struggle of the Germanic and Romance people, based on profound opposition of bodily capacities, weaknesses, styles of life, morals, and forms of state. This struggle is as old as the civilized world, as old as the cultural history of mankind. Ever since the Teutons overcame the Romans in war, the bloody torch of this struggle has often cast its dreadful light over the world, but from the soil watered by the blood of the enemy there always sprang forth a new cultural era, a new step forward for a refreshed and rejuvenated mankind; a new, better race grew out of the empty fields of battle, and from the ashes of the ruined huts of half-barbarians grew the comfortable homes of civilized nations. The struggle between these two great, proud races has ever helped to

*The slave South was far more British than the free states, a fact that was no more a secret in 1861 than it was a century later. JNP.

destroy old, rotted-out structures and to open the era of a new epoch with new and better perceptions for the human race. The titanic struggle of the German emperors—whose greatness was the result of their conquest of the Romans—with the popes was nothing other than another mighty round of these same two antagonists. The religious question was the chief concern then, just as slavery is the main concern today, but the opposition lay then and lies now much deeper—in the utterly different drives of the two different races.

Certainly the rage for slavery is the direct cause of the struggle for the Southern states right now; but we would look in vain for an explanation of the degree of enthusiasm for something so basically evil if we did not have the history of the Romance race before our eyes. Wherever it came to rule, there it rejected the systems of self-government or showed discomfort in acting within the limits of individual liberty without some sort of guardian or leader. The Spaniard, the Frenchman, developed the sytem of absolutism in the times of Philip II and Louis XIV to perfection. Europe seethes under this system even today, and unfortunately it has penetrated so deeply into the blood of this nation that the hankering for absolutism and slavery is something less offensive to these peoples than it is to the Germanic peoples.

So now we see that the peril that slumbered during the foundation of the Union, and the contradictions that were suppressed due to external perils, have now led to battle after a long truce in which both sides gathered strength. The aim of this struggle is to achieve a resolution of the conflict, a final solution that will at last bestow on the chaotic masses of this nation a national, unitary spirit, a national feeling that has been lacking until now.

Anzeiger des Westens, 18 July 1861
(for Tuesday, 16 July 1861

From Washington

Washington City, 9 July 1861

I have been here for four days and cannot yet find my way around: I shall need at least another week to orient myself in the *new* Washington. What a contrast with earlier times! Such liveliness, rushing, and shoving on the once so empty Pennsylvania Street, where before one could have been robbed in broad daylight by thieves and no one would have seen it. Congress is acting more than it is talking, the Capitol is gradually being purged of traitors and spies, and the Southern pride that once stomped on everyone's neck has been humiliated. One actually begins to believe that this country has a government and a future.

I have seen our Frank P. Blair, and he is working with untiring energy as chairman of the Military Committee, where he dedicates much of his attention to the organization of volunteer regiments. He argues on behalf of the German volunteer regiments of Missouri, and I heard him make the following statement to a group of representatives and senators: "By God, gentlemen, I shall always declare that it was the Germans who saved Missouri. Without the Germans and their volunteer regiments Missouri would have been lost for the Union and would already be well along on the same road as Tennessee and Arkansas. I was almost ashamed of my native-born compatriots at Boonville. We could have captured Jackson, Parsons, and the whole band without a stroke of the sword after the encounter and ended the war in Missouri if my native-born countrymen there had told us a tenth of what they all knew. But there was no information to be wrung from them; only the Germans rode in from thirty or forty miles around to give us the information we needed. Unfortunately, a great deal of time was lost due to the great distances involved, so we could not do anything more."

It will interest the Home Guard in St. Louis to know that Captain Sweeny's election as brigadier general of Home Guards was *not confirmed* by the War Department. By order of General Scott, furthermore, Captain Sweeny and his company have been ordered back to Washington City. I read in your newspapers that General Sweeny is still styled a general in Missouri, and I cannot understand that, since the order for his recall went to General Lyon on the sixth. More soon from your

A. F.

Anzeiger des Westens, 18 July 1861
(for Tuesday, 16 July 1861)

The People's Justice

Every civilized race, wherever found on this earth, possesses a certain natural sense of justice that can perhaps be suppressed for a while under the press of circumstances but can never be *extin-*

guished. This sense is more a property of the Germans, the most deep-thinking of all nations, than of any other people on earth. Through centuries it has learned to endure and get along, but woe to anyone who dares fan these embers into a flame. This sense of justice, this inborn and instinctive distinction between good and evil, this hostility against the heaping up of capital and aristocratic titles that is held by a working people used to earning its bread through tedious and honest toil, this hatred of aristocracy whether of birth or wealth, has already toppled thrones and inspired revolutions that are immortally inscribed in the annals of world history.

For that reason no one should abuse the people in a gratuitous or unjust fashion. We know that the people are a mass easily brought into motion by the impulse of a moment, but also that in their hearts the people have an indelible conviction against every injustice, every oppression, every treachery.

Mr. Alexander Kayser,* one of our oldest German fellow-citizens, who owes *everything* he has to the *Germans,* has recently been seized with the unhappy idea of joining the secessionist party and forgetting himself *to such a degree* that he has become a contributor to the *State Journal,* a newspaper deeply detested by all Germans. Under some circumstances we might excuse a *native-born American* for joining the Southern party, but a *German,* who has become everything he is because of Germans, can never be forgiven or justified when he joins hands with the bitterest enemies of his *own* countrymen.

Mr. Alexander Kayser called his own countrymen "dogs" on an occasion we have mentioned earlier, and when he tried to excuse himself he said he only meant "the lickspittles of Börnstein and Blair."

After this prologue can we hardly wonder why the German people of this city took the first occasion to express their feelings about this *degenerate* German?

We do not wish to be misunderstood. We hate *every* act of violence, whichever side perpetrates it. But when a man in the position of Alexander Kayser forgets his origins to such a degree that he

---

*Alexander Kayser, brother of the city engineer Henry Kayser, was born in 1815 in St. Goarshausen on the Rhine and emigrated in 1833. He became a lawyer after clerking for a while in the city administration, and he held several posts in the Democratic party. He served as a lieutenant in the Mexican War, and he married Eloise P. Morrison, granddaughter of Gen. Daniel Bissell. He worked with Börnstein for the election of Thomas Hart Benton to the United States House of Representatives, and the two were guests together at Benton's home after the election. See Richard Edwards, *Edwards's Great West and Her Commercial Metropolis . . .* (St. Louis: *Edwards's Monthly,* 1860), 564–65. SR.

lowers himself to the law of the jungle, then he can expect nothing better from the Germans he so detests. Mr. Alexander Kayser is a well-known man with considerable property, and he is no longer young—under these circumstances it would have been better for him to keep his recent *notions* to himself.

We disapprove of *every* act of violence, but "whoever sows the wind reaps the whirlwind." When Mr. Alexander Kayser, accompanied by his brother,* was leaving the office of Justice of the Peace Schröder on southern Carondelet Avenue, where he had been arguing a case, a crowd of people suddenly gathered and began bombarding the *secessionist* with stones. The infuriated mob grew rapidly in size as Mr. A. Kayser fled their curses and stones into Seventh Street, then toward Third and Convent Street. There the bitterness of the mob reached such a pitch that he would doubtless have been stripped or beat to death if the very Home Guards he has so detested had not thrown themselves into the fray and rescued him from certain death, for the excitement of the crowd was great and plenty of rope was available.

Mr. Kayser was brought by the Home Guards to the Soulard Market building, where the Second Regiment of Home Guards has its headquarters, and there the blood and filth were washed off, and he was kept in hiding until a *priest's robes* could be brought so he could be taken home in a carriage in disguise.

Anzeiger des Westens, 25 July 1861
(for Friday, 19 July 1861)*

General Frémont has met his wife, just arrived from California, in New York, and according to a promise made to Governor Yates of Illinois he is expected in Springfield, Illinois, whither he will be followed by seven thousand of the best firearms. He appears to have spent his time in New York recruiting a general staff.

*Henry Kayser, St. Louis's first city engineer, had worked with Robert E. Lee in improving St. Louis's harbor in 1838. After Lee's departure, Kayser had completed the work, over a fifteen-year span. Late in 1861, when zealous Union officers selected a group of secessionist sympathizers for a special cash assessment, Alexander Kayser was assessed, but Henry was not. JNP.

*On 3 July 1861 President Lincoln, acting on the urging of the Blairs, named Maj. Gen. John C. Frémont, the hero of radical Unionists, as commandant of the Department of the West. In late July the executive committee of the state convention appointed the moderate Unionist Hamilton Rowan Gamble as provisional governor of Missouri, with Willard P. Hall as lieutenant governor. The state thus received an antislavery military administration along with a proslavery civil administration. SR.

Anzeiger des Westens, 1 August 1861
(for Friday, 26 July 1861)

Arrival of General Frémont

General Frémont has met his wife, just arrived from California, in New York, and according to a promise made to Governor Yates of Illinois he is expected in Springfield, Illinois, whither he will be followed by seven thousand of the best firearms. He appears to have spent his time in New York recruiting a general staff.

Colonel *A. Asboth,** once Kossuth's adjutant general and already named a brigadier general in Washington; *Casselmann, Ch. Zagonyi,* *Joseph W. Savoyn, F. M. Dearn,* and *J. C. Wood,* who have taken up quarters in the Everett house.

After most of the staff officers from the Arsenal paid their respects at midday, the Second Home Guard Regiment serenaded him in the evening, after which the general asked Colonel Kallmann* and his staff up to express his thanks and extend his hospitality.

He has aged greatly since the great campaign of 1856, and gray now predominates in his hair and beard. Otherwise he is strong and possessed of his usual iron energy. *All hail Frémont!*

Anzeiger des Westens, 4 September 1861

Karl Ludwig Bernays as a Prophet

Missouri, 23 August 1861

I did not always agree with Mr. C. L. Bernays, but his profound

---

*Col. J. B. Brant, a Massachusetts native, had settled in St. Louis in 1823. After he resigned his army commission in 1839, he entered the construction business. He had built many of the city's tallest (five- and six-story) buildings, and by 1860 he was among the wealthiest men in the city. His second wife was Sarah Benton, niece of Thomas Hart Benton, and thus a first cousin of Jessie Benton Frémont. JNP.

*Alexander Sandor Asboth, 1811–1868, had served in the Austrian Army and under Kossuth before emigrating to America. After serving with Frémont's staff he had a respectable career, retiring a brevet major general and dying as United States minister in Buenos Aires as a result of wounds suffered in the war. See Kaufmann, *Deutschen im Bürgerkrieg,* 479. SR.

*Karoly Zagonyi, commanding major of the Frémont Body Guard, who had served with Kossuth in Hungary, was chiefly noted for his cavalry actions in the taking of Springfield in October 1862. See Robert E. Miller, "Zagonyi," *MHR* 76 (1982): 174–92. SR.

*Hermann Kallmann, colonel of the Second Regiment, United States Reserve Corps, Missouri Volunteers, made up of residents living between Soulard and Chouteau,

vision and broad understanding of things has earned my respect on more than one occasion.

It is uncomfortable for me to praise a man to his face; Mr. C. L. Bernays is far away from here by now, so the publication of what follows appears proper.*

On my last visit to St. Louis I was with Bernays and some friends (I think Dr. Hammer was there) in the rather uncomfortable little back room of the *Anzeiger*'s office. This was at the start of April before the firing on Fort Sumter, when nothing too worrisome had taken place here, when no shots had been fired, and when most people hoped a peaceful solution would be found.

There was a pause in the conversation, and Mr. Bernays held his forehead and said, "No one can mislead me by the appearances of things; the rebellion that has just begun will spread across all the slave states, and even Missouri will be drawn in again and again. Here in St. Louis and all over the state we will have the wildest civil war, and all of us will have to fight for our lives and for our own hearths. The victory will be in doubt until we have leaders other than those we now have, and until we have the will to action that has not yet shown itself."

That is what C. L. Bernays said more than four months ago, and never has a prophecy been so literally fulfilled.

Far West [Friedrich Münch]

Anzeiger des Westens, 28 August 1861*

Our Losses in the Battle at Springfield

Today we are giving a complete list of dead, wounded, and missing from the First (Blair) Regiment, Missouri Volunteers, as well as Major (now Colonel) Osterhaus's command from the Second

---

did active service in southern Missouri with his regiment during 1861. See Rombauer, *Union Cause*, 431. SR.

*Bernays left St. Louis on grounds of health and returned to Germany. He came back, along with Heinrich Börnstein, to try to rescue the political fortunes of Francis P. Blair, Jr., in 1862. SR.

*On 18 June, the day after the battle of Boonville, a group of German recruits was massacred by secessionists at Cole Camp. This incident greatly upset Germans in the countryside. While pursuing General Price and Governor Jackson southward, Colonel Sigel ran into overwhelming enemy forces at Carthage on 5 July and made one of his more illustrious retreats, winning honorable mention if not victory for his handling of artillery. The battle of Wilson's Creek on 10 August resulted in the death of Nathaniel Lyon and the loss of Springfield, but inflicted such heavy losses on the Confederates that a substantial advance into the state was prevented. SR.

(formerly Börnstein) Regiment. The former figures reveal a particularly dreadful result. The regiment lost no less than 44 percent, and it is mostly German names that appear on this black and bloody list. One would hardly have believed there were still so many Germans serving in the Blair Regiment, where virtually all the officers are Americans and where Germans have been systematically pushed out. Major Osterhaus had two horses shot out from under him.

The First Iowa and Second Kansas regiments suffered hardly any less, and General Lyon fell at their head crying, "Come on, brave Iowa boys!" We will omit listing these names, of which most of the German names have already been given, since they would be unknown to most of our readers. But this much we must say, that the primarily German Iowa regiment held up very well and received citations for great valor both from the general and from all the other officers who came near them. Colonel Osterhaus won the very highest praise, which deserves to be stressed because no one had any faith in his staff officers, to such a degree that a placard was set up the night before the battle which read, "We cannot go into battle with such field officers." Colonel Bates was ill at the time and did not take part in the battle, while the conduct of other officers was such that the men shouted to the general, "Give us a leader!," to which he shouted back, "I shall lead you myself." And that was after he had lost a horse and been wounded in one foot. Then he led them into battle on foot up to within forty feet of the enemy, where he received a second wound in the leg that caused him to collapse, reaching for his stricken side. Captain Gottschalk of Dubuque gripped him by the arm to support him and lead him back, but he cried quickly and sharply, "No, no! Lead on!" And in the same instant the captain was wounded in the leg and had to be taken to the rear with the general, while Sergeant Schäfer led Company H. Lyon then mounted another horse and was again at the front, where he received his mortal wound *in less than no time.*

Certainly our worst losses were in Sigel's command, since we learn, for example, that of the sixty men (following the end of the three-month enlistment) of Company C of the Fifth Regiment, thirteen men were left dead, not counting many wounded, while in the First Regiment the largest number of dead in a company was eleven. But this was due to the fact that Captain Totten's battery fired into Sigel's command after they saw a captured secessionist flag being waved in the ranks. Also, most of Sigel's cannon were broken up and had to be left behind.

Incidentally, Colonel Osterhaus says once more in his report what has often been repeated, namely that the day would have been won if the two corps had had a reserve, or if the enemy had had a clear route of retreat. Attack was absolutely necessary, since only by these means could Lyon's whole command be saved, but it was expecting too much to try to surround and destroy an enemy of twenty-five thousand men with about forty-eight hundred effective soldiers. If they had not been caught between two fires, they would have made their escape just as the five Missouri regiments did. For a fleeing enemy one should build bridges of gold.

There is no more doubt that thousands of Indians are serving with the enemy. They are supposed to have become terribly worked up. Only the Cherokees under Ross resisted the call to arms. All other tribes and a part of the Cherokee are in a close alliance with the South.

Captain McDonald of McCulloch's staff is supposed to have admitted that five thousand men in his command were casualties, including over two thousand dead.*

Anzeiger des Westens, 28 August 1861

Hear, Hear!

We recently complained that too little attention was paid to the defenders of our Fatherland on their return to the city, so we are pleased to relate that there was a splendid reception in the Tenth Ward celebrating the return of the Fifth Regiment under Colonel Stifel.* A ladies' committee took charge of the festivities and

---

*The Union lost approximately 235 dead and 1,000 wounded and missing out of some 5,400 committed to battle, the Confederates about 265 dead and 830 wounded out of 10,500. The Confederate force included 5,200 Missouri State Guards, 2,700 Confederate troops from Arkansas, Louisiana, and Texas, and about 2,500 Arkansas militiamen. In addition, some 2,000 unarmed men, including slaves, were assisting the Confederates. JNP.

*Col. Charles G. Stifel, 1819–1900, was born in Württemberg and emigrated in 1837, eventually coming to St. Louis in 1849. He grew wealthy as the owner of the City Brewery at Fourteenth and Chambers. He was involved in early self-defense training and marched the regiment he had organized to the Arsenal on 12 May 1861, where it was mustered in as the Fifth Regiment, United States Reserve Corps, Missouri Volunteers. This unit lost two men dead and seven wounded at Seventh and Walnut on its return due to mob violence. Stifel served a total of ten months with his regiment, including service in western Missouri against Colonel Joe Shelby, before he resigned his commission to return to his business. See Hyde and Conard, *Encyclopedia*, 4:2141–43; Rombauer, *Union Cause*, 464. SR.

elected as their spokeswoman Frau Dr. Doehn. On the arrival of the regiment at its headquarters there were a great number of ladies and several thousand men gathered; children were dressed up in white and carrying American flags; the enthusiasm was beyond description. Still, the high point of the festivities was the following speech by the esteemed spokeswoman, a speech so beautiful and genuinely moving that we publish it not out of courtesy but in order that everyone may read it. Whoever does so will be able to feel the impact this speech had on those present, and "Shame, eternal shame on the coward!" will sound in our souls. If this is how a woman speaks, then a man must indeed be moved. So we express our thanks to the Frau Doktor publicly, and we only note in addition that Colonel Stifel responded with a few touching and gallant words.

Welcome

A joyous welcome indeed, which finds its echo a thousand times over in the hearts of all these women and children, I call out to you, returned warriors. The little ones shout with joy to their father, and the eye of the woman, which has shed many a quiet tear for her distant spouse, has now dried. More than any other, the Fifth Regiment has survived innumerable troubles and dangers, but the greater the sacrifice the greater the fame it has earned for saving Missouri. Oh, if only this joy could have been unsullied! Then we could say to you, lay down your weapons and rest in your family circle and recover from the terrors and deprivations of war. But this time is, alas, still far in the future; at this very moment the country that has become our new homeland is threatened by the enemy as at no other time, and it demands that each of its sons serves with the whole of his strength, to hew a path for liberty with his good right arm so that treason and tyranny are vanquished forever. But men are not the only ones who must sacrifice for the Fatherland, and not just men must shed their blood; women, too, must pay their tribute. They are far from battle, but they bleed in their hearts when they let that which is most precious to them in the entire world march away to a place where death exacts its innumerable victims. Until now the Germans have been in the first ranks of battle, and they cannot give up until the work is finished, until the star-spangled banner waves everywhere in its full glory once again. Now thousands of your brothers flock to the brave *Sigel* to join with his band of heroes to destroy the foe. We have suffered terrible losses, since not only the bold *Lyon*, who launched the war of liberation in Missouri, has found his grave, but hundreds of your brothers have soaked the field of battle with their blood. So shame on those who think they have done enough and lay down their weapons, for they shall suffer the dreadful consequences of their acts with double certainty, should disaster overtake our city.

Unfortunately, we have reached the point where the struggle for an idea, for a principle, has faded into the background. Now you are fighting for your existence, for your woman and child, and you must defend them with your last drop of blood. But it is also your holy duty, ladies, not to discourage or hold back your husband out of petty weakness, for only when the trumpet of war is silent again will your husband be able to return to the hearth and see his own again. Will not everyone reach for his sword with courage and enthusiasm when he knows a *Frémont* is within our walls, who has in a brief time drawn upon himself the full trust and love of all upstanding patriots through his tireless energy? He knows how to value the Germans' contributions, he knows in them the true sons of a free America, and the names of those unworthy of his trust shall forever be branded with infamy. So gather yourselves around this flag before it is too *late*, for only united action and a joyful willingness to sacrifice will win us a successful conclusion to this unhappy war. And so, before we allow ourselves the joy of reunion, give a cheer for the men on whom our hopes for a happy future rest. Long live Frémont! Long live Sigel!

Anzeiger des Westens, 28 August 1861
(for early in the week)

Mrs. Lincoln's Movements—this is all we are reading in the papers from back East. The devil take Mrs. Lincoln's movements. It would be nicer to hear something about Mr. Lincoln's movements. With all due respect to the ladies, and particularly to the president's wife, if she will not be like Mrs. Frémont and actually work personally with her husband for the great cause of the nation, then it would be better if she never made herself the subject of conversation.

Anzeiger des Westens, 28 August 1861
(for early in the week)

General Sigel arrived in the city suddenly yesterday evening at 7 P.M. after taking the 12:30 train from Rolla, which waited for him an hour. He got off at Fourteenth Street, went straight to General Frémont, and spoke with him for half an hour together with General Asboth, Colonel Fiala,* and Colonel Blair. It appears that the general order that named him commander of troops in and around Rolla has not yet arrived there and that he has not yet taken

*Col. John T. Fiala, a topographical engineer who had served in the Hungarian army in 1848 before coming to America, was elected lieutenant colonel of the Second Regiment, United States Reserve Corps, Missouri Volunteers. He became Frémont's topographer and a colonel in his staff and was involved in planning the fortifications of St. Louis built by Hassendeubel under Frémont's order. See Rombauer, *Union Cause*, xii. SR.

command there. He had several extremely interesting details to impart about the battle, particularly about their surprise by a strong enemy body that Dr. Melchior of the Fifth Regiment announced with the words "Lyon's men are coming!," and which the general took to be Iowa men because of the lack of distinguishing insignia and because they were marching under our flag. This was about nine o'clock and led to the loss of the cannon. The artillerymen and their rigs were terribly shot up by this incident, so that only a few men and two horses survived. Colonel Albert* and Lieutenant Schützenbach were the last officers at the general's side, and he owed his own survival to the swiftness of his horse. Incidentally, the general doubtless gave the commander-in-chief an official report on the dead and wounded, which amounts to no more than three hundred of the fifteen hundred men of the Third and Fifth regiments, since many men have been showing up again.*

Despite the fact that Sigel does all he can to keep out of the public eye, it became known that he had made his quarters in Captain Gisecker's house on Gratiot Street.

*Col. Albert Anselm, often called by his first name but listed in this way in both the *St. Louis Directory* and Rombauer, *Union Cause*, 380, was a lieutenant colonel of Sigel's Third Regiment, Missouri Volunteers. He had served under Kossuth in Hungary, and he was working in St. Louis in 1860 as a reporter for the *Mississippi Handels-Zeitung*. He followed Frémont to the East and served under him in West Virginia. See Kaufmann, *Deutschen in Bürgerkrieg*, 478. SR.

*Members of Lyon's officer corps who wrote reminiscences of Wilson's Creek assigned the chief responsibility for the failure to win on General Sigel. The only reason the entire affair was considered a Confederate victory, they argue, was Sigel's pell-mell retreat to Rolla, leaving guns and supplies scattered over the countryside. The Confederates were not chasing him. Before the battle Sigel had insisted on dividing the slim Union forces, taking his brigade (two regiments of German volunteers) around to the rear of the Confederate position. Lyon, with two Kansas, one Iowa, and two Missouri regiments plus a few hundred regulars, attacked Price's front with great initial success. Sigel's surprise thrust from the rear worked at first, but his men fell to looting and were routed by two companies of Louisiana troops that were retreating from Lyon. Lyon was killed leading a charge, and with Sigel in retreat, Lyon's men gradually withdrew in the face of vastly superior numbers. Apparently the Confederates thought they had lost the battle early, but were unable to find an escape route. Both sides were hampered by lack of training, especially Price's Missouri Guard, and by the profusion of uniform colors. Sigel had believed the gray-clad Louisianans were Iowa troops until they were within ten yards of him. Nonetheless, his detractors argue, there was no reason for him to run, since he had five times as many men as his attackers. Colonel Sigel eventually became a major general, but the consensus remained the same. He was superior in theoretical knowledge, incompetent in battle, and "hell on retreat." Frank Blair, who was in Washington (in a congressional session) during the battle, blamed Wilson's Creek and Lyon's death upon Frémont, who had refused to send reinforcements. Even those who denounced Sigel praised some other German officers, especially Maj. Peter J. Osterhaus. JNP.

After eleven a number of patriots led by Frank Böhm's band came to the hero's house and serenaded him.

Sigel made a long speech in German, then in English, in which he stressed the great importance of this particular moment and declared that differences of party and nationality had to be totally set aside, and that we all had to be Americans united.

Endless jubilation rolled from all sides, after which the general retired, for he had earned a rest.

Unfortunately, these splendid festivities were disturbed somewhat by the noisy bawling of an anti-Union man. When General Sigel began his address, this wretch yelled "Damn the Dutch" and the like, besides the familiar hurrah for the rebels, and he was silenced in a singularly direct manner and escorted to the Turner Hall. If General Sigel had not put in a good word for the man, he would have been hung from a lamp post.

Tony Niederwieser posted an honor guard of two men with six-shooter rifles at the general's door, and they were later relieved by other Home Guards.

Anzeiger des Westens, 4 September 1861

A Day of Mourning for Missouri's Hero

Today St. Louis is giving its final homage to its dead lion. *Nathaniel Lyon* has returned to the place from which he arose, a splendid meteor destined to purify the suffocating air of our unhappy state. The man who departs as a dead man from the state where he labored and gained fame marched into the interior as a liberator, full of powerful, creative life. If St. Louis owes any man more thanks than to all the others, it is to Lyon. It was he who stood solid as a rock in the fire during the darkest of days. At that time he proved that "a man is worth much at the right moment," since he freed us of the oppressive presence of Major Bell and led us beyond the passivity of Harney and Hagner,* broke up Camp Jackson, organized the Germans, saved the Arsenal, shattered the plans of our traitorous ex-governor, and began purging the state of traitors and rebels.

*Bell and Hagner were removed by Washington from the Arsenal, and Harney from command, because Frank Blair insisted upon it. JNP.

Unfortunately, he could not complete his great task, and he fell a martyr to the holy cause of our Fatherland on that fearful and glorious day at Springfield, a heavy legacy for Frémont, for all Unionists, and for Germans in particular. Let us show him the respect that is his due today, and in the morning we can set about his revenge. Certainly no further challenge is needed for the entire sorrowful city of St. Louis to follow his coffin all the way to the river's edge, so we can give his body over to the free states to do further honor to the remains of this heroic spirit, until he is given his final resting-place in the soil of his native Connecticut. Do not expect mausoleums or hecatombs, though the latter will not be lacking before the day of reckoning comes. Above all else his memory lives and shall survive as does that of Warren in the Pantheon of eternal fame with the heroes of Plutarch. "And may his shadow never grow less."

Anzeiger des Westens, 4 September 1861

† Dr. Hohlfeldt †

Once more it is one of the very best, the very man who made such a splendid commemoration as lieutenant to Captain Blandowski, who has fallen. This was a man who did not live without a purpose. Born in Loebau, Kingdom of Saxony, he edited a newspaper there that set the tone for revolutionary opinion. As a leader of the people after his election to the Saxon Assembly and the National Assembly as well as the Chamber of Estates, he was one of the most outstanding leaders and left marks of his endeavors every step of the way. He was one of the most prominent on the barricades during the May rising in Dresden in 1849.

When he fled to Switzerland, he despaired along with thousands of others that there would be an end to reaction after Louis Napoleon's coup d'etat, and so he turned his eyes to America, where he took up the study of medicine. He practiced in Collinsville in Madison County, and then here. The start of the war for the Union saw him one of the very first to defend his Fatherland, and he was with Sigel's Regiment on Camp Jackson day, at the battle of Carthage, and at the desperate battle at Camp Dixon (Wilson's Creek); at the last battle a cannonball injured his left hip. He lay near death for several days on the battlefield before he was brought to the hospital in Springfield, and he was taken in to be treated for some days by a woman he had befriended. On the fifteenth, five days after the battle, he died, and he was buried on the sixteenth by his friends and fellow sufferers in the camp for prisoners of war. Colonel Albert gave the eulogy. He was less than fifty, yet his intellectual labors and conscientiousness had turned his hair white, though he had kept his heart young to the end.

Anzeiger des Westens, 4 September 1861
(before 30 August 1861)

Martial Law! Martial Law for the Entire State is the general demand. So much from Far West and Arnold Krekel. Secessionists are becoming bold once more, like the devil, and this boldness will grow until there is some forward movement such as the *Missouri Democrat* reports is taking place from Ironton. But in the meantime the sum of human misery endured by the Union men in the interior of the state mounts up to a terrifying total. Now they are fleeing here from the southwest and west, man, woman, and child, carrying all they have, with sack and pack, no longer stopping here but going on to Illinois or up to Iowa to leave Missouri forever. It is a permanent loss to the state. In the north of Missouri, despite the fact that the secessionists are thickest there, things have yet to deteriorate that far. This is due to the military policies of General Pope, who has formed security committees made up of the wealthiest citizens of every place and county and made them personally and financially responsible for losses to Union people, with payment assured through quartering and extortion. That is already a form of martial law, and it has had a wholesome effect so far, since it makes it unnecessary to place a garrison at every place and on every bridge, etc. But even more is needed. Summary punishment, including execution for spies and other cohorts of rebels, particularly those found bearing arms directed against the government, is needed. That can only take place if there is a formal declaration of martial law, which is needed to accomplish what is needed in several parts of the state. Martial law, then! Martial law over the whole state!

Anzeiger des Westens, 4 September 1861 (after 31 August 1861)

Frémont's Ultimate Measures

What we demanded yesterday with overwhelming justification had already been done by Frémont the night before, though through an oversight of the adjutant general no one had notified the German press.

Of course we mean

The Proclamation of Martial Law
over the Entire State,

and this time we are speaking of *a drumhead law with all of its most extreme consequences.* Whoever reads the following proclamation of the supreme general will see that we are done once and for all with half measures, and that the suppression of rebellion at all costs is to proceed with fearful and bloody seriousness. Whoever plays the traitor now does so at the risk of his head.

"Woe to him whose hands are stained with guiltless blood!"

Whoever is captured with weapons in his hands *has forfeited his life and will be shot,* and whoever is not captured but bears weapons against the United States or otherwise assists the enemy in the field *loses all his property to the United States, while all his slaves shall be freed.*

This goes quite a bit further than the confiscation law of the Congress—it is a measure of war and extreme necessity. In other words, it is a dictatorial act, an act a la Jackson. "*Frémont takes the responsibility.*" The man is risking his total incalculable ability to save the nation as he now risks his head and his life, *Lyon-like.*

Now let someone say he is not the right man in the right place.

Anzeiger des Westens, 18 September 1861*

Rumors!

Ever since Messrs. Blair and Meigs arrived in St. Louis from Washington, *one* view has been that they have come to help General

*Frémont's premature emancipation proclamation greatly weakened his standing with Washington, and he was blamed for the defeat at Wilson's Creek as well as the capture of Col. James Mulligan's Illinois Irishmen at Lexington, Missouri, the latter rather more cogently. Frémont and Blair soon fell out, and this led to a split of the

Frémont in all official acts and to find out what he needs, but the *other* view is that they are representing the cabinet in settling Lyon's business with the commanding general.* Now since the day before yesterday when a telegram arrived saying that the government was doing what it could to give the command in the West to Quartermaster General Meigs and to sack General Frémont with prejudice, there is a third interpretation.

It is also said that this hidden battery is being set up by persons who otherwise know nothing of artillery and have already shot their load in Missouri so far as the Germans are concerned.* Further, many believe that an effort is being made by persons in the highest places to test public sentiment in order to prepare the ground for Frémont's removal. The idea is to reduce the shock of the event, to illuminate the "causes" and the "necessity" through the right newspapers without risking a stormy popular reaction.

Yet others fear that the conflict between the interpretation of government regulations that exists between McClellan, who orders escaped slaves held and returned to their masters, and Frémont, who issues manumissions out of hand to slaves, would push the conclusion of the war into the unforeseeable future.

However that might be and however many thousands of ways there might be for points of view to vary, we can still repeat today what we said yesterday to calm popular agitation, which is that we *refuse* to believe that the government is planning such a disciplinary action.

The motives for this belief can be briefly summarized:

It is well known that the cabinet in Washington is filled with ambitious intriguers from Missouri who have watched their lucky star fade and who wish with deadly serious bitterness to rewin their old dictatorship, and that they have decided it is high time to be rid of General Frémont, but it is still not clear that those in Washington know the situation in Missouri or the consequences for the entire loyal Union of what has already taken place.

---

unconditional Unionists between these two men. SR.

*Postmaster General Montgomery Blair and Quartermaster General Montgomery C. Meigs were investigating Frank Blair's charges of incompetence and corruption against Frémont and his staff. Frémont had proved and continued to prove his incompetence, and his quartermaster, Justus McKinstry, was court-martialed and convicted for selling war contracts. JNP.

*The reference here is to Frank Blair, whose opposition to Frémont's emancipation measure further alienated Germans, some of whom were already complaining because Blair's half-German First Missouri Regiment had no German officers. Frémont was already maneuvering into position for another try at the presidency in 1864; Blair was fully committed to Lincoln and his policies. The German editors' ultimate target was Lincoln, who was not yet committed to abolition. JNP.

The administration *should* and *must* know that the *Germans* of Missouri, Illinois, Iowa, and Kansas have taken upon themselves the largest part of the battles that have been fought to keep Missouri in the Union, and that they claim the right to see that *the men they trust* are not victimized at the expense of the preservation of the Union, or at the sacrifice of the property and blood of citizens.

The administration *must* know that there is no other man in the Union who possesses both the magnanimity of a patriot ready for any sacrifice and the understanding of what has to be done, a man who could serve as a model for Republican cabinet secretaries, since he is endowed with both energy and clemency.

Further, the administration *should* and *must* expect that *the entire German population of Missouri* looks up to General Frémont with profound respect and that under *his* command it goes to meet the enemy with unlimited trust, but *without* him it holds Missouri to be lost.

Without Frémont in the front rank, German divisions and brigades, regiments, and companies of Volunteers or Home Guards remain pious wishes, not just in Missouri but in the entire Northwest.* The storm of disappointment would spread northward like an avalanche until it reached the very pinnacle of government and shook the pillars of the White House.

And *because* President Lincoln and his secretaries are capable of knowing these truths and these justified fears, we want to believe that the administration would not wish to challenge the whole of loyalist Germanity in the West.

No confirmation of these fears has yet come—as we have said, let us wait until the moment of truth.

Anzeiger des Westens, 16 October 1861

Frémont's Oriental Pomp has been mentioned yet again by the *New Yorker Abendzeitung* as an excuse for having published Blair's letter of 1 September, despite the fact that it was personal correspondence. We have noticed no such pomp here in St. Louis. The general himself keeps to a very simple manner. He allows the others to wear the gold braid and the hats decorated with feathers. His office quarters are every bit as republican in their plainness. For a long time his chief of general staff was housed together with

*Frémont was removed, but the Germans still fought. Editorial control of the mass of Germans was less than perfect. JNP.

three or four of his most important staff officers in a basement room, and the sentries were very unprepossessing because they were just there to fulfill their practical function. No one has tried to rationalize the aristocratic manner, the withdrawal from public contact, the luxurious clothing, etc., etc., of General Blenker—least of all the *New Yorker Abendzeitung*.* Yet this would seem to merit more attention and would be more within the competence of that newspaper. We ourselves regard it as a matter of little consequence, though the New Yorkers declare themselves very upset, and they make the accusation that Mrs. Frémont* (whose correspondence with the president was also regarded as scandalous by that news-paper) was received in splendor in Jefferson City by the ill-fated *Garde de Corps* and entered the town mounted in a coach of state drawn by four span of horses, and they further remarked that we passed over this event in silence. Very well, we did remain silent because the whole matter appeared to us uninteresting because it was purely a matter of military etiquette. It struck us personally as very odd, and we certainly knew that nothing to Frémont's benefit could come of it, but we also saw no point in making much noise about it. Americans put an incredibly great stock in external appearance. Think of how much fuss is made over Mrs. Lincoln, *the first lady of the land*, learning French, and so on. Now if such formality is justified anywhere, it is in the military. Frémont's authority is of an entirely different sort than Lincoln's, and even if he does not insist on formalities for himself, he can have them performed in his camp for his wife when she comes for some purpose other than pure *show*. Were they supposed to receive her with a hand lantern and have her dragged on foot in the dirt and rain through dark streets, as happened to the general himself when he was welcomed by General Thomas L. Price?* The joke was funny once and only once: Mrs. Frémont works energetically and valiant-

*General Ludwig Blenker, 1812–1863, served as a police officer in Greece and was a colonel of the Baden-Palatine revolutionary army under Sigel in 1849. In 1861 he was a brigadier general at Bull Run and distinguished himself by keeping his unit together in the panic retreat. He raised great hostility and suspicion among Americans for his elaborate staff, which seemed more suited to a European court than an American brigade. He was soon impelled to resign on suspicion of corruption. See Kaufmann, *Die Deutschen im Bürgerkrieg*, 478; also Rudolf Zewell, "Anton Schütte (1817–1867) . . . ," *Jahrbuch des Instituts für deutsche Geschichte* (Tel Aviv), 11 (1982): 145–48. SR.

*Jessie Benton Frémont, the daughter of Thomas Hart Benton, was a political force in her own right. She acted as her husband's chief adviser during his Missouri command, leading to comments about "General Jessie." SR.

*Price's reception of Frémont in Jefferson City was experienced by Gustav Körner, who could summon up the misery of the evening after more than a generation had passed. See Koerner, *Memoirs*, 2:175. SR.

ly for her country and deserves the greatest recognition. And if the name "Jessie" is used now and then and some good old American-style humbug is committed by her overenthusiastic and indiscreet friends, then this is certainly no crime of the general's. As far as we are concerned, the German press here has been very understanding about this until now.

Anzeiger des Westens, 13 November 1861*

Betrayal Has Run Its Course

and the Blair clique has won. We now know for certain that General Hunter has received the order *to take over General Frémont's command and to withdraw the army from Springfield to winter quarters in St. Louis.*

So the state has fallen victim to Frank Blair's despicable intrigues. Whether our army will allow itself to carry out this shameful role, whether our citizens and soldiers will stand by and watch this act of high treason against their holy cause is up to the people themselves. In any case Blair has bid us farewell—and so we have to him, and we hope never to see him again. He has been tried and found wanting.*

*   *   *

Frémont's Removal

is supposed to have been telegraphed here by Frank P. Blair, who went to Washington specifically for that purpose. Lincoln gave it to him personally. Our press informant added that either *Harney* (?) or *Halleck* of California (perhaps so there could still be a Californian here) would be his successor in the command. Are they actually going to allow General Frémont to fight the battle that looms—*his* battle? An attack has to be made, and it is not clear that Hunter or

*Frémont's advance south was ponderously prepared after he had elaborately fortified St. Louis. Springfield was taken by a dashing cavalry attack by his much-maligned Body Guard under the command of Charles Zagonyi on 25 October. The removal of Frémont and the retreat to winter quarters caused many to fear a mutiny of the politically committed officers and men of Frémont's command. SR.

*The *Anzeiger*'s rejection of Blair has no place in Heinrich Börnstein's memory, though by this time he was far away in Bremen. He would be brought back to St. Louis on leave in 1862 specifically to try to rescue Blair, but to no avail. See Börnstein, *Fünfundsiebzig Jahre*, 2:366–75. SR.

anyone else will be able to get the army to withdraw, although this appears to be the administration's plan.

P.S. A dispatch given elsewhere confirms the unbelievable: *Frémont's sword has been broken before the fight and Mr. Hunter is to lead the army back to St. Louis for winter quarters.* It is as if a choir of a hundred clowns were singing. Should anyone on the Potomac be thinking of winter quarters after the scandal at Ball's Bluff? The people and the army here want a battle first. And the enemy will force one on us on his own terms if we run before him as he has heretofore run before us.

To withdraw now, when Frémont has brought us into the very presence of the enemy, would not only be despicable treachery to the commander in the field, but an act of cowardice and of baseness that no one can easily accept. Let the Eastern English newspapers bleat out sheepish patience and subservience: what Lincoln has done, so be it. We proclaim that we hold this order to be pitiful, since it makes the president appear to be not only incompetent but also unworthy to act as the head of a great nation. This also gives aid and comfort to the enemy. Certainly the army itself would unanimously condemn such an act, and Frémont would not be the man we hold him to be if he made an act of penitence rather than strike the enemy. The people have been tried to the extreme, and the results of such a stupid undertaking by the administration are not to be foreseen.*

Anzeiger des Westens, 13 November 1861

The Pathfinder as Unifier

A work was completed here in St. Louis in utter silence that is unique for this city, something which, despite its manifest advantages, could never have taken place without Frémont. We mean, of course, the unification of the three railways, the Pacific, the Iron Mountain, and the North Missouri, through tracks laid along Levee and Poplar streets. Just think of the enormous advantage that comes from being able to take any line directly from the levee, straight from the boat, as in Chicago, and being able to shift freight

*Once again the *Anzeiger* equates political purity with military skill. Not just the Germans, but other interests as well, pressed the case for political generals—the army was swarming with them. Ironically, Frank Blair was one of the few such generals who demonstrated real military ability. JNP.

from one line to another. Frémont grasped the problem at once, of course, from the point of view of military usefulness and necessity. But this does not prevent him from being the benefactor of the whole of St. Louis, particularly of its mercantile class. Captain E. H. Castle, superintendent of railways for the Western Department, oversaw and led this act of unification, now completed. We wonder whether the adjutant general had fits when he learned that such an office existed? In any case the thing has been done, and there will be an excursion this morning in celebration of the completion that will set out from the foot of Chestnut Street and travel over all of the three rail lines. The superintendents of the three lines, Kissock for the Pacific, Phelps for the Iron Mountain, and Gamble for the North Missouri, will join together to assure the security and comfort of the participants.

Anzeiger des Westens, 13 November 1861

Frémont Is Coming!

According to a telegram that has arrived from Rolla, Major General *Frémont* gave his command over to General Hunter last Sunday and departed from Springfield the evening of the same day.

This hard-tested patriot will arrive in St. Louis either *this evening* or *early tomorrow*, and we cannot fail to call on *the whole of loyal Unionist Germanity* to prepare for the general the reception he deserves.

A man who has done so much for Missouri, for St. Louis, and for Germans as Frémont, who has fallen victim to the most loathsome cabal and the blackest ingratitude of an idiot *administration*, should at the least receive a faithful, unfalsified statement of love and respect from the *people*. This is an opportunity the Germans will not allow to pass.

Loyal St. Louis must receive its noblest martyr grandly and in a manner suited to impress the administration. It should give him a warm, heartfelt German greeting, which will put this treasonous clique of dogs on notice that no act of force by the powerful, even the most corrupt, can ever kill the sense for truth and justice in the life of the people.*

*The impact of Frémont's removal led to what even the cautious Gustav Körner describes as a near mutiny. See Koerner, *Memoirs*, 2:189–91. SR.

Anzeiger des Westens, 20 November 1861

A Sword from the People to Frémont

An assembly of German citizens from all wards, which had served as a committee or deputation at the great Frémont demonstration, has discussed and approved a subscription of ten cents from the half-million German males in the Northwest to pay for the making of a presentation sword for General Frémont. The idea arose from the fact that the administration had taken away or broken the sword of this warrior, and that the gift would symbolize the restoration of his sword by the people. The inscription would be a message to the cabinet in Washington that the mass of the Germans were still behind the man. —We now present this matter to the public so that you would be so good as to spread the word. We hope to be able to give you a copy of the subscription list and all the details tomorrow. If the amount subscribed greatly exceeds the cost of a sword, which is to be expected, then it would be easy to determine another use for the excess by agreement before the money is actually gathered. No one will miss ten cents.

Anzeiger des Westens, 4 December 1861

Emancipation Policy

We must return to the disjointed and superficial remarks we made yesterday. At the outset we should make it clear that when we use the word *emancipation* we are not thinking in terms of something that would have to wait until the conclusion of peace but rather of emancipation on the basis of martial law, as Frémont tried to do, or as the gospel was preached by John Quincy Adams when he was a United States senator.*

It has been estimated that of the ninety thousand slaves who lived in Missouri at the start of Jackson's revolt,* fully forty thousand have been lost; twenty-five thousand are supposed to have been moved to the South, and the remnant have run away to freedom. The fear of Lyon, Frémont, and the Germans has contributed essentially to this process. And if this continues through the

*John Quincy Adams served in the lower house after leaving the presidency. He was never a senator. JNP.
*Missouri had 115,000 slaves at the beginning of the war. JNP.

winter at this pace, slavery will hardly be able to survive another year of this struggle. Frémont's proclamation of 30 August freed many thousands of slaves who made use of it as soon as they knew their rights. And despite General Order No. 3, Halleck cannot halt the disintegration of the institution. This process has virtually freed Missouri of its Negroes, so that there will very soon be no difficulty in dealing with the expansion of slavery by means of legislation.

The same is true of most of the border slave states. In almost every case the slave population has declined significantly as a result of export to the South, despite the fact that these states have not been blessed with a Lyon or a Frémont. Massive evictions on short notice have taken place everywhere, especially in Maryland and Virginia. In West Virginia they are discussing a plan for gradual emancipation. From the outset it was an inevitable result of the rebellion that this institution should collapse in the border slave states. Ways will be found to help the loyal citizens injured by this without causing difficulties for the people at large.

As far as the rebel states themselves are concerned, it is already clear that whenever we occupy them an active war party in our favor must be created. If we expanded the white occupation troops on the coast of the rebel states from eighteen thousand to seventy-five thousand, we still could not hold these points throughout the winter without having them eaten alive by fever. It is necessary to consider what to do and when to do it. Occupy as much land as it is possible to hold. Gather the harvests of cotton, rice, etc., and ship them out. Sow the fields again. Conceive fortifications of the most solid and approved sort and raise a local force for permanent occupation. But since only the slaves are available to do the work, then it is necessary to train a proper number of them in weapons with the greatest possible rapidity so that they can be relied upon. At the same time, nothing could be a finer preparation for or a better transition to freedom than these labors in the field and in defense such as they would have to do later as free men, all under the law of pressing necessity. No people has ever been lifted up to freedom. Freedom is not something that is given—it has to be taken. Alexander II is a rare exception.* But lacking a formal education for freedom, the best preparation has always been a revolution or a war. In this we can teach by example. If now it is the rebel masters who run away from their slaves rather than the other way around, then that is a proper nemesis. Blacks are serving

*Tsar Alexander had just emancipated Russia's serfs. JNP.

to carry out a federal judgment. The matter is simple to carry out. All that has to happen is for Congress to pass from half-measures to whole measures and declare *all* rebel property forfeit, and then it should look upon the blacks who come over as free men liable for military service. Some of them can work fields, build fortifications, etc., or, if they wish, serve in military columns at the same pay as other United States soldiers. There is no hope for the republic without a complete extermination of rebellion or without a hard blow at slavery!

Anzeiger des Westens, 4 December 1861*

Is Price Speaking?

Major General Price has issued a proclamation to the people of Missouri from Osceola in which he pressingly demands fifty thousand men, particularly from the wealthier secessionists, who have done *nothing at all* until now while the poor have been putting their lives in peril for six months and want to go home. He believes these wealthy persons could come bringing their own blankets, bedquilts, clothing, wagons, weapons, and so on, and he promises compensation, since he has seized $250 million worth of property from Unionists. Only make haste, etc. His people are supposed to have occupied *Lexington* again, as the *Evening News* reports, and they are trying to gain passage to the North to destroy the Hannibal–St. Joe Railway, or perhaps they have already done so. Since Price is already much more exposed than ever was the case with Frémont, this might be the right moment to trap him. General Hunter is in Leavenworth and General Sherman in Sedalia. When will the blow come?

Anzeiger des Westens, 11 December 1861

The Proclamations

of Price to his soldiers and to the citizens of central and northern Missouri are given to you today in full text. They are too remark-

*Sterling Price's "Proclamation to the People of Central and North Missouri," a masterpiece of Civil War oratorical style originally published in the *Missouri Army*

able merely to summarize in a few words. They are naturally not dated—they come from his headquarters of the moment, south or north, and despite his assurances that he will never turn back, it is almost too easy to show them to be a tissue of lies. If you listen to Price, his people have always won, even at Boonville where they ran like rabbits, and at Carthage, where they were beaten by Sigel despite a fivefold advantage, or at Springfield, where Frémont's Body Guard mercilessly beat them despite a tenfold advantage.* The enemy is *still* in the state (without Hunter there would be none at all), but Price says he has stolen $250 million and the good days have barely begun. It is obvious that his soldiers have had enough—but he demands fifty thousand more in their place, and he does not demand them once but twenty times—he commands them, he demands them, he beseeches them, he longs for them, he begs them—he squanders this flood of words until his pen has worn out. That ill-favored clergyman *J. W. Tucker* of the old *State Journal* has taken up his quill and fires away ad nauseam in the new Price organ called the *Missouri Army Argus*. He adds, "Who can read these words and hold in his heart that it is possible for anyone to desert General Price in the field before he receives the reinforcement he must quickly have. Soldiers! Brave men! Stand by your *glorious* old leader but a little longer!" —Then he carries on about the many Confederate victories and a recognition of the Confederacy by England. They are in a worse vice than Lyon was at Springfield. Mr. Halleck only has to seize the opportunity.

Anzeiger des Westens, 11 December 1861

Frémont in New York

Although, as previously reported, Frémont has abstained from every festivity in New York, the Germans have still not ceased to greet him. This was particularly the case with the Arion Singing

---

Argus in November 1861, described in graphic terms the poor state of his forces and their lack of basic popular support. He called repeatedly for fifty thousand volunteers, especially from the wealthier classes, and he promised to use Northern property in the state, valued at $200 million, to compensate those who suffered any losses as a result of defending the state. SR.

*The news of Sigel's victory at Carthage must have come as a surprise to Price, who thought he had chased Sigel off the field. Zagonyi's charge at Springfield was indeed dramatic, but it was not strongly contested. Other Union units were attacking at the same time. JNP.

Society, under the leadership of Bergmann, which gathered in front of the Astor House at 9 P.M. Saturday and serenaded the general. In the meantime a committee of eleven payed its respects to the general, consisting of *A. Willmann,* chairman of the Deutsches Centralclub, *Fr. Kapp,** the historian, *Dr. Dulon,** pastor of Bremen and Sigel's father-in-law, *Albert Sigel,** *Wm. Kopp,* former editor of the *New York Demokrat, H. Grube, J. Kupper, Wm. M. Wermerskirch, W. Götze, F. Friedeborn, E. Sigel, Theodor Glaubensklee, Dr. Kessmann,* and *Dr. Tegnitz.*

Friedrich Kapp addressed the general in the name of the committee and the Germans of New York and expressed the strong hope that the views represented and propagated by Frémont in Missouri would soon become the principles of the war and of the administration. Frémont thanked the committee and said that he knew not how to recognize adequately the uniform friendliness shown him by Germans from the borders of Kansas to this place. Captain Tracy of Frémont's military establishment, who was with the late Lyon in the Arsenal at the very start of the war, also described how the St. Louis Germans had been the first to volunteer to help the two hundred isolated United States soldiers and their leader, the sainted Lyon, and then actually took up arms. Mrs. Jessie Frémont was especially charming. Afterward there were various musical entertainments, so that quiet did not descend on the Astor House until after midnight. On Sunday Mr. and Mrs. Frémont visited Beecher's church in Brooklyn, where Frémont was honored by everyone rising when he entered, and Mr. Beecher preached a sermon on human greatness. Two Philadelphia papers have recently decided to support Frémont, and the president is supposed to have said that several members of his cabinet continuously try to incite him to attack Frémont, but now they have decided to pass the responsibility off on others in view of the hostility of congressmen.

*Friedrich Kapp, 1824–1884, was an important New York German author and editor, noted for a history of German immigration and for biographies of Germans who had played a role in American life. He was an ardent supporter of the Union during the war, but returned to Germany afterward. See Wittke, *Refugees of Revolution,* 63. SR.
*Dr. Rudolf Dulon was a noted freethinker and pedagogue who led the famous Feldner School in New York, 1855–1866. Franz Sigel married his daughter and taught in the school for a time. Wittke, *Refugees of Revolution,* 302. SR.
*Albert Sigel, 1827–1884, Franz Sigel's younger brother, was a patriotic and romantic poet of modest importance. He was an officer of the Baden army until the revolution of 1848, after which he emigrated to America. He rose to the rank of colonel in the war, serving in Missouri. See Kaufmann, *Deutschen im Bürgerkrieg,* 553; Paul F. Guenther, "Albert Sigel—St. Louis German Poet," *BMHS* 36 (1980): 156–61. SR.

Anzeiger des Westens, 18 December 1861

To the Friends of Freedom and Frémont

The friends of slavery are more active now than they have ever been. The Blair clique, the *Louisville Journal* and the *Louisville Democrat*, which brought down Frémont more than any others and who continue to oppose any injury to the sacred institution of slavery, as Frank's vote in Congress on 2 December demonstrates,* are stirring up a storm among the old conservatives and peacemongers against any effort to carry on the war energetically. They want to scream in the ears of Congress the lie that slavery is not the origin of the great rebellion and thus not the cause of the war. They want to restrict the war to mere defense, particularly the defense of Washington, a policy that will lead to endless trouble, to the death of a hundred thousand men, and to the waste of hundreds of millions of dollars, and will lead the land into unnameable misery if not humiliation in the end. But we want a short, energetic war, a war that will secure freedom and with it a guarantee of lasting peace and uninterrupted growth and prosperity for Missouri and the whole country. We recommend that support for *Frémont* be multiplied twofold, even tenfold, and as a further demonstration we should all sign the following petition:

Petition of the People to Congress

To the Congress of the United States!

We the undersigned, citizens of ——— in the state of ——— present the following with deepest respect:

Whereas the current fearful rebellion against the federal government obviously has its roots in and draws its nourishment from the system of human slavery in the South; whereas the leading conspirators are slaveowners and as such form an oligarchy which is a conscious enemy of all free institutions; and whereas no lasting peace will be achieveable so long as the cause of this traitorous insurrection is allowed to survive, then for these reasons we pressingly ask a vigilant Congress *to free the slaves of all rebels without condition*, at once by power of the law of war, and, without recognizing the right of property in human beings, to arrange for a just compensation in money for loyal slaveowners for the slaves to be emancipated, as a means of reconciliation and for a friendly settlement of difficulties. In this way the war can be brought rapidly and

*Blair still opposed immediate emancipation without compensation. As his German and Radical support faded, he picked up a following among War Democrats and moderates. Blair controlled the federal patronage in Missouri, and he and Governor Gamble—so much at odds in May—were united in their distaste for Frémont. JNP.

beneficially to an end, and all sections and interests of the country can be indivisibly united on the lasting foundation of general freedom.

Anzeiger des Westens, 18 December 1861

An Anti-Sigel Clique

We have long tried not to see or believe what has now become palpable, that there is now an *anti-Sigel clique* among the German officers. But now we have to draw the attention of our colleagues of the press to the truly laughable beginnings of this clique, whose members we hesitate to name, although two of them are among our closest friends.

This clique is as solidly organized and has in part the same motivation as the old anti-Frémont clique. The two intrigues resemble one another in operation like two eggs.

The readers of this newspaper could not have ignored the long series of articles about developments in the regiment of the Benton Hussars.* Here Governor Gamble, emerging from behind his mask for the first time, has named a *commander utterly disliked* by soldiers and officers, *directly against General Sigel's wishes*, probably in order that this creature of the governor can lead the regiment away from Sigel or even dismember it, as has already begun. In this matter the governor is demoralizing the regiment from the top down. The regiment was recruited *under Sigel* and *for Sigel*, just as the Frémont Body Guard was formed under and for Frémont. What impact should it have, then, when it is led off to a general it does not know and in which it has no faith? Sigel would have to get along without cavalry. How is he supposed to be a division commander and perform his military duties effectively if the cavalry he has collected with such care is taken from him? And what is he to do with this regiment under a commander in whom he has as little confidence as does the regiment itself?

Obviously there is more to the story than this. It has to do with the general himself and with the German organization. The Germans have been removed from the general staff, they are being pushed out of high command, and the German brigades are being

*The Benton Hussars Regiment was the Fifth Missouri Cavalry Regiment, which served at Pea Ridge under Col. Joseph Nemett. See Johnson and Buel, *Battles and Leaders*, 1:337. SR.

destroyed. This goes hand in hand with the blows against the German reserve regiments.

But the Germans have their eyes wide open, and other officers will stand and fall with Sigel. The clique has not yet won, and its burden of guilt will be dreadful.

Anzeiger des Westens, 13 January 1862*

Sigel's Resignation

We have finally confirmed the truth of the report that Sigel has resigned. In the meantime we have, of course, not learned whether his resignation has been accepted or not.

From what we hear, the grounds are nothing more than the manner in which he has been treated, specifically that Curtis* removed him from a command he had been given three days before. He is not complaining about the individual placed over him,* but rather about his continual disparagement.

This was said in the mild manner we have come to expect from the general, whose modesty and calm in conversation is as widely recognized as his decisiveness in deeds.

But he certainly does have special grounds for complaint, such as that he has been subordinated to Curtis, who has never shown any capacity as a commanding general, in whom the earlier commander of the department had no confidence, and who made himself particularly unloved here in the affair of the Benton Hussars. It was

*General Sigel's resignation was not accepted in the end, but offering it precipitated an uproar in the German community nationwide. Gustav Körner was delegated to discuss Sigel's grievances, and the result was Sigel's promotion to major general and his transfer to the Army of the Potomac. This promotion did not take effect until after Sigel had finally proved himself at the Battle of Pea Ridge, 6–8 March 1862. SR.

*Samuel R. Curtis, who had been St. Louis's city engineer from 1850 to 1853, lived in Iowa in 1861. He proved to be the ablest Union commander operating chiefly in the Missouri theater after Lyon's death. Curtis defeated Price decisively twice, at Pea Ridge in northern Arkansas in March 1862 and at Westport (Kansas City) in September 1864. Curtis's victory at Pea Ridge, where he was outnumbered two to one, insured Union control of Missouri for the duration. Governor Jackson then moved his Confederate Missouri capital to central Arkansas, and after Jackson's death in 1863, his successor Thomas C. Reynolds moved it to Marshall, Texas. The battle of Westport was a humiliating finale to Price's quixotic 1864 raid into Missouri, undertaken primarily to draw Union forces away from Atlanta (it did not). After Westport, Union troops chased Price's disintegrating army to the Arkansas River at Fort Smith. JNP.

*Curtis had ties to Frémont's enemies among the St. Louis business elite and therefore was distrusted by the Germans. JNP.

Curtis who imposed a commander on the Benton Hussars Regiment, and who later said that it was an entirely superfluous courtesy to inform the general about it. It was also he who took several companies away from this regiment, and who has finally taken away the whole regiment.

But General Sigel hit time and again on restrictions of which he was only able to speak yesterday. For example, he demanded an answer to his suggestions for a more effective organization for the Third Division, and he has begged in vain for four weeks for stoves and tents for his freezing and overexposed soldiers. He did just get some stoves, but hundreds could have been sent if there had been the will to do it.

It was also said with conviction that the Ninth (German) Wisconsin Regiment and Forty-Third (Körner) Illinois were originally destined for his division, besides the Benton Hussars, but he never set eyes on them, and that commissions had been withdrawn from the general's staff, or at least some of its individual members, without any grounds given.

So one could describe the general's entire career in Missouri from Carthage, where he was placed in a doomed position, until his resignation as a continuous tale of sorrows. Since he is now the highest ranking military German, he has to bear the cross of Germany as well.* Unfortunately that is true, and we cannot suppress this remark even though we do not wish to stoke the fires of alienation and make the gap between ethnic groups even greater than it is.

We ourselves believe that there has been a process of coming to one's senses in a few places, where the facts have been made clear, and some appear inclined to turning around. At least that is how we interpret the latest acts of Governor Gamble and some of the things we hear about General Halleck.* Praise be to them if it is so!

The fact that the story of the resignation of thirty German officers along with Sigel is either a pure rumor or a pure fabrication is symptomatic of the fact that the Germans, who have had a great deal of practice, have tried to avoid making threats to act, let alone proceeding to act, in a separatist manner. Sigel's own discrete, even

*The cross of Germany refers to Ludwig Blenker's resignation under a cloud of corruption. SR.

*Gen. Henry W. Halleck, who succeeded Frémont in command of the Western Department, levied financial assessments against more than fifty Confederate sympathizers in St. Louis to provide for the hundreds of refugees from Confederate guerrilla operations in southwest Missouri who were pouring into the city. Gamble had approved a loyalty test oath for all officeholders, state, county, and municipality. JNP.

delicate, conduct has kept his friends and admirers from making a demonstration on his behalf. They are waiting for events to develop by themselves.

But the jug can only go to the well so many times before it breaks. Not everything that looks like a calculated slight can be borne. Yet German patience is just as proverbial as German patriotism. People grumble about bitter disappointment, but they are very ready to recognize any improvement. And it is not our strong point to be too pretentious.

How are we doing, anyway? Was it not just after Cameron's infamous Know-Nothing order demanding an ability to speak English for entry into the army that it was declared officially not only that German organizations were accepted but also that German officers who spoke English were doubly welcome? And now they do not just want to tear German organizations apart, but they even deem the most experienced and tested general, who happens also to be as good an American and patriot as lives, to be unfit to command Americans?

Still that is all just a temporary misunderstanding. It cannot go on like this. And General Sigel has shown his decisiveness on the one hand through upholding his military honor, and on the other hand through refusing to participate in German particularism or to complain over every slight, thus laying a foundation for clarifying this misunderstanding and bringing the matter to a settlement.

We must recognize one thing further: we will be happy to see any reconciliation or understanding, and we are looking forward to a sign of good will. The best thing of all would be for the general not to be allowed to depart but to be given a command worthy of himself and of us.

Anzeiger des Westens, 29 January 1862

Is the Slavery Question Insoluble?

Missouri, 14 January 1862

In many cases it is true that people lose their capacity to judge developments and conditions here the moment they cease to have American soil under their feet. We can hardly marvel at the wrong-headed evaluations put forward by Europeans, since many of those who have been here for many years see everything in a false light as soon as they reappear in the Old World, even when they are incapable of conscious misrepresentation.

We have all valued Mr. Otto Ruppius* as an important author, and so it is disturbing—no, even amazing—to read the article he has just published in Germany on America, in the *Gartenlaube*.

In the first article he gives a frightfully exaggerated portrayal of the character of the people here, which he determines to be so demoralized that he believes our day of doom has already come— *"The Union is finished, along with the whole republic,"* those are his words. We are just as ready as he is to condemn the lust for profit and the corruption that is so common and grandiose here, and we spurn the conceit with which Americans look down on other countries, and many other things, but we have always abstained from condemnations *wholesale*, which is improper for any sensible or modest person. If we wanted to carry on in the same vein about conditions and shortcomings in the Old World, hardly a hair would be left on the heads over there. But the truth is that there are sunny sides and shadowy sides over there just as there are here, and that both express themselves differently here under a condition of general freedom than there under restrictions. Over there people try to heal the wounds of repression, here the problem is with the excesses of freedom, and in both cases these problems are not about to end. The moral level both here and there is about the same; but the good and the bad fruits are different, bred by independence and compulsion respectively. If we have too much freedom for the level of enlightenment here, it is easier for us to introduce some restrictions than it is for the Europeans to expand freedom as much as they would like.

It is an utterly improper assertion to say that the first great national trial that comes upon us should ruin us. So how would this lead to *the collapse of our entire republic*, even if we accept that this struggle has the worst possible result, which is that a portion of the South should survive as a slavery confederation alongside the Union? Would the result be that the North would also fall to pieces or that it would unite more firmly? Would these bits of the Union fall so far apart that America would return to the wild and have to be repopulated again? Or will this civil war open our eyes to the source of our troubles, the lack of a crowned head, so that we would

*Otto Ruppius published a large number of popular novels, including the sequel to Heinrich Börnstein's *The Mysteries of St. Louis, Der Prairie-Teufel*. He served until his departure for Germany as editor of *Der Salon*, literary supplement of the *Anzeiger*. SR.

cry for a full-blooded European prince and a brood of barons and counts and establish a police state of the European style?

What did Germany become after the Thirty Years War? Did it recover? No one doubts that the people here are capable of accomplishing something, and everyone knows this country has great natural resources, and yet is it to be ruined beyond all hope by a single blow?

Why does Mr. R. not take the other approach, which is that our people will arise from this hard trial improved, strengthened, and morally elevated, and that they will go on to fulfill the high mission foreseen for them only after undergoing such a hard testing? There are weak human natures that believe all days have ended when one lightning bolt strikes, and it seems that Mr. R. is one of these men of little faith.

But I would rather believe him to be of little faith than to follow the sophistic style of his next article, in which he praises the institution of Southern slavery to the skies, and in which he tries to show that the right lies with the South in this struggle. Mason, Slidell,* and their cohorts have presented these ideas in Congress a hundred times over, since it is just the cant of the old slavery argument, which is that (1) white persons cannot work in the South; (2) the world needs cotton, sugar, coffee, and rice, which has to be produced by black labor; (3) Africans do not work without the whip; (4) if blacks were free they would be a burden to the rest of society; (5) blacks never attain social equality with whites, so they are best kept as slaves; (6) all attempts at liberation in Liberia, Jamaica, etc., have been utter disasters; (7) marriages among mulattoes are unfruitful, and so on. So the whole fault of the bloody disruption that will destroy both parts is blamed on the abolitionists, who are a rabble of swindlers and hypocrites, and on the Republican party, which has only egoistic aims in mind.

We can clearly see that Mr. R. has done his homework in America, but what he has to say is terribly out of place in a journal that usually promotes the humane spirit of progress.

And now we come to our main theme: *is the slavery question really insoluble?* Must the growth of enlightenment, which has changed and improved everything and overcome one after another of the perverted institutions of humanity, cease its work at the institution of black slavery and leave it forever untouched? We assume at the outset that every maladjustment arising from human error is capable of a human solution, however difficult it might be; to de-

*Former United States senators James M. Mason of Virginia and John Slidell of Louisiana, both proslavery "ultras." JNP.

clare the failing to be beyond recovery is moral cowardice, and often nothing more than mean and hypocritical self-indulgence.

There is one true sentence among the many uttered by Mr. R., which says that the descendants of Negroes will have great difficulty ever being accepted as social equals by the Anglo-Saxon race, and that even if they were willing to extend the blacks full civil rights it would be better for both of the groups for them to be spacially separated. Messrs. Blair, Lincoln, and others have moved for external colonization. Against this solution there are the following objections: (1) that we have no right to send away people who were born here, who have committed no crime, and who have indeed worked for the common good of their neighbors; (2) that no one would give us a large enough piece of land to colonize our 4 million Africans; (3) that there are no funds to carry out such an enterprise; (4) that it would be utter madness to send away by force the labor power of 4 million people, especially if the South needs them where they are; and (5) that we ourselves have excessive land that is utterly suitable for colonization under our own eyes and under our control, so we do not need to send away those we wish to separate from ourselves.

As I see it the matter can be ordered in this way. (1) We have a respectable mass of mixed persons who stand closer to the Caucasian than the African, and by all the rules of justice these should be admitted to the full enjoyment of civil rights, which we do not deny to half-breed Indians; (2) such emancipated slaves as make free agreements with their old masters or other persons and wish to remain in a relationship of service should be allowed to stay and live where they wish, and any abuses could be regulated by suitable laws; (3) those who wish to participate in colonization and have perhaps saved the necessary capital through hard work and thrift should be given the necessary lands in *Florida*, which could be reduced to the status of a *territory*, and there they could enjoy the rights of all residents of territories. Anglo-Saxon racial pride will have to concede this much, that there would be an *African Territory* among our territories, and eventually there would be a state consisting primarily of Africans.

If you do not want that, then I tell you, "Finish this war by retaining as many of the border states as possible in the Union, and abolish slavery in those states at once. Then let the incurable remnant of the slave states go in the certain expectation that this accursed institution, once it is no longer protected and preserved by the North, will die somehow—probably bloodily—without your doing a thing."

No one will be able to stop the course of history, not even Mr. Ruppius, and when men do not have the will or the reason to do things reasonably or at the right time, it will become a doom that leaves behind it torment and ruin. The present rebellion, insofar as it is a struggle to perpetuate slavery, is an offense to the progressive spirit of the times and will either end by dragging us all down to ruin, as Mr. R. believes, or with the splendid victory of the better cause, which will lead to more victories in the future.

I wanted to correct an editorial remark made in the last number of the *Anzeiger:* I did lose one of my sons at the battle of Wilson's Creek, two others were almost lost to typhus (the elder only recovered after several months in bed), and I lost my eldest grandson on New Year's Day. He was a splendid boy of twelve. This is to answer numerous inquiries from friends.

Far West [Friedrich Münch]

Anzeiger des Westens, 26 February 1862*

From Southwest Missouri: Price's Rear Guard Overrun—Baggage Looted—Prisoners Taken

We have already related that troops under General Curtis entered Springfield last Thursday, when an enemy detail was driven back and the town taken after a brief exchange. Price left town with his troops, leaving a great amount of provisions and baggage behind that fell into the hands of our troops. He also left behind his sick in the hospitals.

After the capture of the town had been assured, our cavalry pursued the retreating enemy along the road to Cassville. They overtook the rear guard, and the enemy fled in all directions after a brief exchange, leaving all baggage behind. Our cavalry pursued the fleeing enemy and took a large number of prisoners—so many that General Curtis said he did not know what to do with them.

This is the last blow against the rebels in southwest Missouri.

Price has had to flee in great haste and disorder to Arkansas, which has totally demoralized his army and rendered it unsuitable for further service.

With the loss of the southwest the enemy loses both of the lead

---

*The recovery of Springfield from the secessionists was the work of an expedition from Rolla led by Brig. Gen. Samuel R. Curtis and Brig. Gen. Franz Sigel, begun on 9 February 1862. SR.

mines in Newton, which he worked very intensely and from which the rebels gained most of their supply of lead.

From now on the southwest will remain in the hands of the federal troops, and Springfield becomes the center of operations against Arkansas and the Indian Territories. All of Missouri has been rewon for the Union, save for the swamp district, and this will soon be cleared by our troops as well.*

Anzeiger des Westens, 26 February 1862

The Taking of Fort Donelson

The more we hear about the three-day battle that led to the capture of Fort Donelson, the more glorious the deeds done there appear. Illinois has the right to take first prize. There were, after all, a full twenty-five infantry regiments and four cavalry regiments from there in the battle, and her people in McClernand's division were in the most exposed positions, while others under General Smith were the first to leave the trenches. These therefore took the heaviest losses, particularly in staff officers, since a good half-dozen Illinois colonels were either killed or critically wounded, among them Morrison, Lawler, Logan, and others. The troops of Illinois, Indiana, Iowa, and Missouri vied with one another in valor and did their duty to the fullest measure.

The fact that the gunboats could not do the work alone is simply a proof that they are no more perfect than anything made by human hands.* We had never hoped to make them invulnerable. It was especially unfortunate, however, that they were rendered virtually incapable of firing after being in combat for only an hour, and then they had to withdraw from the fight and even from the firing line. Since the *Essex* was launched, the American spirit of inventiveness has been at work to construct an invulnerable gunboat, and Mr.

*Union forces under U. S. Grant gained control of the "swamp" area on the west bank of the Mississippi below the mouth of the Ohio in the spring of 1862. Skirmishes and guerrilla raids continued there and in western, central, and northern Missouri for the next two years. Despite frequent rumors, St. Louis was never threatened. JNP.

*These gunboats, designed and built by James B. Eads at the Nelson-Eads shipyard in St. Louis, had forced a small garrison to abandon Fort Henry on the Tennessee River before Grant's army arrived. Fort Donelson, nearby on the Cumberland, was strongly defended. Two of Commodore Andrew H. Foote's gunboats were disabled by the fort's guns after the boats had inflicted considerable damage inside the fort, and the flotilla retired downriver. Meanwhile, Grant with seventeen thousand men had surrounded the fort. After the garrison of twenty-one thousand men failed to break out, Grant attacked and the Confederates surrendered. JNP.

Ericson is supposed to have nearly solved the puzzle in New York. We do not know what happened to the mortar barges that were towed up the Cumberland. In any case, they appear not to have been brought into action.

Even if the rebels generally fought well on this occasion, their valor is not to be compared with that of our own men. The rebels were dug into trenches and had no choice but to fight for their lives. Despite that, a couple of brigades withdrew from this human trap, and this running away, led by Floyd and Pillow, was condemned so roundly by the Confederates who stayed to be an act of cowardice and treachery that we thought it unnecessary to characterize it harshly.* It is possible that if that thief Floyd had not snuck away from Buckner during the night, they might have tried to hold the works through Sunday, and then they would have been able to get reinforcements from Beauregard, who must be in the area. He could certainly see that the fate of Clarksville and Nashville, in fact all of Tennessee, depends on Fort Donelson, and he would have committed his entire army to hold it.*

In fact, we are willing to see the greatest consequences for the fall of Fort Donelson, though everything could still be dissipated through withdrawal or inactivity. But that would be simply impossible after such a great success, with a full view of the fruits that are about to drop into our lap.

In any case, we have achieved far too much already, and our power in Tennessee has grown too great, not to exploit the strategic value of our victory by completely dominating the Tennessee and Cumberland valleys with gunboats, by interrupting the rebels' rail lines, by occupying Nashville, Knoxville, and Memphis, and by mastering not only the lower Mississippi but also the entire moun-

*After the general breakout had failed at Donelson, Confederate brigadiers John B. Floyd and Gideon Pillow, after deciding to surrender, handed the command to Brig. Gen. S. B. Buckner and decamped at night by boat with three thousand men. Separately, Col. Nathan Bedford Forrest escaped with one thousand calvarymen—without horses. Buckner then surrendered the fort and seventeen thousand men to his West Point classmate, U. S. Grant. Floyd, an ex-governor of Virginia, had been secretary of war under Buchanan. After he had resigned to join the Confederacy, his war department accounts were discovered to be $875,000 short. He and his subordinate Pillow were both dismissed from the Confederate army by Jefferson Davis after Donelson. Buckner was exchanged after a few weeks and served the Confederacy competently for the duration. Nearly thirty years later he became governor of Kentucky. JNP.

*Interestingly, in this lengthy *Anzeiger* account of Fort Donelson, U. S. Grant is neither credited with the victory nor even mentioned, though the blundering Frémont and Sigel are consistently treated by the newspaper as military geniuses. Perhaps the problem with Grant was that he was a Democrat at the beginning of the war, owning a slave until 1859. JNP.

tain plateau, making it the controlling position of the entire theater of war. We have already achieved far too much to dissipate it now. From this point everything will move forward by its own force.

To consider the matter from another side, this victory will have a strong impact on Europe. Even if they do not want to take time to evaluate its strategic importance, its immediate results and dimensions have to have an effect on the imagination of the peoples. Blow after blow has fallen since the middle of January, and the question has to be asked whether the rebels have enough vitality to recover from these blows and arise like a phoenix from the consuming flames. Success is the god the European dynasties worship. Even Louis Napoleon Bonaparte believes in it. He has sought to have England retrieve for him his burning chestnuts from the fire, which are due to his bankrupt treasury. If it appears that the rebels are collapsing, he is even less likely to undertake the Herculean task of destroying the Union by himself—a task that would bring upon him the condemnation of all peoples.

This is how far we have been brought by the fall of Fort Donelson. Of course we are not yet to the real end of the rebellion or to the goal of all our trials. But just as we experienced the end of the beginning at Fort Sumter, so now we are experiencing the beginning of the end. Let that end be one of terror and justice, until freedom at last has a secure resting place in this Union.

Anzeiger des Westens, 26 February 1862

Bad Signs

When the beast is down, the ravens gather. Even now we can see the men of compromise and the peacemongers at work again. They are only waiting for a great, decisive victory to start to preach reconciliation and constitutionality; let everything remain as it was, or make conditions even worse than they were before the great bloodbath. Yet we have little fear of such reactionary caterwauling by such men as Stanton, particularly in view of the reawakened spirit of the people.

Another sign of the reactionary spirit is the manner in which the English-language newspapers are singing the praises of *McClellan*. For even if his plans, like those of Scott, pointed the way to the latest victories, still he restrains himself so irresponsibly to avoid bloodshed that he makes it inevitable. He has used his plenitude of power in such a way that he cannot bring his mass of warriors into motion, so that we have to wait for Stanton to be the redeeming Messiah.* Now more than ever it seems to us that it is not McClellan the strategist but McClellan the politician who is being pulled to the center of the stage in an utterly unjustifiable manner. And all of this at a time when he has been compromised by the revelations about the traitor Stone,* so that he has to forbid the press to publish so much as a notice about his arrest.

This has the same motivation as the rabid, poisonous, and gall-filled articles published by the *Missouri Republican* against General Sigel. This is a unique occurrence, since that newspaper has never tried anything similar, so there must be a good reason. First came demonstrations of the most extreme sort against the German press, then the stupidest libels against the most patriotic and successful German general. Statements made in private letters to his father-in-law and to other friends about Halleck or Curtis, which were given in utter confidentiality, are branded as violations of discipline or insubordination, and this most modest and effective of soldiers is branded a troublemaker and a confidence man. Frémont's defense of him and Sigel's own strategic plans have been held back from the public in order to give others the sole credit for

*Edwin M. Stanton had succeeded the corrupt Simon Cameron as secretary of war. He was an efficient and honest administrator, but a tricky politician. Stanton was despised by the *Anzeiger* because he had served in Buchanan's cabinet and because he was at odds with Secretary of the Treasury Salmon P. Chase, a favorite with the Radicals. Like other Radicals, non-Germans included, the *Anzeiger* perceived correctly that victory without emancipation would be an empty vessel, and that only grim dedication to total victory would win the war, but they believed blindly that ideological purity in generals was essential to military success. None of the ablest Union generals—Grant, William T. Sherman, Philip Sheridan, George H. Thomas, and George Gordon Meade—were abolitionists. John A. Logan of Illinois and Frank P. Blair, the best of the political generals, were as dedicated to total victory as any Radical, and a good deal more fitted to achieve it, but they were moderate (slow) emancipationists. On the other side of the coin, extremist members of the Confederate cabinet had tried to deny the Virginia command to Robert E. Lee because he had opposed secession before the war. If Lee had chosen the Union, which he had considered doing, the *Anzeiger* would no doubt have pronounced him unfit. JNP.

*Brig. Gen. Charles P. Stone, commander of Massachusetts troops in Maryland, aware of the delicate political situation there, had forbidden his men to encourage slave insubordination. When one of his officers returned two escapees to their masters, Charles Sumner denounced Stone in the Senate. Sumner's and the *Anzeiger*'s indignation was understandable, but Stone was no traitor; he had acted in the spirit of federal policy. A few weeks later, when elements of his command were trapped and slaughtered at Ball's Bluff, the Radical Congressional Committee on the Conduct of the War forced his arrest. Neither Lincoln nor Stanton could risk defending Stone, though there were no specific charges against him. After a few months he was released and restored to command, but it was clear that temporizing and soft dealing with slavery would no longer do. Total victory and emancipation were becoming essential war aims by spring 1862. JNP.

large-scale plans, and even confidential messages and complaints are seen as worthy of punishment. When people undertake to cripple the highest military leader of the Germans through systematic libel, it looks as if they have decided that they do not need the Germans any more and want to keep the victories for Americans alone, to their own greater glory. But the end has not yet come.

Anzeiger des Westens, 3 March 1862

The Emancipation Movement cannot be brought into motion too rapidly in Missouri. "Strike while the iron is hot." And it is hot now. Dozens of our friends in the interior of the state assure us of that. Rebel slaveowners are now as humiliated and withdrawn as they could possibly be. And Union men among them, especially in the southwestern part of the state, have at last come to see that the dissolution of the peculiar institution is good not only for the common interests of the state but also for their own private interest. If we do not know enough to make use of this positive attitude, then no one will be able to guarantee the future. It is still very problematic to try and conceive what our national situation will be.

For us Germans, emancipation is a matter of life and death. If Missouri remains a slave state, then we will not remain here any longer. No one is fooled about that. We will always be seen as a dangerous, incendiary element, and since the time when we can always be armed will soon pass, it would be inevitable that we would always be outvoted and looked at askance, defeated in all matters and cheated, and it would then be best for us to leave. —If Missouri becomes a free state, on the other hand, then we would be saviors not only in war but also in peace, and they would look on us with respect in the free states; German immigration would then not simply rise but increase twofold and tenfold, and just as we have won voting power through freshly naturalized German soldiers, so also floating and unsteady elements would join us to give us a position of power. What prosperity would flow from this for the people in this state!

When the government here has settled with emancipation, then it should proceed at once to the building of our railways, at the expense of the Union, as a war measure. Just as it places fortresses on the coastline and broadens waterways, so also it should draw Missouri into the net, and it would soon be able to repay all of the costs.

Just as we helped it in its hour of greatest need, so it should help us and make a stride toward the great Pacific Ocean at the same time.

Congress and the administration could show the faith they have in the free, proud future of this country. Energetic intervention for emancipation and railroads is the point of Archimedes for Messrs. Henderson, Hall, Price, Blair, and Rollins,* by which the many failures of the past could be lifted away and a greater future for Missouri and the whole nation could be created. What do they say?

Anzeiger des Westens, 12 March 1862

Major General Sigel

Our readers now know that it is "all right" with Sigel's commission as a major general. The president has named him, and the Senate is sure to confirm him. It is only remarkable that his name was not given as one of the series of major generals in the list of nominations in the announcement yesterday. Instead we read, "A special dispatch to the *New York Tribune* says that the following brigadier generals are nominated as major generals: McDowell, Burnside, Buell, Pope, Curtis, McClernand, C. F. Smith, and Lewis Wallace, acting generals at Fort Donelson.* Ranked in the order as named—so that according to this series McDowell stood before Allen and *Curtis before Sigel*." So only here, at the end, where Curtis's precedent is guaranteed, Sigel's name appears for the first time. It is as if the telegraph could only name Sigel in order to insult him. This proves that Sigel was promoted, since otherwise Curtis's superiority in rank would be unquestioned, and Curtis was also Sigel's elder as brigadier. The telegraph does not waste words. We might be upset that Sigel is below McDowell, the hero of Bull Run, or Curtis, the ingenious leader of the Southwest Expedition, if it were not for the fact that you have to expect this sort of thing in America. But we are at least happy that two major generals cannot be kept together as long as there are fifteen thousand men or fewer to be moved. We feel justified in giving numbers this time, since they had become well known in the press before the War Depart-

*Missouri Sen. John B. Henderson, Rep. Frank Blair, and Rep. James S. Rollins. JNP.
*Irvin McDowell (commander of the Union forces at the Bull Run disaster); Ambrose Burnside; Don Carlos Buell; John Pope; Samuel R. Curtis; John McClernand; and Lew (not Lewis) Wallace. McClernand and Wallace served under Grant at Fort Donelson; Wallace gained undying fame after the war as the author of *Ben Hur*. JNP.

ment issued its ban, so they have become a matter of public knowledge. And if they are divided and Sigel receives an autonomous command, he will know how to find his own way. The wording used also tells us that Sigel is ranked ahead of the hero of Fort Donelson, for it is clear from the conclusion of the message that they stand together, "acting major generals at Fort Donelson." So we are satisfied, and it seems to us that modesty does honor to the man, despite the dictum of Goethe.

Anzeiger des Westens, 19 March 1862

"It All Depends upon Blair"

Emancipation was always a matter of honor for the Germans, particularly in Missouri, and we have already endured one defeat in a municipal election under this banner. But since the start of the war it has become a question of policy and virtually a question of survival for us Missouri Germans. Since the president's special message of 6 March it can be seen that we are not in vain in viewing it as a matter of honor.* We certainly believe that this view of the matter can figure on virtually unanimous support among the Germans, and that they have come to the point where they intend to present the emancipation question as a test in the next general elections. No one running for Congress or governor or the legislature who does not pledge himself by word and hand to vote and work for the emancipation of Missouri can expect votes from Germans.

In these circumstances it is only natural to concern oneself with sounding the mood among the Americans. And here as usual we find how hard it is to bring the masses into motion, and that the secret Union Clubs are inclined, in fact committed, to holding themselves "noncommittal" and to endeavor to resurrect the decayed and discredited old Bell-Everett platform, which said nothing about slavery at all.

And even more than that, we are surprised by the answer we receive almost monotonously when we ask for the opinions of old Republicans on the great question of our day. "It all depends upon what Blair will do," they say. Blair appears to be lord over the body and soul of these gentlemen. We just do not understand that. It is hardly to be understood by anyone. And yet it is so. He has ruled for

*Lincoln proposed to give financial aid to any state that would adopt gradual emancipation. JNP.

so long, he has exercised so much patronage, that the faith in him has grown into a superstition, even into idolatry. They are nothing without him! —Now we do not wish to conspire against Blair. We even think he would join in himself, since he did vote for the president's message in the House. But we do want to comment that he certainly is not the natural leader of this movement. Colonel B. Gratz Brown represented emancipation in the legislature many years ago with a higher intellectual capacity and greater energy than Blair, and he was credited for it throughout the country, so that today his name is much greater in this context than Blair's has ever been. So when so many of our earlier Republican friends among the Americans want to take their cue from Blair, it certainly seems to me to be a peculiar notion. They owe it to their own past to enter into the great struggle for freedom like men. If Mr. Blair wants to come along, so much the better for him. Besides, a greater and a better man than he is had already spoken, namely the president himself. Therefore emancipation, a necessary act, must have precedence over obedience to an accustomed leader.

And yet we are happy to know many a good man among the native-born who have attached themselves to his party.

Anzeiger des Westens, 26 March 1862*

On the Battle of Pea Ridge

Information on the great battle in Arkansas has been maddeningly slow in coming in, and this has caused great anxiety, both because of the large mass of St. Louisans involved, which leads virtually everyone to fear the loss of a relative or friend among the heavy casualties, and because of yesterday's *Missouri Republican*

*The battle of Pea Ridge, Arkansas, 6–8 March 1862, led to the exclusion of large units of secessionist troops from Missouri until 1864, though the state was by no means pacified. First reports of the battle were badly garbled, and the full importance and scale of the battle were unclear for weeks. SR.

Confederate Gen. Earl Van Dorn commanded some twenty-five thousand men at Pea Ridge, including several thousand Creeks, Choctaws, and Cherokees from the Indian Territory. The Union forces under Samuel R. Curtis numbered ten thousand five hundred. After Van Dorn had divided his forces for an unsuccessful front-and-rear assault, Curtis's artillery pounded the Confederates from the front and both flanks, silencing their batteries. A two-pronged infantry charge then drove the Southerners from the field. The Union lost thirteen hundred men (including eight scalped by Indians), and Van Dorn about eighteen hundred. Most of the Indians avoided the war thereafter. JNP.

statement that the numerically superior enemy might dare a new attack. At this moment we are really more interested in divining the future course of events than in looking back. Still, under the present circumstances it is our duty to give out everything we have heard.

A Cincinnati dispatch tells us first of all that the enemy was surely twenty-five thousand strong, and that Sigel was able to cut through seven enemy regiments with only two understrength regiments of his own.

The number of dead and wounded is estimated here at fifteen hundred for our side and twenty-five hundred to three thousand for the enemy. A terrifying picture was drawn of the atrocities committed by the Indians under Pike.

The first account of the *Missouri Republican*, which it received from Lieutenant Willis of Indiana, who brought the body of Colonel Hendricks, 29th Indiana, here, was that Hendricks died instantly and that he was the only higher officer to fall. For a time the battle appeared lost due to the extraordinarily greater numbers of the enemy. We were bombarded with chain-shot and stones. According to this account, the enemy was thirty-five thousand strong and lost eleven hundred dead and twenty-five hundred to three thousand wounded. The Indians ganged up like beasts. We took sixteen hundred prisoners and thirteen cannons, not just five, since *Sigel alone* took *no fewer than ten*. Major Hébert of the Louisiana Volunteers is among the prisoners, and he said that General Frost of Camp Jackson has fallen.* It is known, of course, that he had kept the terms of his parole and had not taken part in fighting until he was exchanged for Colonel Mulligan by General Frémont. For a while he considered going to Europe, and for a while he seemed inclined to use his sword on behalf of the Union. At least that is what he said. But no one was ready to trust him, and he could hardly have expected a command. So in the end this forced him over to the other side, probably because he wanted to quash the accusation of cowardice. And so he has followed his adversary Lyon into the other world at the first opportunity. It was also confirmed that McCulloch, McIntosh, and Rector have fallen. Earl Van Dorn and Price

*Daniel Frost was not killed at Pea Ridge. He had not joined the Confederacy until after he was assessed as a rebel sympathizer late in 1861. In 1863 his wife was banished from St. Louis for disloyalty and deposited behind the Confederate lines. Frost then left the country with her without bothering to resign his commission. After the war Frost returned to his large farm near Florissant and kept a low profile thereafter. Price had captured Col. James Mulligan and his "Irish Brigade" at Lexington in September 1861. JNP.

were supposed to have fled in opposite directions, probably to re-
gather their scattered forces in the Boston Mountains. Sigel pursued some to Batesville and the Ozarks.

We do not yet know where our army stands at present. It is said to
be in or around Bentonville. Until now we have precise information
only on losses from Colonel Phelps's Missouri Regiment and the
29th Indiana.* In the case of the first, they went into battle 275
strong with four companies, of which three captains were seriously
wounded, and Captain Potter of Company C was killed. All other
officers in Companies D and H were wounded. Horses were shot
from under Colonel Phelps and Major Geiger. The 29th Indiana was
in the battle with 410 men and only lost a few officers besides
Colonel Hendricks. There were nine dead and 32 wounded. Even
then the losses amounted to precisely 10 percent.

Finally, the *Abend-Demokrat* gives a very extensive description
of the battle, but it tells us nothing new save that *Sigel* and
Osterhaus were mentioned again and again as the leaders of the
day.

Anzeiger des Westens, 26 March 1862

"Unionizing the City Council"

and the legislature should be the sum total of our effort, says the
Evening News. Unionizing the city council! Are we so far along that
we are to Unionize, i.e. loyalize, the government of this Unionist
and ultrapatriotic city? Where the hell did the people put their eyes
when they elected these worthless elements to rule them early last
year? Or perhaps last year the majority of most wards was not so
Unionist, since Frémont said he found himself in a half-rebel city
when he arrived. It is well known that there was a frightful falling
back between the election of the convention in February and April,
and that Lyon was aware of the increased boldness and overconfi-
dence of secessionists when he stomped on the head of secession on
10 May. It is also certain that the city council was already pretty
impure before it appeared in its current, most unimproved edition.
This was shown by the fact that it rejected an extremely modest

*John S. Phelps of Springfield, a War Democrat, served as military governor of
Arkansas in 1863. He became one of the Missouri's leading attorneys and Democratic politicians after the war. His most noted case was his successful defense of Wild
Bill Hickock, who killed a man on the streets of Springfield in 1865. From 1877 to 1881
he was governor of Missouri. JNP.

Unionist resolution on 11 January 1861, when the First Ward was dishonored by its bogus representative Chester. In those days that was the sort of politics the city council tried to avoid. But now that the weapons of the Union are everywhere victorious, they declare themselves to be for the Union and even stage demonstrations, such as for the funereal passage of the noble Lyon, who was cursed by them so much in life, or for Washington's Birthday. This has told us that the weapons and generals of the United States are the best Unionizers for our city council. Now everyone is a Unionist, and everyone is ready to swear to it. But despite all his protests and declarations, we hold no one to be a Unionist who is not also an emancipationist. Anyone who does not place the interests of his Fatherland and its manifest need for freedom before his own pecuniary advantage, his prejudices, or his *"state pride"* can be taken away from us. If it is a German who is trying to subvert us, then he is utterly contemptible. He rages against his own flesh and blood and sins against the German spirit. We will not support him for that reason, and who is not for us is against us, *in toto.* Germans can only have a homeland in a Missouri that is committed to freedom. This makes the city council very important, if for no other reason than that it names voting judges for all elections.* And we have all too often seen what abuses are possible there. It will not work any other way. We will only achieve true Union through emancipation.

Anzeiger des Westens, 23 April 1862

To the Germans of the State of Missouri

(from the *St. Charles Demokrat*)

Missouri, 31 March 1862

When our compatriots first began to settle in the western parts of this country in large numbers almost thirty years ago, it was inevitable that part of the German immigration would come to the state of Missouri, since this place was so richly endowed by nature and could offer advantages of location to be found nowhere else.

---

*Radicals, called "Charcoals" in St. Louis at this time, won control of the city council in April 1862. Republicans Chauncey I. Filley and James S. Thomas held the mayor's office for the next five years. Filley was too friendly to Frank Blair to be fully satisfactory to the German press. JNP.

Those of us who traveled to Missouri then knew full well that we were going to a *slave state*, but we did not attribute very great importance to that fact. As long as slavery existed in the territory of the United States—we figured—it made no difference whether we had blacks as close neighbors or only as distant ones; we were guaranteed the full enjoyment of all the rights we would ever want by federal law and by the liberal Constitution of the State of Missouri—so we thought. —The thought of coming to terms with slavery was entertained by only a few among us; we were sorry that there were slaves here, but we could not do anything about it; we ourselves wanted nothing to do with slavery, so we were not particularly burdened by it.

I confess along with thousands of others that we deceived ourselves in these last expectations. The first few years, when there were no disputes concerning slavery, went by very quietly for us, but gradually we came to realize that slavery and true freedom could not exist side by side. No law can take away the freedom of thought, and so far as one or another thing is not specifically prohibited, the freedom of writing and speech or of action are totally guaranteed by the law of the land, but in practice we were compelled to live in a state of perpetual guardianship in the hands of slaveowners. Not everyone was equally sensitive to this, because they were not restricted in their ordinary daily lives, and they were bothered little by those things that were not ordinary; but no one can deny the shameful fact that we were not free men in this so-called *free* country as long as the slaveowners could control us at a whim.

Were we allowed to tell the owners of human beings what we thought of black servitude? Were we allowed to tell the slaves, or even indicate to them through silent conduct, that we regarded them to be *human beings* and that they had human rights, too? Yet even if we said nothing whatsoever and did nothing at all, were not those grand gentlemen suspicious of our inner thoughts because we seldom stood out as *praisers* of the institution, and since we did not participate actively in trading and breeding human beings?

Not very long ago in the area where I live, a respected German who let slip a simple comment that blacks were *people*, too, was pressingly visited by a group of those gentlemen, cross-examined, and intensively grilled. It also happened that, less than a year ago, a so-called vigilance committee was formed to observe our deeds and speech, and meetings were held and resolutions drafted that designated Germans as a group as thieves of Negroes and cursed them in other ways as well. We were placed under the surveillance of men we would normally regard as far beneath us, who were nothing but worthless ne'er-do-wells and later proved to be traitors and rebel vagabonds worthy of death on the gallows.

By what right did those people condemn us? Could anyone show where we had done anything to injure the rights of anyone, even the rights of slaveowners? Has anyone among our countrymen ever actually seized a slave, or enticed him away or stolen him? Nothing of the sort! They cannot accuse us for any of our deeds, but they do want to abandon us to revenge for having a superior and more humane sensibility: they believe they can read a sentiment in our hearts that accuses them of inhumanity done on a daily basis, and our crime is our refusal to agree with their sole orthodox doctrine that a portion of mankind exists to be driven, whipped, worked to death, or even burned to death under certain circumstances. —When we were few, our convictions received little attention; since then, not only has the number of Germans risen—especially in certain parts of the state—but also their importance and prosperity, and in many places they have come to overshadow the slaveholders after having started with nothing, and they envy us and would like to make us a sort of slave who would have nothing to say, but who would simply work and be silent.

They have injured our inner feelings no less by the hardness and viciousness with which the preservation of slavery seems to be bound. Many of us have had hungry slaves come to our doors; others have been robbed because the slaves had nothing at their own home, or because they had been raised in savagery; we have seen others walking around in rags and tatters and barefoot in harsh weather; finally, the screams of those being whipped—not children being disciplined, mind you, but men, women, mothers being beaten—often came to our ears; or we were eyewitnesses to the sale of souls, that dreadful show where parents, children, and married couples were pulled apart in the midst of the raw jesting of traders in human flesh. Could any individual's feelings be so hardened that he was not moved by such things? —Even if such things did not happen every day, they came often enough to convince every good man that these crudities had to end, as quickly as possible.

In fact, if slavery were to stay forever in Missouri, Germans would no longer settle in this state, since there is plenty of room in the western free states where they could avoid so much that offends them here; but it would be better for us to make every effort to save from perdition this state we have chosen as our new homeland: in that case we would be accomplishing as great and important a work as history has to offer. If Germans had never come to Missouri, then slavery would be all that much more dominant, and the state would now be in that same dreadful condition into which all the slave states are rapidly sinking. If we reconcile ourselves to the notion of free labor existing alongside slave labor and continuing so into the future, then we will be guilty of holding our state back from the progress of the free states, and we shall never win full freedom for ourselves or our descendants.

Fr[iedrich] M[ünch]

Index

319